DATE		

THE CONTEMPORARY SHAKESPEARE SERIES

VOLUME III

All's Well That Ends Well

*

Henry The Fifth

*

Macbeth

*

King Richard The Third

*

The Taming of the Shrew

Edited by A. L. Rowse

Modern Text with Introduction

UNIVERSITY PRESS OF AMERICA

Copyright © 1985 by A.L. Rowse

University Press of America,® Inc.

4720 Boston Way
Lanham, MD 20706

3 Henrietta Street
London WC2E 8LU England

Distributed to the trade by The Scribner Book Companies

Library of Congress Cataloging in Publication Data
(Revised for vol. 3)

Shakespeare, William, 1564-1616.
  The contemporary Shakespeare series.

  Contents: v. 1. Hamlet. Julius Caesar. The merchant
of Venice. A Midsummer night's dream. Romeo and Juliet.
The tempest —   — v. 3. All's well that ends well.
Henry V. King Richard the Third. Macbeth. The taming
of the shrew.
  I. Rowse, A. L. (Alfred Leslie), 1903-
PR2754.R67   1984b   822.3'3   84-5105
ISBN 0-8191-3922-X (v. 3)

The plays in this volume are also available individually in
paperbound editions from University Press of America.

Book design by Leon Bolognese

WHY A CONTEMPORARY SHAKESPEARE?

The starting point of my project was when I learned both from television and in education, that Shakespeare is being increasingly dropped in schools and colleges because of the difficulty of the language. In some cases, I gather, they are given just a synopsis of the play, then the teacher or professor embroiders from his notes.

This is deplorable. We do not want Shakespeare progressively dropped because of superfluous difficulties that can be removed, skilfully, conservatively, keeping to every line of the text. Nor must we look at the question statically, for this state of affairs will worsen as time goes on and we get further away from the language of 400 years ago—difficult enough in all conscience now.

We must begin by ridding our mind of prejudice, i.e. we must not pre-judge the matter. A friend of mine on New York radio said that he was 'appalled' at the very idea; but when he heard my exposition of what was proposed he found it reasonable and convincing.

Just remember, I do not need it myself: *I live in the Elizabethan age*, Shakespeare's time, and have done for years, and am familiar with its language, and his. But even for me there are still difficulties—still more for modern people, whom I am out to help.

Who, precisely?

Not only students at school and in college, but all readers of Shakespeare. Not only those, but all viewers of the plays, in the theatre, on radio and television— actors too, who increasingly find pronunciation of the words difficult, particularly obsolete ones—and there are many, besides the difficulty of accentuation.

The difficulties are naturally far greater for non-English-speaking peoples. We must remember that he is our greatest asset, and that other peoples use him a great deal in learning our language. There are no Iron Curtains for him—though, during Mao's Cultural Revolution in China, he was prohibited. Now that the ban has been lifted, I learn that the Chinese in thousands flock to his plays.

Now, a good deal that was grammatical four hundred years ago is positively ungrammatical today. We might begin by removing what is no longer good grammar.

For example: plural subjects with a verb in the singular:

'*Is* Bushy, Green and the earl of Wiltshire dead?' Any objection to replacing 'is' correctly by 'are'? Certainly not. I notice that some modern editions already correct—

These high wild hills and rough uneven ways
Draws out our miles and makes them wearisome

to 'draw' and 'make', quite sensibly. Then, why not go further and regularise this Elizabethan usage to modern, consistently throughout?

Similarly with archaic double negatives—'Nor shall you not think neither'—and double comparatives: 'this is more worser than before.' There are hundreds of instances of what is now just bad grammar to begin with.

There must be a few thousand instances of superfluous subjunctives to reduce to simplicity and sense. Today we use the subjunctive occasionally after 'if', when we say 'if it be'. But we mostly say today 'if it is'. Now Shakespeare has hundreds of subjunctives, not only after if, but after though, although, unless, lest, whether, until, till, etc.

I see no point whatever in retaining them. They only add superfluous trouble in learning English, when the great appeal of our language as a world-language is precisely that it has less grammar to learn than almost any. Russian is unbelievably complicated. Inflected languages—German is like Latin in this respect—are really rather backward; it has been a great recommendation that English has been more progressive in this respect in simplifying itself.

Now we can go further along this line: keep a few subjunctives, if you must, but reduce them to a minimum.

Let us come to the verb. It is a great recommendation to modern English that our verbs are comparatively simple to conjugate — unlike even French, for example. In the Elizabethan age there was a great deal more of it, and some of it inconsistent in modern usage. Take Shakespeare's,

'Where is thy husband now? Where be thy brothers?'

Nothing is lost by rendering this as we should today:

Where is your husband now? Where are your brothers?

And so on.

The second and third person singular—all those shouldsts and wouldsts, wilts and shalts, haths and doths, have become completely obsolete. Here a vast simplification may be effected—with no loss as far as I can see, and with advantages from several points of view.

For example, 'st' at the end of a word is rather difficult to say, and more difficult even for us when it is succeeded by a word beginning with 'th'. Try saying, 'Why usurpedst thou this?' Foreigners have the greatest difficulty in pronouncing our 'th' anyway—many never succeed in getting it round their tongues. Many of these tongue-twisters even for us proliferate in Shakespeare, and I see no objection to getting rid of *superfluous* difficulties. Much easier for people to say, 'Why did you usurp this?'—the same number of syllables too.

This pre-supposes getting rid of almost all thous and thees and thines. I have no objection to keeping a few here and there, if needed for a rhyme—even then they are sometimes not necessary.

Some words in Shakespeare have changed their meaning into the exact opposite: we ought to remove that stumbling-block. When Hamlet says, 'By heaven, I'll make a ghost of him that *lets* me', he means *stops*; and we should replace it by stops, or holds me. Shakespeare regularly uses the word 'owe' where we should say own: the meaning has changed. Take a line like, 'Thou dost here usurp the name thou ow'st not': we should say, 'You do here usurp the name you own not', with the bonus of getting rid of two ugly 'sts'.

The word 'presently' in the Elizabethan age did not mean in a few minutes or so, but immediately—instantly has the same number of syllables. 'Prevent' then had its Latin meaning, to go before, or forestall. Shakespeare frequently uses the word 'still' for always or ever.

Let us take the case of many archaic forms of words, simple one-syllable words that can be replaced without the slightest difference to the scansion: 'sith' for since, 'wrack' for wreck, 'holp' for helped, 'writ' for wrote, 'brake' for broke, 'spake' for spoke, 'bare' for bore, etc.

These give no trouble, nor do a lot of other words that he uses: 'repeal' for recall, 'reproof' for disproof, 'decline' for incline. A few words do give more trouble. The linguistic scholar, C. T. Onions, notes that it is sometimes difficult to give the precise meaning Shakespeare attaches to the word 'conceit'; it usually means thought, or fancy, or concept. I do not know that it ever has our meaning; actually the word 'conceited' with him means ingenious or fantastic, as 'artificial' with Elizabethans meant artistic or ingenious.

There is a whole class of words that have completely gone out, of which moderns do not know the meaning. I find no harm in replacing the word 'coistrel' by rascal, which is what it means—actually it has much the same sound—or 'coil' by fuss; we find 'accite' for summon, 'indigest' for formless. Hamlet's word 'reechy', for the incestuous kisses of his mother and her brother-in-law, has gone out of use: the nearest word, I suppose, would be reeky, but filthy would be a suitable modern equivalent.

In many cases it is extraordinary how little one would need to change, how conservative one could be. Take Hamlet's famous soliloquy, 'To be or not to be.' I find only two words that moderns would not know the meaning of, and one of those we might guess:

> . . .When he himself might his *quietus* make
> With a bare bodkin? Who would *fardels* bear. . .

'Quietus' means put paid; Elizabethans wrote the Latin 'quietus est' at the bottom of a bill that was paid—when it was—to say that it was settled. So that you could replace 'quietus' by settlement, same number of syllables, though not the same accentuation; so I would prefer to use the word acquittance, which has both.

'Fardels' means burdens; I see no objection to rendering, 'Who would burdens bear'—same meaning, same number of syllables, same accent: quite simple. I expect all the ladies to know what a bodkin is: a long pin, or skewer. Now let us take something really difficult—perhaps the most difficult passage to render in all Shakespeare. It is the virtuoso comic piece describing all the diseases that horseflesh is heir to, in *The Taming of the Shrew*. The horse is Petruchio's. President Reagan tells me that this is the one Shakespearean part that he played—and a very gallant one too. In Britain last year we saw a fine performance of his on horseback in Windsor Park alongside of Queen Elizabeth II—very familiar ground to William Shakespeare and Queen Elizabeth I, as we know from *The Merry Wives of Windsor*.

Here is a headache for us: Petruchio's horse (not President Reagan's steed) was 'possessed with the glanders, and like to mose in the chine; troubled with the lampass, infected with the fashions, full of windgalls, sped with spavins, rayed with the yellows, past cure of the fives, stark spoiled with the staggers, begnawn with the bots; swayed in the back, and shoulder-shotten; near-legged before, and with a half-cheeked bit, and a headstall of sheep's leather', etc.

What on earth are we to make of that? No doubt it raised a laugh with Elizabethans, much more familiarly acquainted with horseflesh than we are; but I doubt if Hollywood was able to produce a nag for Reagan that qualified in all these respects.

Now, even without his horsemanship, we can clear one fence at the outset: 'mose in the chine'. Pages of superfluous commentary have been devoted to that word 'mose'. There was no such Elizabethan word: it was simply a printer's misprint for 'mourn', meaning dripping or running; so it suggests a running sore. You would need to consult the *Oxford English Dictionary*, compiled on historical lines, for some of the words, others like 'glanders' country folk know and we can guess.

So I would suggest a rendering something like this: 'possessed with glanders, and with a running sore in the back; troubled in the gums, and infected in the glands; full of galls in the fetlocks and swollen in the joints; yellow with jaundice, past cure of the strangles; stark spoiled with the staggers, and gnawed by worms; swayed in the back and shoulder put out; near-legged before, and with a half-cheeked bit and headgear of sheep's leather', etc. That at least makes it intelligible.

Oddly enough, one encounters the greatest difficulty with the least important words and phrases, Elizabethan expletives and malapropisms, or salutations like God 'ild you, Godden, for God shield you, Good-even, and so on. 'God's wounds' was Elizabeth I's favourite swearword; it appears frequently enough in Victorian novels as 'Zounds'— I have never heard anyone use it. The word 'Marry!', as in the phrase 'Marry come up!' has similarly gone out, though a very old gentleman at All Souls, Sir Charles Oman, had heard the phrase in the back-streets of Oxford just after the 1914-18 war. 'Whoreson' is frequent on the lips of coarse fellows in Shakespeare: the equivalent in Britain today would be bloody, in America (I suppose) s.o.b.

Relative pronouns, who and which: today we use who for persons, which for things. In Elizabethan times the two were hardly distinguished and were interchangeable. Provokingly Shakespeare used the personal relative 'who' more frequently for impersonal objects, rivers, buildings, towns; and then he no less frequently uses 'which' for persons. This calls out to be regularised for the modern reader.

Other usages are more confusing. The word 'cousin'

was used far more widely by the Elizabethans for their kin: it included nephews, for instance. Thus it is confusing in the English History plays to find a whole lot of nephews—like Richard III's, whom he had made away with in the Tower of London—referred to and addressed as cousins. That needs regularisation today, in the interests of historical accuracy and to get the relationship clear. The word 'niece' was sometimes used of a grandchild—in fact this is the word Shakespeare used in his will for his little grand-daughter Elizabeth, his eventual heiress who ended up as Lady Barnard, leaving money to her poor relations the Hathaways at Stratford. The Latin word *neptis*, from which niece comes also meant grandchild—Shakespeare's grammar-school education at Stratford was in Latin, and this shows you that he often thought of a word in terms of its Latin derivation.

Malapropisms, misuse of words, sometimes mistaking of meanings, are frequent with uneducated people, and sometimes not only with those. Shakespeare transcribed them from lower-class life to raise a laugh, more frequently than any writer for the purpose. They are an endearing feature of the talk of Mistress Quickly, hostess of the Boar's Inn in East Cheapside, and we have no difficulty in making out what she means. But in case some of us do, and for the benefit of non-native English speakers, I propose the correct word in brackets afterwards: 'You have brought her into such a canaries [quandary]. . .and she's as fartuous [virtuous] a civil, modest wife. . .'

Abbreviations: Shakespeare's text is starred—and in my view, marred—by innumerable abbreviations, which not only look ugly on the page but are sometimes difficult to pronounce. It is not easy to pronounce 'is't', or 'in't', or 'on't', and some others: if we cannot get rid of them altogether they should be drastically reduced. Similarly with 'i'th'', 'o'th'', with which the later plays are liberally bespattered, for "in the" or "of the."

We also have a quite unnecessary spattering of apostrophes in practically all editions of the plays—''d' for the past participle, e.g. 'gather'd'. Surely it is much better to regularise the past participle 'ed', e.g. gathered; and when the last syllable is, far less frequently, to be pronounced, then accent it, gatherèd.

This leads into the technical question of scansion, where a practising poet is necessary to get the accents right, to help the reader, and still more the actor. Most people will hardly notice that, very often, the frequent ending of words in 'ion', like reputation, has to be pronounced with two syllables at the end. So I propose to accent this when necessary, e.g. reputatiòn. I have noticed the word 'ocean' as tri-syllabic, so I accent it, to help, oceàn. A number of words which to us are monosyllables were pronounced as two: hour, fire, tired; I sometimes accent or give them a dieresis, either hoùr or f̈ire. In New England speech words like prayèr, thëre, are apt to be pronounced as two syllables—closer to Elizabethan usage (as with words like gotten) than is modern speech in Britain.

What I notice in practically all editions of Shakespeare's plays is that the editors cannot be relied on to put the accents in the right places. One play edited by a well known Shakespearean editor had, I observed, a dozen accents placed over the wrong syllables. This is understandable, for these people don't write poetry and do not know how to scan. William Shakespeare knew all about scanning, and you need to be both familiar with Elizabethan usage and a practising traditional poet to be able to follow him.

His earlier verse was fairly regular in scansion, mostly iambic pentameter with a great deal of rhyme. As time went on he loosened out, until there are numerous irregular lines—this leaves us much freer in the matter of modernising. Our equivalents should be rhythmically as close as possible, but a strait-jacket need be no part of the equipment. A good Shakespearean scholar tells us, 'there is no necessity for Shakespeare's lines to scan absolutely. He thought of his verse as spoken rather than written and of his rhythmic units in terms of the voice rather than the page.'

There is nothing exclusive or mandatory about my project. We can all read Shakespeare in any edition we like—in the rebarbative olde Englishe spelling of the First Folio, if we wish. Any number of conventional academic editions exist, all weighed down with a burden of notes, many of them superfluous. I propose to make most of them unnecessary—only one occasionally at the foot of very few pages. Let the text be freed of superfluous difficulties, remove obstacles to let it speak for itself, while adhering conservatively to every line.

We really do not need any more editions of the Plays on conventional lines—more than enough of those exist already. But *A Contemporary Shakespeare* on these lines—both revolutionary and conservative—should be a help to everybody all round the world—though especially for younger people, increasingly with time moving away from the language of 400 years ago.

All's Well
That Ends Well

INTRODUCTION

All's Well That Ends Well is a remarkable play from
several points of view, and yet—as Professor C. J.
Sisson says—it has 'suffered at the hands of critics',
who have not perceived its points or how revealing it is.
'In general, the play has been greatly under-rated, not least
as an acting play', with its magnificent *dénouement.* Yet it
has splendid character parts: Parolles, whom Charles I
noted as outstanding in his copy of the Second Folio, one
of Shakespeare's most individual comic creations; the
Countess of Rossillion, whom Bernard Shaw regarded as
'the most beautiful old woman's part ever written'; her
son, the spoiled young aristocrat whom nobody loves—
except Helena, the doctor's lower-class daughter; Helena
herself, who wins him to her bed if not to her love by the
well-known bed-trick, which was welcome to Elizabethan
taste if not to ours.

In short, failure to appreciate the play is in part due to
the change of taste and values since Shakespeare's day; and
with no play is it more important to put it, and see it, in
the perspective of its time. Then to interpret it—the proper,
and modest, role of critics.

The story came from Boccaccio via Painter's *Palace of
Pleasure* (1566). That provided the theme; but, as was
Shakespeare's way, it was one that was very relevant to the
circumstances of the time and released what he had it in

mind to say about them. Crucial to the plot is the sickness of the King, well-nigh fatal, but miraculously cured by a dead doctor's daughter outside the sphere of regular orthodox physicians. She is virtually an empiric—and the conflict between the College of Physicians (referred to as such) and empirics was a topical theme, as we know from Simon Forman's case.[1] Sickness was much in the air: the ageing Queen was moving towards her end in these years 1601–3. Again, as Sisson points out, 'many a royal ward in those days had reason to rebel against his or her disposal in marriage for the benefit of their guardians.' Thus the young Count's 'conduct is natural enough in real Elizabethan life and society.' This historical comment is very helpful to understanding Count Bertram, the character most in need of sympathy—though modern taste would sympathise with him rather than with Helena, the virgin who virtually forces herself upon him.

Where have we met this imbroglio before?—In the case of Shakespeare's young patron, the Earl of Southampton, in which he was closely involved. The spoiled young Earl would not marry—in spite of his duty to his house and the urgent persuasions of his friends. It would seem that Shakespeare's in the Sonnets were not disagreeable to the Countess, his mother, who received a tribute in them. Rather than marry, he preferred to fling off to serve in France, as Bertram does to Italy—both, be it noted, as Generals of Horse, though the King thought it 'a charge too heavy', exactly as the Queen thought in Southampton's case in Ireland. The Earl incurred her displeasure, as the Count did the King's. Both young men served bravely and were wounded.

One hardly needs to go further. In these years, 1601–3, Southampton was languishing sick in the Tower; and 1603

---

[1] cf. my *Simon Forman: Sex and Society in Shakespeare's Age.*

was a bad plague year. In Ireland he was on very familiar terms with a braggadoccio Captain Piers Edmonds, 'culling' him in his arms in his tent. We note that Count Bertram's familiar, the braggart captain Parolles, calls him 'sweetheart'.

A great deal of the time is in this play: we should date it to 1602, the last year of the Queen's life. Pertinent reflections occur on the new and disillusioning society opening out with the new century, the vulgarity of the Jacobean age—the heroic days over—the conflicts of generations and class. Count Bertram is affronted at being married off to a doctor's daughter. The dramatist's comment on that is:

From lowest place when virtuous things proceed,
The place is dignified by the doer's deed.

And

Honours thrive
When rather from our acts we them derive
Than our foregoers.

The elderly King quotes the young Count's father against the latter's generation: 'Let me not live', he used to say,

to be the snuff
Of younger spirits, whose apprehensive senses
All but new things disdain; whose judgements are
Mere fathers of their garments; whose constancies
Expire before their fashions.

The Countess appeals to the King to pardon her son's injurious conduct on the ground of his youth—which was Southampton's mother's plea on behalf of her son for his rebellion:

Natural rebellion done in the blade of youth,
When oil and fire, too strong for reason's force,
O'erbear it and burn on.

Southampton's rebellion was in the immediate background,
in 1601, only a year or two before the play. We have reason to note again and again Shakespeare's
reflections on 'honour', and his constant interest in monu-
ments and tombs—personally characteristic. The mere word
'honour' is

Debauched on every tomb, on every grave
A lying trophy, and as oft is dumb `
Where dust and damned oblivion is the tomb
Of honoured bones indeed.

We detect too the sceptical note characteristic of him, since
it is so often sounded throughout the plays: 'They say
miracles are past, and we have our philosophical persons
to make modern [i.e. normal] and familiar things supernatural and causeless. Hence is it that we make trifles of
terrors, ensconcing ourselves into seeming knowledge when
we should submit ourselves to an unknown fear.' And for
a philosophic reflection of his own, unmistakable for all
the absurd assumption that we cannot tell what Shakespeare
thought himself, when it occurs in different guises again
and again: 'The web of our life is of a mingled yarn, good
and ill together. Our virtues would be proud if our faults
whipped them not, and our crimes would despair if they
were not cherished by our virtues.'
    We see the application of this tolerant scepticism in
experience: 'for young Charbon the Puritan and old Poysam
the Papist, howsoever their hearts are severed in religion,
their heads are both one: they may jowl horns together like
any deer in the herd', i.e. both may be equally cuckolds.

And, we may add, we see the writer's enthusiasm for deer-hunting from early days in everything he wrote. Not much bawdy in this serious play, though he takes an opportunity when it presents itself, and there are the almost regulation references to 'French crowns' and balding from venereal disease, rife in Elizabethan London.

Imperceptive critics are apt to dismiss the rhymed couplets in which he expressed his *sententiae* as 'old-fashioned fustian': but they are characteristic of the age, and ubiquitous in the country: evidently considered appropriate to the thought, like a motto, or indeed the injunction on his gravestone.

> Oft expectation fails, and most of there
> Where most it promises, and oft it hits
> Where hope is coldest and despair most fits.

The language of this play offers no particular difficulties. But a modern edition, which modernises spelling and punctuation—as many sensibly do nowadays—should not keep pointless archaisms like 'vild' for vile, 'yond' for yon. Shakespeare often uses 'in' for words where we should use un, e.g. incertain, inaidable, for uncertain, unaidable; or again, he will use 'un' where the modern usage is in. No sacrosanctity attaches to inconsistency: we are free to modernise. And it is a sheer bonus, in a modern edition, to get rid of such tongue-twisters as 'methink*st* thou', 'should*st* strive', 'may*st* thou', 'should*st* choose', etc.

Though less popular than it deserves, this play—along with its companion piece, *Measure for Measure*—is of special interest philosophically, provoking thought and telling us what Shakespeare thought.

CHARACTERS

BERTRAM, Count of Rossillion
The COUNTESS of Rossillion, Bertram's mother
HELENA, a young girl brought up by the Countess
PAROLLES, Bertram's follower
Rinaldo, STEWARD in the Countess's household
Lavatch, CLOWN in the Countess's household
A Page
The KING of France
LAFEW, an old Lord
The brothers Dumaine, two French LORDS: later Captains
    serving the Duke of Florence
A GENTLEMAN, Astringer to the Court of France
The DUKE of Florence
A WIDOW of Florence
DIANA, the Widow's daughter
MARIANA, a friend of the Widow

LORDS, ATTENDANTS, SOLDIERS, CITIZENS, French and
    Florentine

Act I

SCENE I
The Countess's house.

*Enter Bertram, Count of Rossillion, his mother
the Countess, Helena, and Lord Lafew; all in black*

COUNTESS   In delivering my son from me, I bury a second
husband.

BERTRAM   And I in going, madam, weep over my father's
death anew; but I must attend his majesty's command,
to whom I am now in ward, evermore in subjection.

LAFEW   You shall find of the King a husband, madam;
you, sir, a father. He that so generally is at all times
good must of necessity hold his virtue to you, whose
worthiness would stir it up where it wanted, rather
than lack it where there is such abundance.

COUNTESS   What hope is there of his majesty's
amendment?

LAFEW   He has abandoned his physicians, madam, under
whose practices he has persecuted time with hope, and
finds no other advantage in the process but only the
losing of hope by time.

COUNTESS   This young gentlewoman had a father—O
that 'had', how sad a passage it is!—whose skill was
almost as great as his honesty; had it stretched so far,
would have made nature immortal, and death should
have play for lack of work. Would for the King's sake he
were living! I think it would be the death of the King's
disease.

LAFEW   How called you the man you speak of, madam?

COUNTESS   He was famous, sir, in his profession, and it
was his great right to be so: Gerard de Narbonne.

LAFEW   He was excellent indeed, madam. The King very
lately spoke of him admiringly, and mourningly. He
was skilful enough to have lived still, if knowledge
could be set up against mortality.

BERTRAM   What is it, my good lord, the King languishes
of?

LAFEW   A fistula, my lord.

BERTRAM   I heard not of it before.

LAFEW   I would it were not notorious. Was this gentlewoman the daughter of Gerard de Narbonne?

COUNTESS   His sole child, my lord, and bequeathed to
my overlooking. I have those hopes of her good, that her
education promises her disposition she inherits—which
makes fair gifts fairer. For where an unclean mind carries
virtuous qualities, there commendations go with pity:
they are virtues and traitors too. In her they are the
better for their simpleness. She derives her honesty and
achieves her goodness.

LAFEW   Your commendations, madam, get from her tears.

COUNTESS   It is the best brine a maiden can season
her praise in. The remembrance of her father never
approaches her heart but the tyranny of her sorrows
takes all livelihood from her cheek. No more of this,
Helena; go to, no more, lest it be rather thought you
affect a sorrow than to have it.

HELENA   I do affect a sorrow indeed, but I have it too.

LAFEW   Moderate lamentation is the right of the dead,
excessive grief the enemy to the living.

COUNTESS   If the living is enemy to the grief, the excess
makes it soon mortal.

BERTRAM   Madam, I desire your holy wishes.

LAFEW   How understand we that?

COUNTESS
   Be you blessed, Bertram, and succeed your father
   In manners as in shape! Your blood and virtue
   Contend for empire in you, and your goodness
   Share with your birthright! Love all, trust a few,
   Do wrong to none. Be able for your enemy
   Rather in power than use, and keep your friend
   Under your own life's key. Be checked for silence,
   But never taxed for speech. What heaven more will,
   That you may furnish and my prayers pluck down,
   Fall on your head! Farewell. —My lord,
   He is an unseasoned courtier: good my lord,
   Advise him.
LAFEW   He cannot want the best
   That shall attend his love.
COUNTESS   Heaven bless him! Farewell, Bertram.   *Exit*
BERTRAM   The best wishes that can be forged in your
   thoughts be servants to you! (*To Helena*) Be comfortable
   to my mother, your mistress, and make much of her.
LAFEW   Farewell, pretty lady. You must hold the credit of
   your father.   *Exeunt Bertram and Lafew*
HELENA
   O, were that all! I think not on my father,
   And these great tears grace his remembrance more
   Than those I shed for him. What was he like?
   I have forgotten him. My imagination
   Carries no features in it but Bertram's.
   I am undone: there is no living, none,
   If Bertram is away. It were all one
   That I should love a bright particular star
   And think to wed it, he is so above me.
   In his bright radiance and collateral light
   Must I be comforted, not in his sphere.
   The ambition in my love thus plagues itself:
   The hind that would be mated by the lion
   Must die for love. It was pretty, though a plague,

To see him every hour, to sit and draw
His archèd brows, his hawking eye, his curls,
In our heart's table—heart too capable
Of every line and trick of his sweet looks.
But now he's gone, and my idolatrous fancy
Must sanctify his relics. Who comes here?

Enter Parolles

One that goes with him. I love him for his sake,
And yet I know him a notorious liar,
Think him a great way fool, solely a coward;
Yet these fixed evils sit so fit in him
That they take place when virtue's steely bones
Look bleak in the cold wind. Full oft we see
Cold wisdom waiting on superfluous folly.

PAROLLES   Save you, fair queen!
HELENA   And you, monarch!
PAROLLES   No.
HELENA   And no.
PAROLLES   Are you meditating on virginity?
HELENA   Ay. You have some stain of soldier in you: let
me ask you a question. Man is enemy to virginity; how
may we barricade it against him?
PAROLLES   Keep him out.
HELENA   But he assails, and our virginity, though valiant,
in the defence yet is weak. Unfold to us some warlike
resistance.
PAROLLES   There is none. Man setting down before you
will undermine you and blow you up.
HELENA   Bless our poor virginity from underminers and
blowers-up! Is there no military policy how virgins
might blow up men?
PAROLLES   Virginity being blown down, man will quicklier
be blown up; indeed, in blowing him down again, with
the breach yourselves made you lose your city. It is not

politic in the commonwealth of nature to preserve
virginity. Loss of virginity is rational increase, and
there was never virgin got till virginity was first lost.
That you were made of is mettle to make virgins.
Virginity, by being once lost, may be ten times found;
by being ever kept it is ever lost. It is too cold a
companion. Away with it!

HELENA   I will stand for it a little, though therefore I die
a virgin.

PAROLLES   There's little can be said in it; it is against
the rule of nature. To speak on the part of virginity
is to accuse your mothers, which is most infallible
disobedience. He that hangs himself is a virgin; virginity
murders itself, and should be buried in highways out of
all sanctified limit, as a desperate offendress against
nature. Virginity breeds mites, much like a cheese,
consumes itself to the very paring, and so dies with
feeding its own stomach. Besides, virginity is peevish,
proud, idle, made of self-love which is the most inhibited
sin in the canon. Keep it not; you cannot choose but lose
by it. Out with it! Within ten years it will make itself
two, which is a goodly increase, and the principal itself
not much the worse. Away with it!

HELENA   How might one do, sir, to lose it to her own
liking?

PAROLLES   Let me see. Sure, ill, to like him that never it
likes. It is a commodity will lose the gloss with lying;
the longer kept, the less worth. Off with it while it is
vendible; answer the time of request. Virginity, like an
old courtier, wears her cap out of fashion, richly suited
but unsuitable, just like the brooch and the toothpick,
which wear not now. Your date is better in your pie and
your porridge than in your cheek; and your virginity,
your old virginity, is like one of our French withered
pears: it looks ill, it eats drily; to be sure, 'tis a withered
pear; it was formerly better; yet 'tis a withered pear. Will
you anything with it?

HELENA

Not my virginity, yet . . .
There shall your master have a thousand loves,
A mother, and a mistress, and a friend,
A phoenix, captain, and an enemy,
A guide, a goddess, and a sovereign,
A counsellor, a traitress, and a dear.
His humble ambition, proud humility,
His jarring concord, and his discord dulcet,
His faith, his sweet disaster; with a world
Of pretty, vain, adopted names when blind
Cupid is god-parent. Now shall he—
I know not what he shall. God send him well!
The Court's a learning-place, and·he is one—

PAROLLES

What one, in faith?

HELENA

That I wish well. It is pity—

PAROLLES

What is a pity?

HELENA

That wishing well had not a body in it
Which might be felt: that we, the poorer born,
Whose baser stars do shut us up in wishes,
Might with effects of them follow our friends,
And show what we alone must think, which never
Returns us thanks.

Enter Page

PAGE Monsieur Parolles, my lord calls for you.   *Exit*
PAROLLES Little Helen, farewell. If I can remember you I
  will think of you at Court.
HELENA Monsieur Parolles, you were born under a
  charitable star.

PAROLLES   Under Mars, I.

HELENA   I especially think under Mars.

PAROLLES   Why under Mars?

HELENA   The wars have so kept you under that you must needs be born under Mars.

PAROLLES   When he was predominant.

HELENA   When he was retrograde, I think rather.

PAROLLES   Why think you so?

HELENA   You go so much backward when you fight.

PAROLLES   That's for advantage.

HELENA   So is running away, when fear proposes the safety. But the composition that your valour and fear make in you is a virtue of a good wing, and I like the wear well.

PAROLLES   I am so full of businesses I cannot answer you acutely. I will return perfect courtier, in which my instruction shall serve to naturalize you, so you will be capable of a courtier's counsel, and understand what advice shall thrust upon you. Else you die in your unthankfulness, and your ignorance makes you away. Farewell. When you have leisure, say your prayers; when you have none, remember your friends. Get you a good husband, and use him as he uses you. So, farewell. *Exit*

HELENA

Our remedies oft in ourselves do lie,
Which we ascribe to heaven. The fated sky
Gives us free scope, only does backward pull
Our slow designs when we ourselves are dull.
What power is it which mounts my love so high,
That makes me see, and cannot feed my eye?
The mightiest space in fortune nature brings
To join like likes, and kiss like native things.
Impossible are strange attempts to those
That weigh their pains in sense, and do suppose
What has been cannot be. Who ever strove
To show her merit that did miss her love?

The King's disease—my project may deceive me,
But my intents are fixed, and will not leave me.   *Exit*

SCENE II
The King's palace.

*Flourish of cornets. Enter the King of France with letters,
and attendants*

KING
The Florentines and Senoys [Siennese] are by the ears,
Have fought with equal fortune, and continue
A braving war.
FIRST LORD   So it is reported, sir.
KING
Nay, it is most credible. We here receive it
A certainty, vouched from our cousin Austria,
With caution that the Florentine will move us
For speedy aid. Wherein our dearest friend
Prejudicates the business, and would seem
To have us make denial.
FIRST LORD   His love and wisdom,
Approved so to your majesty, may plead
For amplest credence.
KING   He has armed our answer,
And Florence is denied before he comes.
Yet, for our gentlemen that mean to see
The Tuscan service, freely have they leave
To stand on either part.
SECOND LORD   It well may serve
A nursery to our gentry, who are sick
For breathing and exploit.
KING   What's he comes here?

Enter Bertram, Lafew, and Parolles

FIRST LORD
   It is the Count Rossillion, my good lord,
   Young Bertram.
KING   Youth, you bear your father's face;
   Frank nature, rather curious than in haste,
   Has well composed you. Your father's moral parts
   May you inherit too! Welcome to Paris.
BERTRAM
   My thanks and duty are your majesty's.
KING
   I would I had that corporal soundness now,
   As when your father and myself in friendship
   First tried our soldiership. He did look far
   Into the service of the time, and was
   Discipled of the bravest. He lasted long,
   But on us both did haggish age steal on,
   And wore us out of act. It much repairs me
   To talk of your good father. In his youth
   He had the wit which I can well observe
   Today in our young lords; but they may jest
   Till their own scorn returns to them unnoted
   Ere they can hide their levity in honour.
   So like a courtier, contempt or bitterness
   Was not in his pride or sharpness. If they were,
   His equal had awaked them, and his honour,
   Clock to itself, knew the true minute when
   Exception bid him speak; and at this time
   His tongue obeyed his hand. Who were below him
   He used as creatures of another place,
   And bowed his eminent top to their low ranks,
   Making them proud of his humility,
   In their poor praise he humbled. Such a man
   Might be a copy to these younger times;
   Which, followed well, would demonstrate them now
   But goers backward.

BERTRAM   His good remembrance, sir,
     Lies richer in your thoughts than on his tomb;
     So in approof lives not his epitaph
     As in your royal speech.
KING
     Would I were with him! He would always say—
     I think I hear him now; his worthy words
     He scattered not in ears, but grafted them
     To grow there and to bear—'Let me not live',
     This his good melancholy oft began
     On the catastrophe and heel of pastime,
     When it was out, 'Let me not live', said he,
     'After my flame lacks oil, to be the snuff
     Of younger spirits, whose apprehensive senses
     All but new things disdain; whose judgements are
     Mere fathers of their garments; whose constancies
     Expire before their fashions.' This he wished.
     I, after him, do after him wish too,
     Since I nor wax nor honey can bring home,
     I quickly were dissolvèd from my hive
     To give some labourers room.
SECOND LORD   You're loved, sir;
     They that least lend it you shall lack you first.
KING
     I fill a place, I know. How long is it, Count,
     Since the physician at your father's died?
     He was much famed.
BERTRAM   Some six months since, my lord.
KING
     If he were living I would try him yet.
     Lend me an arm.—The rest have worn me out
     With several applications; nature and sickness
     Debate it at their leisure. Welcome, Count,
     My son is no dearer.
BERTRAM   Thank your majesty.
                              Exeunt. Flourish

SCENE III
The Countess's house.

Enter the Countess, her Steward, and Lavatch her Clown

COUNTESS   I will now hear. What say you of this
gentlewoman?

STEWARD   Madam, the care I have had to even your
content I wish might be found in the calendar of my
past endeavours; for then we wound our modesty, and
make foul the clearness of our deservings, when of
ourselves we publish them.

COUNTESS   What does this knave here? Get you gone,
fellow. The complaints I have heard of you I do not all
believe; it is my slowness that I do not, for I know you
lack not folly to commit them, and have ability enough
to make such knaveries yours.

CLOWN   It is not unknown to you, madam, I am a poor
fellow.

COUNTESS   Well, sir.

CLOWN   No, madam, it is not so well that I am poor,
though many of the rich are damned; but if I may have
your ladyship's good will to go to the world, Isbel your
woman and I will do as we may.

COUNTESS   Will you needs be a beggar?

CLOWN   I do beg your good will in this case.

COUNTESS   In what case?

CLOWN   In Isbel's case and my own. Service is no heritage,
and I think I shall never have the blessing of God till I
have issue of my body; for they say bairns are blessings.

COUNTESS   Tell me your reason why you will marry.

CLOWN   My poor body, madam, requires it. I am driven
on by the flesh, and he must needs go that the devil
drives.

COUNTESS   Is this all your worship's reason?

CLOWN   Faith, madam, I have other holy reasons, such
as they are.

COUNTESS   May the world know them?

CLOWN   I have been, madam, a wicked creature, as you
and all flesh and blood are, and indeed I do marry that I
may repent.

COUNTESS   Your marriage, sooner than your wickedness.

CLOWN   I am out of friends, madam, and I hope to have
friends for my wife's sake.

COUNTESS   Such friends are your enemies, knave.

CLOWN   You are shallow, madam; even great friends, for
the knaves come to do that for me which I am aweary of.
He that ploughs my land spares my team, and gives me
leave to in the crop. If I am his cuckold, he's my drudge.
He that comforts my wife is the cherisher of my flesh
and blood; he that cherishes my flesh and blood loves
my flesh and blood; he that loves my flesh and blood is
my friend; *ergo,* he that kisses my wife is my friend. If
men could be contented to be what they are, there were
no fear in marriage; for young Charbon the puritan and
old Poysam the papist, howsoever their hearts are severed
in religion, their heads are both one: they may jowl
horns together like any deer in the herd.

COUNTESS   Will you ever be a foul-mouthed and calum-
nious knave?

CLOWN   A prophet I, madam, and I speak the truth the
next way:

For I the ballad will repeat
    Which men full true shall find:
Your marriage comes by destiny,
    Your cuckoo sings by kind.

COUNTESS   Get you gone, sir. I'll talk with you more
anon.

STEWARD   May it please you, madam, that he bid Helen
come to you: of her I am to speak.

COUNTESS   Fellow, tell my gentlewoman I would speak
with her—Helen, I mean.

CLOWN
                Was this fair face the cause, said she,
                Why the Grecians sackèd Troy?
                    Ill done, done ill,
                Was this King Priam's joy?
                With that she sighèd as she stood,
                With that she sighèd as she stood,
                And gave this sentence then:
                Among nine bad if one is good,
                Among nine bad if one is good,
                There's yet one good in ten.

COUNTESS   What, one good in ten? You corrupt the song,
fellow.

CLOWN   One good woman in ten, madam, which is a
purifying of the song. Would God would serve the
world so all the year! We'd find no fault with the tithe-
woman if I were the parson. One in ten, said he! If we
might have a good woman born but one every blazing
star or at an earthquake, it would mend the lottery well;
a man may draw his heart out ere he plucks one.

COUNTESS   You'll be gone, sir knave, and do as I command
you!

CLOWN   That man should be at woman's command, and
yet no hurt done! Though honesty is no puritan, yet it
will do no hurt. It will wear the surplice of humility
over the black gown of a big heart. I am going, forsooth.
The business is for Helen to come hither.   *Exit*

COUNTESS   Well, now.

STEWARD   I know, madam, you love your gentlewoman
entirely.

COUNTESS   Faith, I do. Her father bequeathed her to me
and she herself, without other advantage, may lawfully
make title to as much love as she finds. There is more

owing her than is paid, and more shall be paid her than she will demand.

STEWARD   Madam, I was very late more near her than I think she wished me. Alone she was, and did communicate to herself her own words to her own ears; she thought, I dare vow for her, they touched not any stranger sense. Her matter was, she loved your son. Fortune, she said, was no goddess, that had put such difference betwixt their two estates; Love no god, that would not extend his might only where qualities were level; Dian no queen of virgins, that would suffer her poor knight surprised without rescue in the first assault or ransom afterward. This she delivered in the most bitter touch of sorrow that ever I heard virgin exclaim in, which I held my duty speedily to acquaint you with since, in the loss that may happen, it concerns you somewhat to know it.

COUNTESS   You have discharged this honestly; keep it to yourself. Many likelihoods informed me of this before, which hung so tottering in the balance that I could neither believe nor misdoubt. Pray you leave me. Stall this in your bosom, and I thank you for your honest care. I will speak with you further anon.   *Exit Steward*

Enter Helena

COUNTESS
Even so it was with me when I was young.
   If ever we are nature's, these are ours; this thorn
Does to our rose of youth rightly belong;
   Our blood to us, this to our blood is born.
It is the show and seal of nature's truth,
Where love's strong passion is impressed in youth.
By our remembrances of days foregone,
Such were our faults, or then we thought them none.
Her eye is sick of it; I observe her now.

HELENA
  What is your pleasure, madam?
COUNTESS   You know, Helen,
  I am a mother to you.
HELENA
  My honourable mistress.
COUNTESS   Nay, a mother.
  Why not a mother? When I said 'a mother',
  I thought you saw a serpent. What's in 'mother'
  That you start at it? I say I am your mother,
  And put you in the catalogue of those
  That were enwombèd mine. It is often seen
  Adoption strives with nature, and choice breeds
  A native slip to us from foreign seeds.
  You never oppressed me with a mother's groan,
  Yet I express to you a mother's care.
  God's mercy, maiden! Does it curd your blood
  To say I am your mother? What's the matter,
  That this distempered messenger of wet,
  The many-coloured Iris, rounds your eye?
  Why, that you are my daughter?
HELENA   That I am not.
COUNTESS
  I say I am your mother.
HELENA   Pardon, madam.
  The Count Rossillion cannot be my brother.
  I am from humble, he from honoured name;
  No note upon my parents, his all noble.
  My master, my dear lord he is, and I
  His servant live, and will his vassal die.
  He must not be my brother.
COUNTESS   Nor I your mother?
HELENA
  You are my mother, madam; would you were—
  So that my lord your son were not my brother—
  Indeed my mother! Or were you both our mothers

I care no more for than I do for heaven,
So I were not his sister. Can it no other
But, I your daughter, he must be my brother?
COUNTESS
  Yes, Helen, you might be my daughter-in-law.
  God shield you mean it not! 'Daughter' and 'mother'
  So strive upon your pulse. What, pale again?
  My fear has caught your folly. Now I see
  The mystery of your loneliness, and find
  Your salt tears' head. Now to all sense 'tis clear:
  You love my son. Invention is ashamed
  Against the proclamation of your passion
  To say you do not. Therefore tell me true;
  But tell me then, 'tis so; for, look, your cheeks
  Confess it the one to the other, and your eyes
  See it so grossly shown in your behaviour
  That in their kind they speak it; only sin
  And hellish obstinacy tie your tongue,
  That truth should be suspected. Speak, is it so?
  If it is so, you have wound a goodly clew;
  If it is not, forswear it; however, I charge you,
  As heaven shall work in me for your avail,
  To tell me truly.
HELENA   Good madam, pardon me.
COUNTESS
  Do you love my son?
HELENA   Your pardon, noble mistress.
COUNTESS
  Love you my son?
HELENA   Do not you love him, madam?
COUNTESS
  Do not evade; my love has in it a bond
  Whereof the world takes note. Come, come, disclose
  The state of your affection, for your passions
  Have to the full betrayed you.

HELENA   Then I confess,
   Here on my knee, before high heaven and you,
   That before you, and next unto high heaven,
   I love your son.
   My friends were poor, but honest; so is my love.
   Be not offended, for it hurts not him
   That he is loved of me. I follow him not
   By any token of presumptuous suit,
   Nor would I have him till I do deserve him,
   Yet never know how that desert should be.
   I know I love in vain, strive against hope,
   Yet in this captious and untenable sieve
   I still pour in the waters of my love
   And lack not to lose still. Thus, Indian-like,
   Religious in my error, I adore
   The sun that looks upon its worshipper
   But knows of him no more. My dearest madam,
   Let not your hate encounter with my love,
   For loving where you do; but if yourself,
   Whose agèd honour cites a virtuous youth,
   Did ever, in so true a flame of liking,
   Wish chastely and love dearly, that your Dian
   Was both herself and love—O then, give pity
   To her whose state is such that cannot choose
   But lend and give where she is sure to lose;
   That seeks not to find what her search implies,
   But riddle-like lives sweetly where she dies.
COUNTESS
   Had you not lately an intent—speak truly—
   To go to Paris?
HELENA   Madam, I had.
COUNTESS   Wherefore? tell true.
HELENA
   I will tell truth, by grace itself I swear.
   You know my father left me some prescriptions
   Of rare and proved effects, such as his reading
   And manifest experience had collected

For general sovereignty. And that he willed me
In heedfullest reservation to bestow them,
As notes whose faculties inclusive were
More than they were reported. Among the rest
There is a remedy, approved, set down,
To cure the desperate languishings whereof
The King is rendered lost.

COUNTESS   This was your motive
For Paris, was it? Speak.

HELENA
My lord your son made me to think of this,
Else Paris and the medicine and the King
Had from the conversation of my thoughts
Haply been absent then.

COUNTESS   But think you, Helen,
If you should tender your supposèd aid,
He would receive it? He and his physicians
Are of a mind: he, that they cannot help him;
They, that they cannot help. How shall they credit
A poor unlearnèd virgin, when the schools,
Embowelled of their doctrine, have left off
The danger to itself?

HELENA   There's something in it
More than my father's skill, which was the greatest
Of his profession, that his good receipt
Shall for my legacy be sanctified
By the luckiest stars in heaven. And would your honour
But give me leave to try success, I'd venture
The well-lost life of mine on his grace's cure
By such a day, and hour.

COUNTESS   Do you believe it?

HELENA
Ay, madam, knowingly.

COUNTESS
Why, Helen, you shall have my leave and love,
Means and attendants, and my loving greetings

To those of mine in Court. I'll stay at home
And pray God's blessing into your attempt.
Be gone tomorrow, and be sure of this,
What I can help you to, you shall not miss.   *Exeunt*

Act II

SCENE I
The King's Palace.

Enter the King with Lords; Bertram and Parolles;
attendants. Flourish of cornets

KING
   Farewell, young lords; these warlike principles
   Do not throw from you; and you, my lords, farewell.
   Share the advice between you; if both gain all,
   The gift does stretch itself as it is received,
   And is enough for both.
FIRST LORD   It is our hope, sir,
   As experienced soldiers, to return
   And find your grace in health.
KING
   No, no, it cannot be; and yet my heart
   Will not confess it owns the malady
   That does my life besiege. Farewell, young lords.
   Whether I live or die, be you the sons
   Of worthy Frenchmen. Let higher Italy—
   Except those that inherit but the fall
   Of the last monarchy—see that you come
   Not to woo honour, but to wed it. When
   The bravest seeker shrinks, find what you seek,
   That fame may cry you loud. I say farewell.
FIRST LORD
   Health at your bidding serve your majesty!

KING
   Those girls of Italy, take heed of them:
   They say our French lack language to deny
   If they demand. Beware of being captives
   Before you serve.
BOTH LORDS   Our hearts receive your warnings.
KING
   Farewell. *(To some attendants)* Come hither to me.

He withdraws

FIRST LORD
   O my sweet lord, that you will stay behind us!
PAROLLES
   'Tis not his fault, the spark.
SECOND LORD   O, 'tis brave wars!
PAROLLES
   Most wonderful! I have seen those wars.
BERTRAM
   I am commanded here, frustrated with
   'Too young', and 'The next year', and ''Tis too early'.
PAROLLES
   If your mind stands to it, boy, steal away bravely.
BERTRAM
   I shall stay here the forehorse to a smock,
   Creaking my shoes on the plain masonry,
   Till honour is bought up, and no sword worn
   But one to dance with. By heaven, I'll steal away!
FIRST LORD
   There's honour in the theft.
PAROLLES   Commit it, Count.
SECOND LORD   I am your accessary; and so farewell.
BERTRAM   I grow to you, and our parting is a tortured
   body.
FIRST LORD   Farewell, captain.
SECOND LORD   Sweet Monsieur Parolles!

PAROLLES   Noble heroes, my sword and yours are kin.
Good sparks and lustrous, a word, good metals. You
shall find in the regiment of the Spinii one Captain
Spurio, with his scar, an emblem of war, here on his
sinister cheek; it was this very sword entrenched it. Say
to him I live, and observe his reports for me.
FIRST LORD   We shall, noble captain.   *Exeunt the Lords*
PAROLLES   Mars dote on you for his novices! (*To Bertram*)
What will you do?
BERTRAM   Stay: the King.
PAROLLES   Use a more spacious ceremony to the noble
lords; you have restrained yourself within the list of too
cold an adieu. Be more expressive to them, for they wear
themselves in the cap of the time; there do muster true
gait, eat, speak, and move, under the influence of the
most received star; and though the devil leads the
measure, such are to be followed. After them, and take a
more dilated farewell.
BERTRAM   And I will do so.
PAROLLES   Worthy fellows, and like to prove most sinewy
sword-men.   *Exeunt Bertram and Parolles*

Enter Lafew. The King comes forward

LAFEW   (*kneeling*)
Pardon, my lord, for me and for my tidings.
KING
I'll sue you to stand up.
LAFEW
Then here's a man stands that has brought his pardon,
I would you had kneeled, my lord, to ask me mercy,
And that at my bidding you could so stand up.
KING
I would I had, so I had broken your pate
And asked you mercy for it.

LAFEW   Good faith, a hit!
But, my good lord, 'tis thus: will you be cured
Of your infirmity?
KING   No.
LAFEW   O, will you eat
No grapes, my royal fox? Yes, but you will
My noble grapes, and if my royal fox
Could reach them. I have seen a medicine
That is able to breathe life into a stone,
Quicken a rock, and make you dance canary
With sprightly fire and motion; whose simple touch
Is powerful to araise King Pepin, nay,
To give great Charlemagne a pen in his hand
And write to her a love-line.
KING   What 'her' is this?
LAFEW
Why, Doctor She! My lord, there's one arrived,
If you will see her. Now by my faith and honour—
If seriously I may convey my thoughts
In this my light deliverance—I have spoken
With one that in her sex, her years, profession,
Wisdom, and constancy has amazed me more
Than I dare blame my weakness. Will you see her,
For that is her demand, and know her business?
That done, laugh well at me.
KING   Now, good Lafew,
Bring in the wonderment, that we with you
May spend our wonder too, or take off yours
By wondering how you took it.
LAFEW   Nay, I'll show you,
And not be all day either.
KING
Thus he his special nothing ever prologues.
LAFEW
Nay, come your ways.

Enter Helena

KING   This haste has wings indeed.
LAFEW
  Nay, come your ways.
  This is his majesty: say your mind to him.
  A traitor you do look like, but such traitors
  His majesty seldom fears. I am Cressid's uncle
  That dare leave two together. Fare you well.   *Exit*
KING
  Now, fair one, does your business follow us?
HELENA
  Ay, my good lord.
  Gerard de Narbonne was my father,
  In what he did profess, well found.
KING   I knew him.
HELENA
  The rather will I spare my praises towards him;
  Knowing him is enough. On his bed of death
  Many receipts he gave me; chiefly one,
  Which, as the dearest issue of his practice,
  And of his old experience the only darling,
  He bade me store up as a triple eye,
  Safer than my own two, more dear. I have so,
  And hearing your high majesty is touched
  With that malignant cause wherein the honour
  Of my dear father's gift stands chief in power,
  I come to tender it and my appliance,
  With all bound humbleness.
KING   We thank you, maiden,
  But may not be so credulous of cure,
  When our most learnèd doctors leave us, and
  The congregated college have concluded
  That labouring art can never ransom nature
  From her unaidible estate. I say we must not
  So stain our judgement or corrupt our hope,
  To prostitute our past-cure malady

To empirics, or to dissever so
Our great self and our credit, to esteem
A senseless help, when help past sense we deem.

HELENA

My duty then shall pay me for my pains.
I will no more enforce my office on you,
Humbly entreating from your royal thoughts
A modest one to bear me back again.

KING

I cannot give you less, to be called grateful.
You thought to help me, and such thanks I give
As one near death to those that wish him live.
But what at full I know, you know no part;
I knowing all my peril, you no art.

HELENA

What I can do can do no hurt to try,
Since you set up your stand against remedy.
He that of greatest works is finisher
Oft does them by the weakest minister.
So holy writ in babes has judgement shown,
When judges have been babes; great floods have flown
From simple sources; and great seas have dried
When miracles have by the greatest been denied.
Oft expectation fails, and most oft there
Where most it promises, and oft it hits
Where hope is coldest and despair most fits.

KING

I must not hear you. Fare you well, kind maid.
Your pains, not used, must by yourself be paid;
Proffers not taken reap thanks for their reward.

HELENA

Inspirèd merit so by breath is barred.
It is not so with Him that all things knows
As it is with us that base our guess on shows;
But most it is presumption in us when
The help of heaven we count the act of men.

Dear sir, to my endeavours give consent.
Of heaven, not me, make an experiment.
I am not an impostor, that proclaim
Myself against the level of my aim,
But know I think, and think I know most sure,
My art is not past power, nor you past cure.
KING
Are you so confident? Within what space
Hope you my cure?
HELENA   The greatest grace lending grace,
Ere twice the horses of the sun shall bring
Their fiery torcher his diurnal ring,
Ere twice in murk and occidental damp
Moist Hesperus has quenched her sleepy lamp;
Or four and twenty times the pilot's glass
Has told the thievish minutes how they pass,
What is infirm from your sound parts shall fly,
Health shall live free and sickness freely die.
KING
Upon your certainty and confidence
What dare you venture?
HELENA   Tax of impudence,
A strumpet's boldness, a divulgèd shame;
Traduced by odious ballads my maiden's name;
Seared otherwise, nor worse of worst, extended
With vilest torture let my life be ended.
KING
I think in you some blessèd spirit does speak
His powerful sound within an organ weak;
And what impossibility would slay
In common sense, sense saves another way.
Your life is dear, for all that life can rate
Worth name of life in you has estimate:
Youth, beauty, wisdom, courage—all
That happiness and prime can happy call.
You this to hazard needs must intimate

Skill infinite, or monstrous desperate.
Sweet practiser, your physic I will try,
That ministers your own death if I die.

HELENA
If I break time, or flinch in property
Of what I spoke, unpitied let me die,
And well deserved. Not helping, death is my fee;
But if I help, what do you promise me?

KING
Make your demand.

HELENA   But will you make it even?

KING
Ay, by my sceptre and my hopes of heaven.

HELENA
Then shall you give me with your kingly hand
What husband in your power I will command:
Exempted be from me the arrogance
To choose from forth the royal blood of France
My low and humble name to propagate,
With any branch or image of your state;
But such a one, your vassal, whom I know
Is free for me to ask, you to bestow.

KING
Here is my hand; the premises observed,
Your will by my performance shall be served.
So make the choice of your own time, for I,
Your resolved patient, on you still rely.
More should I question you, and more I must,
Though more to know could not be more to trust:
From whence you came, how tended on—but rest
Unquestioned welcome, and undoubted blessed.
Give me some help here, ho! If you proceed
As high as word, my deed shall match your deed.

                                    Flourish. Exeunt

SCENE II
The Countess's house.

Enter the Countess and the Clown

COUNTESS   Come on, sir. I shall now put you to the height of your breeding.

CLOWN   I will show myself highly fed and lowly taught. I know my business is but to the Court.

COUNTESS   To the Court! Why, what place make you special, when you put off that with such contempt? But to the Court!

CLOWN   Truly, madam, if God has lent a man any manners he may easily put it off at Court. He that cannot make a leg, put off his cap, kiss his hand, and say nothing, has neither leg, hands, lip, nor cap; and indeed such a fellow, to say precisely, were not for the Court. But for me, I have an answer will serve all men.

COUNTESS   Indeed, that's a bountiful answer that fits all questions.

CLOWN   It is like a barber's chair that fits all buttocks: the pin-buttock, the squat-buttock, the brawn-buttock, or any buttock.

COUNTESS   Will your answer serve fit to all questions?

CLOWN   As fit as ten groats is for the hand of an attorney, as your French crown for your taffeta whore, as Tib's rush ring for Tom's forefinger; as a pancake for Shrove Tuesday, a morris for May-day, as the nail to its hole, the cuckold to his horn; as a scolding quean to a wrangling knave, as the nun's lip to the friar's mouth; nay, as the pudding to its skin.

COUNTESS   Have you, I say, an answer of such fitness for all questions?

CLOWN   From below your duke to beneath your constable, it will fit any question.

COUNTESS   It must be an answer of most monstrous size
that must fit all demands.
CLOWN   But a trifle, in good faith, if the learned should
speak truth of it. Here it is, and all that belongs to it.
Ask me if I am a courtier; it shall do you no harm to
learn.
COUNTESS   To be young again, if we could! I will be a
fool in question, hoping to be the wiser by your answer.
I pray you, sir, are you a courtier?
CLOWN   O Lord, sir!—There's a simple putting off. More,
more, a hundred of them.
COUNTESS   Sir, I am a poor friend of yours that loves
you.
CLOWN   O Lord, sir!—Quick, quick; spare not me.
COUNTESS   I think, sir, you can eat none of this homely
meat.
CLOWN   O Lord, sir!—Nay, put me to it, I warrant you.
COUNTESS   You were lately whipped, sir, as I think.
CLOWN   O Lord, sir!—Spare not me.
COUNTESS   Do you cry 'O Lord, sir!' at your whipping,
and 'spare not me'? Indeed your 'O Lord, sir!' is very
sequent to your whipping: you would answer very well
to a whipping, if you were but bound to it.
CLOWN   I never had worse luck in my life in my 'O Lord,
sir!' I see things may serve long, but not serve ever.
COUNTESS
I play the noble housewife with the time,
To entertain it so merrily with a fool.
CLOWN
O Lord, sir!—Why, there it serves well again.
COUNTESS
An end, sir! To your business: give Helen this,
And urge her to a present answer back.
Commend me to my kinsmen and my son.
This is not much.

CLOWN   Not much commendation to them?

COUNTESS   Not much employment for you. You understand me?

CLOWN   Most fruitfully. I am there before my legs.

COUNTESS   Haste you again.

Exeunt

SCENE III
The King's palace.

Enter Bertram, Lafew, and Parolles

LAFEW   They say miracles are past, and we have our philosophical persons to make normal and familiar, things supernatural and causeless. Hence is it that we make trifles of terrors, ensconcing ourselves into seeming knowledge when we should submit ourselves to an unknown fear.

PAROLLES   Why, 'tis the rarest argument of wonder that has shot out in our latter times.

BERTRAM   And so it is.

LAFEW   To be relinquished of the artists—

PAROLLES   So I say—both of Galen and Paracelsus.

LAFEW   Of all the learnèd and authentic fellows—

PAROLLES   Right, so I say.

LAFEW   That gave him out incurable—

PAROLLES   Why, there it is, so say I too.

LAFEW   Not to be helped.

PAROLLES   Right, as it were a man assured of a—

LAFEW   Uncertain life and sure death.

PAROLLES   Just, you say well. So would I have said.

LAFEW   I may truly say it is a novelty to the world.

PAROLLES   It is indeed. If you will have it in showing, you shall read it in what-do-you-call there.

LAFEW   A showing of a heavenly effect in an earthly
   actor.
PAROLLES   That's it, I would have said the very same.
LAFEW   Why, your dolphin is not lustier. Before me, I
   speak in respect—
PAROLLES   Nay, 'tis strange, 'tis very strange, that is the
   brief and the tedious of it; and he's of a most villainous
   spirit that will not acknowledge it to be the—
LAFEW   Very hand of heaven.
PAROLLES   Ay, so I say.
LAFEW   In a most weak—
PAROLLES   And feeble minister, great power, great
   transcendence, which should indeed give us a further
   use to be made than alone the recovery of the King, as to
   be—
LAFEW   Generally thankful.

   Enter the King, Helena, and attendants

PAROLLES   I would have said it, you say well. Here comes
   the King.
LAFEW   Lustig, as the German says. I'll like a maid the
   better while I have a tooth in my head. Why, he's able to
   lead her a coranto [a dance].
PAROLLES   *Mor du vinager!* Is not this Helen?
LAFEW   Before God, I think so.
KING
   Go, call before me all the lords in Court.
                                    Exit an attendant
   Sit, my preserver, by your patient's side,
   And with this healthful hand, whose banished sense
   You have recalled, a second time receive
   The confirmation of my promised gift,
   Which but attends your naming.

   Enter four Lords

Fair maid, send forth your eye. This youthful parcel
Of noble bachelors stand at my bestowing,
Over whom both sovereign power and father's voice
I have to use. Your frank election make;
You have power to choose, and they none to forsake.

HELENA
To each of you one fair and virtuous mistress
Fall, when love pleases! Yet, to each but one!

LAFEW
I'd give my bay horse and his furniture
My mouth no more were broken than these boys',
And claimed as little beard.

KING   Peruse them well.
Not one of those but had a noble father.

HELENA
Gentlemen,
Heaven has through me restored the King to health.

ALL THE LORDS
We understand it, and thank heaven for you.

HELENA
I am a simple maid, and therein wealthiest
That I protest I simply am a maid.
Please it your majesty, I have done already.
The blushes in my cheeks thus whisper me:
'We blush that you should choose, but, be refused,
Let the white death sit on your cheek for ever,
We'll never come there again.'

KING   Make choice and see,
Who shuns your love shuns all his love in me.

HELENA
Now, Dian, from your altar do I fly,
And to imperial Love, that god most high,
Do my sighs stream. (To First Lord) Sir, will you hear
    my suit?

FIRST LORD
  And grant it.
HELENA   Thanks, sir. All the rest is mute.
LAFEW   I had rather be in this choice than throw an ace
  for my life.
HELENA   (to Second Lord)
  The honour, sir, that flames in your fair eyes
  Before I speak, too threateningly replies.
  Love make your fortunes twenty times above
  Her that so wishes, and her humble love!
SECOND LORD
  No better, if you please.
HELENA   My wish receive,
  Which great Love grant. And so I take my leave.
LAFEW Do all they deny her? If they were sons of mine I
  would have them whipped, or I would send them to
  the Turk to make eunuchs of.
HELENA   (to Third Lord)
  Be not afraid that I your hand should take;
  I'll never do you wrong, for your own sake.
  Blessing upon your vows, and in your bed
  Find fairer fortune if you ever wed!
LAFEW   These boys are boys of ice; they'll none have her.
  Sure, they are bastards to the English; the French never
  got them.
HELENA   (to Fourth Lord)
  You are too young, too happy, and too good
  To make yourself a son out of my blood.
FOURTH LORD   Fair one, I think not so.
LAFEW   There's one grape yet. I am sure your father drank
  wine; but if you are not an ass, I am a youth of fourteen;
  I have known you already.
HELENA   (to Bertram)
  I dare not say I take you, but I give
  Me and my service, ever while I live,
  Into your guiding power. This is the man.

KING
    Why, then, young Bertram, take her, she's your wife.
BERTRAM
    My wife, my lord! I shall beseech your highness,
    In such a business give me leave to use
    The help of my own eyes.
KING   Know you not, Bertram,
    What she has done for me?
BERTRAM   Yes, my good lord,
    But never hope to know why I should marry her.
KING
    You know she has raised me from my sickly bed.
BERTRAM
    But follows it, my lord, to bring me down
    Must answer for your raising? I know her well:
    She had her breeding at my father's charge.
    A poor physician's daughter my wife! Disdain
    Rather corrupt me ever!
KING
    It is only title you disdain in her, which
    I can build up. Strange is it that our bloods,
    Of colour, weight, and heat, poured all together,
    Would quite confound distinction, yet stands off
    In differences so mighty. If she is
    All that is virtuous, save what you dislike—
    A poor physician's daughter—you dislike
    Of virtue for the name. But do not so.
    From lowest place when virtuous things proceed,
    The place is dignified by the doer's deed.
    Where great additions swell us and virtue none,
    It is a dropsied honour. Good alone
    Is good, without a name: vileness is so;
    The property by what it is should go,
    Not by the title. She is young, wise, fair;
    In these to nature she's immediate heir,
    And these breed honour; that is honour's scorn

Which challenges itself as honour's born
And is not like the sire. Honours thrive
When rather from our acts we them derive
Than our foregoers. The mere word's a slave,
Debauched on every tomb, on every grave
A lying trophy, and as oft is dumb
Where dust and damned oblivion are the tomb
Of honoured bones indeed. What should be said?
If you can like this creature as a maid,
I can create the rest. Virtue and she
Are her own dower; honour and wealth from me.

BERTRAM
I cannot love her nor will strive to do it.

KING
You wrong yourself if you should strive to choose.

HELENA
That you are well restored, my lord, I'm glad.
Let the rest go.

KING
My honour's at the stake, which to defeat,
I must produce my power. Here, take her hand,
Proud, scornful boy, unworthy this good gift,
That do in vile contempt so shackle up
My love and her desert; that can not dream
We, poising us in her defective scale,
Shall weigh you to the beam; that will not know
It is in us to plant your honour where
We please to have it grow. Check your contempt.
Obey our will which travails in your good.
Believe not your disdain, but forthrightly
Do your own fortunes that obedient right
Which both your duty owes and our power claims.
Or I will throw you from my care for ever
Into the staggers and the careless lapse
Of youth and ignorance; both my revenge and hate
Loosing upon you in the name of justice,
Without all terms of pity. Speak. Your answer.

BERTRAM
  Pardon, my gracious lord; for I submit
  My fancy to your eyes. When I consider
  What great creation and what share of honour
  Fly where you bid it, I find that she, who late
  Was in my nobler thoughts most base, is now
  The praisèd of the King; who, so ennobled,
  Is as it were born so.
KING   Take her by the hand
  And tell her she is yours; to whom I promise
  A counterpoise, if not to your estate,
  A balance more replete.
BERTRAM   I take her hand.
KING
  Good fortune and the favour of the King
  Smile upon this contract, whose ceremony
  Shall follow swiftly on the new-born brief,
  And be performed tonight. The solemn feast
  Shall more attend upon the coming space,
  Expecting absent friends. As you love her
  Your love's to me religious; else, does err.
                    Exeunt all but Parolles and Lafew
LAFEW   Do you hear, monsieur? A word with you.
PAROLLES   Your pleasure, sir.
LAFEW   Your lord and master did well to make his
  recantation.
PAROLLES   Recantation! My lord! My master!
LAFEW   Ay. Is it not a language I speak?
PAROLLES   A most harsh one, and not to be understood
  without bloody succeeding. My master!
LAFEW   Are you companion to the Count Rossillion?
PAROLLES   To any Count, to all Counts, to what is man.
LAFEW   To what is Count's man; Count's master is of
  another style.

PAROLLES   You are too old, sir; let it satisfy you, you are
too old.

LAFEW   I must tell you, fellow, I write man, to which title
age cannot bring you.

PAROLLES   What I dare too well do, I dare not do.

LAFEW   I did think you for two mealtimes to be a pretty
wise fellow. You did make tolerable vent of your travel;
it might pass. Yet the scarfs and the bannerets you
about did manifoldly dissuade me from believing you a
vessel of too great a burden. I have now found you;
when I lose you again I care not. Yet are you good for
nothing but taking up, and that you are scarce worth.

PAROLLES   Had you not the privilege of antiquity upon
you—

LAFEW   Do not plunge yourself too far in anger, lest you
hasten your trial; which if—Lord have mercy on you for
a hen! So, my good window of lattice, fare you well;
your casement I need not open, for I look through you.
Give me your hand.

PAROLLES   My lord, you give me most egregious indignity.

LAFEW   Ay, with all my heart; and you are worthy of it.

PAROLLES   I have not, my lord, deserved it.

LAFEW   Yes, good faith, every dram of it, and I will not
spare you a scruple.

PAROLLES   Well, I shall be wiser.

LAFEW   Even as soon as you can, for you have to drink a
bellyful of the contrary. If ever you are bound in your
scarf and beaten, you shall find what it is to be proud of
your bondage. I have a desire to hold my acquaintance
with you, or rather my knowledge, that I may say, when
you default, 'He is a man I know'.

PAROLLES   My lord, you do me most insupportable
vexation.

LAFEW   I would it were hell-pains for your sake, and my
poor doing eternal; for doing I am past, as I will by you,
in what motion age will give me leave.   *Exit*

PAROLLES   Well, you have a son shall take this disgrace off me, scurvy, old, filthy, scurvy lord! Well, I must be patient, there is no fettering of authority. I'll beat him, by my life, if I can meet him with any convenience, if he were double and double a lord. I'll have no more pity on his age than I would have on—I'll beat him if I could but meet him again.

Enter Lafew

LAFEW   Fellow, your lord and master's married, there's news for you; you have a new mistress.
PAROLLES   I most unfeignedly beseech your lordship to make some reservation of your wrongs. He is my good lord: whom I serve above is my master.
LAFEW   Who? God?
PAROLLES   Ay, sir.
LAFEW   The devil it is that's your master. Why do you garter up your arms in this fashion? Do you make hose of your sleeves? Do other servants so? You were best set your lower part where your nose stands. By my honour, if I were but two hours younger I'd beat you. I think you are a general offence and every man should beat you. I think you were created for men to breathe themselves upon you.
PAROLLES   This is hard and undeserved measure, my lord.
LAFEW   Go to, sir. You were beaten in Italy for picking a kernel out of a pomegranate. You are a vagabond and no true traveller. You are more saucy with lords and honourable personages than the commission of your birth and virtue gives you heraldry. You are not worth another word, else I'd call you knave. I leave you.   *Exit*

Enter Bertram

PAROLLES   Good, very good, it is so then. Good, very

good; let it be concealed awhile.

BERTRAM

Undone and forfeited to cares for ever!

PAROLLES   What's the matter, sweetheart?

BERTRAM

Although before the solemn priest I have sworn,
I will not bed her.

PAROLLES

What, what, sweetheart?

BERTRAM

O my Parolles, they have married me!
I'll to the Tuscan wars and never bed her.

PAROLLES

France is a dog-hole and it no more merits
The tread of a man's foot. To the wars!

BERTRAM

There's letters from my mother: what the import is I
know not yet.

PAROLLES

Ay, that would be known. To the wars, my boy, to the
wars!
He wears his honour in a box unseen
That hugs his kicky-wicky here at home,
Spending his manly marrow in her arms,
Who should sustain the bound and high curvet
Of Mars's fiery steed. To other regions!
France is a stable, we that dwell in it, jades.
Therefore to the wars!

BERTRAM

It shall be so. I'll send her to my house,
Acquaint my mother with my hate to her
And wherefore I am fled; write to the King
That which I durst not speak. His present gift
Shall furnish me to those Italian fields
Where noble fellows strike. War is no strife
To the dark house and the detested wife.

PAROLLES
  Will this capriccio hold in you, for sure?
BERTRAM
  Go with me to my chamber and advise me.
  I'll send her straight away. Tomorrow
  I'll to the wars, she to her single sorrow.
PAROLLES
  Why, these balls bound, there's noise in it. 'Tis hard:
  A young man married is a man that's marred.
  Therefore away, and leave her bravely; go.
  The King has done you wrong, but hush, 'tis so.

                                              Exeunt

SCENE IV
The King's Palace.

Enter Helena and the Clown

HELENA   My mother greets me kindly. Is she well?
CLOWN   She is not well, but yet she has her health; she's
  very merry, but yet she is not well. But thanks be given
  she's very well and wants nothing in the world; but yet
  she is not well.
HELENA   If she is very well, what does she ail that she is
  not very well?
CLOWN   Truly, she is very well indeed, but for two things.
HELENA   What two things?
CLOWN   One, that she is not in heaven, whither God
  send her quickly! The other, that she's on earth, from
  whence God send her quickly!

Enter Parolles

PAROLLES   Bless you, my fortunate lady.
HELENA   I hope, sir, I have your good will to have my
  own good fortune.

PAROLLES   You had my prayers to lead them on, and to
keep them on have them still. O, my knave! How does
my old lady?

CLOWN   So that you had her wrinkles and I her money, I
would she did as you say.

PAROLLES   Why, I say nothing.

CLOWN   Well, you are the wiser man, for many a man's
tongue shakes out his master's undoing. To say nothing,
to do nothing, to know nothing, and to have nothing, is
to be a great part of your title, which is within a very
little of nothing.

PAROLLES   Away! You are a knave.

CLOWN   You should have said, sir, 'Before a knave you
are a knave'; that's 'Before me, you are a knave'. This
had been truth, sir.

PAROLLES   Go to, you are a witty fool: I have found you.

CLOWN   Did you find me in your self, sir, or were you
taught to find me? The search, sir, was profitable; and
much fool may you find in you, even to the world's
pleasure and the increase of laughter.

PAROLLES
A good knave in faith, and well fed.
Madam, my lord will go away tonight;
A very serious business calls on him.
The great prerogative and rite of love,
Which as your due time claims, he does acknowledge,
But puts it off to a compelled restraint:
Whose want and whose delay are strewed with sweets,
Which they distil now in the curbèd time,
To make the coming hour o'erflow with joy
And pleasure drown the brim.

HELENA   What's his will else?

PAROLLES
That you will take your instant leave of the King,
And make this haste as your own good proceeding,

Strengthened with what apology you think
May make it probable need.

HELENAWhat more commands he?

PAROLLES
That, having this obtained, you immediately
Attend his further pleasure.

HELENA
In everything I wait upon his will.

PAROLLES
I shall report it so.*Exit*

HELENA
I pray you. Come, boy.*Exeunt*

SCENE V
The same.

Enter Lafew and Bertram

LAFEWBut I hope your lordship thinks not him a soldier.

BERTRAMYes, my lord, and of very valiant proof.

LAFEWYou have it from his own deliverance.

BERTRAMAnd by other warranted testimony.

LAFEWThen my dial goes not true: I took this lark for a bunting.

BERTRAMI do assure you, my lord, he is very great in knowledge, and accordingly valiant.

LAFEWI have then sinned against his experience and transgressed against his valour, and my state that way is dangerous, since I cannot yet find in my heart to repent. Here he comes. I pray you make us friends; I will pursue the amity.

Enter Parolles

PAROLLES   (*to Bertram*) These things shall be done, sir.

LAFEW   Pray you, sir, who's his tailor?

PAROLLES   Sir!

LAFEW   O, I know him well. Ay, sir, he, sir, is a good workman, a very good tailor.

BERTRAM   (*aside to Parolles*) Is she gone to the King?

PAROLLES   She is.

BERTRAM   Will she away tonight?

PAROLLES   As you will have her.

BERTRAM

I have written my letters, casketed my treasure,
Given order for our horses; and tonight,
When I should take possession of the bride,
End ere I do begin.

LAFEW   (*aside*). A good traveller is something at the latter end of a dinner; but one that lies three thirds and uses a known truth to pass a thousand nothings with, should be once heard and thrice beaten. (*Aloud*) God save you, captain!

BERTRAM   Is there any unkindness between my lord and you, monsieur?

PAROLLES   I know not how I have deserved to run into my lord's displeasure.

LAFEW   You have made shift to run into it, boots and spurs and all, like him that leaped into the custard; and out of it you'll run again rather than suffer question for your residence.

BERTRAM   It may be you have mistaken him, my lord.

LAFEW   And shall do so ever, though I took him at his prayers. Fare you well, my lord, and believe this of me: there can be no kernel in this light nut. The soul of this man is his clothes. Trust him not in matter of heavy consequence. I have kept some of them tame, and know their natures. Farewell, monsieur; I have spoken better of you than you have or will to deserve at my hand, but we must do good against evil.   *Exit*

PAROLLES   An idle lord, I swear.
BERTRAM   I think not so.
PAROLLES   Why, do you not know him?
BERTRAM
   Yes, I do know him well, and common speech
   Gives him a worthy pass. Here comes my clog.

Enter Helena

HELENA
   I have, sir, as I was commanded from you,
   Spoken with the King, and have procured his leave
   For present parting; only he desires
   Some private speech with you.
BERTRAM   I shall obey his will.
   You must not marvel, Helen, at my course,
   Which holds not colour with the time, nor does
   The ministration and requirèd office
   On my particular. Prepared I was not
   For such a business, therefore am I found
   So much unsettled. This drives me to entreat you
   That now at once you take your way for home,
   And rather muse than ask why I entreat you.
   For my respects are better than they seem,
   And my appointments have in them a need
   Greater than shows itself at the first view
   To you that know them not. This to my mother.

He gives Helena a letter

   It will be two days ere I shall see you, so
   I leave you to your wisdom.
HELENA   Sir, I can nothing say
   But that I am your most obedient servant.
BERTRAM
   Come, come, no more of that.

HELENA   And ever shall
With true observance seek to eke out that
Wherein toward me my homely stars have failed
To equal my great fortune.
BERTRAM   Let that go.
My haste is very great. Farewell. Hie home.
HELENA
Pray, sir, your pardon.
BERTRAM   Well, what would you say?
HELENA
I am not worthy of the wealth I own,
Nor dare I say 'tis mine—and yet it is;
But, like a timorous thief, most fain would steal
What law does vouch my own.
BERTRAM   What would you have?
HELENA
Something, and scarce so much; nothing indeed.
I would not tell you what I would, my lord.
Faith, yes:
Strangers and foes do sunder and not kiss.
BERTRAM
I pray you, stay not, but in haste to horse.
HELENA
I shall not break your bidding, good my lord.
Where are my other men? Monsieur, farewell.   *Exit*
BERTRAM
Go you toward home, where I will never come
While I can shake my sword or hear the drum.
Away, and for our flight.
PAROLLES   Bravely. Coragio!   *Exeunt*

Act III

SCENE I
The Duke of Florence's Palace.

Flourish. Enter the Duke of Florence, and two French
Lords, with soldiers

DUKE
So that from point to point now have you heard
The fundamental reasons of this war,
Whose great decision has much blood let forth,
And more thirsts after.
FIRST LORD   Holy seems the quarrel
Upon your grace's part, black and fearful
On the opposer.
DUKE
Therefore we marvel much our cousin France
Would in so just a business shut his bosom
Against our borrowing prayers.
SECOND LORD   Good my lord,
The reasons of our state I cannot yield,
But like a common and an outside man
That the great figure of a council frames
By self-unable motion; therefore dare not
Say what I think of it, since I have found
Myself in my uncertain grounds to fail
As often as I guessed.
DUKE   Be it his pleasure.
FIRST LORD
But I am sure the younger of our nature
That surfeit on their ease will day by day

Come here for physic.

DUKE   Welcome shall they be,
And all the honours that can fly from us
Shall on them settle. You know your places well;
When better fall, for your avails they fell.
Tomorrow to the field.   *Flourish. Exeunt*

SCENE II
The Countess's house.

Enter the Countess and the Clown

COUNTESS   It has happened all as I would have had it,
save that he comes not along with her.
CLOWN   By my faith, I take my young lord to be a very
melancholy man.
COUNTESS   By what observance, I pray you?
CLOWN   Why, he will look upon his boot and sing, mend
the ruff and sing, ask questions and sing, pick his teeth
and sing. I knew a man that had this trick of melancholy
hold a goodly manor for a song.
COUNTESS   Let me see what he writes, and when he
means to come.

She opens the letter

CLOWN   I have no mind to Isbel since I was at Court. Our
old lings and our Isbels of the country are nothing like
your old ling and your Isbels of the Court. The brains of
my Cupid's knocked out, and I begin to love as an old
man loves money, with no stomach.
COUNTESS   What have we here?
CLOWN   Even that you have there.   *Exit*
COUNTESS   *(reading the letter aloud) I have sent you a
daughter-in-law; she has recovered the King and undone*

me. I have wedded her, not bedded her, and sworn to make the 'not' eternal. You shall hear I am run away; know it before the report comes. If there is breadth enough in the world I will hold a long distance. My duty to you.

Your unfortunate son,

Bertram.

This is not well, rash and unbridled boy,
To fly the favours of so good a King,
To pluck his indignation on your head
By the misprizing of a maid too virtuous
For the contempt of empire.

Enter Clown

CLOWN   O madam, yonder is heavy news within, between two soldiers and my young lady.

COUNTESS   What is the matter?

CLOWN   Nay, there is some comfort in the news, some comfort: your son will not be killed so soon as I thought he would.

COUNTESS   Why should he be killed?

CLOWN   So say I, madam, if he runs away, as I hear he does. The danger is in standing to it; that's the loss of men, though it is the getting of children. Here they come will tell you more. For my part, I only hear your son was run away.   *Exit*

Enter Helena and the two French Lords

FIRST LORD
Save you, good madam.

HELENA
Madam, my lord is gone, for ever gone.

SECOND LORD
  Do not say so.
COUNTESS
  Think upon patience. Pray you, gentlemen—
  I have felt so many quirks of joy and grief
  That the first face of neither on the start
  Can woman me unto it. Where is my son, I pray you?
SECOND LORD
  Madam, he's gone to serve the Duke of Florence.
  We met him thitherward, for thence we came,
  And, after some dispatch in hand at Court,
  Thither we bend again.
HELENA
  Look on his letter, madam: here's my passport.

              (She reads the letter aloud)

  When you can get the ring upon my finger, which never
  shall come off, and show me a child begotten of your
  body that I am father to, then call me husband; but in
  such a 'then' I write a 'never'.
  This is a dreadful sentence.
COUNTESS   Brought you this letter, gentlemen?
FIRST LORD   Ay, madam, and for the contents' sake are
  sorry for our pains.
COUNTESS
  I pray you, lady, have a better cheer.
  If you engross all the griefs are yours
  You rob me of a moiety. He was my son,
  But I do wash his name out of my blood
  And you are all my child. Towards Florence is he?
SECOND LORD
  Ay, madam.
COUNTESS   And to be a soldier?

SECOND LORD
  Such is his noble purpose; and, believe it,
  The Duke will lay upon him all the honour
  That good convenience claims.
COUNTESS   Return you thither?
FIRST LORD
  Ay, madam, with the swiftest wing of speed.
HELENA   *(reading)*
  Till I have no wife I have nothing in France.
  It is bitter.
COUNTESS   Find you that there?
HELENA   Ay, madam.
FIRST LORD   It is but the boldness of his hand, haply,
  which his heart was not consenting to.
COUNTESS
  Nothing in France until he has no wife!
  There's nothing here that is too good for him
  But only she; and she deserves a lord
  That twenty such rude boys might tend upon
  And call her, hourly, mistress. Who was with him?
FIRST LORD   A servant only, and a gentleman whom I
  have sometime known.
COUNTESS   Parolles, was it not?
FIRST LORD   Ay, my good lady, he.
COUNTESS
  A very tainted fellow, and full of wickedness.
  My son corrupts a well-derivèd nature
  With his inducement.
FIRST LORD   Indeed, good lady,
  The fellow has a deal of that too much
  Which profits him much to have.
COUNTESS   You are welcome, gentlemen.
  I will entreat you, when you see my son,
  To tell him that his sword can never win
  The honour that he loses. More I'll entreat you
  Written to bear along.

SECOND LORD   We serve you, madam,
    In that and all your worthiest affairs.
COUNTESS
    Not so, but as we change our courtesies.
    Will you draw near? *Exeunt the Countess and the Lords*
HELENA
    'Till I have no wife I have nothing in France.'
    Nothing in France until he has no wife!
    You shall have none, Rossillion, none in France,
    Then have you all again. Poor lord, is it I
    That chase you from your country, and expose
    Those tender limbs of yours to the event
    Of the none-sparing war? And is it I
    That drive you from the sportive Court, where you
    Were shot at with fair eyes, to be the mark
    Of smoky muskets? O you leaden messengers,
    That ride upon the violent speed of fire,
    Fly with false aim, move the recovering air
    That sings with piercing, do not touch my lord.
    Whoever shoots at him, I set him there.
    Whoever charges on his forward breast,
    I am the miscreant that do hold him to it;
    And though I kill him not, I am the cause
    His death was so effected. Better it were
    I met the ravenous lion when he roared
    With sharp constraint of hunger; better it were
    That all the miseries which nature owns
    Were mine at once. No, come you home, Rossillion,
    Whence honour but of danger wins a scar,
    As oft it loses all. I will be gone;
    My being here it is that holds you hence.
    Shall I stay here to do it? No, no, although
    The air of paradise did fan the house
    And angels officed all. I will be gone,
    That pitiful rumour may report my flight

To consolate your ear. Come, night; end, day!
For with the dark, poor thief, I'll steal away.   *Exit*

SCENE III
Florence. Before the Duke's palace.

*Flourish. Enter the Duke of Florence, Bertram, Parolles,
soldiers, drum and trumpets*

DUKE
  The general of our horse you are, and we,
  Great in our hope, lay our best love and credence
  Upon your promising fortune.
BERTRAM   Sir, it is
  A charge too heavy for my strength; but yet
  We'll strive to bear it for your worthy sake
  To the extreme edge of hazard.
DUKE   Then go you forth,
  And fortune play upon your prosperous helm
  As your auspicious mistress!
BERTRAM   This very day,
  Great Mars, I put myself into your file;
  Make me but like my thoughts and I shall prove
  A lover of your drum, hater of love.   *Exeunt*

SCENE IV
The Countess's house.

Enter the Countess and the Steward

COUNTESS
  Alas! and would you take the letter of her?
  Might you not know she would do as she has done
  By sending me a letter? Read it again.

STEWARD   (*reading*)
   I am Saint Jaquès' pilgrim, thither gone.
    Ambitious love has so in me offended
   That barefoot plod I the cold ground upon,
    With sainted vow my faults to have amended.
   Write, write, that from the bloody course of war
    My dearest master, your dear son, may hie.
   Bless him at home in peace, while I from far
    His name with zealous fervour sanctify.
   His taken labours bid him me forgive;
    I, his despiteful Juno, sent him forth
   From courtly friends, with camping foes to live
    Where death and danger dog the heels of worth.
   He is too good and fair for death and me;
    Whom I myself embrace to set him free.
COUNTESS
   Ah, what sharp stings are in her mildest words!
   Rinaldo, you did never lack advice so much
   As letting her pass so. Had I spoken with her,
   I could have well diverted her intents,
   Which thus she has prevented.
STEWARD   Pardon me, madam.
   If I had given you this at overnight
   She might have been overtaken; yet she writes
   Pursuit would be but vain.
COUNTESS   What angel shall
   Bless this unworthy husband? He cannot thrive,
   Unless her prayers, whom heaven delights to hear
   And loves to grant, reprieve him from the wrath
   Of greatest justice. Write, write, Rinaldo,
   To this unworthy husband of his wife.
   Let every word weigh heavy of her worth
   That he does weigh too light. My greatest grief,
   Though little he does feel it, set down sharply.
   Dispatch the most convenient messenger.

When haply he shall hear that she is gone,
He will return; and hope I may that she,
Hearing so much, will speed her foot again,
Led hither by pure love. Which of them both
Is dearer to me I have no skill in sense
To make distinction. Provide this messenger.
My heart is heavy and my age is weak;
Grief would have tears, and sorrow bids me speak.

Exeunt

SCENE V
Outside the walls of Florence.

*A tucket afar off. Enter Widow of Florence, her
daughter Diana, and Mariana, with citizens*

WIDOW   Nay, come, for if they do approach the city, we
shall lose all the sight.
DIANA   They say the French Count has done most
honourable service.
WIDOW   It is reported that he has taken their greatest
commander, and that with his own hand he slew the
Duke's brother.

Tucket

We have lost our labour; they are gone a contrary way.
Hark! You may know by their trumpets.
MARIANA   Come, let's return again and suffice ourselves
with the report of it. Well, Diana, take heed of this
French Earl. The honour of a maid is her name, and no
legacy is so rich as chastity.
WIDOW   I have told my neighbour how you have been
solicited by a gentleman his companion.

MARIANA   I know that knave, hang him! one Parolles; a
   filthy officer he is in those suggestions for the young
   Earl. Beware of them, Diana: their promises, enticements,
   oaths, tokens, and all these engines of lust, are not the
   things they pass for. Many a maid has been seduced by
   them, and the misery is, example, that so terribly shows
   in the wreck of maidenhood, cannot for all that dissuade
   others, but that they are limed with the twigs that
   threaten them. I hope I need not to advise you further;
   but I hope your own grace will keep you where you are,
   though there is no further danger known but the chastity
   which is so lost.
DIANA   You shall not need to fear me.

Enter Helena

WIDOW   I hope so. Look, here comes a pilgrim. I know
   she will lie at my house; thither they send one another.
   I'll question her. God save you, pilgrim! Whither are
   bound?
HELENA
   To Saint Jaques le Grand.
   Where do the palmers lodge, I do beseech you?
WIDOW
   At the Saint Francis here beside the gate.
HELENA
   Is this the way?

A march afar

WIDOW
   Ay, for sure, it is. Hark you, they come this way.
   If you will tarry, holy pilgrim,
   But till the troops come by,
   I will conduct you where you shall be lodged;

The rather for I think I know your hostess
As ample as myself.

HELENA   Is it yourself?

WIDOW
If you shall please so, pilgrim.

HELENA
I thank you and will stay upon your leisure.

WIDOW
You came, I think, from France?

HELENA   I did so.

WIDOW
Here you shall see a countryman of yours
That has done worthy service.

HELENA   His name, I pray you?

DIANA
The Count Rossillion. Know you such a one?

HELENA
But by the ear, that hears most nobly of him;
His face I know not.

DIANA   Whatsoever he is,
He's bravely taken here. He stole from France,
As it is reported, for the King had married him
Against his liking. Think you it is so?

HELENA
Ay, surely, merely the truth. I know his lady.

DIANA
There is a gentleman that serves the Count
Reports but coarsely of her.

HELENA   What's his name?

DIANA
Monsieur Parolles.

HELENA   O, I believe with him,
In argument of praise or to the worth
Of the great Count himself, she is too mean
To have her name repeated. All her deserving
Is a reservèd chastity, and that
I have not heard examined.

DIANA   Alas, poor lady!
'Tis a hard bondage to become the wife
Of a detesting lord.

WIDOW
I warrant, good creature, wheresoever she is,
Her heart weighs sadly. This young maid might do her
A shrewd turn if she pleased.

HELENA   How do you mean?
Maybe the amorous Count solicits her
In the unlawful purpose?

WIDOW   He does indeed,
And bargains with all that can in such a suit
Corrupt the tender honour of a maid.
But she is armed for him and keeps her guard
In chastity's defence.

Drum and colours. Enter Bertram, Parolles, with soldiers

MARIANA   The gods forbid else!

WIDOW
So, now they come.
That is Antonio, the Duke's eldest son;
That Escalus.

HELENA   Which is the Frenchman?

DIANA   He—
That with the plume. 'Tis a most gallant fellow.
I would he loved his wife; if he were chaster
He were much goodlier. Is't not a handsome gentleman?

HELENA
I like him well.

DIANA
'Tis pity he is not chaste. Yon's that same knave
That leads him to these places. Were I his lady
I would poison that vile rascal.

HELENA   Which is he?

DIANA   That jackanapes with scarfs. Why is he
  melancholy?
HELENA   Perchance he's hurt in the battle.
PAROLLES   Lose our drum! Well!
MARIANA   He's very vexed at something. Look, he has
  spied us.
WIDOW   Indeed, hang you!
MARIANA   And your courtesy, for a ring-carrier!
                    Exeunt Bertram, Parolles, and soldiers
WIDOW
  The troop is past. Come, pilgrim, I will bring you
  Where you shall host. Of enjoined penitents
  There are four or five, to great Saint Jaquès bound,
  Already at my house.
HELENA   I humbly thank you.
  Please it this matron and this gentle maid
  To eat with us tonight; the charge and thanking
  Shall be for me and, to requite you further,
  I will bestow some precepts on this virgin,
  Worthy the note.
WIDOW *and* MARIANA
       We'll take your offer kindly.   *Exeunt*

SCENE VI
Camp before Florence.

Enter Bertram and the two French Lords

FIRST LORD   Nay, good my lord, put him to it, let him
  have his way.
SECOND LORD   If your lordship finds him not a rascal,
  hold me no more in your respect.
FIRST LORD   On my life, my lord, a bubble.
BERTRAM   Do you think I am so far deceived in him?
FIRST LORD   Believe it, my lord, in my own direct

knowledge; without any malice, but to speak of him as
if my kinsman, he's a most notable coward, an infinite
and endless liar, an hourly promise-breaker, the owner of
no one good quality worthy your lordship's entertainment.
SECOND LORD   It were fit you knew him; lest, reposing
too far in his virtue which he has not, he might at some
great and trusty business in a main danger fail you.
BERTRAM   I would I knew in what particular action to
try him.
SECOND LORD   None better than to let him fetch off his
drum, which you hear him so confidently undertake to do.
FIRST LORD   I, with a troop of Florentines, will suddenly
surprise him; such I will have whom I am sure he
knows not from the enemy. We will bind and hoodwink
him so, that he shall suppose no other but that he is
carried into the camp of the adversaries, when we bring
him to our own tents. Be but your lordship present at
his examination. If he does not for the promise of his
life, and in the highest compulsion of base fear, offer to
betray you and deliver all the intelligence in his power
against you, and that with the divine forfeit of his soul
upon oath, never trust my judgement in anything.
SECOND LORD   O, for the love of laughter, let him fetch
his drum; he says he has a stratagem for it. When your
lordship sees the bottom of his success in it, and to what
metal this counterfeit lump of ore will be melted, if you
give him not John Drum's entertainment your inclining
cannot be removed. Here he comes.

Enter Parolles

FIRST LORD   O, for the love of laughter, hinder not the
honour of his design; let him fetch off his drum in any
hand.
BERTRAM   How now, monsieur! This drum sticks sorely
in your disposition.

SECOND LORD   A pox on it! Let it go, it is but a drum.

PAROLLES   But a drum! Is it but a drum? A drum so lost!
There was excellent command: to charge in with our
horse upon our own wings and to rend our own soldiers!

SECOND LORD   That was not to be blamed in the command
of the service; it was a disaster of war that Caesar
himself could not have prevented, if he had been there
to command.

BERTRAM   Well, we cannot greatly condemn our luck;
some dishonour we had in the loss of that drum, but it
is not to be recovered.

PAROLLES   It might have been recovered.

BERTRAM   It might, but it is not now.

PAROLLES   It is to be recovered. But that the merit of service
is seldom attributed to the true and exact performer, I
would have that drum or another, or *hic jacet.* [Here he
lies.]

BERTRAM   Why, if you have a stomach, to it, monsieur!
If you think your mystery in stratagem can bring this
instrument of honour again into its native quarter, be
magnanimous in the enterprise and go on. I will grace
the attempt for a worthy exploit. If you speed well in it
the Duke shall both speak of it and extend to you what
further becomes his greatness, even to the utmost syllable
of your worthiness.

PAROLLES   By the hand of a soldier, I will undertake it.

BERTRAM   But you must not now slumber in it.

PAROLLES   I'll about it this evening, and I will at once pen
down my dilemmas, encourage myself in my certainty,
put myself into my mortal preparation. And by midnight
look to hear further from me.

BERTRAM   May I be bold to acquaint his grace you are
gone about it?

PAROLLES   I know not what the success will be, my lord,
but the attempt I vow.

BERTRAM   I know you are valiant, and to the capability
of your soldiership will subscribe for you. Farewell.

PAROLLES   I love not many words.   *Exit*

FIRST LORD   No more than a fish loves water. Is not this a
strange fellow, my lord, that so confidently seems to
undertake this business; which he knows is not to be
done, damns himself to do, and dares better be damned
than to do it.

SECOND LORD   You do not know him, my lord, as we do.
Certain it is that he will steal himself into a man's
favour and for a week escape a great deal of discoveries;
but when you find him out you know him ever after.

BERTRAM   Why, do you think he will make no deed at
all of this that so seriously he does address himself
unto?

FIRST LORD   None in the world, but return with an
invention, and clap upon you two or three probable
lies. But we have almost run him down. You shall see
his fall tonight; for indeed he is not for your lordship's
respect.

SECOND LORD   We'll make you some sport with the fox
ere we cage him. He was first shown up by the old Lord
Lafew. When his disguise and he are parted tell me
what a sprat you shall find him; which you shall see
this very night.

FIRST LORD   I must go look to my twigs. He shall be
caught.

BERTRAM   Your brother, he shall go along with me.

FIRST LORD   As it pleases your lordship. I'll leave you.
                                                    Exit

BERTRAM
Now will I lead you to the house and show you
The lass I spoke of.

SECOND LORD   But you say she's chaste.

BERTRAM
That's all the fault. I spoke with her but once
And found her wondrous cold. But I sent to her
By this same coxcomb that we have in the wind
Tokens and letters which she did re-send,
And this is all I have done. She's a fair creature;
Will you go see her?
SECOND LORD   With all my heart, my lord.   *Exeunt*

SCENE VII
Florence. The Widow's house.

Enter Helena and the Widow

HELENA
If you misdoubt me that I am not she,
I know not how I shall assure you further
But I shall lose the grounds I work upon.
WIDOW
Though my estate is fallen, I was well born,
Nothing acquainted with these businesses,
And would not put my reputation now
In any staining act.
HELENA   Nor would I wish you.
First give me trust the Count he is my husband,
And what to your sworn counsel I have spoken
Is so from word to word; and then you cannot,
By the good aid that I of you shall borrow,
Err in bestowing it.
WIDOW   I should believe you,
For you have shown me that which well approves
You are great in fortune.
HELENA   Take this purse of gold,
And let me buy your friendly help thus far,
Which I will over-pay, and pay again

When I have found it. The Count he woos your daughter,
Lays down his wanton siege before her beauty,
Resolved to carry her. Let her, in fine, consent
As we'll direct her how 'tis best to bear it.
Now his importunate blood will naught deny
That she'll demand. A ring the Count does wear
That downward has succeeded in his house
From son to son some four or five descents
Since the first father wore it. This ring he holds
In most rich choice; yet, in his idle fire,
To buy his will it would not seem too dear,
However repented after.
WIDOW   Now I see
The bottom of your purpose.
HELENA
You see it lawful then. It is no more
But that your daughter, ere she seems as won,
Desires this ring; appoints him an encounter;
In short, delivers me to fill the time,
Herself most chastely absent. After,
To marry her I'll add three thousand crowns
To what is passed already.
WIDOW   I have yielded.
Instruct my daughter how she shall persèver
That time and place with this deceit so lawful
May prove coherent. Every night he comes
With music of all sorts, and songs composed
To her unworthiness. It nothing helps us
To chide him from our eaves, for he persists
As if his life lay on it.
HELENA   Why then tonight
Let us assay our plot, which, if it speed,
Is wicked meaning in a lawful deed,
And lawful meaning in a lawful act,
Where both not sin, and yet a sinful fact.
But let us about it.   *Exeunt*

Act IV

SCENE I
Outside the Florentine camp.

Enter the First French Lord, with Soldiers in ambush

FIRST LORD   He can come no other way but by this hedgecorner. When you sally upon him speak what terrible language you will; though you understand it not yourselves, no matter; for we must not seem to understand him, unless some one among us, whom we must produce for an interpreter.

FIRST SOLDIER   Good captain, let me be the interpreter.

FIRST LORD   Are you not acquainted with him? Knows he not your voice?

FIRST SOLDIER   No, sir, I warrant you.

FIRST LORD   But what mish-mash have you to speak to us again?

FIRST SOLDIER   Even such as you speak to me.

FIRST LORD   He must think us some band of foreigners in the adversary's entertainment. Now he has a smack of all neighbouring languages, therefore we must every one be a man of his own fancy, not to know what we speak one to another; so we seem to know is to know straight our purpose—choughs' language, gabble enough and good enough. As for you, interpreter, you must seem very politic. But couch, ho! Here he comes to beguile two hours in a sleep, and then to return and swear the lies he forges.

Enter Parolles

PAROLLES   Ten o'clock. Within these three hours it will
be time enough to go home. What shall I say I have
done? It must be a very plausible invention that carries
it. They begin to suspect me, and disgraces have of late
knocked too often at my door. I find my tongue is too
foolhardy, but my heart has the fear of Mars before it
and of his creatures, not daring the reports of my tongue.
FIRST LORD   This is the first truth that ever your own
tongue was guilty of.
PAROLLES   What the devil should move me to undertake
the recovery of this drum, being not ignorant of the
impossibility, and knowing I had no such purpose? I
must give myself some hurts, and say I got them in an
exploit. Yet slight ones will not carry it: they will say
'Came you off with so little?' And great ones I dare not
give. Wherefore, what's the instance? Tongue, I must
put you into a butter-woman's mouth, and buy myself
another of Bajazeth's mule, if you prattle me into these
perils.
FIRST LORD   Is it possible he should know what he is,
and be that he is?
PAROLLES   I would the cutting of my garments would
serve the turn, or the breaking of my Spanish sword.
FIRST LORD   We cannot afford you so.
PAROLLES   Or the baring of my beard, and to say it was in
stratagem.
FIRST LORD   It would not do.
PAROLLES   Or to drown my clothes and say I was stripped.
FIRST LORD   Hardly serve.
PAROLLES   Though I swore I leaped from the window of
the citadel—
FIRST LORD   How deep?
PAROLLES   Thirty fathom.
FIRST LORD   Three great oaths would scarce make that be
believed.

PAROLLES   I would I had any drum of the enemy's; I
would swear I recovered it.
FIRST LORD   You shall hear one anon.
PAROLLES   A drum now of the enemy's—

Alarum within

FIRST LORD   *Throca movousus, cargo, cargo, cargo.*
ALL   *Cargo, cargo, cargo, villianda par corbo, cargo.*

They seize him

PAROLLES
O, ransom, ransom!

They blindfold him

Do not hide my eyes.
FIRST SOLDIER   *Boskos thromuldo boskos.*
PAROLLES
I know you are the Muskos' regiment,
And I shall lose my life for want of language.
If there be here German, or Dane, Low Dutch,
Italian, or French, let him speak to me,
I'll discover that which shall undo the Florentine.
FIRST SOLDIER   *Boskos vauvado.* I understand you, and
can speak your tongue. *Kerelybonto.* Sir, betake you to
your faith, for seventeen poniards are at your bosom.
PAROLLES   O!
FIRST SOLDIER   O, pray, pray, pray! *Manka revania dulche.*
FIRST LORD   *Oscorbidulchos volivorco.*
FIRST SOLDIER
The General is content to spare you yet,
And, blindfold as you are, will lead you on
To gather from you. Haply you may inform
Something to save your life.

PAROLLES   O, let me live,
And all the secrets of our camp I'll show,
Their force, their purposes; nay, I'll speak that
Which you will wonder at.
FIRST SOLDIER   But will you faithfully?
PAROLLES
If I do not, damn me.
FIRST SOLDIER   *Acordo linta.*
Come on, you are granted space.
                              Exit with Parolles guarded

                    A short alarum within

FIRST LORD
Go tell the Count Rossillion and my brother
We have caught the woodcock and will keep him muffled
Till we do hear from them.
SECOND SOLDIER   Captain, I will.
FIRST LORD
He will betray us all unto ourselves:
Inform on that.
SECOND SOLDIER
So I will, sir.
FIRST LORD
Till then I'll keep him dark and safely locked.   *Exeunt*

SCENE II
The Widow's house.

                Enter Bertram and Diana

BERTRAM
They told me that your name was Fontibell.

DIANA
  No, my good lord, Diana.
BERTRAM   Titled goddess,
  And worth it, with addition! But, fair soul,
  In your fine frame has love no quality?
  If the quick fire of youth light not your mind
  You are no maiden but a monument.
  When you are dead you should be such a one
  As you are now; for you are cold and stern,
  And now you should be as your mother was
  When your sweet self was got.
DIANA
  She then was chaste.
BERTRAM   So should you be.
DIANA   No.
  My mother did but duty—such, my lord,
  As you owe to your wife.
BERTRAM   No more of that!
  I pray you do not strive against my vows.
  I was compelled to her, but I love you
  By love's own sweet constraint, and will for ever
  Do you all rights of service.
DIANA   Ay, so you serve us
  Till we serve you; but when you have our roses,
  You barely leave our thorns to prick ourselves,
  And mock us with our bareness.
BERTRAM   How have I sworn!
DIANA
  It is not the many oaths that make the truth,
  But the plain single vow that is vowed true.
  What is not holy, that we swear not by,
  But take the highest to witness. Then, pray you, tell me:
  If I should swear by Love's great attributes
  I loved you dearly, would you believe my oaths
  When I did love you ill? This has no holding,
  To swear by him whom I protest to love

That I will work against him. Therefore your oaths
Are words, and poor conditions but unsealed—
At least in my opinion.
BERTRAM   Change it, change it.
Be not so holy-cruel. Love is holy,
And my integrity never knew the crafts
That you do charge men with. Stand no more off,
But give yourself unto my sick desires,
Who then recovers. Say you are mine, and ever
My love as it begins shall so persèver.
DIANA
I see that men make vows in such a flame
That we'll forsake ourselves. Give me that ring.
BERTRAM
I'll lend it you, my dear, but have no power
To give it from me.
DIANA   Will you not, my lord?
BERTRAM
It is an honour belonging to our house,
Bequeathèd down from many ancestors,
Which were the greatest obloquy in the world
In me to lose.
DIANA   My honour is such a ring;
My chastity's the jewel of our house,
Bequeathèd down from many ancestors,
Which were the greatest obloquy in the world
In me to lose. Thus your own self's wisdom
Brings in the champion Honour on my part
Against your vain assault.
BERTRAM   Here, take my ring.
My house, my honour, yea, my life be yours,
And I'll be bidden by you.
DIANA
When midnight comes, knock at my chamber window;
I'll order take my mother shall not hear.
Now will I charge you in the band of truth,

When you have conquered my yet maiden bed,
Remain there but an hour, nor speak to me.
My reasons are most strong and you shall know them
When back again this ring shall be delivered.
And on your finger in the night I'll put
Another ring, that what in time proceeds
May token to the future our past deeds.
Adieu till then; then, fail not. You have won
A wife of me, though there my hope is done.

BERTRAM
A heaven on earth I have won by wooing thee.   *Exit*

DIANA
For which live long to thank both heaven and me!
You may so in the end.
My mother told me just how he would woo
As if she sat in his heart. She says all men
Have the like oaths. He had sworn to marry me
When his wife's dead; therefore I'll lie with him
When I am buried. Since Frenchmen are so braid [false].
Marry that will, I live and die a maid.
Only, in this disguise, I think it no sin
To cozen him that would unjustly win.   *Exit*

SCENE III
The Florentine camp.

Enter the two French Lords, and soldiers

FIRST LORD   You have not given him his mother's letter?
SECOND LORD   I have delivered it an hour since. There is
something in it that stings his nature, for on reading it
he changed almost into another man.
FIRST LORD   He has much worthy blame laid upon him
for shaking off so good a wife and so sweet a lady.

SECOND LORD   Especially he has incurred the everlasting displeasure of the King, who had even tuned his bounty to sing happiness to him. I will tell you a thing, but you shall let it dwell darkly with you.

FIRST LORD   When you have spoken it 'tis dead, and I am the grave of it.

SECOND LORD   He has perverted a young gentlewoman here in Florence, of a most chaste renown, and this night he fleshes his will in the spoil of her honour. He has given her his monumental ring, and thinks himself made in the unchaste composition.

FIRST LORD   Now, God lay our rebellious flesh! As we are ourselves, what things are we!

SECOND LORD   Merely our own traitors. And as in the common course of all treasons we ever see them reveal themselves till they attain to their abhorred ends, so he that in this action contrives against his own nobility, in his proper stream overflows himself.

FIRST LORD   Is it not meant damnable in us to be trumpeters of our unlawful intents? We shall not then have his company tonight?

SECOND LORD   Not till after midnight, for he is dieted to his hour.

FIRST LORD   That approaches apace. I would gladly have him see his company analysed, that he might take a measure of his own judgements wherein so curiously he had set this counterfeit.

SECOND LORD   We will not meddle with him till he comes, for his presence must be the whip of the other.

FIRST LORD   In the meantime, what hear you of these wars?

SECOND LORD   I hear there is an overture of peace.

FIRST LORD   Nay, I assure you, a peace concluded.

SECOND LORD   What will Count Rossillion do then? Will he travel further, or return again into France?

FIRST LORD   I perceive by this demand you are not altogether of his counsel.

SECOND LORD   Let it be forbidden, sir; so should I be a great deal of his act.

FIRST LORD   Sir, his wife some two months sincc fled from his house. Her pretence is a pilgrimage to Saint Jaques le Grand; which holy undertaking with most austere sanctimony she accomplished; and there residing, the tenderness of her nature became as a prey to her grief; in fine, made a groan of her last breath, and now she sings in heaven.

SECOND LORD   How is this borne out?

FIRST LORD   The stronger part of it by her own letters, which make her story true even to the point of her death. Her death itself, which could not be her office to say is come, was faithfully confirmed by the rector of the place.

SECOND LORD   Has the Count all this intelligence?

FIRST LORD   Ay, and the particular confirmations, point from point, to the full arming of the verity.

SECOND LORD   I am heartily sorry that he'll be glad of this.

FIRST LORD   How mightily sometimes we make comforts of our losses!

SECOND LORD   And how mightily some other times we drown our gain in tears! The great dignity that his valour has here acquired for him shall at home be encountered with a shame as ample.

FIRST LORD   The web of our life is of a mingled yarn, good and ill together. Our virtues would be proud if our faults whipped them not, and our crimes would despair if they were not cherished by our virtues.

Enter a Messenger

How now? Where's your master?

MESSENGER   He met the Duke in the street, sir, of whom he has taken a solemn leave: his lordship will next morning for France. The Duke has offered him letters of commendations to the King.

SECOND LORD   They shall be no more than needful there, if they were more than they can commend.

Enter Bertram

FIRST LORD   They cannot be too sweet for the King's tartness. Here's his lordship now. How now, my lord? Is it not after midnight?

BERTRAM   I have tonight dispatched sixteen businesses a month's length apiece. By an abstract of success: I have congied with the Duke, done my adieu with his nearest, buried a wife, mourned for her, writ to my lady mother I am returning, entertained my convoy, and between these main parcels of dispatch effected many nicer needs; the last was the greatest, but that I have not ended yet.

SECOND LORD   If the business is of any difficulty, and this morning your departure hence, it requires haste of your lordship.

BERTRAM   I mean, the business is not ended, as fearing to hear of it hereafter. But shall we have this dialogue between the Fool and the Soldier? Come, bring forth this counterfeit image who has deceived me like a doublemeaning prophesier.

SECOND LORD   Bring him forth.   *Exeunt the Soldiers*
Has sat in the stocks all night, poor gallant knave.

BERTRAM   No matter. His heels have deserved it in usurping his spurs so long. How does he carry himself?

SECOND LORD   I have told your lordship already: the stocks carry him. But to answer you as you would be understood, he weeps like a wench that had spilt her milk. He has confessed himself to Morgan, whom he supposes to be a friar, from the time of his remembrance to this very instant disaster of his setting in the stocks. And what think you he has confessed?

BERTRAM   Nothing of me, has he?

SECOND LORD   His confession is taken, and it shall be read to his face; if your lordship is in it, as I believe you are, you must have the patience to hear it.

Enter Parolles muffled

BERTRAM   A plague upon him! Muffled! He can say nothing of me.

FIRST LORD   *(aside to Bertram)* Hush, hush! Blindman comes. *(Aloud) Portotartarossa.*

FIRST SOLDIER   He calls for the tortures. What will you say without them?

PAROLLES   I will confess what I know without constraint. If you pinch me like a pasty I can say no more.

FIRST SOLDIER   *Bosko chimurcho.*

FIRST LORD   *Boblibindo chicurmurco.*

FIRST SOLDIER   You are a merciful general. Our General bids you answer to what I shall ask you out of a note.

PAROLLES   And truly, as I hope to live.

FIRST SOLDIER   *(reading) First demand of him how many horse the Duke is strong.* What say you to that?

PAROLLES   Five or six thousand, but very weak and unserviceable. The troops are all scattered and the commanders very poor rogues, upon my reputation and credit, and as I hope to live.

FIRST SOLDIER   Shall I set down your answer so?

PAROLLES   Do. I'll take the sacrament on it, how and which way you will.

BERTRAM   All's one to him. What a past-saving slave is this!

FIRST LORD   You are deceived, my lord; this is Monsieur Parolles, the gallant militarist—that was his own phrase—that had the whole theory of war in the knot of his scarf, and the practice in the scabbard of his dagger.

SECOND LORD   I will never trust a man again for keeping
  his sword clean, nor believe he can have everything in
  him by wearing his apparel neatly.
FIRST SOLDIER   Well, that's set down.
PAROLLES   'Five or six thousand horse' I said—I will say
  true—'or thereabouts' set down, for I'll speak truth.
FIRST LORD   He's very near the truth in this.
BERTRAM   But I give him no thanks for it, in the nature
  he delivers it.
PAROLLES   'Poor rogues' I pray you say.
FIRST SOLDIER   Well, that's set down.
PAROLLES   I humbly thank you, sir. A truth's a truth, the
  rogues are marvellous poor.
FIRST SOLDIER   (reading) Demand of him of what strength
  they are a-foot. What say you to that?
PAROLLES   By my faith, sir, if I were to live this present
  hour, I will tell true. Let me see: Spurio, a hundred
  and fifty; Sebastian, so many; Corambus, so many;
  Jaques, so many; Guiltian, Cosmo, Lodowick, and Gratii,
  two hundred fifty each; my own company, Chitopher,
  Vaumond, Bentii, two hundred fifty each. So that the
  muster-file, rotten and sound, upon my life, amounts
  not to fifteen thousand poll; half of which dare not
  shake the snow from off their cassocks lest they shake
  themselves to pieces.
BERTRAM   What shall be done to him?
FIRST LORD   Nothing but let him have thanks. Demand
  of him my condition, and what credit I have with the
  Duke.
FIRST SOLDIER   Well, that's set down. (Reading) You shall
  demand of him whether one Captain Dumaine is in the
  camp, a Frenchman; what his reputation is with the
  Duke, what his valour, honesty, and expertness in wars;
  or whether he thinks it not possible with well-weighing
  sums of gold to corrupt him to a revolt. What say you to
  this? What do you know of it?

PAROLLES   I beseech you, let me answer to the particular of the interogatories. Demand them singly.

FIRST SOLDIER   Do you know this Captain Dumaine?

PAROLLES   I know him: he was a patcher's prentice in Paris, from whence he was whipped for getting the sheriff's fool with child, a dumb innocent that could not say him nay.

BERTRAM   Nay, by your leave, hold your hands—though I know his brains are forfeit to the next tile that falls.

FIRST SOLDIER   Well, is this captain in the Duke of Florence's camp?

PAROLLES   Upon my knowledge he is, and lousy.

FIRST LORD   Nay, look not so upon me; we shall hear of your lordship anon.

FIRST SOLDIER   What is his reputation with the Duke?

PAROLLES   The Duke knows him for no other but a poor officer of mine, and wrote to me this other day to turn him out of the band. I think I have his letter in my pocket.

FIRST SOLDIER   Sure, we'll search.

PAROLLES   Seriously, I do not know; either it is there or it is upon a file with the Duke's other letters in my tent.

FIRST SOLDIER   Here it is; here's a paper. Shall I read it to you?

PAROLLES   I do not know if it is it or no.

BERTRAM   Our interpreter does it well.

FIRST LORD   Excellently.

FIRST SOLDIER   (reading)
Dian, the Count's a fool, and full of gold.

PAROLLES   That is not the Duke's letter, sir; that is an advertisement to a respectable maid in Florence, one Diana, to take heed of the allurement of one Count Rossillion, a foolish idle boy, but for all that very ruttish. I pray you, sir, put it up again.

FIRST SOLDIER   Nay, I'll read it first by your favour.

PAROLLES   My meaning in it, I protest, was very honest
in the behalf of the maid; for I knew the young Count to
be a dangerous and lascivious boy, who is a whale to
virginity, and devours up all the fry it finds.

BERTRAM   Damnable both-sides rogue!

FIRST SOLDIER   (reading)
When he swears oaths, bid him drop gold, and
   take it;
After he scores he never pays the score.
Half-won is match well made; match, and well
   make it.
He never pays after-debts, take it before.
And say a soldier, Dian, told you this:
Men are to meddle with, boys are not to kiss;
For count of this, the Count's a fool, I know it,
Who pays before, but not when he does owe it.
         Yours, as he vowed to you in your ear,
                         Parolles.

BERTRAM   He shall be whipped through the army, with
this rhyme in his forehead.

SECOND LORD   This is your devoted friend, sir, the
manifold linguist, and the armipotent soldier.

BERTRAM   I could endure anything before but a cat, and
now he's a cat to me.

FIRST SOLDIER   I perceive, sir, by the General's looks, we
shall be forced to hang you.

PAROLLES   My life, sir, in any case! Not that I am afraid
to die, but that, my offences being many, I would repent
out the remainder of nature. Let me live, sir, in a
dungeon, in the stocks, or anywhere, so I may live.

FIRST SOLDIER   We'll see what may be done, so you confess
freely. Therefore once more to this Captain Dumaine:
you have answered to his reputation with the Duke and
to his valour; what is his honesty?

PAROLLES   He will steal, sir, an egg out of a cloister. For
rapes and ravishments he parallels Nessus. He professes
not keeping of oaths; in breaking them he is stronger
than Hercules. He will lie, sir, with such volubility that
you would think truth were a fool. Drunkenness is his
best virtue, for he will be swine-drunk, and in his sleep
he does little harm, save to his bedclothes about him;
but they know his conditions and lay him in straw. I
have but little more to say, sir, of his honesty: he has
everything that an honest man should not have; what
an honest man should have, he has nothing.

FIRST LORD   I begin to love him for this.

BERTRAM   For this description of your honesty? A pox
upon him! For me, he's more and more a cat.

FIRST SOLDIER   What say you to his expertness in war?

PAROLLES   Faith, sir, he has led the drum before the
English tragedians—to belie him I will not—and more
of his soldiership I know not, except in that country he
had the honour to be the officer at a place there called
Mile-end, to instruct for the doubling of files. I would do
the man what honour I can, but of this I am not certain.

FIRST LORD   He has out-villained villainy so far that the
rarity redeems him.

BERTRAM   A pox on him! He's a cat still.

FIRST SOLDIER   His qualities being at this poor price, I
need not to ask you if gold will corrupt him to revolt.

PAROLLES   Sir, for a quarter he will sell the fee-simple of
his salvation, the inheritance of it, and cut the entail
from all remainders, and a perpetual succession for it
perpetually.

FIRST SOLDIER   What's his brother, the other Captain
Dumaine?

SECOND LORD   Why does he ask him of me?

FIRST SOLDIER   What is he?

PAROLLES   Even a crow of the same nest; not altogether so
great as the first in goodness, but greater a great deal in

evil. He excels his brother for a coward, yet his brother
is reputed one of the best that is. In a retreat he outruns
any lackey; however, in coming on he has the cramp.

FIRST SOLDIER   If your life is saved will you undertake to
betray the Florentine?

PAROLLES   Ay, and the captain of his horse, Count
Rossillion.

FIRST SOLDIER   I'll whisper with the General and know
his pleasure.

PAROLLES   I'll no more drumming. A plague of all
drums! Only to seem to deserve well, and to beguile the
supposition of that lascivious young boy, the Count,
have I run into this danger. Yet who would have suspected
an ambush where I was taken?

FIRST SOLDIER   There is no remedy, sir, but you must die.
The General says you that have so traitorously discovered
the secrets of your army, and made such pestiferous
reports of men very nobly held, can serve the world for
no honest use; therefore you must die. Come, headsman,
off with his head.

PAROLLES   O Lord, sir, let me live, or let me see my
death!

FIRST SOLDIER   That shall you, and take your leave of all
your friends.

He unmuffles him

So: look about you. Know you any here?

BERTRAM   Good morrow, noble captain.

SECOND LORD   God bless you, Captain Parolles.

FIRST LORD   God save you, noble captain.

SECOND LORD   Captain, what greeting will you to my
Lord Lafew? I am for France.

FIRST LORD   Good captain, will you give me a copy
of the sonnet you writ to Diana in behalf of the Count

Rossillion? If I were not a very coward I'd compel it of
you; but fare you well.

Exeunt Bertram and the Lords

FIRST SOLDIER   You are undone, captain—all but your
scarf; that has a knot in it yet.

PAROLLES   Who cannot be crushed with a plot?

FIRST SOLDIER   If you could find out a country where but
women were that had received so much shame, you
might begin an impudent nation. Fare you well, sir. I
am for France too; we shall speak of you there.

Exeunt the Soldiers

PAROLLES

Yet am I thankful. If my heart were great
It would burst at this. Captain I'll be no more,
But I will eat and drink and sleep as soft
As captain shall. Simply the thing I am
Shall make me live. Who knows himself a braggart,
Let him fear this; for it will come to pass
That every braggart shall be found an ass.
Rust, sword; cool, blushes; and Parolles live
Safest in shame; being fooled, by foolery thrive.
There's place and means for every man alive.
I'll after them.   *Exit*

SCENE IV
The Widow's house.

Enter Helena, the Widow, and Diana

HELENA

That you may well perceive I have not wronged you
One of the greatest in the Christian world
Shall be my surety; before whose throne 'tis needful,
Ere I can perfect my intents, to kneel.
Time was, I did him a desirèd office,

Dear almost as his life, which gratitude
Through flinty Tartar's bosom would peep forth
And answer thanks. I duly am informed
His grace is at Marseillès, to which place
We have convenient convoy. You must know
I am supposèd dead. The army breaking,
My husband hies him home where, heaven aiding,
And by the leave of my good lord the King,
We'll be before our welcome.
WIDOW   Gentle madam,
You never had a servant to whose trust
Your business was more welcome.
HELENA   Nor you, mistress,
Ever a friend whose thoughts more truly labour
To recompense your love. Doubt not but heaven
Has brought me up to be your daughter's dower,
As it has fated her to be my motive
And helper to a husband. But, O strange men!
That can such sweet use make of what they hate,
When saucy trusting of the cozened thoughts
Defiles the pitchy night. So lust does play
With what it loathes for that which is away.
But more of this hereafter. You, Diana,
Under my poor instructions yet must suffer
Something in my behalf.
DIANA   Let death and honesty
Go with your impositions, I am yours,
Upon your will to suffer.
HELENA   Yet, I pray you.
But with the word the time will bring on summer,
When briars shall have leaves as well as thorns
And be as sweet as sharp. We must away;
Our wagon is prepared, and time revives us.
All's well that ends well; ever the fine's the crown.
Whatever the course, the end is the renown.   *Exeunt*

SCENE V
The Countess's house.

Enter the Countess, Lafew, and the Clown

LAFEW   No, no, no, your son was misled with a snipped taffeta fellow there, whose villainous saffron would have made all the unbaked and doughy youth of a nation in his colour. Your daughter-in-law had been alive at this hour, and your son here at home, more advanced by the King than by that red-tailed bumble-bee I speak of.

COUNTESS   I would I had not known him; it was the death of the most virtuous gentlewoman that ever nature had praise for creating. If she had partaken of my flesh and cost me the dearest groans of a mother I could not have owed her a more rooted love.

LAFEW   'Twas a good lady, 'twas a good lady. We may pick a thousand salads ere we light on such another herb.

CLOWN   Indeed, sir, she was the sweet-marjoram of the salad, or, rather, the herb rue.

LAFEW   They are not herbs, you knave, they are scented herbs.

CLOWN   I am no great Nebuchadnezzar, sir, I have not much skill in grass.

LAFEW   Which do you profess yourself, a knave or a fool?

CLOWN   A fool, sir, at a woman's service, and a knave at a man's.

LAFEW   Your distinction?

CLOWN   I would cozen the man of his wife and do his service.

LAFEW   So you were a knave at his service indeed.

CLOWN   And I would give his wife my bauble, sir, to do her service.

LAFEW   I will subscribe for you, you are both knave and
fool.

CLOWN   At your service.

LAFEW   No, no, no.

CLOWN   Why, sir, if I cannot serve you I can serve as
great a prince as you are.

LAFEW   Who's that? A Frenchman?

CLOWN   Faith, sir, he has an English name; but his
physiognomy is hotter in France than there.

LAFEW   What prince is that?

CLOWN   The Black Prince, sir, alias the prince of darkness,
alias the devil.

LAFEW   Hold, there's my purse. I give you not this to
tempt you from your master you talk of; serve him still.

CLOWN   I am a woodland fellow, sir, that always loved a
great fire, and the master I speak of ever keeps a good
fire. But sure he is the prince of the world; let his
nobility remain in his Court. I am for the house with
the narrow gate, which I take to be too little for pomp to
enter; some that humble themselves may, but the many
will be too chill and tender, and they'll be for the
flowery way that leads to the broad gate and the great
fire.

LAFEW   Go your ways. I begin to be aweary of you, and I
tell you so before, because I would not fall out with you.
Go your ways. Let my horses be well looked to, without
any tricks.

CLOWN   If I put any tricks upon them, sir, they shall be
jades' tricks, which are their own right by the law of
nature.   *Exit*

LAFEW   A shrewd knave and an unhappy.

COUNTESS   So he is. My lord that's gone made himself
much sport out of him; by his authority he remains
here, which he thinks is a patent for his sauciness; and
indeed he has no pace, but runs where he will.

LAFEW   I like him well, 'tis not amiss. And I was about
  to tell you, since I heard of the good lady's death
  and that my lord your son was upon his return home, I
  moved the King my master to speak in the behalf of my
  daughter; which, in the minority of them both, his
  majesty out of a self-gracious remembrance did first
  propose. His highness has promised me to do it; and to
  stop up the displeasure he has conceived against your
  son there is no fitter matter. How does your ladyship
  like it?
COUNTESS   With very much content, my lord, and I
  wish it happily effected.
LAFEW   His highness comes post from Marseilles, of
  as able body as when he numbered thirty. He will
  be here tomorrow, or I am deceived by him that in such
  intelligence has seldom failed.
COUNTESS   It rejoices me that I hope I shall see him ere I
  die. I have letters that my son will be here tonight. I
  shall beseech your lordship to remain with me till they
  meet together.
LAFEW   Madam, I was thinking with what manners I
  might safely be admitted.
COUNTESS   You need but plead your honourable privilege.
LAFEW   Lady, of that I have made a bold charter but, I
  thank my God, it holds yet.

Enter Clown

CLOWN   O madam, yonder's my lord your son with a
  patch of velvet on his face; whether there is a scar under
  it or no, the velvet knows, but it is a goodly patch of
  velvet. His left cheek is a cheek of two pile and a half,
  but his right cheek is worn bare.
LAFEW   A scar nobly got, or a noble scar, is a good livery
  of honour; so likely is that.
CLOWN   But it is your ulcerated face.

LAFEW   Let us go see your son, I pray you. I long to talk
with the young noble soldier.

CLOWN   Faith, there's a dozen of them with delicate fine
hats, and most courteous feathers which bow the head
and nod at every man.   *Exeunt*

Act V

SCENE I
Marseilles. A street.

Enter Helena, the Widow, and Diana, with two attendants

HELENA
But this exceeding posting day and night
Must wear your spirits low. We cannot help it;
But since you have made the days and nights as one
To wear your gentle limbs in my affairs,
Be bold you do so grow in my requital
As nothing can unroot you.

Enter a Gentleman to the King

In happy time!
This man may help me to his majesty's ear,
If he would spend his power. God save you, sir!
GENTLEMAN
And you.
HELENA
Sir, I have seen you in the court of France.
GENTLEMAN
I have been sometimes there.
HELENA
I do presume, sir, that you are not fallen
From the report that goes upon your goodness;
And therefore, goaded with most sharp occasions
Which lay nice manners by, I put you to
The use of your own virtues, for ever which

I shall continue thankful.
GENTLEMAN   What is your will?
HELENA
    That it will please you
    To give this poor petition to the King,
    And aid me with that store of power you have
    To come into his presence.
GENTLEMAN
    The King is not here.
HELENA   Not here, sir?
GENTLEMAN   Not indeed.
    He hence removed last night, and with more haste
    Than is his use.
WIDOW   Lord, how we lose our pains!
HELENA
    All's well that ends well yet,
    Though time seems so adverse and means unfit.
    I do beseech you, whither is he gone?
GENTLEMAN
    Indeed, as I take it, to Rossillion;
    Whither I am going.
HELENA   I do beseech you, sir,
    Since you are likely to see the King before me,
    Commend the paper to his gracious hand,
    Which I presume shall render you no blame,
    But rather make you thank your pains for it.
    I will come after you with what good speed
    Our means will make us means.
GENTLEMAN   This I'll do for you.
HELENA
    And you shall find yourself to be well thanked,
    Whatever falls more. We must to horse again.
    Go, go, provide.   *Exeunt*

SCENE II
Before the Countess's house.

Enter the Clown and Parolles

PAROLLES   Good Master Lavatch, give my Lord Lafew
this letter. I have ere now, sir, been better known to you,
when I have held familiarity with fresher clothes; but I
am now, sir, muddied in Fortune's mood, and smell
somewhat strong of her strong displeasure.

CLOWN   Truly, Fortune's displeasure is but sluttish if it
smells so strongly as you speak of. I will henceforth eat
no fish of Fortune's buttering. Pray, allow me the wind.

PAROLLES   Nay, you need not to stop your nose, sir. I
spoke but by a metaphor.

CLOWN   Indeed, sir, if your metaphor stinks I will stop
my nose, or against any man's metaphor. Pray, get you
further.

PAROLLES   Pray you, sir, deliver me this paper.

CLOWN   Foh! Pray stand away. A paper from Fortune's
close-stool, to give to a nobleman! Look, here he comes
himself.

Enter Lafew

Here is a purr of Fortune's sir, or of Fortune's cat, but not
a musk-cat, that has fallen into the unclean fishpond
of her displeasure and, as he says, is muddied with it.
Pray you, sir, use the carp as you may, for he looks
like a poor, decayed, ingenious, foolish, rascally knave.
I do pity his distress in my similes of comfort, and
leave him to your lordship.   *Exit*

PAROLLES   My lord, I am a man whom Fortune has cruelly
scratched.

LAFEW   And what would you have me to do? It is too late

to pare her nails now. Wherein have you played the knave with Fortune that she should scratch you, who of herself is a good lady and would not have knaves thrive long under her? There's a quarter for you. Let the justices make you and Fortune friends; I am for other business.

PAROLLES   I beseech your honour to hear me one single word.

LAFEW   You beg a single penny more. Come, you shall have it, save your word.

PAROLLES   My name, my good lord, is Parolles.

LAFEW   You beg more than 'word' then. God's passion! Give me your hand. How does your drum?

PAROLLES   O my good lord, you were the first that found me.

LAFEW   Was I, in truth? And I was the first that lost you.

PAROLLES   It lies in you, my lord, to bring me in some grace, for you did bring me out.

LAFEW   Out upon you, knave! Do you put upon me at once both the office of God and the devil? One brings you in grace and the other brings you out.

Trumpets sound

The King's coming; I know by his trumpets. Fellow, inquire further after me. I had talk of you last night. Though you are a fool and a knave you shall eat. Get on, follow.

PAROLLES   I praise God for you.   *Exeunt*

SCENE III
The Countess's house.

Flourish. Enter the King, the Countess, Lafew, the two French Lords, with attendants

KING
  We lost a jewel of her, and our esteem
  Was made much poorer by it; but your son,
  As mad in folly, lacked the sense to know
  Her estimation home.
COUNTESS   It is past, my liege,
  And I beseech your majesty to make it
  Natural rebellion done in the blade of youth,
  When oil and fire, too strong for reason's force,
  Overbear it and burn on.
KING   My honoured lady,
  I have forgiven and forgotten all,
  Though my revenges were high bent upon him
  And watched the time to shoot.
LAFEW   This I must say—
  But first I beg my pardon—the young lord
  Did to his majesty, his mother, and his lady
  Offence of mighty note, but to himself
  The greatest wrong of all. He lost a wife
  Whose beauty did astonish the survey
  Of richest eyes, whose words all ears took captive,
  Whose dear perfection hearts that scorned to serve
  Humbly called mistress.
KING   Praising what is lost
  Makes the remembrance dear. Well, call him hither;
  We are reconciled, and the first view shall kill
  All repetition. Let him not ask your pardon;
  The nature of his great offence is dead,
  And deeper than oblivion we do bury
  The incensing relics of it. Let him approach
  A stranger, no offender; and inform him
  So it is our will he should.
ATTENDANT   I shall, my liege.   *Exit*

KING
  What says he to your daughter? Have you spoken?
LAFEW
  All that he is has reference to your highness.
KING
  Then shall we have a match. I have letters sent me
  That sets him high in fame.

Enter Bertram

LAFEW   He looks well on it.
KING
  I am not a day of season,
  For you may see a sunshine and a hail
  In me at once. But to the brightest beams
  Distracted clouds give way; so stand you forth:
  The time is fair again.
BERTRAM   My high-repented blames,
  Dear sovereign, pardon to me.
KING   All is whole.
  Not one word more of the consumèd time.
  Let's take the instant by the forward top;
  For we are old, and on our quickest decrees
  The inaudible and noiseless foot of time
  Steals ere we can effect them. You remember
  The daughter of this lord?
BERTRAM
  Admiringly, my liege. At first
  I stuck my choice upon her, ere my heart
  Durst make too bold a herald of my tongue;
  Where, the impression of my eye infixing,
  Contempt his scornful perspective did lend me,
  Which warped the line of every other favour,
  Scorned a fair colour or expressed it stolen,
  Extended or contracted all proportions
  To a most hideous object. Thence it came

That she whom all men praised, and whom myself,
Since I have lost, have loved, was in my eye
The dust that did offend it.
KING   Well excused.
That you did love her, strikes some scores away
From the great account; but love that comes too late,
Like a remorseful pardon slowly carried,
To the great sender turns a sour offence,
Crying 'That's good that's gone'. Our rash faults
Make trivial price of serious things we have,
Not knowing them until we know their grave.
Oft our displeasures, to ourselves unjust,
Destroy our friends and after weep their dust;
Our own love waking cries to see what's done,
While shameful hate sleeps out the afternoon.
Be this sweet Helen's knell, and now forget her.
Send forth your amorous token for fair Magdalen.
The main consents are had, and here we'll stay
To see our widower's second marriage-day.
COUNTESS
Which better than the first, O dear heaven, bless!
Or, ere they meet, in me, O nature, cease!
LAFEW
Come on, my son, in whom my house's name
Must be digested, give a favour from you
To sparkle in the spirits of my daughter,
That she may quickly come.

Bertram gives Lafew a ring

By my old beard
And every hair that's on it, Helen that's dead
Was a sweet creature; such a ring as this,
The last that ever I took her leave at court,
I saw upon her finger.
BERTRAM   Hers it was not.

KING
  Now pray you let me see it; for my eye,
  While I was speaking, oft was fastened to it.
  This ring was mine, and when I gave it Helen
  I bade her, if her fortunes ever stood
  Necessitied to help, that by this token
  I would relieve her. Had you that craft to rob her
  Of what should help her most?
BERTRAM   My gracious sovereign,
  However it pleases you to take it so,
  The ring was never hers.
COUNTESS   Son, on my life,
  I have seen her wear it, and she reckoned it
  At her life's rate.
LAFEW   I am sure I saw her wear it.
BERTRAM
  You are deceived, my lord, she never saw it.
  In Florence was it from a casement thrown me,
  Wrapped in a paper which contained the name
  Of her that threw it. Noble she was, and thought
  I stood engaged; but when I had subscribed
  To my own fortune, and informed her fully
  I could not answer in that course of honour
  As she had made the overture, she ceased
  In heavy satisfaction, and would never
  Receive the ring again.
KING   Plutus himself,
  That knows the touch and multiplying medicine,
  Has not in nature's mystery more science
  Than I have in this ring. 'Twas mine, 'twas Helen's,
  Whoever gave it you; then if you know
  That you are well acquainted with yourself,
  Confess 'twas hers, and by what rough enforcement
  You got it from her. She called the saints to surety
  That she would never put it from her finger
  Unless she gave it to yourself in bed,

Where you have never come, or sent it us
Upon her great disaster.
BERTRAM   She never saw it.
KING
You speak it falsely, as I love my honour,
And make conjectural fears to come into me
Which I wish to shut out. If it should prove
That you are so inhuman—it will not prove so,
And yet I know not; you did hate her deadly,
And she is dead; which nothing but to close
Her eyes myself could win me to believe,
More than to see this ring. Take him away.
My fore-past proofs, however the matter falls,
Shall tax my fears of little vanity,
Having vainly feared too little. Away with him.
We'll sift this matter further.
BERTRAM   If you shall prove
This ring was ever hers, you shall as easy
Prove that I husbanded her bed in Florence,
Where yet she never was.   *Exit, guarded*
KING
I am wrapped in dismal thinkings.

Enter a Gentleman (the Astringer)

GENTLEMAN   Gracious sovereign,
Whether I have been to blame or no, I know not:
Here's a petition from a Florentine
Who has for four or five removes come short
To tender it herself. I undertook it,
Vanquished thereto by the fair grace and speech
Of the poor supplant who, by this, I know,
Is here attending. Her business looks in her
With an importunate visage, and she told me,
In a sweet verbal brief, it did concern
Your highness with herself.

KING   (*reading the letter*) *Upon his many protestations to marry me when his wife was dead, I blush to say it, he won me. Now is the Count Rossillion a widower; his vows are forfeited to me and my honour's paid to him. He stole from Florence, taking no leave, and I follow him to his country for justice. Grant it me, O King! In you it best lies; otherwise a seducer flourishes, and a poor maid is undone.*

Diana Capilet.

LAFEW   I will buy me a son-in-law in a fair, and toll for this. I'll none of him.

KING

The heavens have thought well of you, Lafew,
To bring forth this discovery. Seek these suitors.
Go speedily, and bring again the Count.

Exeunt some attendants

I am afraid the life of Helen, lady,
Was foully snatched.

COUNTESS   Now justice on the doers!

Enter Bertram, guarded

KING

I wonder, sir, since wives are monsters to you,
And that you fly them as you swear them lordship,
Yet you desire to marry.

Enter the Widow and Diana

What woman is that?

DIANA

I am, my lord, a wretched Florentine,
Derivèd from the ancient Capilet.
My suit, as I do understand, you know,
And therefore know how far I may be pitied.

WIDOW
    I am her mother, sir, whose age and honour
    Both suffer under this complaint we bring,
    And both shall cease, without your remedy.
KING
    Come hither, Count. Do you know these women?
BERTRAM
    My lord, I neither can nor will deny
    But that I know them. Do they charge me further?
DIANA
    Why do you look so strange upon your wife?
BERTRAM
    She's none of mine, my lord.
DIANA   If you shall marry
    You give away this hand, and that is mine,
    You give away heaven's vows, and those are mine,
    You give away myself, which is known mine;
    For I by vow am so embodied yours
    That she who marries you must marry me—
    Either both or none.
LAFEW   Your reputation comes too short for my daughter;
    you are no husband for her.
BERTRAM
    My lord, this is a silly, desperate creature
    Whom sometimes I have laughed with. Let your highness
    Lay a more noble thought upon my honour
    Than just to think that I would sink it here.
KING
    Sir, for my thoughts, you have them ill to friend
    Till your deeds gain them; fairer prove your honour
    Than in my thought it lies!
DIANA   Good my lord,
    Ask him upon his oath if he does think
    He had not my virginity.

KING
  What say you to her?
BERTRAM   She's impudent, my lord,
  And was a common gamester to the camp.
DIANA
  He does me wrong, my lord; if I were so
  He might have bought me at a common price.
  Do not believe him. O behold this ring
  Whose high respect and rich validity
  Did lack a parallel; yet for all that
  He gave it to a commoner of the camp,
  If I am one.
COUNTESS   He blushes and it's it.
  Of six preceding ancestors, that gem
  Conferred by testament to the sequent issue,
  Has it been owned and worn. This is his wife:
  That ring's a thousand proofs.
KING   I thought you said
  You saw one here in court could witness it.
DIANA
  I did, my lord, but loth am to produce
  So bad an instrument: his name is Parolles.
LAFEW
  I saw the man today, if man he is.
KING
  Find him and bring him hither.   *Exit an attendant*
BERTRAM   What of him?
  He's quoted for a most perfidious slave
  With all the spots of the world taxed and debauched,
  Whose nature sickens but to speak a truth.
  Am I or that or this for what he'll utter,
  That will speak anything?
KING   She has that ring of yours.
BERTRAM
  I think she has. Certain it is I liked her
  And boarded her in the wanton way of youth.

She knew her distance and did angle for me,
Madding my eagerness with her restraint,
As all impediments in fancy's course
Are motives of more fancy. And in fine
Her infinite cunning with her common grace
Subdued me to her rate. She got the ring,
And I had that which any inferior might
At market-price have bought.
DIANA   I must be patient.
You that have turned off a first so noble wife
May justly forgo me. I pray you yet—
Since you lack virtue I will lose a husband—
Send for your ring, I will return it home,
And give me mine again.
BERTRAM   I have it not.
KING
What ring was yours, I pray you?
DIANA   Sir, much like
The same upon your finger.
KING
Know you this ring? This ring was his of late.
DIANA
And this was it I gave him, being abed.
KING
The story then goes false you threw it him
Out of a casement?
DIANA   I have spoken the truth.

Enter Parolles

BERTRAM
My lord, I do confess the ring was hers.
KING
You startle swiftly; every feather starts you.—
Is this the man you speak of?
DIANA   Ay, my lord.

KING
> Tell me, fellow—but tell me true I charge you,
> Not fearing the displeasure of your master,
> Which on your just proceeding I'll keep off—
> Of him and of this woman here what know you?

PAROLLES   So please your majesty, my master has been an honourable gentleman. Tricks he has had in him, which gentlemen have.

KING   Come, come, to the purpose. Did he love this woman?

PAROLLES   Faith, sir, he did love her; but how?

KING   How, I pray you?

PAROLLES   He did love her, sir, as a gentleman loves a woman.

KING   How is that?

PAROLLES   He loved her, sir, and loved her not.

KING   As you are a knave and no knave. What an equivocal companion is this!

PAROLLES   I am a poor man, and at your majesty's command.

LAFEW   He's a good drum, my lord, but a bad orator.

DIANA   Do you know he promised me marriage?

PAROLLES   Faith, I know more than I'll speak.

KING   But will you not speak all you know?

PAROLLES   Yes, so please your majesty. I did go between them as I said; but more than that, he loved her, for indeed he was mad for her and talked of Satan and of Limbo and of furies and I know not what. Yet I was in that credit with them at that time that I knew of their going to bed and of other motions, as promising her marriage and things which would derive me ill will to speak of; therefore I will not speak what I know.

KING   You have spoken all already, unless you can say they are married. But you are too slim in your evidence— therefore, stand aside.
> This ring you say was yours?

DIANA   Ay, my good lord.
KING
  Where did you buy it? Or who gave it you?
DIANA
  It was not given me, and I did not buy it.
KING
  Who lent it you?
DIANA   It was not lent me either.
KING
  Where did you find it then?
DIANA   I found it not.
KING
  If it were yours by none of all these ways
  How could you give it him?
DIANA   I never gave it him.
LAFEW   This woman's an easy glove, my lord; she goes off
  and on at pleasure.
KING
  This ring was mine; I gave it his first wife.
DIANA
  It might be yours or hers for aught I know.
KING
  Take her away, I do not like her now.
  To prison with her. And away with him.
  Unless you tell me where you had this ring
  You die within this hour.
DIANA   I'll never tell you.
KING
  Take her away.
DIANA   I'll put in bail, my lord.
KING
  I think you now some common customer.
DIANA
  By Jove, if ever I knew man it was you.

KING
  Wherefore have you accused him all this while?
DIANA
  Because he's guilty and he is not guilty.
  He knows I am no maid, he'll swear to it;
  I'll swear I am a maid and he knows not.
  Great king, I am no strumpet; by my life
  I am either maid or else this old man's wife.
KING
  She does abuse our ears. To prison with her.
DIANA
  Good mother, fetch my bail. Stay, royal sir;
                                        Exit the Widow
  The jeweller that owns the ring is sent for
  And he shall surety me. But for this lord
  Who has abused me as he knows himself,
  Though yet he never harmed me, here I quit him.
  He knows himself my bed he has defiled,
  And at that time he got his wife with child.
  Dead though she be she feels her young one kick.
  So there's my riddle: one that's dead is quick.
  And now behold the meaning.

               Enter the Widow, with Helena

KING   Is there no exorcist
  Beguiles the truer office of my eyes?
  Is it real that I see?
HELENA   No, my good lord,
  It is but the shadow of a wife you see,
  The name and not the thing.
BERTRAM   Both, both. O pardon!
HELENA
  O my good lord, when I was like this maid
  I found you wondrous kind. There is your ring,
  And, look you, here's your letter. This it says:

When from my finger you can get this ring . . .
And is by me with child, etc. This is done.
Will you be mine now you are doubly won?

BERTRAM

If she, my liege, can make me know this clearly
I'll love her dearly, ever, ever dearly.

HELENA

If it appears not plain and prove untrue
Deadly divorce step between me and you!
O my dear mother, do I see you living?

LAFEW

My eyes smell onions, I shall weep anon.
(To Parolles) Good Tom Drum, lend me a handkerchief.
So, I thank you. Wait on me home, I'll make sport with
    you. Let your curtsies alone, they are scurvy ones.

KING

Let us from point to point this story know
To make the even truth in pleasure flow.
(To Diana) If you are yet a fresh uncroppèd flower
Choose you your husband and I'll pay your dower;
For I can guess that by your honest aid
You kept a wife herself, yourself a maid.
Of that and all the progress more and less
Resolvèdly more leisure shall express.
All yet seems well, and if it ends so meet,
The bitter past, more welcome is the sweet.

Flourish

EPILOGUE

Spoken by the King

The King's a beggar, now the play is done.
All is well ended if this suit is won,
That you express content; which we will pay
With strife to please you, day exceeding day.
Ours be your patience then and yours our parts;
Your gentle hands lend us and take our hearts.   *Exeunt*

Henry V

INTRODUCTION

With *Henry V* in 1599 Shakespeare completed the quartet of English history plays begun with *Richard II* in 1595 and continued with the two parts of *Henry IV* in 1597–8. We should notice the variety, how different these plays are, from the lyricism of *Richard II*, through the mixture of comedy with history in *Henry IV*, to *Henry V* which is different again, with something of a patriotic epic about it. This may not be to everybody's taste today, though it certainly spoke again to the hearts of the generation of 1940 when Britain was in mortal danger. In particular we find the boastful slanging-matches between English and French both naif and tiresome, as simpler Elizabethans did not: they liked that sort of thing.

In the long set speeches of the first Act, in which the claim of Henry V to the French crown (he was more than half-French) is set out at tedious length, Shakespeare is simply versifying as he goes along from the Chronicles, principally Holinshed. And we should notice that he is always better when creating out of his own head. His 'source' he relies on for the framework, the plot, the facts—sometimes wrong, as in blaming the Archbishop of Canterbury for inciting Henry to war (he needed no encouragement). The fun is all Shakespeare's—as Dr. Johnson observed, and Shakespeare corroborates in his portrait of himself as Berowne in *Love's Labour's Lost:* his original bent was all for comedy.

Henry V is enlivened by comic scenes, particularly in the scenes around the Welsh, Irish, and Scots captains, in which Shakespeare caricatured their respective brogues with his usual linguistic virtuosity. Pistol also appears again with his extraordinary lingo—(Shakespeare must have had some particular individual in mind)—a braggart from the wars such as he observed in Elizabethan London. But the most fabulous comic of all, Falstaff, had to be omitted as too outsize. His weight would have broken the bounds of the play; Shakespeare had to change his plan for the very different scheme he had in mind, the depiction of Henry V as the hero-King he was to the Elizabethans and the evocation of the nostalgic memories of Agincourt.

Here again the King in action is not to everybody's taste. Professor Dover Wilson, however, says sympathetically, 'Henry V is a play which men of action have been wont silently to admire, and literary men—at any rate during the last hundred and thirty years—volubly to contemn.' So much the worse for the literary men, such liberal doctrinaires as Hazlitt, for example: showing no generosity of imagination, still less political or historical understanding.

For Henry is, above all, a political type, an ideal ruler, who rises to the challenge of the tremendous responsibility for other men's lives that the ruler, whether King or President, so bears. And Henry does not bear it lightly: his soul is exposed to us in the wonderful night scene before Agincourt, in which he argues the issue fairly with a common soldier and then lays the matter before God in prayer:

Upon the King! Let us our lives, our souls,
Our debts, our careful wives,
Our children, and our sins, lay on the King!
We must bear all . . .

We have still more reason to appreciate and understand the dire responsibility resting upon those in ultimate control, in a nuclear age, of the release of nuclear power. For a fuller appreciation of Henry V's character and the political issues I must refer the reader to my longer Introduction to the play in my *Prefaces to Shakespeare's Plays*. Here we must concentrate on the drama.

The dramatist met the difficulties of the extended field of action overseas by a direct appeal to the imagination of the audience, with a descriptive chorus before each Act. With his usual courtesy he asks pardon for

> The flat unraisèd spirits that have dared
> On this unworthy scaffold to bring forth
> So great an object. Can this cockpit hold
> The vasty fields of France? Or may we cram
> Within this wooden O the very casques
> That did affright the air at Agincourt?

The wooden O was the Globe Theatre which the Burbages had erected on the South Bank of the Thames, using the timbers of the old Theatre in Shoreditch which had given Shakespeare his earlier opportunities. Henceforth the Globe was to be the Company's permanent home.

At each appearance as Chorus Shakespeare wooed the sympathy and applause of the audience. In the Sonnet which concludes the play as Epilogue we have him in his own person:

> Thus far, with rough and all-unable pen,
> Our bending author has pursued the story—

and opportunity should always be taken to cast the author himself as Chorus. He concludes with a reference to his own *Henry VI* trilogy, the historical sequel, with which he had first won success:

Which oft our stage has shown.

But what a prodigious development had been registered in his work as a dramatist in those past seven or eight years!

We are given indications of the contemporary scene as always, here in direct references. The long war with Spain was approaching a climax with the quasi-national resistance in Ireland under a great leader, O'Neill. The effort to equip the largest army yet sent across the Irish Channel appears in

> The armourers, accomplishing the knights,
> With busy hammers closing rivets up,
> Give dreadful note of preparatiòn.

The army was under the command of Essex, who was given a grand send-off from the City:

> How London doth pour out her citizens

like 'antique Rome' fetching 'their conquering Caesar in—

> As, by a lower but loving likelihood
> Were now the General of our gracious Empress—
> As in good time he may—from Ireland coming,
> Bringing rebellion broachèd on his sword,
> How many would the peaceful city quit
> To welcome him!

The Irish crisis stoked up the fires of patriotism once more, so much to the fore in this play as in the earlier history plays. We have Irish references in this, not only in Captain MacMorris, but yet again to the Irish kern, riding barelegged.

For the modern reader the play presents greater linguistic

difficulties than any, and modernisation is more necessary than ever. We have a whole scene in French, in which the Princess Katherine (ancestress of Elizabeth I) is learning English: a good deal of her love-scene with Henry is in French, while French phrases abound. All this is translated, the whole of the first, Act III, Scene 4, in the Appendix, the rest in footnotes or in brackets.

How did Shakespeare come by all this French? Well, about this time he was lodging in the City in Silver Street, with a French family, the Montjoies, who were tire-makers or headdress makers. Shakespeare was on confidential terms with Madame Montjoie, the betrothal of whose daughter he performed on her behalf. The French herald in the play, Montjoy, is given a considerable part, and the reference to people wearing their own hair pinpoints the association. No doubt Shakespeare received help from that quarter.

The respective brogues of the Welsh, Irish and Scotch captains has been rendered less outlandish than the original, leaving enough of it to indicate the flavour. After all, actors can supply their own accents—Mrs. Quickly, for example, should be rendered in demotic Cockney. Even so some of her malapropisms are reduced or explained for the reader; others may be guessed at, like Shakespeare's bawdy, where he never fails to make a sexual innuendo to tickle the audience.

A favourite word, puissance or puissant, gives difficulty: with Shakespeare it was pronounced as a tri-syllable, pù-issance. I have replaced it: the adjective 'powerful' is conveniently tri-syllabic. Words like hour, tire or tired, prayer, were pronounced as two syllables. The personal 'who' and impersonal 'which' are interchangeable and used quite inconsistently by Shakespeare: I have regularised them to accord with modern usage. Similarly with 'on' and 'of' which are used interchangeably. Shakespeare's ungrammatical use of 'who' for 'whom' points the way the language is moving, with careless writers, today. The use of the subordinate verb to be, 'is come' for 'has come', is oddly in accordance with French usage, and should be regularised—let alone redundant 'that', as in 'if that', 'for that', etc.

It is worth noting that the phrase several times repeated on Pistol's flamboyant lips—he regularly talks inflated nonsense—'And that's the humour of it' is a joke, kindly enough, against the 'Humour' plays which Ben Jonson patented just at this time. Shakespeare welcomed his play, *Every Man in his Humour*, to the Chamberlain's Men in 1598, and himself acted in Ben's *Every Man out of his Humour* next year, the year of *Henry V*. To know these connexions makes the stage-life of the time more real to us.

CHARACTERS

CHORUS

KING HENRY THE FIFTH
DUKE OF GLOUCESTER
DUKE OF BEDFORD } brothers of the King
DUKE OF CLARENCE
DUKE OF EXETER, uncle of the King
DUKE OF YORK, cousin of the King
EARL OF SALISBURY
EARL OF WESTMORLAND
EARL OF WARWICK
EARL OF HUNTINGDON
ARCHBISHOP OF CANTERBURY
BISHOP OF ELY
RICHARD EARL OF CAMBRIDGE
HENRY LORD SCROOP } conspirators
SIR THOMAS GREY
SIR THOMAS ERPINGHAM
CAPTAIN FLUELLEN
CAPTAIN GOWER } officers
CAPTAIN JAMY
CAPTAIN MACMORRIS
JOHN BATES
ALEXANDER COURT } soldiers
MICHAEL WILLIAMS
BARDOLPH
NYM } camp-followers
PISTOL
BOY
HOSTESS QUICKLY, now married to Pistol

CHARLES THE SIXTH, King of France

LEWIS, the Dauphin
DUKE OF BURGUNDY
DUKE OF ORLEANS
DUKE OF BRITAINE
DUKE OF BOURBON
CHARLES DELABRETH, Constable of France
GRANDPRÉ
RAMBURES } French Lords
THE GOVERNOR OF HARFLEUR
MONTJOY, a French Herald
AMBASSADORS to the King of England
MONSIEUR LE FER, a French soldier
ISABEL, Queen of France
KATHERINE, daughter of the King of France
ALICE, a lady attending on her

LORDS, LADIES, OFFICERS, SOLDIERS, CITIZENS,
MESSENGERS, HERALDS, ATTENDANTS

Prologue

Flourish. Enter Chorus

CHORUS
O for a Muse of fire, that would ascend
The brightest heaven of inventiòn,
A kingdom for a stage, princes to act,
And monarchs to behold the swelling scene!
Then should the warlike Harry, like himself,
Assume the state of Mars, and at his heels,
Leashed in like hounds, should famine, sword, and fire
Crouch for employment. But pardon, gentles all,
The flat unraisèd spirits that have dared
On this unworthy scaffold to bring forth
So great an object. Can this cockpit hold
The vasty fields of France? Or may we cram
Within this wooden O the very casques
That did affright the air at Agincourt?
O, pardon! since a crookèd figure may
Attest in little place a milliòn,
And let us, ciphers to this great account,
On your imaginary forces work.
Suppose within the girdle of these walls
Are now confined two mighty monarchies,
Whose high uprearèd and abutting fronts
The perilous narrow ocean parts asunder.
Piece out our imperfections with your thoughts:
Into a thousand parts divide one man,
And make an imaginary universe.
Think, when we talk of horses, that you see them
Printing their proud hoofs in the receiving earth;
For 'tis your thoughts that now must deck our kings,

Carry them here and there, jumping over times,
Turning the accomplishment of many years
Into an hour-glass: now for which supply,
Admit me Chorus to this history,
Who Prologue-like your humble patience pray,
Gently to hear, kindly to judge, our play.   *Exit*

Act I

SCENE I
Westminster. The palace.

Enter the Archbishop of Canterbury and the Bishop of Ely

CANTERBURY

    My lord, I'll tell you. That self bill is urged
    Which in the eleventh year of the last King's reign
    Was likely, and had indeed against us passed,
    But that the contentious and unquiet time
    Did push it out of farther questiòn.

ELY

    But how, my lord, shall we resist it now?

CANTERBURY

    It must be thought on. If it passes against us,
    We lose the better half of our possession.
    For all the temporal lands which men devout
    By testament have given to the Church
    Would they strip from us. Being valued thus—
    As much as would maintain, to the King's honour,
    Full fifteen earls, and fifteen hundred knights,
    Six thousand and two hundred good esquires;
    And, to relief of lepers and weak age,
    Of indigent faint souls past corporal toil,
    A hundred almshouses right well supplied;
    And, to the coffers of the King beside,
    A thousand pounds by the year. Thus runs the bill.

ELY
  This would drink deep.
CANTERBURY   It would drink the cup and all.
ELY
  But what prevention?
CANTERBURY
  The King is full of grace and fair regard.
ELY
  And a true lover of the holy Church.
CANTERBURY
  The courses of his youth promised it not.
  The breath no sooner left his father's body
  But that his wildness, mortified in him,
  Seemed to die too. Yea, at that very moment,
  Consideration like an angel came
  And whipped the offending Adam out of him,
  Leaving his body as a paradise
  To envelop and contain celestial spirits.
  Never was such a sudden scholar made;
  Never came reformation in a flood
  With such a heady current scouring faults.
  Nor ever Hydra-headed wilfulness
  So soon did lose its seat, and all at once,
  As in this King.
ELY   We are blessèd in the change.
CANTERBURY
  Hear him but reason in divinity,
  And all-admiring, with an inward wish,
  You would desire the King were made a prelate.
  Hear him debate of commonwealth affairs,
  You would say it has been all in all his study.
  List his discourse of war, and you shall hear
  A fearful battle rendered you in music.
  Turn him to any cause of policy,
  The Gordian knot of it he will unloose,
  Familiar as his garter; that, when he speaks,

The air, a chartered libertine, is still,
And the mute wonder lurks then in men's ears
To steal his sweet and honeyed sentences.
So that the art and practical part of life
Must be the mistress to the theory—
Which is a wonder how his grace should glean it,
Since his addiction was to courses vain,
His companies unlettered, rude, and shallow;
His hours filled up with riots, banquets, sports,
And never noted in him any study,
Any retirement, any sequestration,
From open haunts and popularity.

ELY

The strawberry grows underneath the nettle,
And wholesome berries thrive and ripen best
Neighboured by fruit of baser quality.
And so the Prince obscured his contemplation
Under the veil of wildness—which, no doubt,
Grew like the summer grass, fastest by night,
Unseen, yet growing in capacity.

CANTERBURY

It must be so, for miracles are ceased;
And therefore we must needs admit the means
How things are pèrfected.

ELY   But, my good lord,
How now for mitigation of this bill
Urged by the Commons? Does his majesty
Incline to it, or no?

CANTERBURY   He seems impartial,
Or rather swaying more upon our part
Than cherishing the exhibiters against us.
For I have made an offer to his majesty—
Upon our spiritual Convocation,
And in regard of causes now in hand,
Which I have opened to his grace at large
As touching France—to give a greater sum

Than ever at one time the clergy yet
Did to his predecessors part with free.

ELY

How did this offer seem received, my lord?

CANTERBURY

With good acceptance of his majesty,
Save that there was not time enough to hear—
As I perceived his grace would fain have done—
The several and unhidden passages
Of his true titles to some certain dukedoms,
And generally to the crown and seat of France,
Derived from Edward, his great-grandfather.

ELY

What was the impediment that broke this off?

CANTERBURY

The French ambassador upon that instant
Craved audience, and the hour, I think, is come
To give him hearing. Is it four o'clock?

ELY

It is.

CANTERBURY

Then go we in to know his embassy;
Which I could with a ready guess declare
Before the Frenchman speaks a word of it.

ELY

I'll wait upon you, and I long to hear it.

Exeunt

SCENE II
The same.

*Enter the King, Gloucester, Bedford, Clarence,
Exeter, Warwick, Westmorland, and attendants*

KING HENRY
   Where is my gracious Lord of Canterbury?
EXETER
   Not here in presence.
KING HENRY   Send for him, good uncle.
WESTMORLAND
   Shall we call in the ambassador, my liege?
KING HENRY
   Not yet, my cousin; we would be resolved,
   Before we hear him, of some things of weight
   That tax our thoughts, concerning us and France.

Enter the Archbishop of Canterbury and the Bishop
of Ely

CANTERBURY
   God and His angels guard your sacred throne,
   And make you long become it!
KING HENRY   Sure, we thank you.
   My learnèd lord, we pray you to proceed,
   And justly and religiously unfold
   Why the law Salic that they have in France
   Either should or should not bar us in our claim.
   And God forbid, my dear and faithful lord,
   That you should fashion, wrest, or bow your reading,
   Or nicely charge your understanding soul
   With opening titles miscreate, whose right
   Suits not in native colours with the truth.
   For God does know how many now in health
   Shall drop their blood in approbatiòn
   Of what your reverence shall incite us to.
   Therefore take heed how you impawn our person,
   How you awake our sleeping sword of war.
   We charge you in the name of God, take heed;
   For never two such kingdoms did contend
   Without much fall of blood, whose guiltless drops

Are every one a woe, a sore complaint
Against him whose wrongs give edge unto the swords
That make such waste in brief mortality.
Under this conjuration speak, my lord,
For we will hear, note, and believe in heart
That what you speak is in your conscience washed
As pure as sin with baptism.

CANTERBURY
Then hear me, gracious sovereign, and you peers,
That owe yourselves, your lives, and services
To this imperial throne. There is no bar
To make against your highness' claim to France
But this, which they produce from Pharamond:
'In terram Salicam mulieres ne succedant'—
'No woman shall succeed in Salic land'.
Which Salic land the French unjustly gloss
To be the realm of France, and Pharamond
The founder of this law and female bar.
Yet their own authors faithfully affirm
That the land Salic is in Germany,
Between the floods of Sala and of Elbe.
Where Charles the Great, having subdued the Saxons,
There left behind and settled certain French,
Who, holding in disdain the German women
For some dishonest manners of their life,
Established then this law: to wit, no female
Should be inheritrix in Salic land.
Which Salic, as I said, between Elbe and Sala,
Is at this day in Germany called Meisen.
Then does it well appear the Salic law
Was not devisèd for the realm of France.
Nor did the French possess the Salic land
Until four hundred one-and-twenty years
After defunction of King Pharamond,
Idly supposed the founder of this law,
Who died within the year of our redemption

Four hundred twenty-six. And Charles the Great
Subdued the Saxons, and did seat the French
Beyond the river Sala, in the year
Eight hundred five. Besides, their writers say,
King Pepin, who deposèd Childeric,
Did, as heir general, being descended
Of Blithild, who was daughter to King Clothair,
Make claim and title to the crown of France.
Hugh Capet also—who usurped the crown
Of Charles the Duke of Lorraine, sole heir male
Of the true line and stock of Charles the Great—
To find his title with some shows of truth,
Though in pure truth it was corrupt and naught,
Conveyed himself as the heir to the Lady Lingard,
Daughter to Charlemain, who was the son
To Lewis the Emperor, and Lewis the son
Of Charles the Great. Also King Lewis the Ninth,
Who was sole heir to the usurper Capet,
Could not keep quiet in his consciènce,
Wearing the crown of France, till satisfied
That fair Queen Isabel, his grandmother,
Was lineal of the Lady Ermengard,
Daughter to Charles the foresaid Duke of Lorraine.
By which marriage the line of Charles the Great
Was re-united to the crown of France.
So that, as clear as is the summer's sun,
King Pepin's title, and Hugh Capet's claim,
King Lewis's satisfaction, all appear
To hold in right and title of the female.
So do the kings of France unto this day,
Howbeit they would hold up this Salic law
To bar your highness claiming from the female,
And rather choose to hide them in a net
Than amply to unbar their crookèd titles
Usurped from you and your progenitors.

KING HENRY
   May I with right and conscience make this claim?
CANTERBURY
   The sin upon my head, dread sovereign!
   For in the Book of Numbers is it written,
   When the man dies, let the inheritance
   Descend unto the daughter. Gracious lord,
   Stand for your own, unwind your bloody flag,
   Look back into your mighty ancestors.
   Go, my dread lord, to your great-grandsire's tomb,
   From whom you claim; invoke his warlike spirit,
   And your great-uncle's, Edward the Black Prince,
   Who on the French ground played a tragedy,
   Making defeat on the full power of France;
   While his most mighty father on a hill
   Stood smiling to behold his lion's whelp
   Forage in blood of French nobility.
   O noble English, that could entertain
   With half their forces the full pride of France,
   And let another half stand laughing by,
   All out of work and cold for actiòn!
ELY
   Awake remembrance of these valiant dead,
   And with your powerful arm renew their feats.
   You are their heir, you sit upon their throne,
   The blood and courage that renownèd them
   Runs in your veins; and my thrice-mighty liege
   Is in the very May-morn of his youth,
   Ripe for exploits and mighty enterprises.
EXETER
   Your brother kings and monarchs of the earth
   Do all expect that you should rouse yourself,
   As did the former lions of your blood.
WESTMORLAND
   They know your grace has cause and means and might—
   So has your highness. Never King of England

Had nobles richer and more loyal subjects,
Whose hearts have left their bodies here in England
And lie pavilioned in the fields of France.
CANTERBURY
   O, let their bodies follow, my dear liege,
   With blood and sword and fire to win your right!
   In aid whereof we of the spiritualty
   Will raise your highness such a mighty sum
   As never did the clergy at one time
   Bring in to any of your ancestors.
KING HENRY
   We must not only arm to invade the French
   But lay down our proportions to defend
   Against the Scot, who will make road upon us
   With all advantages.
CANTERBURY
   They of those marches, gracious sovereign,
   Shall be a wall sufficient to defend
   Our inland from the pilfering borderers.
KING HENRY
   We do not mean the coursing snatchers only,
   But fear the main intention of the Scot,
   Who has been ever a giddy neighbour to us.
   For you shall read that my great-grandfather
   Never went with his forces into France
   But that the Scot on his unfurnished kingdom
   Came pouring, like the tide into a breach,
   With ample and brim fullness of his force,
   Galling the gleanèd land with hot assaults,
   Girding with grievous siege castles and towns;
   That England, being empty of defence,
   Shook and trembled at the ill neighbourhood.
CANTERBURY
   She has been then more feared than harmed, my liege;
   For hear her but exampled by herself:
   When all her chivalry has been in France,

And she a mourning widow of her nobles,
She has herself not only well defended
But taken and impounded as a stray
The King of Scots: whom she did send to France
To fill King Edward's fame with prisoner kings,
And make her chronicle as rich with praise
As is the ooze and bottom of the sea
With sunken wreck and sumless treasuries.

ELY
But there's a saying very old and true:
    'If that you will France win,
    Then with Scotland first begin.'
For once the eagle England being in prey,
To her unguarded nest the weasel Scot
Comes sneaking, and so sucks her princely eggs,
Playing the mouse in absence of the cat,
To wreck and havoc more than she can eat.

EXETER
It follows then the cat must stay at home;
Yet that is but a crushed necessity,
Since we have locks to safeguard necessaries,
And pretty traps to catch the petty thieves.
While the armèd hand does fight abroad,
The advisèd head defends itself at home;
For government, though high, and low, and lower,
Put into parts, does keep in one consent,
Agreeing in a full and natural close,
Like music.

CANTERBURY   True: therefore does heaven divide
The state of man in divers functiòns,
Setting endeavour in continual motion;
To which is fixèd as an aim or butt
Obedience; for so work the honey-bees,
Creatures that by a rule in nature teach
The act of order to a peopled kingdom.
They have a king, and officers of sorts,

Where some, like magistrates, correct at home;
Others, like merchants, venture trade abroad.
Others, like soldiers, armèd in their stings,
Make booty of the summer's velvet buds:
Which pillage they with merry march bring home
To the tent-royal of their emperor.
Who, busied in his majesties, surveys
The singing masons building roofs of gold,
The civil citizens kneading up the honey,
The poor mechanic porters crowding in
Their heavy burdens at his narrow gate,
The sad-eyed justice, with his surly hum,
Delivering to executors pale
The lazy yawning drone. I this infer,
That many things, having full reference
To one consent, may work contrariously,
As many arrows loosèd several ways
Come to one mark;
As many several ways meet in one town,
As many fresh streams meet in one salt sea,
As many lines close in the dial's centre.
So may a thousand actions, once afoot,
End in one purpose, and be all well borne
Without defeat. Therefore to France, my liege!
Divide your happy England into four;
Whereof take you one quarter into France,
And you with that shall make all Gallia shake.
If we, with thrice such powèrs left at home,
Cannot defend our own doors from the dog,
Let us be worried, and our nation lose
The name of hardiness and policy.

KING HENRY

Call in the messengers sent from the Dauphin.

Exeunt some attendants

Now are we well resolved, and by God's help
And yours, the noble sinews of our power,

France being ours, we'll bend it to our awe,
Or break it all to pieces. Or there we'll sit,
Ruling in large and ample empery
Over France and her almost kingly dukedoms,
Or lay these bones in an unworthy urn,
Tombless, with no remembrance over them.
Either our history shall with full mouth
Speak freely of our acts, or else our grave,
Like Turkish mute, shall have a tongueless mouth,
Not worshipped with a waxen epitaph.

Enter Ambassadors of France

Now are we well prepared to know the pleasure
Of our fair cousin Dauphin; for we hear
Your greeting is from him, not from the King.
AMBASSADOR
May it please your majesty to give us leave
Freely to render what we have in charge,
Or shall we sparingly show you far off
The Dauphin's meaning and our embassy?
KING HENRY
We are no tyrant, but a Christian king,
Unto whose grace our passion is as subject
As are our wretches fettered in our prisons:
Therefore with frank and with uncurbèd plainness
Tell us the Dauphin's mind.
AMBASSADOR   Thus then, in short:
Your highness, lately sending into France,
Did claim some certain dukedoms, in the right
Of your great predecessor, King Edward the Third.
In answer of which claim, the Prince our master
Says that you savour too much of your youth,
And bids you be advised there's naught in France
That can be with a nimble galliard won;
You cannot revel into dukedoms there.

He therefore sends you, meeter for your spirit,
This tun of treasure; and, in lieu of this,
Desires you let the dukedoms that you claim
Hear no more of you. This the Dauphin speaks.

KING HENRY
What treasure, uncle?

EXETER   Tennis-balls, my liege.

KING HENRY
We are glad the Dauphin is so pleasant with us.
His present, and your pains, we thank you for.
When we have matched our rackets to these balls,
We will in France, by God's grace, play a set
Shall strike his father's crown into the hazard.
Tell him he has made a match with such a wrangler
That all the courts of France will be disturbed
With chases. And we understand him well,
How he comes over us with our wilder days,
Not measuring what use we made of them.
We never valued this poor seat of England,
And therefore, living hence, did give ourself
To barbarous licence; as it is ever common
That men are merriest when away from home.
But tell the Dauphin I will keep my state,
Be like a king, and show my sail of greatness,
When I do rouse me in my throne of France.
For then I have laid by my majesty,
And plodded like a man for working-days;
But I will rise there with so full a glory
That I will dazzle all the eyes of France,
Yea, strike the Dauphin blind to look on us.
And tell the pleasant Prince this mock of his
Has turned his balls to gun-stones, and his soul
Shall stand sore chargèd for the wasteful vengeance
That shall fly with them. For many a thousand widows
Shall this his mock mock out of their dear husbands;
Mock mothers from their sons, mock castles down;

And some are yet ungotten and unborn
That shall have cause to curse the Dauphin's scorn.
But this lies all within the will of God,
To whom I do appeal, and in whose name,
Tell you the Dauphin, I am coming on,
To revenge me as I may, and to put forth
My rightful hand in a well-hallowed cause.
So get you hence in peace; and tell the Dauphin
His jest will savour but of shallow wit
When thousands weep more than did laugh at it.
Convey them with safe conduct. Fare you well.

Exeunt Ambassadors

EXETER

This was a merry message.

KING HENRY

We hope to make the sender blush at it.
Therefore, my lords, omit no happy hour
That may give furtherance to our expedition;
For we have now no thought in us but France,
Save those to God, that run before our business.
Therefore let our proportions for these wars
Be soon collected, and all things thought upon
That may with reasonable swiftness add
More feathers to our wings; for, God before,
We'll chide this Dauphin at his father's door.
Therefore let every man now task his thought
That this fair action may on foot be brought. *Exeunt*

Prologue to Act II

Flourish. Enter Chorus

CHORUS
Now all the youth of England are on fire,
And silken dalliance in the wardrobe lies.
Now thrive the armourers, and honour's thought
Reigns solely in the breast of every man.
They sell the pasture now to buy the horse,
Following the mirror of all Christian kings
With wingèd heels, as English Mercuries.
For now sits expectation in the air,
And hides a sword from hilt unto the point
With crowns imperial, crowns and coronets,
Promised to Harry and his followers.
The French, advised by good intelligence
Of this most dreadful preparatiòn,
Shake in their fear, and with pale policy
Seek to divert the English purposes.
O England! model to your inward greatness,
Like little body with a mighty heart,
What might you do, that honour would you do,
Were all your children kind and natural!
But see, your fault France has in you found out,
A nest of hollow bosoms, which he fills
With treacherous crowns. And three corrupted men—
One, Richard Earl of Cambridge, and the second,
Henry Lord Scroop of Masham, and the third,
Sir Thomas Grey, knight, of Northumberland—
Have, for the gilt of France—O guilt indeed!—
Confirmed conspiracy with fearful France.
And by their hands this grace of kings must die,

153

If hell and treason hold their promises,
Ere he takes ship for France, and in Southampton.
Linger your patience on, and we'll digest
The abuse of distance, forge a play.
The sum is paid; the traitors are agreed;
The King is set from London; and the scene
Is now transported, gentles, to Southampton.
There is the playhouse now, there must you sit,
And thence to France shall we convey you safe
And bring you back, charming the narrow seas
To give you gentle pass; for, if we may,
We'll not offend one stomach with our play.
But till the King comes forth, and not till then,
Unto Southampton do we shift our scene.   *Exit*

Act II

SCENE I
London. A street.

Enter Corporal Nym and Lieutenant Bardolph

BARDOLPH   Well met, Corporal Nym.

NYM   Good morrow, Lieutenant Bardolph.

BARDOLPH   What, are Ancient[1] Pistol and you friends yet?

NYM   For my part, I care not. I say little; but when time shall serve, there shall be smiles—but that shall be as it may. I dare not fight, but I will wink and hold out my iron. It is a simple one, but what though? It will toast cheese, and it will endure cold as another man's sword will—and there's an end.

BARDOLPH   I will bestow a breakfast to make you friends, and we'll be all three sworn brothers to France. Let it be so, good Corporal Nym.

NYM   Faith, I will live so long as I may, that's the certain of it; and when I cannot live any longer, I will do as I may. That is my rest, that is the rendezvous of it.

BARDOLPH   It is certain, Corporal, that he is married to Nell Quickly, and certainly she did you wrong, for you were betrothed to her.

NYM   I cannot tell; things must be as they may. Men may sleep, and they may have their throats about them at that time, and some say knives have edges: it must be as it may—though patience is a tired mare, yet she will plod; there must be conclusions—well, I cannot tell.

---

[1]Ensign.

Enter Pistol and Hostess Quickly

BARDOLPH   Here comes Ancient Pistol and his wife. Good
    Corporal, be patient here.
NYM   How now, my host Pistol?
PISTOL
    Base tike, call you me host?
    Now by this hand I swear I scorn the term;
    Nor shall my Nell keep lodgers.
HOSTESS   No, by my word, not long; for we cannot lodge
    and board a dozen or fourteen gentlewomen that live
    honestly by the prick of their needles but it will be
    thought we keep a bawdy-house straight.

Nym draws his sword

    O well-a-day, Lady, if he is not drawn now! We shall see
    wilful adultery and murder committed.
BARDOLPH   Good Lieutenant! Good Corporal! Offer
    nothing here.
NYM   Pish!
PISTOL
    Pish for you, Iceland dog! you prick-eared cur of Iceland!
HOSTESS   Good Corporal Nym, show your valour, and
    put up your sword.
NYM   Will you shog off? I would have you *solus*. [alone].

He sheathes his sword

PISTOL
    '*Solus*', egregious dog? O viper vile!
    The '*solus*' in your most marvellous face!
    The '*solus*' in your teeth and in your throat,
    And in your hateful lungs, yea, in your maw, by God!
    And, which is worse, within your nasty mouth!

I do retort the '*solus*' in your bowels,
For I can take, and Pistol's cock is up,
And flashing fire will follow.

NYM   I am not Barbason; you cannot conjure me. I have
an humour to knock you indifferently well. If you grow
foul with me, Pistol, I will scour you with my rapier, as
I may, in fair terms. If you would walk off, I would prick
your guts a little, in good terms, as I may, and that's the
humour of it.

PISTOL
O braggart vile, and damnèd furious wight!
The grave does gape, and doting death is near:
Therefore exhale!

They both draw

BARDOLPH   Hear me, hear me what I say! He that strikes
the first stroke, I'll run him up to the hilt, as I am a
soldier.

He draws

PISTOL
An oath of much might, and fury shall abate.

Pistol and Nym sheathe their swords

Give me your fist, your forefoot to me give;
Your spirits are most tall.

NYM   I will cut your throat one time or other, in fair
terms, that is the humour of it.

PISTOL
'*Couple a gorge!*'[2]
That is the word. I you defy again!

---

[2]Cut a throat.

O hound of Crete, think you my spouse to get?
No, to the hospital go,
And from the powdering tub of infamy
Fetch forth the leper kite of Cressid's kind,
Doll Tearsheet she by name, and her espouse.
I have, and I will hold, the quondam[3] Quickly
For the only she; and—*pauca,*[4] there's enough.
Go to!

Enter the Boy

BOY   My host Pistol, you must come to my master—and
you, Hostess: he is very sick, and would to bed. Good
Bardolph, put your face between his sheets, and do the
office of a warming-pan. Faith, he's very ill.
BARDOLPH   Away, you rogue!
HOSTESS   By my word, he'll yield the crow a pudding one
of these days; the King has killed his heart. Good
husband, come home presently.   *Exit with Boy*
BARDOLPH   Come, shall I make you two friends? We
must to France together: why the devil should we keep
knives to cut one another's throats?
PISTOL
Let floods o'erswell, and fiends for food howl on!
NYM   You'll pay me the eight shillings I won of you at
betting?
PISTOL
Base is the slave that pays!
NYM   That now I will have; that's the humour of it.
PISTOL
As manhood shall compound. Push home!

They draw

---

[3]Former.
[4]Briefly.

BARDOLPH   By this sword, he that makes the first thrust,
I'll kill him! By this sword, I will.

PISTOL
Sword is an oath, and oaths must have their course.

He sheathes his sword

BARDOLPH   Corporal Nym, if you will be friends, be
friends: if you will not, why then be enemies with me
too. Pray put up.

NYM   I shall have my eight shillings I won of you at
betting?

PISTOL
A crown shall you have, and present pay;
And liquor likewise will I give to you,
And friendship shall combine, and brotherhood.
I'll live by Nym, and Nym shall live by me.
Is not this just? For I shall sutler be
Unto the camp, and profits will accrue.
Give me your hand.

Nym sheathes his sword

NYM   I shall have my crown?

PISTOL
In cash most justly paid.

NYM   Well then, that's the humour of it.

Enter Hostess

HOSTESS   As ever you came of women, come in quickly
to Sir John. Ah, poor heart! he is so shaked of a burning
quotidian fever that it is most lamentable to behold.
Sweet men, come to him.

NYM   The King has run bad humours on the knight,
that's the truth of it.
PISTOL
Nym, you have spoken the right;
His heart is fracted and corroborate.
NYM   The King is a good king, but it must be as it may:
he passes some humours and careers.
PISTOL
Let us condole the knight; for, lambkins, we will live.

Exeunt

SCENE II
Southampton. A chamber.

Enter Exeter, Bedford, and Westmorland

BEDFORD
Before God, his grace is bold to trust these traitors.
EXETER
They shall be apprehended by and by.
WESTMORLAND
How smooth and even they do bear themselves!
As if allegiance in their bosoms sat,
Crownèd with faith and constant loyalty.
BEDFORD
The King has note of all that they intend,
By interception which they dream not of.
EXETER
Nay, but the man that was his bedfellow,
Whom he has dulled and cloyed with gracious favours —
That he should, for a foreign purse, so sell
His sovereign's life to death and treachery!

*Sound trumpets. Enter the King, Scroop, Cambridge,
Grey, and attendants*

KING HENRY
  Now sits the wind fair, and we will aboard.
  My Lord of Cambridge, and my kind Lord of Masham,
  And you, my gentle knight, give me your thoughts.
  Think you not that the powers we bear with us
  Will cut their passage through the force of France,
  Doing the execution and the act
  For which we have in head assembled them?
SCROOP
  No doubt, my liege, if each man does his best.
KING HENRY
  I doubt not that, since we are well persuaded
  We carry not a heart with us from hence
  That grows not in a fair consent with ours;
  Nor leave any behind that does not wish
  Success and conquest to attend on us.
CAMBRIDGE
  Never was monarch better feared and loved
  Than is your majesty. There's not, I think, a subject
  That sits in heart-grief and uneasiness
  Under the sweet shade of your government.
GREY
  True: those that were your father's enemies
  Have steeped their galls in honey, and do serve you
  With hearts created of duty and of zeal.
KING HENRY
  We therefore have great cause of thankfulness,
  And shall forget the office of our hand
  Sooner than quittance of desert and merit
  According to the weight and worthiness.
SCROOP
  So service shall with steelèd sinews toil,
  And labour shall refresh itself with hope
  To do your grace incessant services.

KING HENRY
   We judge no less. Uncle of Exeter,
   Enlarge the man committed yesterday
   That railed against our person. We consider
   It was excess of wine that set him on,
   And on his more advice we pardon him.
SCROOP
   That's mercy, but too much security.
   Let him be punished, sovereign, lest example
   Breed, by his sufferance, more of such a kind.
KING HENRY
   O, let us yet be merciful.
CAMBRIDGE
   So may your highness, and yet punish too.
GREY
   Sir,
   You show great mercy if you give him life
   After the taste of much correction.
KING HENRY
   Alas, your too much love and care of me
   Are heavy orisons against this poor wretch!
   If little faults, proceeding on distemper,
   Shall not be winked at, how shall we stretch our eye
   When capital crimes, chewed, swallowed, and digested,
   Appear before us? We'll yet enlarge that man,
   Though Cambridge, Scroop, and Grey, in their dear
      care
   And tender preservation of our person
   Would have him punished. And now to our French
      causes:
   Who are the late commissioners?
CAMBRIDGE
   I one, my lord.
   Your highness bade me ask for it today.

SCROOP
    So did you me, my liege.
GREY
    And I, my royal sovereign.
KING HENRY
    Then, Richard Earl of Cambridge, there is yours;
    There yours, Lord Scroop of Masham; and, sir knight,
    Grey of Northumberland, this same is yours.
    Read them, and know I know your worthiness.
    My Lord of Westmorland, and uncle Exeter,
    We will aboard tonight. —Why, how now, gentlemen?
    What see you in those papers, that you lose
    So much complexion? Look you, how they change!
    Their cheeks are paper. —Why, what read you there
    That have so cowarded and chased your blood
    Out of appearance?
CAMBRIDGE   I do confess my fault,
    And do submit me to your highness' mercy.
GREY, SCROOP
    To which we all appeal.
KING HENRY
    The mercy that was quick in us but late
    By your own counsel is suppressed and killed.
    You must not dare, for shame, to talk of mercy,
    For your own reasons turn into your bosoms
    As dogs upon their masters, worrying you.
    See you, my princes, and my noble peers,
    These English monsters! My Lord of Cambridge here—
    You know how apt our love was to accord
    To furnish him with all appertinents
    Belonging to his honour. And this man
    Has, for a few light crowns, lightly conspired,
    And sworn unto the practices of France,
    To kill us here in Hampton. To which also
    This knight, no less for bounty bound to us
    Than Cambridge is, has likewise sworn. But O,

What shall I say to you, Lord Scroop, you cruel,
Ungrateful, savage, and inhuman creature?
You that did bear the key of all my counsels,
That knew the very bottom of my soul,
That almost might have coined me into gold,
Would you have practised on me, for your use?
May it be possible that foreign hire
Could out of you extract one spark of evil
That might annoy my finger? It is so strange
That, though the truth of it stands off as gross
As black and white, my eye will scarcely see it.
Treason and murder ever kept together,
As two yoke-devils sworn to either's purpose,
Working so grossly in a natural cause
That astonishment did not whoop at them.
But you, against all proportion, did bring in
Wonder to wait on treason and on murder:
And whatsoever cunning fiend it was
That wrought upon you so preposterously
Has got the voice in hell for excellence.
All other devils that suggest by treasons
Do botch and bungle up damnatiòn
With patches, colours, and with forms, being fetched
From glistering semblances of piety.
But he that tempered you bade you stand up,
Gave you no instance why you should do treason,
Unless to dub you with the name of traitor.
If that same demon that has gulled you thus
Should with his lion gait walk the whole world,
He might return to vast Tartary back,
And tell the legions, 'I can never win
A soul so easy as that Englishman's.'
O, how have you with deep mistrust infected
The sweetness of affiance! Show men dutiful?
Why, so did you. Seem they grave and learnèd?
Why, so did you. Come they of noble family?

Why, so did you. Seem they religious?
Why, so did you. Or are they spare in diet,
Free from gross passion or of mirth or anger,
Constant in spirit, not swerving with the blood,
Garnished and decked in modest complement,
Not working with the eye without the ear,
And but in purgèd judgement trusting neither?
Such and so finely sifted did you seem:
And thus your fall has left a kind of blot
To mark the thoughtful man and best endued
With some suspicion. I will weep for you;
For this revolt of yours, I think, is like
Another fall of man. Their faults are open.
Arrest them to the answer of the law;
And God acquit them of their practices!

EXETER   I arrest you of high treason, by the name of
Richard Earl of Cambridge.
I arrest you of high treason, by the name of Henry Lord
Scroop of Masham.
I arrest you of high treason, by the name of Thomas
Grey, knight, of Northumberland.

SCROOP
Our purposes God justly has discovered,
And I repent my fault more than my death.
Which I beseech your highness to forgive,
Although my body pays the price of it.

CAMBRIDGE
For me, the gold of France did not seduce,
Although I did admit it as a motive
The sooner to effect what I intended.
But God be thankèd for prevention,
Which I in sufferance heartily will rejoice,
Beseeching God and you to pardon me.

GREY
Never did faithful subject more rejoice
At the discovery of most dangerous treason

Than I do at this hour joy o'er myself,
Prevented from a damnèd enterprise.
My fault, but not my body, pardon, sovereign.
KING HENRY
God quit you in His mercy! Hear your sentence.
You have conspired against our royal person,
Joined with an enemy proclaimed, and from his coffers
Received the golden earnest of our death.
Wherein you would have sold your King to slaughter,
His princes and his peers to servitude,
His subjects to oppression and contempt,
And his whole kingdom into desolation.
Touching our person seek we no revenge,
But we our kingdom's safety must so tender,
Whose ruin you have sought, that to her laws
We do deliver you. Get you therefore hence,
Poor miserable wretches, to your death;
The taste whereof God of His mercy give
You patience to endure, and true repentance
Of all your dire offences. Bear them hence.

Exeunt Cambridge, Scroop, and Grey, guarded

Now, lords, for France; the enterprise whereof
Shall be to you, as us, like glorious.
We doubt not of a fair and lucky war,
Since God so graciously has brought to light
This dangerous treason lurking in our way
To hinder our beginnings. We doubt not now
But every rub is smoothèd on our way.
Then forth, dear countrymen! Let us deliver
Our armament into the hand of God,
Putting it straight in expeditiòn.
Cheerily to sea! The signs of war advance!
No King of England if not King of France!
Flourish. Exeunt

SCENE III
London. Before the Boar's Head.

Enter Pistol, Hostess, Nym, Bardolph, and Boy

HOSTESS   Pray, honey-sweet husband, let me bring you to
Staines.

PISTOL

No, for my manly heart does grieve.
Bardolph, be blithe! Nym, rouse your vaunting veins!
Boy, bristle your courage up! For Falstaff, he is dead,
And we must grieve therefor.

BARDOLPH   Would I were with him, wheresoever he is,
either in heaven or in hell!

HOSTESS   Nay, sure, he's not in hell: he's in Arthur's
bosom, if ever man went to Arthur's bosom. He made a
finer end, and went away as it had been any christened
child; he departed even just between twelve and one,
even at the turning of the tide. For after I saw him
fumble with the sheets, and play with flowers, and
smile upon his fingers' ends, I knew there was but one
way; for his nose was as sharp as a pen, and he talked of
green fields. 'How now, Sir John?' said I, 'What, man, be
of good cheer!' So he cried out, 'God, God, God!' three or
four times. Now I, to comfort him, bid him he should
not think of God—I hoped there was no need to trouble
himself with any such thoughts yet. So he bade me lay
more clothes on his feet; I put my hand into the bed,
and felt them, and they were as cold as any stone; then I
felt to his knees, and so upward and upward, and all
was as cold as any stone.

NYM   They say he cried out for sack.

HOSTESS   Ay, that he did.

BARDOLPH   And for women.

HOSTESS   Nay, that he did not.

BOY   Yes, that he did, and said they were devils incarnate.

HOSTESS   He could never abide carnation, 'twas a colour he never liked.

BOY   He said once, the devil would have him about women.

HOSTESS   He did in some sort, indeed, handle women; but then he was rheumatic, and talked of the Whore of Babylon.

BOY   Do you not remember, he saw a flea stick upon Bardolph's nose, and he said it was a black soul burning in hell?

BARDOLPH   Well, the fuel is gone that maintained that fire—that's all the riches I got in his service.

NYM   Shall we be off? The King will be gone from Southampton.

PISTOL

   Come, let's away. My love, give me your lips.

   Look to my chattels and my movables.

   Let senses rule. The word is 'Pitch and pay!'

   Trust none;

   For oaths are straws, men's faiths are wafer-cakes,

   And Holdfast is the only dog, my duck.

   Therefore, *Caveto* [Take care] be your counsellor.

   Go, clear your crystals. Yoke-fellows in arms,

   Let us to France, like horse-leeches, my boys,

   To suck, to suck, the very blood to suck!

BOY   And that's but unwholesome food, they say.

PISTOL

   Touch her soft mouth, and march.

BARDOLPH   Farewell, Hostess.

He kisses her

NYM   I cannot kiss, that is the humour of it; but adieu.

PISTOL
    Let housewifery appear. Keep close, I you command.
HOSTESS   Farewell! Adieu!   *Exeunt*

SCENE IV
France. The King's palace.

*Flourish. Enter the French King, the Dauphin, the Dukes
of Berri and Brittany, the Constable and others*

FRENCH KING
    Thus come the English with full power upon us,
    And more than carefully it us concerns
    To answer royally in our defences.
    Therefore the Dukes of Berri and of Brittany,
    Of Brabant and of Orleans, shall make forth,
    And you, Prince Dauphin, with all swift dispatch,
    To line and new repair our towns of war
    With men of courage and with means defendant;
    For England's near approaches make as fierce
    As waters to the sucking of a gulf.
    It fits us then to be as provident
    As fear may teach us, out of late examples
    Left by the fatal and neglected English
    Upon our fields.
DAUPHIN   My most redoubted father,
    It is most meet we arm us against the foe;
    For peace itself should not so dull a kingdom,
    Though war nor any quarrel were in question,
    But that defences, musters, preparations,
    Should be maintained, assembled, and collected,
    As if a war's in expectatìon.
    Therefore, I say, 'tis meet we all go forth
    To view the sick and feeble parts of France:
    And let us do it with no show of fear—

No, with no more than if we heard that England
Were busied with a Whitsun morris-dance.
For, my good liege, she is so idly kinged,
Her sceptre so fantastically borne
By a vain, giddy, shallow, changeable youth,
That fear attends her not.
CONSTABLE   O, peace, Prince Dauphin!
You are too much mistaken in this King.
Question your grace the late ambassadors,
With what great state he heard their embassy,
How well supplied with noble counsellors,
How modest in objection, and with that
How terrible in constant resolution.
And you shall find his vanities foregone
Were but the outside of the Roman Brutus,
Covering discretion with a coat of folly;
As gardeners do with ordure hide those roots
That shall first spring and be most delicate.
DAUPHIN
Well, it is not so, my Lord High Constable;
But though we think it so, it is no matter.
In cases of defence, it is best to weigh
The enemy more mighty than he seems.
So the proportions of defence are filled;
Which of a weak and niggardly projection
Do like a miser spoil his coat with scanting
A little cloth.
FRENCH KING   Think we King Harry strong;
And, princes, look you strongly arm to meet him.
The kindred of him has been fleshed upon us,
And he is bred out of that bloody strain
That haunted us in our familiar paths.
Witness our too much memorable shame
When Crécy battle fatally was struck,
And all our princes captived by the hand
Of that black name, Edward, Black Prince of Wales.

While his mountain sire, on mountain standing,
Up in the air, crowned with the golden sun,
Saw his heroical seed, and smiled to see him,
Mangle the work of nature, and deface
The patterns that by God and by French fathers
Had twenty years been made. This is a stem
Of that victorious stock; and let us fear
The native mightiness and fate of him.

Enter a Messenger

MESSENGER
Ambassadors from Harry King of England
Do crave admittance to your majesty.
FRENCH KING
We'll give them present audience. Go and bring them.
                    Exeunt Messenger and certain lords
You see this chase is hotly followed, friends.
DAUPHIN
Turn head, and stop pursuit, for coward dogs
Most spend their mouths when what they seem to
    threaten
Runs far before them. Good my sovereign,
Take up the English short, and let them know
Of what a monarchy you are the head.
Self-love, my liege, is not so vile a sin
As self-neglecting.

Enter lords, with Exeter and attendants

FRENCH KING   From our brother of England?
EXETER
From him; and thus he greets your majesty:
He wills you, in the name of God Almighty,
That you divest yourself, and lay apart
The borrowed glories that by gift of heaven,

By law of nature and of nations, belong
To him and to his heirs. Namely, the crown,
And all wide-stretchèd honours that pertain
By custom and the ordinance of times
Unto the crown of France. That you may know
It is no sinister nor awkward claim
Picked from the worm-holes of long-vanished days,
Nor from the dust of old oblivion raked,
He sends you this most memorable line,
In every branch truly demonstrative,
Willing you overlook this pedigree.
And when you find him evenly derived
From his most famed of famous ancestors,
Edward the Third, he bids you then resign
Your crown and kingdom, indirectly held
From him, the native and true challenger.

FRENCH KING
Or else what follows?

EXETER
Bloody constraint; for if you hide the crown
Even in your hearts, there will he rake for it.
Therefore in fierce tempest is he coming,
In thunder and in earthquake, like a Jove,
That, if requiring fail, he will compel.
And bids you, in the bowels of the Lord,
Deliver up the crown, and to take mercy
On the poor souls for whom this hungry war
Opens his vasty jaws; and on your head
Turning the widows' tears, the orphans' cries,
The dead men's blood, deprivèd maidens' groans,
For husbands, fathers, and betrothèd lovers
That shall be swallowed in this controversy.
This is his claim, his threatening, and my message—
Unless the Dauphin is in presence here,
To whom expressly I bring greeting too.

FRENCH KING

    For us, we will consider of this further.
    Tomorrow shall you bear our full intent
    Back to our brother of England.

DAUPHIN   For the Dauphin,

    I stand here for him. What to him from England?

EXETER

    Scorn and defiance, slight regard, contempt,
    And anything that may not misbecome
    The mighty sender, does he prize you at.
    Thus says my King: that if your father's highness
    Does not, in grant of all demands at large,
    Sweeten the bitter mock you sent his majesty,
    He'll call you to so hot an answer of it
    That caves and womby vaultages of France
    Shall chide your trespass, and return your mock
    In second accent of his ordinance.

DAUPHIN

    Say, if my father renders fair return,
    It is against my will, for I desire
    Nothing but odds with England. To that end,
    As matching to his youth and vanity,
    I did present him with the Paris balls.

EXETER

    He'll make your Paris Louvre shake for it,
    Were it the mistress Court of mighty Europe:
    And, be assured, you'll find a difference,
    As we his subjects have in wonder found,
    Between the promise of his greener days
    And these he masters now. Now he weighs time
    Even to the utmost grain; that you shall read
    In your own losses, if he stays in France.

FRENCH KING

    Tomorrow shall you know our mind at full.

Flourish

EXETER
    Dispatch us with all speed, lest our King
    Comes here himself to question our delay,
    For he is footed in this land already.
FRENCH KING
    You shall be soon dispatched with fair conditions.
    A night is but small breath and little pause
    To answer matters of this consequence.   *Exeunt*

Prologue to Act III

Flourish. Enter Chorus

CHORUS

Thus with imagined wing our swift scene flies
In motion of no less celerity
Than that of thought. Suppose that you have seen
The well-appointed King at Hampton pier
Embark his royalty, and his brave fleet
With silken streamers the young Phoebus fanning.
Play with your fancies, and in them behold
Upon the hempen tackle ship-boys climbing;
Hear the shrill whistle which does order give
To sounds confused; behold the threaden sails,
Borne with the invisible and creeping wind,
Draw the huge bottoms through the furrowed sea,
Breasting the lofty surge. O, do but think
You stand upon the shore and can behold
A city on the inconstant billows dancing;
For so appears this fleet majestical,
Holding due course to Harfleur. Follow, follow!
Grapple your minds to sternage of this navy,
And leave your England, as dead midnight still,
Guarded with grandsires, babies, and old women,
Either past or not arrived to pith and power.
For who is he whose chin is but enriched
With one appearing hair that will not follow
These culled and choice-drawn cavaliers to France?
Work, work your thoughts, and therein see a siege:
Behold the ordnance on their carriages,
With fatal mouths gaping on girded Harfleur.
Suppose the ambassador from the French comes back;

Tells Harry that the King does offer him
Katherine his daughter and, with her to dowry,
Some petty and unprofitable dukedoms.
The offer likes not; and the nimble gunner
With linstock now the devilish cannon touches,

Alarum, and chambers go off

And down goes all before them. Still be kind,
And eke out our performance with your mind.   *Exit*

Act III

SCENE I
France. Before Harfleur.

*Alarum. Enter the King, Exeter, Bedford, Gloucester, other
lords, and soldiers with scaling-ladders*

KING HENRY
    Once more unto the breach, dear friends, once more,
    Or close the wall up with our English dead!
    In peace there's nothing so becomes a man
    As modest stillness and humility.
    But when the blast of war blows in our ears,
    Then imitate the action of the tiger;
    Stiffen the sinews, conjure up the blood,
    Disguise fair nature with hard-featured rage.
    Then lend the eye a terrible aspèct;
    Let it pry through the portage of the head
    Like the brass cannon; let the brow o'erwhelm it
    As fearfully as does a gallèd rock
    O'erhang and thrusts out its confounded base,
    Swilled with the wild and wasteful oceàn.
    Now set the teeth, and stretch the nostril wide,
    Hold hard the breath, and bend up every spirit
    To its full height! On, on, you noblest English,
    Whose blood is fetched from fathers of war-proof!—
    Fathers that, like so many Alexanders,
    Have in these parts from morn till even fought,
    And sheathed their swords for lack of argument.
    Dishonour not your mothers; now attest
    That those whom you called fathers did beget you!

Be copy now to men of grosser blood,
And teach them how to war. And you, good yeomen,
Whose limbs were made in England, show us here
The mettle of your pasture; let us swear
That you are worth your breeding—which I doubt not;
For there is none of you so mean and base
That has not noble lustre in your eyes.
I see you stand like greyhounds in the slips,
Straining upon the start. The game's afoot!
Follow your spirit, and upon this charge
Cry, 'God for Harry, England, and Saint George!'
Exeunt. Alarum, and chambers go off

SCENE II
The same.

Enter Nym, Bardolph, Pistol, and Boy

BARDOLPH   On, on, on, on, on! To the breach, to the
breach!
NYM   Pray, Corporal, stay—the knocks are too hot, and,
for my own part, I have not a case of lives. The humour
of it is too hot, that is the very plainsong of it.
PISTOL
The plainsong is most just; for humours do abound.
Knocks go and come; God's vassals drop and die;
          And sword and shield,
          In bloody field,
     Do win immortal fame.
BOY   Would I were in an alehouse in London! I would
give all my fame for a pot of ale, and safety.
PISTOL   And I:
          If wishes would prevail with me,
          My purpose should not fail with me,
               But thither would I hie.

BOY   As duly,
                But not as truly,
             As bird does sing on bough.

Enter Fluellen

FLUELLEN   Up to the breach, you dogs! Forward, you
   rascals!

He drives them forward

PISTOL
   Be merciful, great Duke, to men of mould!
   Abate your rage, abate your manly rage,
   Abate your rage, great Duke!
   Good fellow bate your rage! Use lenity, sweet chuck!
NYM   These are good humours! Your honour wins bad
   humours.   *Exeunt all but the Boy*
BOY   As young as I am, I have observed these three
   swashbucklers. I am boy to them all three, but all they
   three, though they would serve me, could not be man to
   me; for indeed three such buffoons do not amount to a
   man. For Bardolph, he is white-livered and red-faced;
   by means whereof he faces it out, but fights not. For
   Pistol, he has a killing tongue, and a quiet sword;
   by means whereof he breaks words, and keeps whole
   weapons. For Nym, he has heard that men of few words
   are the best men; and therefore he scorns to say his
   prayers, lest he should be thought a coward. But his few
   bad words are matched with as few good deeds; for he
   never broke any man's head but his own, and that was
   against a post, when he was drunk. They will steal
   anything, and call it purchase. Bardolph stole a lutecase,
   bore it twelve leagues, and sold it for three halfpence.
   Nym and Bardolph are sworn brothers in filching, and
   in Calais they stole a fire-shovel—I knew by that piece

of service the men would carry coals. They would have me as familiar with men's pockets as their gloves or their handkerchiefs. Which makes much against my manhood, if I should take from another's pocket to put into mine; for it is plain pocketing up of wrongs. I must leave them, and seek some better service. Their villainy goes against my weak stomach, and therefore I must cast it up.   *Exit*

Enter Fluellen, Gower following

GOWER   Captain Fluellen, you must come presently to the mines. The Duke of Gloucester would speak with you.

FLUELLEN   To the mines? Tell you the Duke, it is not so good to come to the mines, for, look you, the mines are not according to the discipline of the war. The concavities of it are not sufficient; for, look you, the adversary, you may discuss unto the Duke, look you, has dug himself four yard under the countermines. By Jesu, I think he will plow up all, if there is not better direction.

GOWER   The Duke of Gloucester, to whom the order of the siege is given, is altogether directed by an Irishman, a very valiant gentleman, in faith.

FLUELLEN   It is Captain Macmorris, is it not?

GOWER   I think it is.

FLUELLEN   By Jesu, he is an ass, as in the world; I will verify as much in his beard. He has no more direction in the true discipline of the wars, look you, of the Roman discipline, than has a puppy-dog.

Enter Captain Macmorris and Captain Jamy

GOWER   Here he comes, and the Scots captain, Captain Jamy, with him.

FLUELLEN   Captain Jamy is a marvellous valorous

gentleman, that is certain, and of great expedition and knowledge in the ancient wars, upon my particular knowledge of his direction. By Jesu, he will maintain his argument as well as any military man in the world, in the discipline of the pristine wars of the Romans.

JAMY   I say good-day, Captain Fluellen.

FLUELLEN   Good-even to your worship, good Captain James.

GOWER   How now, Captain Macmorris, have you quit the mines? Have the pioneers given over?

MACMORRIS   By Chrish, la, 'tish ill done! The work ish given over, the trompet sounds the retreat. By my hand I swear, and my father's soul, the work ish ill done: it ish given over. I would have blowed up the town, so Chrish save me, la, in an hour. O, 'tish ill done, 'tish ill done—by my hand, 'tish ill done!

FLUELLEN   Captain Macmorris, I beseech you now, will you give me, look you, a few disputations with you, as partly touching or concerning the discipline of the war, the Roman wars, in the way of argument, look you, and friendly communication?—partly to satisfy my opinion, and partly for the satisfaction, look you, of my mind—as touching the direction of the military discipline, that is the point.

JAMY   It sall be vary gud, gud feith, gud captens bath, and I sall quit you with gud leve, as I may pick occasion: that sall I, for sure.

MACMORRIS   It is no time to discourse, so Chrish save me! The day is hot, and the weather, and the wars, and the King, and the Dukes—it is no time to discourse, the town is besieged, and the trumpet calls us to the breach, and we talk and, be Chrish, do nothing. 'Tis shame for us all: so God save me 'tis shame to stand still, it is shame, by my hand—and there are throats to be cut, and works to be done, and there ish nothing done, so Chrish save me, la!

JAMY   By the mess, ere theise eyes of mine take themselves
to slomber, ay'll de gud service, or ay'll lie i'th'grund for
it, ay, or go to death! And ay'll pay't as valorously as I
may, that sall I suerly do, that is the breff and the long.
Sure, I wad full fain hear some question 'tween you
tway.

FLUELLEN   Captain Macmorris, I think, look you, under
your correction, there is not many of your nation—

MACMORRIS   Of my nation? What ish my nation? Ish a
villain, and a bastard, and a knave, and a rascal. What
ish my nation? Who talks of my nation?

FLUELLEN   Look you, if you take the matter otherwise
than is meant, Captain Macmorris, peradventure I shall
think you do not use me with that affability as in
discretion you ought to use me, look you, being as good
a man as yourself, both in the discipline of war, and in
the derivation of my birth, and in other particularities.

MACMORRIS   I do not know you so good a man as myself.
So Chrish save me, I will cut off your head.

GOWER   Gentlemen both, you will mistake each other.

JAMY   Ah, that's a foul fault!

A parley is sounded

GOWER   The town sounds a parley.

FLUELLEN   Captain Macmorris, when there is better
opportunity to be required, look you, I will be so bold as
to tell you, I know the discipline of war; and there is an
end.   *Exeunt*

SCENE III
The same.

*Some citizens of Harfleur appear on the walls. Enter the
King and all his train before the gates*

KING HENRY

How yet resolves the Governor of the town?
This is the latest parley we will admit:
Therefore to our best mercy give yourselves,
Or, like to men proud of destructiòn,
Defy us to our worst. For, as I am a soldier,
A name that in my thoughts becomes me best,
If I begin the battery once again,
I will not leave the half-achievèd Harfleur
Till in her ashes she lie burièd.
The gates of mercy shall be all shut up,
And the fleshed soldier, rough and hard of heart,
In liberty of bloody hand shall range
With conscience wide as hell, mowing like grass
Your fresh fair virgins, and your flowering infants.
What is it then to me, if impious war,
Arrayed in flames, like to the prince of fiends,
Does, with his smirched complexion, all fierce feats
Enlinked to waste and desolatiòn?
What is it to me, when you yourselves are cause,
If your pure maidens fall into the hand
Of hot and forcing violatiòn?
What rein can hold licentious wickedness
When down the hill it holds its fierce career?
We may as fruitless spend our vain command
Upon the enragèd soldiers in their spoil
As send precepts to the leviathan
To come ashore. Therefore, you men of Harfleur,
Take pity of your town and of your people
While yet my soldiers are in my command—
While yet the cool and temperate wind of grace
O'erblows the filthy and contagious clouds
Of heady murder, spoil, and villainy.
If not, why, in a moment look to see
The blind and bloody soldier with foul hand

Defile the locks of your shrill-shrieking daughters;
Your fathers taken by the silver beards,
And their most reverend heads dashed to the walls;
Your naked infants spitted upon pikes,
While the mad mothers with their howls confused
Do break the clouds, as did the wives of Jewry
At Herod's bloody-hunting slaughtermen.
What say you? Will you yield, and this avoid?
Or, guilty in defence, be thus destroyed?

Enter the Governor on the wall

GOVERNOR
Our expectation has this day an end.
The Dauphin, whom of succours we entreated,
Returns us that his forces are yet not ready
To raise so great a siege. Therefore, great King,
We yield our town and lives to your soft mercy.
Enter our gates, dispose of us and ours,
For we no longer are defensible.
KING HENRY
Open your gates.

Exit Governor

Come, uncle Exeter,
Go you and enter Harfleur; there remain,
And fortify it strongly against the French.
Use mercy to them all. For us, dear uncle,
The winter coming on, and sickness growing
Upon our soldiers, we will retire to Calais.
Tonight in Harfleur will we be your guest;
Tomorrow for the march are we addressed.

Flourish, and enter the town

SCENE IV[1]
Rouen. The palace.

Enter Katherine and Alice, an old gentlewoman

KATHERINE   Alice, tu as été en Angleterre, et tu parles
bien le langage.

ALICE   Un peu, madame.

KATHERINE   Je te prie, m'enseignez—il faut que j'apprenne
à parler. Comment appelez-vous la main en anglais?

ALICE   La main? Elle est appelée the hand.

KATHERINE   The hand. Et les doigts?

ALICE   Les doigts? Ma foi, j'oublie les doigts, mais je me
souviendrai. Les doigts? Je pense qu'ils sont appelés the
fingers; oui, the fingers.

KATHERINE   La main, the hand; les doigts, the fingers. Je
pense que je suis le bon écolier; j'ai gagné deux mots
d'anglais vitement. Comment appelez-vous les ongles?

ALICE   Les ongles? Nous les appelons the nails.

KATHERINE   The nails. Écoutez: dites-moi si je parle
bien—the hand, the fingers, et de nails.

ALICE   C'est bien dit, madame. Il est fort bon anglais.

KATHERINE   Dites-moi l'anglais pour le bras.

ALICE   The arm, madame.

KATHERINE   Et le coude?

ALICE   The elbow.

KATHERINE   The elbow. Je m'en fais la répétition de tous
les mots que vous m'avez appris dès à présent.

ALICE   Il est trop difficile, madame, comme je pense.

KATHERINE   Excusez-moi, Alice; écoutez—the hand, the
finger, the nails, the arm, the bilbow.

ALICE   The elbow, madame.

KATHERINE   O Seigneur Dieu, je m'en oublie! The elbow.
Comment appelez-vous le col?

---

[1]This scene is translated in the Appendix.

ALICE   The neck, madame.

KATHERINE   The neck. Et le menton?

ALICE   The chin.

KATHERINE   The chin. Le col, the neck; le menton, the chin.

ALICE   Oui. Sauf votre honneur, en vérité, vous prononcez les mots aussi droit que les natifs d'Angleterre.

KATHERINE   Je ne doute point d'apprendre, par la grace de Dieu, et en peu de temps.

ALICE   N'avez-vous pas déjà oublié ce que je vous ai enseigné?

KATHERINE   Non, je réciterai à vous promptement: the hand, the finger, the mails—

ALICE   The nails, madame.

KATHERINE   The nails, the arm, the ilbow—

ALICE   Sauf votre honneur, the elbow.

KATHERINE   Ainsi dis-je: the elbow, the neck, et the chin. Comment appelez-vous le pied et la robe?

ALICE   Le foot, madame, et le count.[2]

KATHERINE   Le foot, et le count? O Seigneur Dieu! Ils sont mots de son mauvais, corruptible, gros, et impudique, et non pour les dames d'honneur d'user. Je ne voudrais prononcer ces mots devant les seigneurs de France pour tout le monde. Foh! Le foot et le count! Néanmoins, je réciterai une autre fois ma leçon ensemble. The hand, the finger, the nails, the arm, the elbow, the neck, the chin, the foot, le count.

ALICE   Excellent, madame!

KATHERINE   C'est assez pour une fois. Allons-nous à dîner.   *Exeunt*

---

[2]Bawdy, of course.

SCENE V
The same.

Enter the King of France, the Dauphin,
the Duke of Brittany, the Constable of France,
and others

FRENCH KING

'Tis certain he has passed the River Somme.

CONSTABLE

And if he is not fought with now, my lord,
Let us not live in France: let us quit all,
And give our vineyards to a barbarous people.

DAUPHIN

O Dieu vivant![3] Shall a few sprays of us,
The emptying of our fathers' lustfulness,
Our scions, put in wild and savage stock,
Spirt up so suddenly into the clouds,
And overlook their grafters?

BRITTANY

Normans, but bastard Normans, Norman bastards!
Mort de ma vie![4] If they march along
Unfought with now, but I will sell my dukedom
To buy a sloppy and a dirty farm
In that crabbèd isle of Albion.

CONSTABLE

Dieu de batailles![5] Where have they this mettle?
Is not their climate foggy, raw, and dull,
On which, as in despite, the sun looks pale,
Killing their fruit with frowns? Can sodden water,

---

[3]O living God.
[4]Death of my life.
[5]God of battles.

A drench for over-reined jades, their barley broth,
Warm up their cold blood to such valiant heat?
And shall our quick blood, spirited with wine,
Seem frosty? O, for honour of our land,
Let us not hang like roping icicles
Upon our houses' thatch, while a more frosty people
Sweat drops of gallant youth in our rich fields!—
Poor we call them 'in their native lords.
DAUPHIN
By faith and honour,
Our madams mock at us, and plainly say
Our mettle is bred out, and they will give
Their bodies to the lust of English youth,
To new-store France with bastard warriors.
BRITAINE
They bid us to the English dancing-schools,
And teach lavoltas high and swift corantos,
Saying our grace is only in our heels,
And that we are most lofty runaways.
FRENCH KING
Where is Montjoy the Herald? Speed him hence,
Let him greet England with our sharp defiance.
Up, Princes, and with spirit of honour edged,
Sharper than your swords, hie to the field!
Charles Delabreth, High Constable of France,
You Dukes of Orleans, Bourbon, and of Berri,
Alençon, Brabant, Bar, and Burgundy,
Jaques Chatillon, Rambures, Vaudemont,
Beaumont, Grandpré, Roussi, and Faulconbridge,
Foix, Lestrake, Bouciqualt, and Charolois,
High Dukes, great Princes, Barons, Lords, and Knights,
For your great seats, now quit you of great shames.
Bar Harry England, that sweeps through our land
With pennons painted in the blood of Harfleur!
Rush on his host, as does the melted snow
Upon the valleys, whose low vassal seat

The Alps do spit and void their snot upon!
Go down upon him, you have power enough,
And in a captive chariot into Rouen
Bring him our prisoner.
CONSTABLE   This becomes the great.
Sorry am I his numbers are so few,
His soldiers sick, and famished in their march.
For I am sure, when he shall see our army,
He'll drop his heart into the sink of fear,
And for achievement offer us his ransom.
FRENCH KING
Therefore, Lord Constable, haste on Montjoy,
And let him say to England that we send
To know what willing ransom he will give.
Prince Dauphin, you shall stay with us in Rouen.
DAUPHIN
Not so, I do beseech your majesty.
FRENCH KING
Be patient, for you shall remain with us.
Now forth, Lord Constable, and Princes all,
And quickly bring us word of England's fall.   *Exeunt*

SCENE VI
The English camp.

Enter Captains Gower and Fluellen

GOWER   How now, Captain Fluellen? Come you from
the bridge?
FLUELLEN   I assure you, there is very excellent service
committed at the bridge.
GOWER   Is the Duke of Exeter safe?
FLUELLEN   The Duke of Exeter is as magnanimous as
Agamemnon, and a man that I love and honour with
my soul, and my heart, and my duty, and my life, and

my living, and my uttermost power. He has not—God
be praised and blessed!—any hurt in the world, but
keeps the bridge most valiantly, with excellent discipline.
There is an ancient lieutenant there at the bridge, I
think in my very conscience he is as valiant a man as
Mark Antony, and he is a man of no estimation in the
world, but I did see him do as gallant service.

GOWER   What do you call him?

FLUELLEN   He is called Ancient Pistol.

GOWER   I know him not.

Enter Pistol

FLUELLEN   Here is the man.

PISTOL

Captain, I you beseech to do me favours.

The Duke of Exeter does love you well.

FLUELLEN   Ay, I praise God, and I have merited some
love at his hands.

PISTOL

Bardolph, a soldier firm and sound of heart,

And of buxom valour, has, by cruel fate,

And giddy Fortune's furious fickle wheel,

That goddess blind,

That stands upon the rolling restless stone—

FLUELLEN   By your patience, Ancient Pistol: Fortune is
painted blind, with a muffler afore her eyes, to signify
to you that Fortune is blind. And she is painted also
with a wheel, to signify to you, which is the moral of it,
that she is turning, and inconstant, and mutability,
and variation; and her foot, look you, is fixed upon a
spherical stone, which rolls, and rolls, and rolls. In
good truth, the poet makes a most excellent description
of it. Fortune is an excellent moral.

PISTOL
>Fortune is Bardolph's foe, and frowns on him;
>For he has stolen a pax, and hanged must he be—
>A damnèd death!
>Let gallows gape for dog; let man go free,
>And let not hemp his windpipe suffocate.
>But Exeter has given sentence of death
>For pax of little price.
>Therefore go speak—the Duke will hear your voice;
>And let not Bardolph's vital thread be cut
>With edge of penny cord and vile reproach.
>Speak, Captain, for his life, and I will you requite.

FLUELLEN   Ancient Pistol, I do partly understand your meaning.

PISTOL
>Why then, rejoice therefor!

FLUELLEN   Certainly, Ancient, it is not a thing to rejoice at, for if, look you, he was my brother, I would desire the Duke to use his good pleasure, and put him to execution; for discipline ought to be used.

PISTOL
>Die and be damned! and *figo* for your friendship.

FLUELLEN   It is well.

PISTOL
>The fig of Spain!   *Exit*

FLUELLEN   Very good.

GOWER   Why, this is an arrant counterfeit rascal, I remember him now—a pimp, a cutpurse.

FLUELLEN   I'll assure you, he uttered as brave words at the bridge as you shall see in a summer's day. But it is very well; what he has spoken to me, that is well, I warrant you, when time is served.

GOWER   Why, 'tis a gull, a fool, a rogue, that now and then goes to the wars, to grace himself at his return into London under the form of a soldier. And such fellows are perfect in the great commanders' names, and they will teach you by rote where services were done. At such and such a sconce, at such a breach, at such a convoy; who came off bravely, who was shot, who disgraced, what terms the enemy stood on. And this they learn perfectly in the phrase of war, which they trick up with new-tuned oaths. And what a beard of the general's cut and a horrid suit of the camp will do among foaming bottles and ale-washed wits is wonderful to be thought of. But you must learn to know such slanders of the age, or else you may be marvellously mistaken.

FLUELLEN   I tell you what, Captain Gower; I do perceive he is not the man that he would gladly make show to the world he is. If I find a hole in his coat, I will tell him my mind.

(Drum within)

Hark you, the King is coming, and I must speak with him from the bridge.

Drum and colours. Enter the King and soldiers,
with Gloucester

God bless your majesty!

KING HENRY
How now, Fluellen, came you from the bridge?

FLUELLEN   Ay, so please your majesty. The Duke of Exeter has very gallantly maintained the bridge. The French is gone off, look you, and there is gallant and most brave passages. Indeed, the adversary was in possession of the bridge, but he is enforced to retire, and the Duke of Exeter is master of the bridge. I can tell your majesty, the Duke is a brave man.

KING HENRY   What men have you lost, Fluellen?

FLUELLEN   The perdition of the adversary has been very great, reasonable great. For my part, I think the Duke has lost never a man, but one that is like to be executed for robbing a church, one Bardolph, if your majesty knows the man: his face is all bubbles and whelks, and knobs, and flames of fire; and his lips blow at his nose, and it is like a coal of fire, sometimes blue, and sometimes red; but his nose is executed, and his fire is out.

KING HENRY   We would have all such offenders so cut off. And we give express charge that in our marches through the country there be nothing compelled from the villages, nothing taken but paid for, none of the French upbraided or abused in disdainful language. For when lenity and cruelty play for a kingdom, the gentler gamester is the soonest winner.

Tucket. Enter Montjoy

MONTJOY   You know me by my habit.

KING HENRY   Well then, I know you: what shall I know of you?

MONTJOY   My master's mind.

KING HENRY   Unfold it.

MONTJOY   Thus says my King: 'Say you to Harry of England, Though we seemed dead, we did but sleep. Advantage is a better soldier than rashness. Tell him we could have rebuked him at Harfleur, but that we thought not good to bruise an injury till it was full ripe. Now we speak upon our cue, and our voice is imperial: England shall repent his folly, see his weakness, and admire our sufferance. Bid him therefore consider of his ransom, which must proportion the losses we have borne, the subjects we have lost, the disgrace we have digested; which in weight to re-answer, his pettiness would bow under. For our losses, his exchequer is too poor; for the effusion of our blood, the muster of his kingdom too faint a number; and for our disgrace, his own person kneeling at our feet but a weak and worthless satisfaction.

To this add defiance: and tell him for conclusion, he
has betrayed his followers, whose condemnation is
pronounced.' So far my King and master; so much my
office.

KING HENRY

What is your name? I know your quality.

MONTJOY   Montjoy.

KING HENRY

You do your office fairly. Turn you back,
And tell your King I do not seek him now,
But could be willing to march on to Calais
Without impeachment. For, to say the truth,
Though it is no wisdom to confess so much
Unto an enemy of craft and vantage,
My people are with sickness much enfeebled,
My numbers lessened, and those few I have
Almost no better than so many French—
Who when they were in health, I tell you Herald,
I thought upon one pair of English legs
Did march three Frenchmen. Yet forgive me, God,
That I do brag thus! This your air of France
Has blown that vice in me—I must repent.
Go, therefore, tell your master here I am;
My ransom is this frail and worthless trunk;
My army but a weak and sickly guard.
Yet, God before, tell him we will come on,
Though France himself, and such another neighbour,
Stand in our way. There's for your labour, Montjoy.
Go bid your master well advise himself:
If we may pass, we will; if we are hindered,
We shall your tawny ground with your red blood
Discolour. And so, Montjoy, fare you well.
The sum of all our answer is but this:
We would not seek a battle as we are,
Nor, as we are, we say we will not shun it.
So tell your master.

MONTJOY
  I shall deliver so. Thanks to your highness.   *Exit*
GLOUCESTER
  I hope they will not come upon us now.
KING HENRY
  We are in God's hand, brother, not in theirs.
  March to the bridge; it now draws toward night.
  Beyond the river we'll encamp ourselves,
  And on tomorrow bid them march away.

                                        Exeunt

SCENE VII
The French camp.

Enter the Constable of France, Rambures, Orleans,
Dauphin, with others

CONSTABLE Tut! I have the best armour of the world.
  Would it were day!
ORLEANS You have an excellent armour; but let my
  horse have his due.
CONSTABLE It is the best horse of Europe.
ORLEANS Will it never be morning?
DAUPHIN My Lord of Orleans, and my Lord High
  Constable, you talk of horse and armour?
ORLEANS You are as well provided of both as any prince
  in the world.
DAUPHIN What a long night is this! I will not change
  my horse with any that treads but on four pasterns. *Ça,*
  ha! He bounds from the earth as if his entrails were
  hairs—*le cheval volant,* the Pegasus, *chez les narines de*
  feu![6] When I bestride him, I soar, I am a hawk. He
  trots the air; the earth sings when he touches it; the

---

[6]The flying horse, with nostrils of fire.

basest horn of his hoof is more musical than the pipe of
Hermes.

ORLEANS   He's of the colour of the nutmeg.

DAUPHIN   And of the heat of the ginger. It is a beast for
Perseus: he is pure air and fire; and the dull elements of
earth and water never appear in him, but only in patient
stillness while his rider mounts him. He is indeed a
horse, and all other jades you may call beasts.

CONSTABLE   Indeed, my lord, it is a most absolute and
excellent horse.

DAUPHIN   It is the prince of palfreys; his neigh is like the
bidding of a monarch, and his countenance enforces
homage.

ORLEANS   No more, cousin.

DAUPHIN   Nay, the man has no wit that cannot, from the
rising of the lark to the lodging of the lamb, vary
deserved praise on my palfrey. It is a theme as fluent as
the sea: turn the sands into eloquent tongues, and my
horse is argument for them all. It is a subject for a
sovereign to reason on, and for a sovereign's sovereign to
ride on; and for the world, familiar to us and unknown,
to lay apart their particular functions and wonder at
him. I once wrote a sonnet in his praise, and began thus:
'Wonder of nature—'.

ORLEANS   I have heard a sonnet begin so to one's mistress.

DAUPHIN   Then did they imitate that which I composed
to my courser, for my horse is my mistress.

ORLEANS   Your mistress bears well.

DAUPHIN   Me well, which is the prescript praise and
perfection of a good and particular mistress.

CONSTABLE   Nay, for I thought yesterday your mistress
shrewdly shook your back.

DAUPHIN   So perhaps did yours.

CONSTABLE   Mine was not bridled.

DAUPHIN   O, then perhaps she was old and gentle, and
you rode like a kern of Ireland, your French hose off,

and in your straight breeks.

CONSTABLE   You have good judgement in horsemanship.

DAUPHIN   Be warned by me, then: they that ride so, and ride not warily, fall into foul bogs. I had rather have my horse to my mistress.

CONSTABLE   I had as soon have my mistress a jade.

DAUPHIN   I tell you, Constable, my mistress wears his own hair.

CONSTABLE   I could make as true a boast as that, if I had a sow to my mistress.

DAUPHIN   'Le chien est retourné à son propre vomissement, et la truie lavée au bourbier':[7] You make use of anything.

CONSTABLE   Yet do I not use my horse for my mistress, or any such proverb so little kin to the purpose.

RAMBURES   My Lord Constable, the armour that I saw in your tent tonight—are those stars or suns upon it?

CONSTABLE   Stars, my lord.

DAUPHIN   Some of them will fall tomorrow, I hope.

CONSTABLE   And yet my sky shall not want.

DAUPHIN   That may be, for you bear many superfluously, and it would be more honour some were away.

CONSTABLE   Even as your horse bears your praises, who would trot as well were some of your brags dismounted.

DAUPHIN   Would I were able to load him with his desert! Will it never be day? I will trot tomorrow a mile, and my way shall be paved with English faces.

CONSTABLE   I will not say so, for fear I should be faced out of my way; but I would it were morning, for I would fain be about the ears of the English.

RAMBURES   Who will go to hazard with me for twenty prisoners?

---

[7]The dog has returned to its own vomit, and the washed sow to the mire.

CONSTABLE   You must first go yourself to hazard ere you
have them.

DAUPHIN   'Tis midnight: I'll go arm myself.   *Exit*

ORLEANS   The Dauphin longs for morning.

RAMBURES   He longs to eat the English.

CONSTABLE   I think he will eat all he kills.

ORLEANS   By the white hand of my lady, he's a gallant
prince.

CONSTABLE   Swear by her foot, that she may tread out the
oath.

ORLEANS   He is simply the most active gentleman of
France.

CONSTABLE   Doing is activity, and he will ever be doing.

ORLEANS   He never did harm, that I heard of.

CONSTABLE   And will do none tomorrow: he will keep
that good name still.

ORLEANS   I know him to be valiant.

CONSTABLE   I was told that by one that knows him better
than you.

ORLEANS   What's he?

CONSTABLE   Well, he told me so himself, and he said he
cared not who knew it.

ORLEANS   He needs not; it is no hidden virtue in him.

CONSTABLE   By my faith, sir, but it is; never anybody
saw it but his lackey. It is a hooded valour, and when it
appears it will dwindle.

ORLEANS   Ill will never said well.

CONSTABLE   I will cap that proverb with 'There is flattery
in friendship.'

ORLEANS   And I will take up that with 'Give the devil
his due!'

CONSTABLE   Well placed! There stands your friend for
the devil. Go for the very eye of that proverb with 'A pox
on the devil!'

ORLEANS   You are the better at proverbs by how much 'A
fool's bolt is soon shot.'

CONSTABLE   You have shot over.

ORLEANS   It is not the first time you were overshot.

Enter a Messenger

MESSENGER   My Lord High Constable, the English lie within fifteen hundred paces of your tents.

CONSTABLE   Who has measured the ground?

MESSENGER   The Lord Grandpré.

CONSTABLE   A valiant and most expert gentleman. Would it were day! Alas, poor Harry of England! He longs not for the dawning as we do.

ORLEANS   What a wretched and peevish fellow is this King of England, to mope with his fat-brained followers so far out of his knowledge.

CONSTABLE   If the English had any apprehension they would run away.

ORLEANS   That they lack; for if their heads had any intellectual armour, they could never wear such heavy head-pieces.

RAMBURES   That island of England breeds very valiant creatures: their mastiffs are of unmatchable courage.

ORLEANS   Foolish curs, that run winking into the mouth of a Russian bear, and have their heads crushed like rotten apples! You may as well say that's a valiant flea that dares eat his breakfast on the lip of a lion.

CONSTABLE   Just, just: and the men do sympathize with the mastiffs in robustious and rough coming on, leaving their wits with their wives. And then, give them great meals of beef, and iron and steel; they will eat like wolves, and fight like devils.

ORLEANS   Ay, but these English are sadly out of beef.

CONSTABLE   Then shall we find tomorrow they have only stomachs to eat, and none to fight. Now is it time to arm. Come, shall we about it?

ORLEANS
It is now two o'clock: but, let me see—by ten
We shall have each a hundred Englishmen.   *Exeunt*

Prologue to Act IV

Flourish. Enter Chorus

CHORUS
Now entertain conjecture of a time
When creeping murmur and the poring dark
Fill the wide vessel of the universe.
From camp to camp, through the foul womb of night,
The hum of either army stilly sounds,
That the fixed sentinels almost receive
The secret whispers of each other's watch.
Fire answers fire, and through their paly flames
Each army sees the other's umbered face.
Steed threatens steed, in high and boastful neighs,
Piercing the night's dull ear; and from the tents
The armourers, accomplishing the knights,
With busy hammers closing rivets up,
Give dreadful note of preparatiòn.
The country cocks do crow, the clocks do toll,
And the third hour of drowsy morning name.
Proud of their numbers, and secure in soul,
The confident and over-lusty French
Do the low-rated English play at dice,
And chide the cripple tardy-gaited night
Which like a foul and ugly witch does limp
So tediously away. The poor condemnèd English,
Like sacrifices, by their watchful fires
Sit patiently, and inly ruminate
The morning's danger. And their gesture sad,
Investing lank-lean cheeks and war-worn coats,
Presents them new unto the gazing moon
So many horrid ghosts. O now, who will behold

The royal Captain of this ruined band
Walking from watch to watch, from tent to tent,
Let him cry, 'Praise and glory on his head!'
For forth he goes and visits all his host,
Bids them good morrow with a modest smile,
And calls them brothers, friends, and countrymen.
Upon his royal face there is no note
How dread an army has enrounded him,
Nor does he dedicate one jot of colour
Unto the weary and all-watchèd night,
But freshly looks, and overbears discomfort
With cheerful semblance and sweet majesty;
That every wretch, pining and pale before,
Beholding him, plucks comfort from his looks.
A largess universal, like the sun,
His liberal eye does give to every one,
Thawing cold fear, that mean and gentle all
Behold, as may unworthiness define,
A little touch of Harry in the night.
And so our scene must to the battle fly;
Where—O for pity!—we shall much disgrace,
With four or five most vile and ragged foils,
Right ill-disposed in brawl ridiculous,
The name of Agincourt. Yet sit and see,
Minding true things by what their mockeries be.   *Exit*

Act IV

SCENE I
The English camp.

Enter the King, Bedford, and Gloucester

KING HENRY
> Gloucester, 'tis true that we are in great danger:
> The greater therefore should our courage be.
> Good morrow, brother Bedford. God Almighty!
> There is some soul of goodness in things evil,
> Would men observingly distil it out;
> For our bad neighbour makes us early stirrers,
> Which is both healthful, and good husbandry.
> Besides, they are our outward consciences,
> And preachers to us all, admonishing
> That we should dress us fairly for our end.
> Thus may we gather honey from the weed,
> And make a moral of the devil himself.

Enter Erpingham

> Good morrow, old Sir Thomas Erpingham!
> A good soft pillow for that good white head
> Were better than a churlish turf of France.

ERPINGHAM
> Not so, my liege—this lodging likes me better,
> Since I may say, 'Now lie I like a king.'

KING HENRY
> 'Tis good for men to love their present pains
> Upon example: so the spirit is eased;

And when the mind is quickened, out of doubt
The organs, though defunct and dead before,
Break up their drowsy grave and newly move
With cast-off slough and fresh legerity.
Lend me your cloak, Sir Thomas. Brothers both,
Commend me to the princes in our camp;
Do my good morrow to them, and anon
Desire them all to my paviliòn.
GLOUCESTER   We shall, my liege.
ERPINGHAM
Shall I attend your grace?
KING HENRY   No, my good knight.
Go with my brothers to my lords of England.
I and my bosom must debate awhile,
And then I would no other company.
ERPINGHAM
The Lord in heaven bless you, noble Harry!
                              Exeunt all but the King
KING HENRY
God-a-mercy, old heart, you speak cheerfully.

Enter Pistol

PISTOL
Qui va là? [Who goes there?]
KING HENRY   A friend.
PISTOL
Discuss unto me, are you officer,
Or are you base, common, and popular?
KING HENRY   I am a gentleman of a company.
PISTOL
Trail you the powerful pike?
KING HENRY   Even so. What are you?
PISTOL
As good a gentleman as the Emperor.
KING HENRY   Then you are a better than the King.

PISTOL

    The King's a good lad, and a heart of gold,
    A lad of life, an imp of fame;
    Of parents good, of fist most valiant.
    I kiss his dirty shoe, and from heartstring
    I love the lovely bully. What is your name?

KING HENRY   Harry le Roy.

PISTOL

    Le Roy? A Cornish name. Are you of Cornish crew?

KING HENRY   No, I am a Welshman.

PISTOL

    Know you Fluellen?

KING HENRY   Yes.

PISTOL

    Tell him I'll knock his leek about his pate
    Upon Saint Davy's day.

KING HENRY   Do not you wear your dagger in your cap
    that day, lest he knock that about yours.

PISTOL

    Are you his friend?

KING HENRY   And his kinsman too.

PISTOL

    The *figo* for you then!

KING HENRY   I thank you. God be with you!

PISTOL

    My name is Pistol called.   *Exit*

KING HENRY   It sorts well with your fierceness.

Enter Fluellen and Gower

GOWER   Captain Fluellen!

FLUELLEN   So! In the name of Jesu Christ, speak lower. It
is the greatest admiration in the universal world, when
the true and ancient prerogatives and laws of the wars
are not kept. If you would take the pains but to examine
the wars of Pompey the Great, you shall find, I warrant

you, that there is no tiddle-taddle nor pibble-pabble in Pompey's camp. I warrant you, you shall find the ceremonies of the wars, and the cares of it, and the forms of it, and the sobriety of it, and the modesty of it, to be otherwise.

GOWER   Why, the enemy is loud, you hear him all night.

FLUELLEN   If the enemy is an ass, and a fool, and a prating coxcomb, is it meet, think you, that we should also, look you, be an ass, and a fool, and a prating coxcomb? In your own conscience now?

GOWER   I will speak lower.

FLUELLEN   I pray you and beseech you that you will.

Exeunt Gower and Fluellen

KING HENRY

Though it appears a little out of fashion,
There are much care and valour in this Welshman.

Enter three soldiers, John Bates, Alexander Court, and Michael Williams

COURT   Brother John Bates, is not that the morning which breaks yonder?

BATES   I think it is; but we have no great cause to desire the approach of day.

WILLIAMS   We see yonder the beginning of the day, but I think we shall never see the end of it. Who goes there?

KING HENRY   A friend.

WILLIAMS   Under what captain serve you?

KING HENRY   Under Sir Thomas Erpingham.

WILLIAMS   A good old commander, and a most kind gentleman. I pray you, what thinks he of our state?

KING HENRY   Even as men wrecked upon a sand, that look to be washed off the next tide.

BATES   He has not told his thought to the King?

KING HENRY   No, nor is it meet he should. For though I speak it to you, I think the King is but a man, as

I am. The violet smells to him as it does to me; the
element shows to him as it does to me; all his senses
have but human conditions. His ceremonies laid by, in
his nakedness he appears but a man; and though his
affections are higher mounted than ours, yet when they
stoop, they stoop with the like wing. Therefore, when
he sees reason of fears, as we do, his fears, out of doubt,
are of the same relish as ours are. Yet, in reason, no man
should possess him with any appearance of fear, lest he,
by showing it, should dishearten his army.

BATES   He may show what outward courage he will, but I
believe, as cold a night as it is, he could wish himself in
Thames up to the neck. And so I would he were, and I
by him, at all adventures, so we were quit here.

KING HENRY   By my word, I will speak my conscience of
the King: I think he would not wish himself anywhere
but where he is.

BATES   Then I would he were here alone; so should he be
sure to be ransomed, and many poor men's lives saved.

KING HENRY   I dare say you love him not so ill to wish
him here alone, howsoever you speak this to feel other
men's minds. I think I could not die anywhere so
contented as in the King's company, his cause being just
and his quarrel honourable.

WILLIAMS   That's more than we know.

BATES   Ay, or more than we should seek after; for we
know enough if we know we are the King's subjects. If
his cause is wrong, our obedience to the King wipes the
crime of it out of us.

WILLIAMS   But if the cause is not good, the King himself
has a heavy reckoning to make, when all those legs, and
arms, and heads, chopped off in a battle, shall join
together at the latter day, and cry all, 'We died at such a
place'. Some swearing, some crying for a surgeon; some
upon their wives left poor behind them, some upon the
debts they owe, some upon their children rawly left. I

am afraid there are few die well that die in a battle, for
how can they charitably dispose of anything when blood
is their argument? Now, if these men do not die well, it
will be a black matter for the King that led them to it,
whom to disobey were against all proportion of subjection.

KING HENRY   So, if a son that is by his father sent about
merchandise does sinfully miscarry upon the sea, the
imputation of his wickedness, by your rule, should
be imposed upon his father that sent him. Or if a
servant, under his master's command, transporting a
sum of money, is assailed by robbers, and dies in many
unreconciled iniquities, you may call the business of
the master the author of the servant's damnation. But
this is not so. The King is not bound to answer the
particular endings of his soldiers, the father of his son,
nor the master of his servant; for they purpose not their
death when they purpose their services. Besides, there is
no king, be his cause never so spotless, if it comes to the
arbitrament of swords, can try it out with all unspotted
soldiers. Some, peradventure, have on them the guilt of
premeditated and contrived murder; some, of beguiling
virgins with the broken seals of perjury; some, making
the wars their bulwark, that have before gored the
gentle bosom of peace with pillage and robbery. Now, if
these men have defeated the law, and outrun native
punishment, though they can outstrip men they have
no wings to fly from God. War is his beadle, war is his
vengeance; so that here men are punished for before-
breach of the King's laws, in now the King's quarrel.
Where they feared the death, they have borne life away;
and where they would be safe, they perish. Then if they
die unprepared, no more is the King guilty of their
damnation than he was before guilty of those impieties
for which they are now visited. Every subject's duty is
the King's, but every subject's soul is his own. Therefore
should every soldier in the wars do as every sick man in

his bed, wash every mote out of his conscience; and
dying so, death is to him advantage. Or not dying, the
time was blessedly lost wherein such preparation was
gained; and in him that escapes, it were not sin to think
that, making God so free an offer, he let him outlive
that day to see his greatness, and to teach others how
they should prepare.

WILLIAMS 'Tis certain, every man that dies ill, the ill
upon his own head—the King is not to answer it.

BATES I do not desire he should answer for me, and yet I
determine to fight lustily for him.

KING HENRY I myself heard the King say he would not
be ransomed.

WILLIAMS Ay, he said so, to make us fight cheerfully:
but when our throats are cut he may be ransomed, and
we never the wiser.

KING HENRY If I live to see it, I will never trust his word
after.

WILLIAMS You pay him out then! That's a perilous shot
out of a pop-gun, that a poor and private displeasure
can do against a monarch! You may as well go about to
turn the sun to ice, with fanning in its face with a
peacock's feather. You'll never trust his word after! Come,
it is a foolish saying.

KING HENRY Your reproof is something too round. I should
be angry with you, if the time was convenient.

WILLIAMS Let it be a quarrel between us, if you live.

KING HENRY I embrace it.

WILLIAMS How shall I know you again?

KING HENRY Give me any gage of yours and I will wear
it in my bonnet. Then, if ever you dare acknowledge it, I
will make it my quarrel.

WILLIAMS Here's my glove: give me another of yours.

KING HENRY There.

WILLIAMS This will I also wear in my cap. If ever you
come to me and say, after tomorrow, 'This is my glove,'

by this hand, I will give you a box on the ear.

KING HENRY   If ever I live to see it, I will challenge it.

WILLIAMS   You dare as well be hanged.

KING HENRY   Well, I will do it, though I take you in the King's company.

WILLIAMS   Keep your word. Fare you well.

BATES   Be friends, you English fools, be friends! We have French quarrels enough, if you could tell how to reckon.

KING HENRY   Indeed, the French may lay twenty French crowns to one they will beat us, for they bear them on their shoulders. But it is no English treason to cut French crowns, and tomorrow the King himself will be a clipper.   *Exeunt Soldiers*

Upon the King! Let us our lives, our souls,
Our debts, our careful wives,
Our children, and our sins, lay on the King!
We must bear all. O hard condition,
Twin-born with greatness, subject to the breath
Of every fool, whose sense no more can feel
But his own wringing! What infinite heart's ease
Must kings neglect that private men enjoy!
And what have kings that privates have not too,
Save ceremony, save general ceremony?
And what are you, you idol ceremony?
What kind of god are you, that suffer more
Of mortal griefs than do your worshippers?
What are your rents? What are your comings-in?
O ceremony, show me but your worth!
What is your soul of adoration?
Are you aught else but place, degree, and form,
Creating awe and fear in other men?
Wherein you are less happy, being feared,
Than they in fearing.
What drink you oft, instead of homage sweet,
But poisoned flattery? O, be sick, great greatness,
And bid your ceremony give you cure!

Think you the fiery fever will go out
With titles blown from adulatiòn?
Will it give place to bowing and low bending?
Can you, when you command the beggar's knee,
Command the health of it? No, you proud dream,
That play so subtly with a king's repose.
I am a king that find you, and I know
It is not the balm, the sceptre, and the ball,
The sword, the mace, the crown imperial,
The intertissued robe of gold and pearl,
The stuffed title running before the king,
The throne he sits on, nor the tide of pomp
That beats upon the high shore of this world—
No, not all these, thrice-gorgeous ceremony,
Not all these, laid in bed majestical,
Can sleep so soundly as the wretched slave,
Who, with a body filled, and vacant mind,
Gets him to rest, crammed with distressful bread;
Never sees horrid night, the child of hell,
But, like a lackey, from the rise to set,
Sweats in the eye of Phoebus, and all night
Sleeps in Elysium. Next day after dawn
Does rise and help Hyperion to his horse;
And follows so the ever-running year
With profitable labour to his grave.
And but for ceremony, such a wretch,
Winding up days with toil, and nights with sleep,
Had the fore-hand and vantage of a king.
The slave, a member of the country's peace,
Enjoys it, but in gross brain little knows
What watch the king keeps to maintain the peace,
Whose hours the peasant best advantages.

Enter Erpingham

ERPINGHAM
  My lord, your nobles, suspicious of your absence,
  Seek through your camp to find you.
KING HENRY   Good old knight,
  Collect them all together at my tent.
  I'll be before you.
ERPINGHAM   I shall do it, my lord.   *Exit*
KING HENRY
  O God of battles, steel my soldiers' hearts;
  Possess them not with fear; take from them now
  The sense of reckoning, if the opposèd numbers
  Pluck their hearts from them. Not today, O Lord,
  O not today, think not upon the fault
  My father made in compassing the crown!
  I Richard's body have interrèd new,
  And on it have bestowed more contrite tears
  Than from it issued forcèd drops of blood.
  Five hundred poor I have in yearly pay,
  Who twice a day their withered hands hold up
  Toward heaven, to pardon blood. And I have built
  Two chantries where the sad and solemn priests
  Sing still for Richard's soul. More will I do,
  Though all that I can do is nothing worth,
  Since my penitence comes after all,
  Imploring pardon.

Enter Gloucester

GLOUCESTER
  My liege!
KING HENRY   My brother Gloucester's voice? Ay,
  I know your errand, I will go with thee.
  The day, my friends, and all things stay for me.
                             Exeunt

SCENE II
The French camp.

Enter the Dauphin, Orleans, Rambures, and others

ORLEANS
    The sun does gild our armour: up, my lords!
DAUPHIN
    Montez à cheval! My horse! *Varlet! Lacquais!*[1]
    Ha!
ORLEANS
        O brave spirit!
DAUPHIN   *Via! Les eaux et la terre!*[2]
ORLEANS
    Rien plus? L'air et le feu?[3]
DAUPHIN   *Ciel,*[4] *cousin Orleans!*

Enter the Constable

    Now, my Lord Constable!
CONSTABLE
    Hark how our steeds for present service neigh!
DAUPHIN
    Mount them and make incision in their hides,
    That their hot blood may spin in English eyes
    And blind them with superfluous courage, ha!
RAMBURES
    What, will you have them weep our horses' blood?
    How shall we then behold their natural tears?

---

[1]Mount your horse. Groom! Lackey!
[2]Water and land.
[3]Nothing more? Air and fire.
[4]Sky.

Enter a Messenger

MESSENGER
  The English are embattled, you French peers.
CONSTABLE
  To horse, you gallant Princes, straight to horse!
  Do but behold yon poor and starvèd band,
  And your fair show shall suck away their souls,
  Leaving them but the shales and husks of men.
  There is not work enough for all our hands,
  Scarce blood enough in all their sickly veins
  To give each naked cutlass then a stain
  That our French gallants shall today draw out,
  And sheathe for lack of sport. Let us but blow on them,
  The vapour of our valour will o'erturn them.
  'Tis positive against all exceptions, lords,
  That our superfluous lackeys, and our peasants,
  Who in unnecessary action swarm
  About our squares of battle, were enough
  To purge this field of such a wretched foe,
  Though we upon this mountain's basis by
  Took stand for idle speculatiòn:
  But that our honours must not. What's to say?
  A very little little let us do,
  And all is done. Then let the trumpets sound
  The signal flourish and the note to mount;
  For our approach shall so much dare the field
  That England shall couch down in fear and yield.

Enter Grandpré

GRANDPRÉ
  Why do you stay so long, my lords of France?
  Yon island carrions, desperate of their bones,
  Ill-favouredly become the morning field.
  Their ragged banners poorly are let loose,

And our air shakes them passing scornfully.
Big Mars seems bankrupt in their beggared host,
And faintly through a rusty helmet peeps.
The horsemen sit like fixèd candlesticks,
With torch-staves in their hand; and their poor jades
Droop down their heads, dropping the hides and hips,
The gum down-roping from their pale-dead eyes;
And in their pale dull mouths the jointed bit
Lies foul with chewed grass, still and motionless.
And their executors, the knavish crows,
Fly over them all, impatient for their hour.
Description cannot suit itself in words
To demonstrate the life of such a battle
In life so lifeless as it shows itself.

CONSTABLE
They have said their prayers, and they stay for death.

DAUPHIN
Shall we go send them dinners, and fresh suits,
And give their fasting horses provender,
And after fight with them?

CONSTABLE
I stay but for my pennant. To the field!
I will the banner from a trumpeter take,
And use it for my haste. Come, come away!
The sun is high, and we outwear the day.   *Exeunt*

SCENE III
The English camp.

Enter Gloucester, Bedford, Exeter, Erpingham,
Salisbury and Westmorland, with soldiers

GLOUCESTER

Where is the King?

BEDFORD

The King himself has gone to view their army.

WESTMORLAND

Of fighting men they have full three-score thousand.

EXETER

There's five to one: besides, they all are fresh.

SALISBURY

God's arm strike with us! It is a fearful odds.

Good-bye you, Princes all: I'll to my charge.

If we no more meet till we meet in heaven,

Then joyfully, my noble Lord of Bedford,

My dear Lord Gloucester, and my good Lord Exeter,

And my kind kinsman, warriors all, adieu!

BEDFORD

Farewell, good Salisbury, and good luck go with you!

EXETER

Farewell, kind lord: fight valiantly today—

And yet I do you wrong to mind you of it,

For you are framed of the firm truth of valour.

Exit Salisbury

BEDFORD

He is as full of valour as of kindness,

Princely in both.

Enter the King

WESTMORLAND   O that we now had here

But one ten thousand of those men in England

That do no work today!

KING HENRY   What's he that wishes so?

My cousin Westmorland? No, my fair cousin.

If we are marked to die, we are enough

To do our country loss: and if to live,

The fewer men, the greater share of honour.
God's will! I pray you wish not one man more.
By Jove, I am not covetous for gold,
Nor care I who does feed upon my cost;
It grieves me not if men my garments wear;
Such outward things dwell not in my desires.
But if it is a sin to covet honour,
I am the most offending soul alive.
No, faith, cousin, wish not a man from England:
God's peace! I would not lose so great an honour
As one man more I think would share from me
For the best hope I have. O, do not wish one more!
Rather proclaim it, Westmorland, through my host,
That he who has no stomach to this fight,
Let him depart: his passport shall be made,
And crowns for convoy put into his purse.
We would not die in that man's company
That fears his fellowship to die with us.
This day is called the Feast of Crispian:
He that outlives this day, and comes safe home,
Will stand a-tiptoe when this day is named,
And rouse him at the name of Crispian.
He that shall see this day, and live old age,
Will yearly on the vigil feast his neighbours,
And say, 'Tomorrow is Saint Crispian.'
Then will he strip his sleeve, and show his scars,
And say, 'These wounds I had on Crispin's day.'
Old men forget; when all shall be forgotten
But he'll remember, with advantages,
What feats he did that day. Then shall our names,
Familiar in his mouth as household words,
Harry the King, Bedford and Exeter,
Warwick and Talbot, Salisbury and Gloucester,
Be in their flowing cups freshly remembered.
This story shall the good man teach his son;
And Crispin Crispian shall never go by,

From this day to the ending of the world,
But we in it shall be rememberèd —
We few, we happy few, we band of brothers.
For he today that sheds his blood with me
Shall be my brother; be he never so vile,
This day shall gentle his conditiòn;
And gentlemen in England now abed
Shall think themselves accursed they were not here,
And hold their manhoods cheap, while any speaks
That fought with us upon Saint Crispin's day.

Enter Salisbury

SALISBURY
My sovereign lord, bestow yourself with speed.
The French are bravely in their order set,
And will with all expedition charge on us.
KING HENRY
All things are ready, if our minds are so.
WESTMORLAND
Perish the man whose mind is backward now!
KING HENRY
You do not wish more help from England, cousin?
WESTMORLAND
God's will, my liege, would you and I alone,
Without more help, could fight this royal battle!
KING HENRY
Why, now you have unwished five thousand men,
Which likes me better than to wish us one.
You know your places. God be with you all!

Tucket. Enter Montjoy

MONTJOY
Once more I come to know of you, King Harry,
If for your ransom you will now compound,

Before your most assurèd overthrow:
For certainly you are so near the gulf
You needs must be swallowed. Besides, in mercy,
The Constable desires that you will mind
Your followers of repentance, that their souls
May make a peaceful and a sweet retreat
From off these fields, where, wretches, their poor bodies
Must lie and fester.
KING HENRY   Who has sent you now?
MONTJOY
The Constable of France.
KING HENRY
I pray you bear my former answer back:
Bid them achieve me, and then sell my bones.
Good God, why should they mock poor fellows thus?
The man that once did sell the lion's skin
While the beast lived, was killed in hunting him.
Many of our bodies shall no doubt
Find native graves; upon which then, I trust,
Shall witness live in brass of this day's work.
And those that leave their valiant bones in France,
Dying like men, though buried in your dunghills,
They shall be famed. For there the sun shall greet them,
And draw their honours reeking up to heaven,
Leaving their earthly parts to choke your clime,
The smell whereof shall breed a plague in France.
Mark then abounding valour in our English,
That being dead, like to the bullet's crashing,
Break out into a second course of mischief,
Killing in rebound of mortality.
Let me speak proudly: tell the Constable
We are but warriors for the working-day;
Our gayness and our gilt are all besmirched
With rainy marching in the painful field.
There's not a piece of feather in our host—
Good argument, I hope, we will not fly—

And time has worn us into slovenry.
But, by the mass, our hearts are in the trim;
And my poor soldiers tell me, yet ere night
They'll be in fresher robes, or they will pluck
The gay new coats o'er the French soldiers' heads,
And turn them out of service. If they do this—
As, if God please, they shall—my ransom then
Will soon be levied. Herald, save you your labour;
Come you no more for ransom, gentle Herald.
They shall have none, I swear, but these my joints,
Which if they have as I will leave 'em them
Shall yield them little, tell the Constable.

MONTJOY

I shall, King Harry. And so fare you well:
You never shall hear herald any more.   *Exit*

KING HENRY

I fear you will once more come again for a ransom.

Enter York

YORK

My lord, most humbly on my knee I beg
The leading of the vanguard.

KING HENRY

Take it, brave York. Now, soldiers, march away:
And how you please, God, then dispose the day!

                                               Exeunt

SCENE IV
The battle-field.

Alarum. Excursions. Enter Pistol, French Soldier, Boy

PISTOL

   Yield, cur!

FRENCH SOLDIER   *Je pense que vous êtes le gentilhomme de bonne qualité.*[5]

PISTOL

   Calitie! 'Calen o custure me!'

   Are you a gentleman? What is your name? Discuss.

FRENCH SOLDIER   *O Seigneur Dieu!* [O, Lord God!]

PISTOL

   O Signieur Dew should be a gentleman:

   Consider my words, O Signieur Dew, and mark.

   O Signieur Dew, you die on point of fox,

   Except, O Signieur, you do give to me

   Egregious ransom.

FRENCH SOLDIER   *O, prenez miséricorde! Ayez pitié de moy!*[6]

PISTOL

   Moy shall not serve: I will have forty moys,

   For I will fetch your rim out at your throat

   In drops of crimson blood!

FRENCH SOLDIER   *Est-il impossible d'échapper la force de ton bras?*[7]

PISTOL

   Brass, cur?

   You damnèd and most lustful mountain goat,

   Offer me brass?

FRENCH SOLDIER   *O, pardonne-moy!* [Pardon me.]

PISTOL

   Say you me so? Is that a ton of moys?

   Come hither, boy: ask me this slave in French

   What is his name.

---

[5] I think that you are a gentleman of quality.

[6] Have mercy! Have pity on me!

[7] Is it impossible to escape the force of your arm?

BOY   *Écoutez: comment êtes-vous appelé?* [Hark: what are you called?]

FRENCH SOLDIER   *Monsieur le Fer.*

BOY   He says his name is Master Fer.

PISTOL   Master Fer! I'll fer him, and firk him, and ferret him. Discuss the same in French unto him.

BOY   I do not know the French for fer, and ferret, and firk.

PISTOL

Bid him prepare, for I will cut his throat.

FRENCH SOLDIER   *Que dit-il, monsieur?*

BOY   *Il me commande à vous dire que vous faites vous prêt, car ce soldat içi est disposé tout à cette heure de couper votre gorge.*[8]

PISTOL

Owy, cuppele gorge, permafoy,

Peasant, unless you give me crowns, brave crowns;

Or mangled shall you be by this my sword.

FRENCH SOLDIER   *O, je vous supplie, pour l'amour de Dieu, me pardonner! Je suis le gentilhomme de bonne maison. Gardez ma vie, et je vous donnerai deux cents écus.*

PISTOL

What are his words?

BOY   He prays you to save his life. He is a gentleman of a good house, and for his ransom he will give you two hundred crowns.

PISTOL

Tell him my fury shall abate, and I

The crowns will take.

FRENCH SOLDIER   *Petit monsieur, que dit-il?*

BOY   *Encore qu'il est contre son jurement de pardonner aucun prisonnier; néanmoins, pour les écus que vous*

---

[8]What does he say, sir? He bids me say prepare yourself, for this soldier here is disposed to cut your throat at once.

l'avez promis, il est content à vous donner la liberté, le
franchisement.[9]

FRENCH SOLDIER   *Sur mes genoux je vous donne mille*
remercîments; et je m'estime heureux que je suis tombé
entre les mains d'un chevalier, je pense, le plus brave,
vaillant, et très distingué seigneur d'Angleterre.

PISTOL

Expound unto me, boy.

BOY   He gives you upon his knees a thousand thanks;
and he esteems himself happy that he has fallen into
the hands of one—as he thinks—the most brave, valorous,
and thrice-worthy signieur of England.

PISTOL

As I suck blood, I will some mercy show.

Follow me!   *Exit*

BOY   *Suivez-vous le grand capitaine.*

                              (Exit French Soldier)

I did never know so full a voice issue from so empty a
heart; but the saying is true, 'The empty vessel makes
the greatest sound.' Bardolph and Nym had ten times
more valour than this roaring devil in the old play,
that everyone may pare his nails with a wooden dagger.
They are both hanged—and so would this be, if he
durst steal anything adventurously. I must stay with
the lackeys, with the luggage of our camp. The French
might have a good prey of us, if he knew of it, for
there is none to guard it but boys.

                                                      Exit

---

[9]Although it is against his oath to grant pardon to any prisoner,
nevertheless for the crowns you have promised he is content to
give you liberty, freely.

SCENE V
The same.

Enter the Constable, Orleans, Bourbon, Dauphin,
and Rambures

CONSTABLE   *O diable!* [O, the devil!]
ORLEANS   *O Seigneur! Le jour est perdu, tout est perdu!*
    [O Lord, the day is lost, all is lost!]
DAUPHIN
Mort de ma vie! All is confounded, all!
Reproach and everlasting shame
Sits mocking in our plumes. *O méchante fortune!* [O ill
    fortune!]

A short alarum

Do not run away!
CONSTABLE   Why, all our ranks are broken.
DAUPHIN
O pèrdurable shame! Let's stab ourselves.
Are these the wretches that we played at dice for?
ORLEANS
Is this the King we sent to for his ransom?
BOURBON
Shame, and eternal shame, nothing but shame!
Let's die in honour! Once more back again!
And he that will not follow Bourbon now,
Let him go hence, and with his cap in hand,
Like a base pander, hold the chamber-door
While by a slave, no gentler than my dog,
His fairest daughter is contaminated.
CONSTABLE
Disorder that has spoiled us, friend us now!
Let us on heaps go offer up our lives.

ORLEANS
  We are enough yet living in the field
  To smother up the English in our throngs,
  If any order might be thought upon.
BOURBON
  The devil take order now! I'll to the throng.
  Let life be short, else shame will be too long.   *Exeunt*

SCENE VI
The same.

Alarum. Enter the King and his train, Exeter and others,
with prisoners

KING HENRY
  Well have we done, thrice-valiant countrymen;
  But all's not done—yet keep the French the field.
EXETER
  The Duke of York commends him to your majesty.
KING HENRY
  Lives he, good uncle? Thrice within this hour
  I saw him down; thrice up again, and fighting.
  From helmet to the spur all blood he was.
EXETER
  In which array, brave soldier, does he lie,
  Larding the plain; and by his bloody side,
  Yoke-fellow to his honour-owning wounds,
  The noble Earl of Suffolk also lies.
  Suffolk first died; and York, hacked all over,
  Comes to him, where in gore he lay insteeped,
  And takes him by the beard, kisses the gashes
  That bloodily did yawn upon his face.
  He cries aloud, 'Tarry, my cousin Suffolk!
  My soul shall yours keep company to heaven.
  Tarry, sweet soul, for mine, then fly abreast,

As in this glorious and well-fought field
We kept together in our chivalry!'
Upon these words I came and cheered him up;
He smiled to me in the face, reached me his hand,
And, with a feeble grip, says, 'Dear my lord,
Commend my service to my sovereign.'
So did he turn, and over Suffolk's neck
He threw his wounded arm, and kissed his lips,
And so espoused to death, with blood he sealed
A testament of noble-ending love.
The pretty and sweet manner of it forced
Those waters from me which I would have stopped;
But I had not so much of man in me,
And all my mother came into my eyes
And gave me up to tears.
KING HENRY   I blame you not;
For, hearing this, I must perforce compound
With mistful eyes, or they will issue too.

Alarum

But hark! what new alarum is this same?
The French have reinforced their scattered men.
Then every soldier kill his prisoners!
Give the word through.   *Exeunt*

SCENE VII
The same.

Enter Fluellen and Gower

FLUELLEN   Kill the boys and the luggage? 'Tis expressly
against the law of arms; 'tis as arrant a piece of knavery,
mark you now, as can be offert—in your conscience
now, is it not?

GOWER   'Tis certain there's not a boy left alive, and the
cowardly rascals that ran from the battle have done this
slaughter. Besides, they have burnt and carried away all
that was in the King's tent, wherefore the King most
worthily has caused every soldier to cut his prisoner's
throat. O, 'tis a gallant King!

FLUELLEN   Ay, he was born at Monmouth, Captain Gower.
What call you the town's name where Alexander the
Big was born?

GOWER   Alexander the Great.

FLUELLEN   Why, I pray you, is not 'big' great? The big, or
the great, or the mighty, or the huge, or the magnanimous,
are all one reckoning, save the phrase is a little variations.

GOWER   I think Alexander the Great was born in Macedon;
his father was called Philip of Macedon, as I take it.

FLUELLEN   I think it is in Macedon where Alexander is
born. I tell you, Captain, if you look in the maps of the
world, I warrant you shall find, in the comparison
between Macedon and Monmouth, that the situation,
look you, is both alike. There is a river in Macedon, and
there is also moreover a river at Monmouth — it is called
Wye at Monmouth, but it is out of my brains what is
the name of the other river; but 'tis all one, 'tis alike as
my fingers is to my fingers, and there is salmon in both.
If you mark Alexander's life well, Harry of Monmouth's
life comes after it indifferent well; for there is figures in
all things. Alexander, God knows and you know, in his
rages, and his furies, and his wraths, and his cholers, and
his moods, and his displeasures, and his indignations,
and also being a little intoxicated in his brains, did in
his ales and his angers, look you, kill his best friend
Cleitus.

GOWER   Our King is not like him in that: he never killed
any of his friends.

FLUELLEN   It is not well done, mark you now, to take the
tales out of my mouth, ere it is made and finished. I speak
but in the figure and comparison of it. As Alexander
killed his friend Cleitus, being in his ales and his cups,
so also Harry Monmouth, being in his right wits and
his good judgement, turned away the fat knight with
the great-belly doublet—he was full of jests, and gibes,
and knaveries, and mocks: I have forgot his name.
GOWER   Sir John Falstaff.
FLUELLEN   That is he. I'll tell you, there is good men born
at Monmouth.
GOWER   Here comes his majesty.

*Alarum. Enter King Henry and Bourbon, with prisoners;
also Warwick, Gloucester, Exeter, and others. Flourish*

KING HENRY
I was not angry since I came to France
Until this instant. Take a trumpet, Herald;
Ride you unto the horsemen on yon hill.
If they will fight with us, bid them come down,
Or void the field: they do offend our sight.
If they'll do neither, we will come to them,
And make them scurry away as swift as stones
Enforcèd from the old Assyrian slings.
Besides, we'll cut the throats of those we have,
And not a man of them that we shall take
Shall taste our mercy. Go and tell them so.

Enter Montjoy

EXETER
Here comes the Herald of the French, my liege.
GLOUCESTER
His eyes are humbler than they used to be.

KING HENRY

    How now, what means this, Herald? Know you not

    That I have fined these bones of mine for ransom?

    Come you again for ransom?

MONTJOY   No, great King;

    I come to you for charitable licence,

    That we may wander over this bloody field

    To book our dead, and then to bury them,

    To sort our nobles from our common men.

    For many of our princes—woe the while!—

    Lie drowned and soaked in mercenary blood.

    So do our vulgar drench their peasant limbs

    In blood of princes, and their wounded steeds

    Struggle fetlock-deep in gore, and with wild rage

    Yerk out their armèd heels at their dead masters,

    Killing them twice. O, give us leave, great King,

    To view the field in safety, and dispose

    Of their dead bodies!

KING HENRY   I tell you truly, Herald,

    I know not if the day is ours or no;

    For yet many of your horsemen do peer

    And gallop over the field.

MONTJOY   The day is yours.

KING HENRY

    Praisèd be God, and not our strength, for it!

    What is this castle called that stands hard by?

MONTJOY

    They call it Agincourt.

KING HENRY

    Then call we this the field of Agincourt,

    Fought on the day of Crispin Crispian.

FLUELLEN   Your grandfather of famous memory, if it please
your majesty, and your great-uncle Edward the Black
Prince of Wales, as I have read in the chronicles, fought
a most brave battle here in France.

KING HENRY   They did, Fluellen.

FLUELLEN   Your majesty says very true. If your majesty is remembered of it, the Welshmen did good service in a garden where leeks did grow, wearing leeks in their Monmouth caps, which your majesty knows to this hour is an honourable badge of the service; and I do believe your majesty takes no scorn to wear the leek upon Saint Davy's day.

KING HENRY

I wear it for a memorable honour;

For I am Welsh, you know, good countryman.

FLUELLEN   All the water in Wye cannot wash your majesty's Welsh blood out of your body, I can tell you that. God bless it and preserve it, as long as it pleases his grace, and his majesty too!

KING HENRY   Thanks, good my countryman.

FLUELLEN   By Jesu, I am your majesty's countryman, I care not who knows it; I will confess it to all the world. I need not to be ashamed of your majesty, praised be God, so long as your majesty is an honest man.

KING HENRY

God keep me so!

Enter Williams

Our heralds go with him.

Bring me just notice of the numbers dead

On both our parts.   *Exeunt Heralds with Montjoy*

Call yonder fellow hither.

EXETER   Soldier, you must come to the King.

KING HENRY   Soldier, why wear you that glove in your cap?

WILLIAMS   If it please your majesty, it is the gage of one that I should fight with, if he is alive.

KING HENRY   An Englishman?

WILLIAMS   If it please your majesty, a rascal that swaggered
with me last night: who, if he lives and ever dares to
challenge this glove, I have sworn to take him a box on
the ear. Or if I can see my glove in his cap, which he
swore as he was a soldier he would wear if alive, I will
strike it out soundly.

KING HENRY   What think you, Captain Fluellen, is it fit
this soldier should keep his oath?

FLUELLEN   He is a craven and a villain else, if it please
your majesty, in my conscience.

KING HENRY   It may be his enemy is a gentleman of great
sort, quite from the answer of his degree.

FLUELLEN   Though he is as good a gentleman as the devil
is, as Lucifer and Belzebub himself, it is necessary, look
your grace, that he should keep his vow and his oath. If
he is perjured, see you now, his reputation is as arrant a
villain and a saucy knave as ever his black shoe trod
upon God's ground and his earth, in my conscience, la!

KING HENRY   Then keep your vow, man, when you meet
the fellow.

WILLIAMS   So I will, my liege, as I live.

KING HENRY   Whom serve you under?

WILLIAMS   Under Captain Gower, my liege.

FLUELLEN   Gower is a good captain, and is good knowledge
and literatured in the wars.

KING HENRY   Call him hither to me, soldier.

WILLIAMS   I will, my liege.   *Exit*

KING HENRY   Here, Fluellen, wear you this favour for me,
and stick it in your cap. When Alençon and myself were
down together, I plucked this glove from his helm. If
any man challenges this, he is a friend to Alençon, and
an enemy to our person: if you encounter any such,
apprehend him, if you do me love.

FLUELLEN   Your grace does me as great honour as can be
desired in the hearts of his subjects. I would fain see the
man that has but two legs that shall find himself

aggrieved at this glove, that is all: but I would fain see it
once, and please God of his grace that I might see.

KING HENRY   Know you Gower?

FLUELLEN   He is my dear friend, please you.

KING HENRY   Pray go seek him, and bring him to my
tent.

FLUELLEN   I will fetch him.   *Exit*

KING HENRY
My Lord of Warwick, and my brother Gloucester,
Follow Fluellen closely at the heels.
The glove which I have given him for a favour
May haply purchase him a box on the ear.
It is the soldier's: I by bargain should
Wear it myself. Follow, good cousin Warwick.
If the soldier strikes him, as I judge
By his blunt bearing he will keep his word,
Some sudden mischief may arise of it.
For I do know Fluellen valiant,
And, touched with choler, hot as gunpowder,
And quickly will return an injury.
Follow, and see there is no harm between them.
Go you with me, uncle of Exeter.   *Exeunt*

SCENE VIII
Before King Henry's pavilion.

Enter Gower and Williams

WILLIAMS   I warrant it is to knight you, Captain.

Enter Fluellen

FLUELLEN   God's will and his pleasure, Captain, I beseech
you now, come apace to the King. There is more good
toward you, peradventure, than is in your knowledge to
dream of.

WILLIAMS   Sir, know you this glove?
FLUELLEN   Know the glove? I know the glove is a glove.
WILLIAMS   I know this; and thus I challenge it.

He strikes him

FLUELLEN   'Sblood! an arrant traitor as any's in the
  universal world, or in France, or in England!
GOWER   How now, sir? You villain!
WILLIAMS   Do you think I'll be denied?
FLUELLEN   Stand away, Captain Gower: I will give treason
  his payment into blows, I warrant you.
WILLIAMS   I am no traitor.
FLUELLEN   That's a lie in your throat. I charge you in his
  majesty's name, apprehend him: he's a friend of the
  Duke Alençon's.

Enter Warwick and Gloucester

WARWICK   How now, how now, what's the matter?
FLUELLEN   My Lord of Warwick, here is — praised be God
  for it! — a most contagious treason come to light, look
  you, as you shall desire in a summer's day. Here is his
  majesty.

Enter the King and Exeter

KING HENRY   How now, what's the matter?
FLUELLEN   My liege, here is a villain and a traitor, that,
  look your grace, has struck the glove which your majesty
  took out of the helmet of Alençon.
WILLIAMS   My liege, this was my glove, here is the fellow
  of it; and he that I gave it to in change promised to wear
  it in his cap. I promised to strike him if he did. I met
  this man with my glove in his cap, and I have been as
  good as my word.

FLUELLEN   Your majesty hear now, saving your majesty's
manhood, what an arrant, rascally, beggarly, lousy knave
it is. I hope your majesty bears me testimony and witness,
and will avouch, that this is the glove of Alençon that
your majesty gave me, in your conscience, now.

KING HENRY   Give me your glove, soldier. Look, here is
the fellow of it.
It was I indeed you promised to strike,
And you have given me most bitter terms.

FLUELLEN   Please your majesty, let his neck answer for it,
if there is any martial law in the world.

KING HENRY   How can you make me satisfaction?

WILLIAMS   All offences, my lord, come from the heart:
never came any from mine that might offend your
majesty.

KING HENRY   It was ourself you did abuse.

WILLIAMS   Your majesty came not like yourself: you
appeared to me but as a common man—witness the
night, your garments, your lowliness. And what your
highness suffered under that shape, I beseech you take
it for your own fault, and not mine; for had you been as
I took you for, I made no offence. Therefore, I beseech
your highness, pardon me.

KING HENRY
Here, uncle Exeter, fill this glove with crowns,
And give it to this fellow. Keep it, fellow,
And wear it for an honour in your cap
Till I do challenge it. Give him the crowns;
And, Captain, you must needs be friends with him.

FLUELLEN   By this day and this light, the fellow has
mettle enough in his belly. Hold, there is twelve pence
for you, and I pray you to serve God, and keep you out of
brawls, and brabbles, and quarrels, and dissensions,
and I warrant you it is the better for you.

WILLIAMS   I will none of your money.

FLUELLEN   It is with a good will: I can tell you it will
   serve you to mend your shoes. Come, wherefore should
   you be so bashful?—your shoes are not so good; 'tis a
   good shilling, I warrant you, or I will change it.

Enter an English Herald

KING HENRY   Now, Herald, are the dead numbered?
HERALD
   Here is the number of the slaughtered French.

He gives him a paper

KING HENRY
   What prisoners of good sort are taken, uncle?
EXETER
   Charles Duke of Orleans, nephew to the King;
   John Duke of Bourbon, and Lord Bouciqualt;
   Of other lords and barons, knights and squires,
   Full fifteen hundred, besides common men.
KING HENRY
   This note does tell me of ten thousand French
   That in the field lie slain. Of princes, in this number,
   And nobles bearing banners, there lie dead
   One hundred twenty-six: added to these,
   Of knights, esquires, and gallant gentlemen,
   Eight thousand and four hundred; of which,
   Five hundred were but yesterday dubbed knights.
   So that, in these ten thousand they have lost,
   There are but sixteen hundred mercenaries;
   The rest are princes, barons, lords, knights, squires,
   And gentlemen of blood and quality.
   The names of those their nobles that lie dead:
   Charles Delabreth, High Constable of France,
   Jaques of Chatillon, Admiral of France,
   The Master of the Cross-bows, Lord Rambures,

Great Master of France, the brave Sir Guichard Dauphin,
John Duke of Alençon, Antony Duke of Brabant,
The brother to the Duke of Burgundy,
And Edward Duke of Bar: of lusty earls,
Grandpré and Roussi, Faulconbridge and Foix,
Beaumont and Marle, Vaudemont and Lestrake.
Here was a royal fellowship of death!
Where is the number of our English dead?

The Herald gives him another paper

Edward the Duke of York, the Earl of Suffolk,
Sir Richard Chichele, Davy Gam, esquire;
None else of name; and of all other men
But five-and-twenty. O God, your arm was here!
And not to us, but to your arm alone,
Ascribe we all! When, without stratagem,
But in plain shock and even play of battle,
Was ever known so great and little loss
On one part and on the other? Take it, God,
For it is only yours.
EXETER   But wonderful!
KING HENRY
Come, go we in procession to the village:
And be it death proclaimèd through our host
To boast of this, or take that praise from God
Which is his only.
FLUELLEN   Is it not lawful, please your majesty, to tell
how many is killed?
KING HENRY
Yes, Captain, but with this acknowledgement,
That God fought for us.
FLUELLEN Yes, my conscience, he did us great good.
KING HENRY
Do we all holy rites:
Let there be sung *Non Nobis* and *Te Deum*,

The dead with charity enclosed in clay;
And then to Calais, and to England then,
Where never from France arrived more happy men.

Exeunt

Prologue to Act V

Flourish. Enter Chorus

CHORUS

Now grant to those that have not read the story
That I may prompt them; and of such as have,
I humbly pray them to admit the excuse
Of time, of numbers, and due course of things,
Which cannot in their huge and proper life
Be here presented. Now we bear the King
Toward Calais. Grant him there: there seen,
Heave him away upon your wingèd thoughts
Athwart the sea. Behold, the English beach
Pales in the flood with men, with wives, and boys,
Whose shouts and claps outvoice the deep-mouthed sea,
Which like a mighty herald before the King
Seems to prepare his way. So let him land,
And solemnly see him set on to London.
So swift a pace has thought that even now
You may imagine him upon Blackheath,
Where now his lords desire him to have borne
His bruisèd helmet and his bended sword
Before him through the city. He forbids it,
Being free from vainness and self-glorious pride,
Giving full trophy, signal, and ostent
Quite from himself to God. But now behold,
In the quick forge and working-house of thought,
How London does pour out her citizens:
The Mayor and all his brethren in best sort,
Like the senators of the antique Rome,
With the plebeians swarmìng at their heels,
Go forth and fetch their conquering Caesar in.

239

As, by a lower but loving likelihood,
Were now the General of our gracious Empress—
As in good time he may—from Ireland coming,
Bringing rebellion spitted on his sword,
How many would the peaceful city quit
To welcome him! Much more, and much more cause,
Did they this Harry. Now in London place him—
As yet the lamentation of the French
Invites the King of England's stay at home.
The Emperor's coming in behalf of France
To order peace between them; and omit
All the occurrences, whatever chanced,
Till Harry's back-return again to France.
There must we bring him; and myself have played
The interim, by remembering you 'tis past.
Then brook abridgement, and your eyes advance,
After your thoughts, straight back again to France.

Exit

Act V

SCENE I
The English camp.

Enter Fluellen and Gower

GOWER   Nay, that's right; but why wear you your leek today? Saint Davy's day is past.

FLUELLEN   There is occasion and cause why and wherefore in all things. I will tell you as my friend, Captain Gower: the rascally, scurvy, beggarly, lousy, bragging knave Pistol—which you and yourself and all the world know to be no better than a fellow, look you now, of no merit—he is come to me and brings me bread and salt yesterday, look you, and bid me eat my leek. It was in a place where I could not breed contention with him; but I will be so bold as to wear it in my cap till I see him once again, and then I will tell him a little piece of my desire.

Enter Pistol

GOWER   Why, here he comes, swelling like a turkey-cock.

FLUELLEN   'Tis no matter for his swelling nor his turkey-cock. God bless you, Ancient Pistol! you scurvy, lousy knave, God bless you!

PISTOL
Ha, are you bedlam? Do you thirst, base Troyan,
To have me fold up Parca's fatal web?
Hence! I am qualmish at the smell of leek.

FLUELLEN   I beseech you heartily, scurvy, lousy knave, at
  my desire, and my request, and my petition, to eat, look
  you, this leek. Because, look you, you do not love it, nor
  your affection, and your appetite, and your digestion,
  does not agree with it, I would desire you to eat it.

PISTOL
  Not for Cadwallader and all his goats!

FLUELLEN   There is one goat for you. (*He strikes him*)
  Will you be so good, scurvy knave, as eat it?

PISTOL
  Base Troyan, you shall die!

FLUELLEN   You say very true, scurvy knave, when God's
  will is. I will desire you to live in the meantime, and eat
  your victuals—come, there is sauce for it. (*He strikes
  him again*) You called me yesterday mountain-squire,
  but I will make you today a squire of low degree. I pray
  you fall to—if you can mock a leek, you can eat a leek.

GOWER   Enough, Captain, you have astonished him.

FLUELLEN   I say, I will make him eat some part of my
  leek, or I will beat his pate four days. Bite, I pray you, it
  is good for your green wound and your bloody coxcomb.

PISTOL   Must I bite?

FLUELLEN   Yes, certainly, and out of doubt, and out of
  question too, and ambiguity.

PISTOL   By this leek, I will most horribly revenge—I eat
  and eat, I swear—

FLUELLEN   Eat, I pray you; will you have some more
  sauce to your leek? There is not enough leek to swear by.

PISTOL   Quiet your cudgel, you do see I eat.

FLUELLEN   Much good do you, scurvy knave, heartily.
  Nay, pray you throw none away, the skin is good for
  your broken coxcomb. When you take occasion to see
  leeks hereafter, I pray you mock at them, that is all.

PISTOL   Good!

FLUELLEN   Ay, leeks are good. Hold you, there is a groat
  to heal your pate.

PISTOL   Me a groat?

FLUELLEN   Yes, verily and in truth you shall take it, or I
have another leek in my pocket which you shall eat.

PISTOL   I take your groat in earnest of revenge.

FLUELLEN   If I owe you anything, I will pay you in
cudgels—you shall be a woodmonger, and buy nothing
of me but cudgels. Good-bye to you, and keep you, and
heal your pate.   *Exit*

PISTOL
All hell shall stir for this!

GOWER   Go, go, you are a counterfeit cowardly knave.
Will you mock at an ancient tradition, begun upon an
honourable respect, and worn as a memorable trophy of
predeceased valour, and dare not make good in your
deeds any of your words? I have seen you mocking and
jeering at this gentleman twice or thrice. You thought,
because he could not speak English in the native garb,
he could not therefore handle an English cudgel. You
find it otherwise, and henceforth let a Welsh correction
teach you a good English disposition. Fare you well. *Exit*

PISTOL
Does Fortune play the housewife with me now?
News have I that my Nell is dead in hospital
Of malady of France,
And there my rendezvous is quite cut off.
Old I do wax, and from my weary limbs
Honour is cudgellèd. Well, bawd I'll turn,
And something lean to cutpurse of quick hand.
To England will I steal, and there I'll—steal;
And patches will I get unto these cudgelled scars,
And swear I got them in the Gallia wars.
                                                   Exit

SCENE II
France. The King's palace.

Enter, at one door, King Henry, Exeter, Bedford, Gloucester,
Clarence, Warwick, Westmorland, Huntingdon, and
other Lords; at another, the French King, Queen
Isabel, the Princess Katherine, Alice,
and other French; the Duke of Burgundy
and his train

KING HENRY

 Peace to this meeting, wherefor we are met!
 Unto our brother France, and to our sister,
 Health and fair time of day. Joy and good wishes
 To our most fair and princely cousin Katherine.
 And, as a branch and member of this royalty,
 By whom this great assembly is contrived,
 We do salute you, Duke of Burgundy;
 And, Princes French, and peers, health to you all!

FRENCH KING

 Right joyous are we to behold your face,
 Most worthy brother England: fairly met!
 So are you, Princes English, every one.

QUEEN ISABEL

 So happy be the issue, brother England,
 Of this good day, and of this gracious meeting,
 As we are now glad to behold your eyes—
 Your eyes which hitherto have borne in them,
 Against the French that met them in their bent,
 The fatal balls of murdering basilisks.
 The venom of such looks, we fairly hope,
 Have lost their quality, and that this day
 Shall change all griefs and quarrels into love.

KING HENRY

 To cry 'Amen' to that, thus we appear.

QUEEN ISABEL
  You English Princes all, I do salute you.
BURGUNDY
  My duty to you both, on equal love,
  Great Kings of France and England! That I have laboured
  With all my wits, my pains, and strong endeavours,
  To bring your most imperial majesties
  Unto this bar and royal interview,
  Your mightiness on both parts best can witness.
  Since, then, my office has so far prevailed
  That face to face, and royal eye to eye,
  You have now greeted, let it not disgrace me
  If I demand, before this royal view,
  What rub or what impediment there is
  Why the naked, poor, and mangled peace—
  Dear nurse of arts, plenties, and joyful births—
  Should not in this best garden of the world,
  Our fertile France, put up her lovely visage?
  Alas, she has from France too long been chased,
  And all her husbandry does lie on heaps,
  Corrupting in its own fertility.
  Her vine, the merry cheerer of the heart,
  Unprunèd dies; her hedges even-pleached,
  Like prisoners wildly overgrown with hair,
  Put forth disordered twigs; her fallow leas
  The darnel, hemlock, and rank fumitory
  Do root upon; while the coulter rusts
  That should deracinate such savagery.
  The even mead, that erst brought sweetly forth
  The freckled cowslip, burnet, and green clover,
  Wanting the scythe, all uncorrected, rank,
  Conceives by idleness, and nothing breeds
  But hateful docks, rough thistles, hemlocks, burs,
  Losing both beauty and utility.
  And as our vineyards, fallows, meads, and hedges,
  Defective in their natures, grow to wildness,

Even so our houses and ourselves and children
Have lost, or do not learn for want of time,
The sciences that should become our country;
But grow like savages—as soldiers will
That nothing do but meditate on blood—
To swearing and stern looks, diffused attire,
And everything that seems unnatural.
Which to reduce into our former favour
You are assembled; and my speech entreats
That I may know the bar why gentle peace
Should not expel these inconveniences,
And bless us with her former qualities.

KING HENRY

If, Duke of Burgundy, you would the peace
Whose want gives growth to imperfectiòns
Which you have cited, you must buy that peace
With full accord to all our just demands,
Whose tenors and particular effects
You have, enscheduled briefly, in your hands.

BURGUNDY

The King has heard them, though to them as yet
There is no answer made.

KING HENRY   Well then, the peace
Which you before so urged lies in his answer.

FRENCH KING

I have but with a cursory eye
O'erglanced the articles. Please it as yet your grace
To appoint some of your Council presently
To sit with us once more, with better heed
To re-survey them, we will suddenly
Pass our accept and pèremptory answer.

KING HENRY

Brother, we shall. Go, uncle Exeter,
And brother Clarence, and you, brother Gloucester,
Warwick, and Huntingdon, go with the King.
And take with you free power to ratify,

Augment, or alter, as your wisdoms best
Shall see advantageable for our dignity,
Anything in or out of our demands,
And we'll agree thereto. Will you, fair sister,
Go with the Princes, or stay here with us?

QUEEN ISABEL
Our gracious brother, I will go with them.
Haply a woman's voice may do some good,
When articles too nicely are insisted on.

KING HENRY
Yet leave our cousin Katherine here with us;
She is our capital demand, comprised
Within the fore-rank of our articles.

QUEEN ISABEL
She has good leave.
                    Exeunt all but Henry, Katherine, and Alice

KING HENRY   Fair Katherine, and most fair,
Will you please deign to teach a soldier terms
Such as will enter at a lady's ear
And plead his love-suit to her gentle heart?

KATHERINE   Your majesty shall mock at me; I cannot
speak your English.

KING HENRY   O fair Katherine, if you will love me soundly
with your French heart, I will be glad to hear you
confess it brokenly with your English tongue. Do you
like me, Kate?

KATHERINE   *Pardonnez-moi,* I cannot tell what is 'like
me'.

KING HENRY   An angel is like you, Kate, and you are like
an angel.

KATHERINE   *Que dit-il? que je suis semblable à les
anges?*[1]

---

[1]What does he say? That I am like the angels? Thus truly,
saving your grace, he says.

ALICE   *Oui, vraiment, sauf votre grâce, ainsi dit-il.*

KING HENRY   I said so, dear Katherine, and I must not blush to affirm it.

KATHERINE   *O bon Dieu! Les langues des hommes sont pleines de tromperies.*

KING HENRY   What says she, fair one? that the tongues of men are full of deceits?

ALICE   *Oui,* that the tongues of men are full of deceits — that is the *Princesse.*

KING HENRY   The Princess is the better Englishwoman. In faith, Kate, my wooing is fit for your understanding. I am glad you can speak no better English; for if you could, you would find me such a plain king that you would think I had sold my farm to buy my crown. I know no ways to mince it in love, but directly to say, 'I love you': then if you urge me farther than to say, 'Do you, in faith?' I wear out my suit. Give me your answer, in faith, do; and so clap hands, and a bargain. How say you, lady?

KATHERINE   *Sauf votre honneur* [saving your honour] I understand well.

KING HENRY   Well, if you would put me to verses, or to dance for your sake, Kate, why, you undo me. For the one, I have neither words nor measure; and for the other, I have no strength in measure, yet a reasonable measure in strength. If I could win a lady at leapfrog, or by vaulting into my saddle with my armour on my back, under the correction of bragging be it spoken, I should quickly leap into a wife. Or if I might buffet for my love, or bound my horse for her favours, I could lay on like a butcher, and sit like a jackanapes, never off. But, before God, Kate, I cannot look callow, nor gasp out my eloquence, nor I have cunning in protestation: only downright oaths, which I never use till urged, nor ever break for urging. If you can love a fellow of this temper, Kate, whose face is not worth sunburning, that never looks in his glass for love of anything he sees there, let your eye be your cook. I speak to you plain soldier. If you can love me for this, take me; if not, to say to you that I shall die is true—but for your love, by the Lord, no—yet I love you too. And while you live, dear Kate, take a fellow of plain and uncoined constancy; for he perforce must do you right, because he has not the gift to woo in other places. For these fellows of infinite tongue, that can rhyme themselves into ladies' favours, they do always reason themselves out again. What! A speaker is but a prater, a rhyme is but a ballad. A good leg will fall; a straight back will stoop; a black beard will turn white; a curled pate will grow bald; a fair face will wither; a full eye will wax hollow. But a good heart, Kate, is the sun and the moon—or rather, the sun, and not the moon; for it shines bright and never changes, but keeps its course truly. If you would have such a one, take me; and take me, take a soldier; take a soldier, take a king. And what say you then to my love? Speak, my fair, and fairly, I pray you.

KATHERINE   Is it possible that I should love the *ennemi* of *France?*

KING HENRY   No, it is not possible you should love the enemy of France, Kate; but in loving me you should love the friend of France. For I love France so well that I will not part with a village of it—I will have it all mine: and Kate, when France is mine, and I am yours, then yours is France, and you are mine.

KATHERINE   I cannot tell what is that.

KING HENRY   No, Kate? I will tell you in French, which I am sure will hang upon my tongue like a new-married wife about her husband's neck, hardly to be shaken off.

*Je—quand sur la possession de France, et quand vous
avez la possession de moi,* —let me see, what then? Saint
Denis be my speed!—*donc vôtre est France, et vous êtes
mienne.*[2] It is as easy for me, Kate, to conquer the
kingdom as to speak so much more French. I shall never
move you in French, unless it be to laugh at me.

KATHERINE   *Sauf votre honneur, le français que vous
parlez, il est meilleur que l'anglais lequel je parle.*[3]

KING HENRY   No, faith, it is not, Kate; but your speaking
of my tongue, and I yours, most truly-falsely, must
needs be granted to be much at one. But Kate, do you
understand thus much English—can you love me?

KATHERINE   I cannot tell.

KING HENRY   Can any of your neighbours tell, Kate? I'll
ask them. Come, I know you love me; and at night,
when you come into your closet, you'll question this
gentlewoman about me. And I know, Kate, you will to
her dispraise those parts in me that you love with your
heart. But, good Kate, mock me mercifully; the rather,
gentle Princess, because I love you cruelly. If ever you
are mine, Kate, as I have a saving faith within me tells
me you shall, I get you by fighting, and you must
therefore needs prove a good soldier-breeder. Shall not
you and I, between Saint Denis and Saint George,
compound a boy, half French, half English, that shall
go to Constantinople and take the Turk by the beard?
Shall we not? What say you, my fair flower-de-luce?

KATHERINE   I do not know that.

KING HENRY   No, it is hereafter to know, but now to
promise. Do but now promise, Kate, you will endeavour
for your French part of such a boy, and for my English

---

[2]When, on possession of France and you have possession
of me, then France is yours and you are mine.
[3]Saving your honour, the French that you speak is better
than the English that I speak.

moiety take the word of a king and a bachelor. How answer you, *la plus belle Katherine du monde, mon très cher et devin déesse?*[4]

KATHERINE   Your majesty has *fausse* [false] French enough to deceive the most *sage demoiselle* [wise girl] that is *en France.*

KING HENRY   Now fie upon my false French! By my honour, in true English, I love you, Kate. By which honour I dare not swear you love me, yet my blood begins to flatter me that you do, notwithstanding the poor and untempering effect of my visage. Now blast my father's ambition! He was thinking of civil wars when he got me; therefore was I created with a stubborn outside, with an aspect of iron, that when I come to woo ladies I frighten them. But in faith, Kate, the older I wax, the better I shall appear. My comfort is that old age, that ill layer-up of beauty, can do no more spoil upon my face. You have me, if you have me, at the worst; and you shall find me, if you have me, better and better; and therefore tell me, most fair Katherine, will you have me? Put off your maiden blushes, confirm the thoughts of your heart with the looks of an empress, take me by the hand, and say, 'Harry of England, I am yours. Which word you shall no sooner bless my ear with but I will tell you aloud, 'England is yours, Ireland is yours, France is yours, and Henry Plantagenet is yours,' Though I speak it before his face, if he is not fellow with the best king, you shall find the best king of good fellows. Come, your answer in broken music—for your voice is music, and your English broken. Therefore, Queen of all, Katherine, break your mind to me in broken English—will you have me?

---

[4]The most lovely Katherine in the world, my dear and divine goddess.

KATHERINE   That is as it shall please the *Roi mon père.* [King my father.]

KING HENRY   Nay, it will please him well, Kate—it shall please him, Kate.

KATHERINE   Then it shall also content me.

KING HENRY   Upon that I kiss your hand, and I call you my Queen.

KATHERINE   *Laissez, mon seigneur, laissez, laissez! Ma foi, je ne veux point que vous abaissiez votre grandeur en baisant la main d'une—notre Seigneur—indigne serviteur. Excusez-moi, je vous supplie, mon très puissant seigneur.*[5]

KING HENRY   Then I will kiss your lips, Kate.

KATHERINE   *Les dames et demoiselles pour être baisées devant leurs noces, il n'est pas la coûtume de France.*

KING HENRY   Madam my interpreter, what says she?

ALICE   That it is not the fashion *pour les* ladies of *France*—I cannot tell what is *baiser en* Anglish.

KING HENRY   To kiss.

ALICE   Your majesty *entend* better *que moi.* [understands better than I.]

KING HENRY   It is not a fashion for the maids in France to kiss before they are married, would she say?

ALICE   *Oui, vraiment.* [Yes, truly.]

KING HENRY   O Kate, nice customs curtsy to great kings. Dear Kate, you and I cannot be confined within the weak list of a country's fashion. We are the makers of manners, Kate, and the liberty that follows our places stops the mouth of all find-faults. As I will do yours for upholding the nice fashion of your country in denying me a kiss; therefore, patiently, and yielding. (*He kisses her*) You have witchcraft in your lips, Kate: there is more eloquence in a sugar touch of them than in the tongues of the French Council, and they should sooner

---

[5]Let be, my lord. Faith, I do not wish you to lower your greatness by kissing the hand of an unworthy servitor.

persuade Harry of England than a general petition of monarchs. Here comes your father.

Enter the French King and Queen, Burgundy, and English and French Lords

BURGUNDY   God save your majesty! My royal cousin, teach you our Princess English?

KING HENRY   I would have her learn, my fair cousin, how perfectly I love her, and that is good English.

BURGUNDY   Is she not apt?

KING HENRY   Our tongue is rough, cousin, and my condition is not smooth; so that, having neither the voice nor the heart of flattery about me, I cannot so conjure up the spirit of love in her that it will appear in its true likeness.

BURGUNDY   Pardon the frankness of my mirth, if I answer you for that. If you would conjure in her, you must make a circle; if conjure up love in her in its true likeness, it must appear naked and blind. Can you blame her, then, being a maid yet rosed over with the virgin crimson of modesty, if she denies the appearance of a naked blind boy in her naked seeing self? It is, my lord, a hard condition for a maid to consent to.

KING HENRY   Yet they do wink and yield, as love is blind and enforces.

BURGUNDY   They are then excused, my lord, when they see not what they do.

KING HENRY   Then, good my lord, teach your cousin to consent winking.

BURGUNDY   I will wink on her to consent, my lord, if you will teach her to know my meaning: for maids, well summered and warm kept, are like flies at Bartholomewtide, blind, though they have their eyes. And then they will endure handling, which before would not abide looking on.

KING HENRY   This moral ties me over to time and a hot summer; and so I shall catch the fly, your cousin, in the latter end, and she must be blind too.

BURGUNDY   As love is, my lord, before it loves.

KING HENRY   It is so; and you may, some of you, thank love for my blindness, who cannot see many a fair French city for one fair French maid that stands in my way.

FRENCH KING   Yes, my lord, you see them perspectively, the cities turned into a maid; for they are all girdled with maiden walls, that war has never entered.

KING HENRY   Shall Kate be my wife?

FRENCH KING   So please you.

KING HENRY   I am content, so the maiden cities you talk of may wait on her: so the maid that stood in the way for my wish shall show me the way to my will.

FRENCH KING
We have consented to all terms of reason.

KING HENRY
Is it so, my lords of England?

WESTMORLAND
The King has granted every article:
His daughter first, and then, in sequel, all,
According to their firm proposèd natures.

EXETER
Only he has not yet subscribèd this:
Where your majesty demands that the King of France, having any occasion to write for matter of grant, shall name your highness in this form, and with this addition, in French, *Notre très cher fils Henri, Roi d'Angleterre, Héritier de France:* and thus in Latin, *Praeclarissimus filius noster Henricus, Rex Angliae et Haeres Franciae.*[6]

---

[6]Our dearest son, Henry, King of England, Heir of France.

FRENCH KING

    And this I have not, brother, so denied
    But your request shall make me let it pass.

KING HENRY

    I pray you then, in love and dear alliance,
    Let that one article rank with the rest,
    And thereupon give me your daughter.

FRENCH KING

    Take her, fair son, and from her blood raise up
    Issue to me, that the contending kingdoms
    Of France and England, whose very shores look pale
    With envy of each other's happiness,
    May cease their hatred; and this dear conjunction
    Plant neighbourhood and Christian-like accord
    In their sweet bosoms, that never war advance
    His bleeding sword between England and fair France.

LORDS   Amen!

KING HENRY

    Now welcome, Kate; and bear me witness all
    That here I kiss her as my sovereign Queen.

Flourish

QUEEN ISABEL

    God, the best maker of all marriages,
    Combine your hearts in one, your realms in one!
    As man and wife, being two, are one in love,
    So be there between your kingdoms such a spousal
    That never may ill office, or mad jealousy,
    Which troubles oft the bed of blessèd marriage,
    Thrust in between the compact of these kingdoms
    To make divorce of their incorporate league;
    That English may as French, French Englishmen,
    Receive each other, God speak this 'Amen'!

ALL   Amen!

KING HENRY

    Prepare we for our marriage; on which day,
    My Lord of Burgundy, we'll take your oath,
    And all the peers', for surety of our leagues.
    Then shall I swear to Kate, and you to me,
    And may our oaths well kept and prosperous be!

                             Sennet. Exeunt

Epilogue

Enter Chorus

CHORUS
    Thus far, with rough and all-unable pen,
        Our bending author has pursued the story,
    In little room confining mighty men,
        Mangling by starts the full course of their glory.
    Small time, but in that small most greatly lived
        This star of England. Fortune made his sword,
    By which the world's best garden he achieved,
        And of it left his son imperial lord.
    Henry the Sixth, in infant bands crowned King
        Of France and England, did this King succeed,
    Whose state so many had the managing
        That they lost France, and made his England bleed:
    Which oft our stage has shown; and, for their sake,
        In your fair minds let this acceptance take.   *Exit*

Appendix to Act III, Scene IV

Enter Princess Katherine and Alice, an old gentlewoman

KATHERINE   Alice, you have been in England, and you speak the language well.

ALICE   A little, madam.

KATHERINE   Pray, teach me—I must learn to speak it. How do you call *la main* in English?

ALICE   *La main?* It is called the hand.

KATHERINE   The hand. And *les doigts?*

ALICE   *Les doigts?* Faith, I forget *les doigts*, but I shall remember. I think that they are called the fingers; yes, the fingers.

KATHERINE   *La main*, the hand; *les doigts*, the fingers. I think I am a good pupil; I have learned two words of English quickly. How do you call *les ongles?*

ALICE   *Les ongles?* We call them the nails.

KATHERINE   The nails. Listen: tell me if I speak well— the hand, the fingers, and the nails.

ALICE   Well said, madam. It is very good English.

KATHERINE   Tell me the English for *le bras.*

ALICE   The arm, madam.

KATHERINE   And *le coude?*

ALICE   The elbow.

KATHERINE   The elbow. I will repeat all the words you have taught me up to this.

ALICE   That is too difficult, madam, as I think.

KATHERINE   Excuse me, Alice; listen—the hand, the fingers, the nails, the arm, the bilbow.

ALICE   The elbow, madam.

KATHERINE   O Lord, I forget! The elbow. How do you call *le col?*

ALICE   The neck, madam.

KATHERINE   The neck. And *le menton?*

ALICE   The chin.

KATHERINE   The chin. *Le col,* the neck; *le menton,* the chin.

ALICE   Yes. Saving your honour, truly, you pronounce the words as well as the natives of England.

KATHERINE   I don't doubt I shall learn, by God's grace, and in little time.

ALICE   You haven't already forgotten what I have taught you?

KATHERINE   No. I will recite to you at once: the hand, the finger, the mails.

ALICE   The nails, madam.

KATHERINE   The nails, the arm, the ilbow.

ALICE   Saving your honour, the elbow.

KATHERINE   So I say: the elbow, the neck, and the chin. How do you call *le pied* and *la robe?*

ALICE   The foot, madam, and the count. [gown]

KATHERINE   The foot, and the count? O Lord, they are bad words, unsuitable, gross, vulgar, not for ladies of honour to use. I wouldn't want to pronounce those words before the lords of France, for all the world. Foh! The foot and the count! Still, I will recite once more my lesson together: the hand, the finger, the nails, the arm, the neck, the chin, the foot, the count.

ALICE   Excellent, madam.

KATHERINE   It's enough for once. Let's go to dinner.

Exeunt

Macbeth

INTRODUCTION

N o play of Shakespeare reflects more clearly the circumstances of the time and what was going on around him than *Macbeth,* for all the remoteness and primitiveness of the story. In 1603 the Scottish King, James I, came to the English throne, with a family and cousinage of Stuart relations, Scots councillors, lords and attendants. For the first time London was made suddenly aware of the Scots. King and Queen took to the delights of the English theatre, masques etc, and James took the Lord Chamberlain's Company under his own patronage as the King's Men. He doubled the rate of remuneration for performances at Court, from Queen Elizabeth's £10 to £20; Shakespeare and his fellows in the Company became Grooms of the Chamber, with an allowance of scarlet for appearance on official occasions in procession. Even the unimaginative Sir Edmund Chambers accepts the early tradition of an agreeable letter from King James to Shakespeare, once in Sir William Davenant's hands, but then lost — as most letters would be in the course of time.[1]

The Scottish succession solved the problem of the unity of the two kingdoms and ended the anxiety as to what would happen when the ageless Queen Elizabeth I died.

---

1. E.K. Chambers, *William Shakespeare,* 1. 76.

But anxiety was renewed when a gang of young Catholic desperados plotted to blow up King and Parliament in the alarming—and never to be forgotten—Gunpowder Plot of 1605. An immense feeling of relief gave the new King an access of popularity—though a marked contrast with the great Queen before him. For one thing, a Calvinist, he was an addicted believer in witchcraft; his book on the subject, his dialogue on *Demonology,* was reprinted and Parliament passed a severe law against witchcraft and sorcery. He shortly began to renew the practice of touching for the King's Evil, a quasi-sacramental rite bespeaking the Divine Right of kings. The Jesuit doctrine of equivocation, by which the Jesuit Provincial, Garnet, covered up his knowledge of the plot, made a widespread ill impression.

All this is in the play. In accordance with his frequent practice Shakespeare looked up a story that would answer the circumstances of the time, and have popular appeal. He found it in the Scottish section of Holinshed's Chronicles, as usual adapting it for his own dramatic purposes. So much for those critics who ignore—or are ignorant of—the contemporary experience (and his own) that went into his plays. As Dr Johnson, greatest of Shakespeare critics, reminds us: 'in order to make a true estimate of the abilities and merit of a writer, it is always necessary to examine the genius of his age, and the opinion of his contemporaries.' In other words, we must see the work in the perspective of its time, and also make it intelligible to ours—the dual purpose of *A Contemporary Shakespeare.*

Johnson adduces the supernatural element crucial to this play, the witches or fairies—'fairies' to the Elizabethans could be malevolent—and he notices that Shakespeare, with the dramatic extremism of his imagination, 'multiplies all the circumstances of horror.' As to its effectiveness, he has a famous phrase: 'he that peruses Shakespeare looks round alarmed, and starts to find himself alone.' The classic Doctor was a man of imagination—and truly, to see Lady Macbeth's sleep-walking scene on the stage, the desolation of it all, one's hair stands on end.

On the question of historical perspective Johnson also says a definitive word, all the more remarkable coming out of the Augustan age with its sceptical rationality, when cultivated minds might dismiss such horrors. 'Shakespeare was in no danger of such censures, since he only turned the system that was then universally admitted to his advantage, and was far from over-burdening the credulity of his age.' As for the remote Gothic—or, rather, Celtic—horrors of the play, our own civilised age sees worse on every hand. Ireland is still with us—as always. Ulster had surrendered to James I, who was planning to plant its waste spaces with Scots *(hinc illae lacrimae)*. We have a couple of references to the Celtic kerns and gallowglasses from both sides of those narrow cousinly waters. The Scots originally came out of Ireland; they formed one primitive world: to what point their endless, murderous scuffling?

The play belongs to 1606. Evidences of its impact appear shortly; next year *The Puritan* recalls the apparition of the murdered Banquo (putative ancestor of the Stuarts) at Macbeth's appalling feast, as does *The Knight of the Burning Pestle*. In April 1611 Simon Forman saw *Macbeth* at the Globe, and gives a fairly full account of it, specially interested in the supernatural, the witches or fairies, Banquo's apparition, the sleep-walking scene with the Doctor noting her words—as he would be.[1]

We must let the play as such speak for itself, and look for touches revealing of its author in person. His profession

---

1. v. my *Simon Forman: Sex and Society in Shakespeare's Age.*, 303-4.

appears, as always:

> Life's but a walking shadow, a poor player
> That struts and frets his hour upon the stage
> And then is heard no more.

Macbeth sees the fulfilment of the witches' first two prophecies of his future

> As happy prologues to the swelling Act
> Of the imperial theme.

Or again the association appears unconsciously in an image: the heavens, 'troubled with man's act, threaten his bloody stage.'

The countryman's early addiction to falconry recurs, with the image of a mousing owl hawking at a falcon and killing it. And it is a countryman that knows that sometimes a sow will eat her farrow. On the other hand is his regularly expressed dislike of dogs—except for hounds. We see the more philosophic Shakespeare face to face in such thoughts as

> There's no art
> To find the mind's construction in the face.

Or

> I am in this earthly world, where to do harm
> Is often laudable, to do good sometimes
> Accounted dangerous folly.

When Macbeth makes the polite reference to King James's supposed ancestor, that under Banquo

> My Genius is rebuked, as it is said,
> Mark Antony's was by Caesar—

i.e. Augustus, we see that *Antony and Cleopatra* is not far away in that teeming mind.

The text of *Macbeth* offers problems. It is one of the shortest of the plays and has evidently been cut, perhaps for political reasons—the subject, the murder of a king, was brimstone enough. Again, the version we have, from the First Folio, may have been an abridged acting version, for it also has interpolated Middleton's Hecate and songs from his play, *The Witch*. There is a good deal of mislineation. As G.K. Hunter sums up, 'when there was too little material the compositor would take to "losing space" by printing short lines. When he was "saving space" he joined up lines.' There is no sacrosanctity about the usages of Jacobean compositors: a modern editor is free to remove barriers for the reader today. Thus there is no point in adhering to Jacobean spellings of Cathness for Caithness, Menteth for Menteith; or Seyward and Seyton for Siward and Seton; or Birnan for Birnam wood as familiar to us as folklore. That kind of thing is Shakespearean archaeology, not helpful to the reader.

Nor is there any point in retaining antique spellings in a supposedly modern edition: 'skir' for scour, 'enow' for enough, 'accompt' for account, 'howlet' for owlet, 'wrack' for wreck; or shortenings like 'nea'er' for nearer, 'whe'er' for whether, liable to confuse. What point is there in keeping 'ingredience' for ingredients? Some words have different meanings and need to be replaced for intelligibility. The word 'modern' meant normal, ordinary, or usual; 'ecstasy' meant frenzy, 'jealousy' suspicion, 'doubt' fear as well as doubt, 'luxury' lust. And so on. Fairly frequently Shakespeare dropped a first syllable for the sake of scansion: for example, 'filed' for defiled; we sometimes have to add one. He was very free in his usage, and very often inconsistent and variable, for Elizabethan language was in a much more fluid, less settled, state. So we may claim no less freedom to be more consistent and regularise, in modernising for the sake of clarity and intelligibility for the reader.

CHARACTERS

DUNCAN, King of Scotland

MALCOLM }
DONALBAIN } his sons

MACBETH, Thane of Glamis, later of Cawdor, later
King of Scotland

BANQUO
MACDUFF
LENNOX
ROSS   Thanes of Scotland
MENTEITH
ANGUS
CAITHNESS

FLEANCE, Banquo's son
SIWARD, Earl of Northumberland
YOUNG SIWARD, his son
SETON, Macbeth's armour-bearer
SON OF MACDUFF
A Captain, An English Doctor, A Scottish Doctor, A
Porter, An Old Man

LADY MACBETH
WIFE OF MACDUFF
Gentlewoman attendant on Lady Macbeth, Three Weird
Sisters, Three other Witches
HECAT
Apparitions, Three Murderers, Other Murderers, Lords,
Gentlemen, Officers, Soldiers, Attendants, Messengers

Act I

SCENE I
A desert heath.

Thunder and lightning. Enter three Witches.

FIRST WITCH
  When shall we three meet again?
  In thunder, lightning, or in rain?
SECOND WITCH
  When the hurly-burly's done,
  When the battle's lost and won.
THIRD WITCH
  That will be ere the set of sun.
FIRST WITCH
  Where the place?
SECOND WITCH   Upon the heath.
THIRD WITCH
  There to meet with Macbeth.
FIRST WITCH
  I come, Grey Malkin. [Grey Cat]
SECOND WITCH   Padock [Toad] calls!
THIRD WITCH   Anon!
ALL
  Fair is foul, and foul is fair.
  Hover through the fog and filthy air.   *Exeunt*

SCENE II
A camp near Forres.

Alarum within
Enter KING DUNCAN, MALCOLM, DONALBAIN, LENNOX,
with Attendants, meeting a bleeding SERGEANT

KING
    What bloody man is that? He can report,
    As seems well by his plight, of the revolt
    The newest state.
MALCOLM   This is the sergeant
    Who like a good and hardy soldier fought
    Against my captivity. Hail, brave friend!
    Say to the King the knowledge of the broil
    As you did leave it.
CAPTAIN   Doubtful it stood,
    As two spent swimmers that do cling together
    And choke their art. The merciless Macdonald—
    Worthy to be a rebel, for to that
    The multiplying villanies of nature
    Do swarm upon him—from the Western Isles
    Of kerns and gallowglasses is supplied;
    And fortune on his damnèd quarrel smiling
    Showed like a rebel's whore. But all's too weak:
    For brave Macbeth—well he deserves that name—
    Disdaining fortune, with his brandished steel,
    Which smoked with bloody execution,
    Like valour's minion carved out his passage
    Till he faced the slave—
    Who never shook hands nor bade farewell to him
    Till he unseamed him from the nave to the chaps,
    And fixed his head upon our battlements.
KING
    O valiant cousin! Worthy gentleman!
CAPTAIN
    As, whence the sun begins its reflection,
    Shipwrecking storms and direful thunders;

So, from that spring whence comfort seemed to come,
Discomfort swells. Mark, King of Scotland, mark!
No sooner justice had, with valour armed,
Compelled these skipping kerns to trust their heels
But the Norwegian lord, surveying vantage,
With furbished arms and new supplies of men,
Began a fresh assault.

KING   Dismayed not this
Our captains, Macbeth and Banquo?

CAPTAIN   Yes—
As sparrows, eagles, or the hare, the lion.
If I say truth I must report they were
As cannons overcharged with double cracks;
So they
Doubly redoubled strokes upon the foe.
Except they meant to bathe in reeking wounds
Or memorize another Golgotha
I cannot tell.
— But I am faint; my gashes cry for help.

KING
So well your words become you as your wounds,
They smack of honour both. Go get him surgeons.

Exit Sergeant and Attendants

Enter ROSS *and* ANGUS

Who comes here?

MALCOLM   The worthy Thane of Ross.

LENNOX
What a haste looks through his eyes!
So should he look that seems to speak things strange.

ROSS
God save the King!

KING
Whence came you, worthy thane?

ROSS   From Fife, great King,
   Where the Norwegian banners flout the sky
   And fan our people cold.
   Norway himself, with terrible numbers,
   Assisted by that most disloyal traitor,
   The Thane of Cawdor, began a dismal conflict—
   Till Bellona's bridegroom, lapped in proof,
   Confronted him with self-comparisons,
   Point against sword rebellious, arm against arm,
   Curbing his lavish spirit; and to conclude,
   The victory fell on us—
KING   Great happiness!
ROSS
   —That now Sweno, the Norways' king,
   Craves compositiòn;
   Nor would we deign him burial of his men
   Till he disbursèd at Saint Colm's Inch
   Ten thousand dollars to our general use.
KING
   No more than Thane of Cawdor shall deceive
   Our bosom interest. Go pronounce his present death,
   And with his former title greet Macbeth.
ROSS
   I'll see it done.
KING
   What he has lost, noble Macbeth has won.   *Exeunt*

SCENE III
A heath.

Thunder. Enter the three Witches

FIRST WITCH   Where have you been, sister?
SECOND WITCH   Killing swine.

THIRD WITCH   Sister, where you?
FIRST WITCH
A sailor's wife had chestnuts in her lap,
And munched and munched and munched. 'Give me,'
   said I.
'Begone, you witch!' the rump-fed rascal cries.
Her husband's to Aleppo gone, master of the *Tiger*.
      But in a sieve I'll thither sail
      And like a rat without a tail
      I'll do, I'll do, and I'll do.
SECOND WITCH
      I'll give you a wind.
FIRST WITCH
      You are kind.
THIRD WITCH
      And I another.
FIRST WITCH
      I myself have all the other.
      And the very ports they blow
      All the quarters that they know
      In the shipman's card.
      I'll drain him dry as hay;
      Sleep shall neither night nor day
      Hang upon his penthouse lid.
      He shall live a man forbid.
      Weary sev'n-nights nine times
        nine
      Shall he dwindle, peak, and pine.
      Though his bark cannot be lost,
      Yet it shall be tempest-tossed.
      Look what I have!
SECOND WITCH   Show me, show me!
FIRST WITCH
      Here I have a pilot's thumb,
      Wrecked as homeward he did come.

Drum within

THIRD WITCH
    A drum! a drum!
    Macbeth does come.
ALL
    The Weird Sisters, hand in hand,
    Posters of the sea and land,
    Thus do go, about, about;
    Thrice to thine, and thrice to mine,
    And thrice again, to make up nine.
    Peace! The charm's wound up.

Enter MACBETH *and* BANQUO

MACBETH
    So foul and fair a day I have not seen.
BANQUO
    How far is it called to Forres? What are these,
    So withered and so wild in their attire,
    That look not like the inhabitants of the earth,
    And yet are on it? Live you? Or are you aught
    That man may question? You seem to understand me
    By each at once her choppy finger laying
    Upon her skinny lips. You should be women;
    And yet your beards forbid me to interpret
    That you are so.
MACBETH   Speak if you can! What are you?
FIRST WITCH
    All hail, Macbeth! Hail to you, Thane of Glamis!
SECOND WITCH
    All hail, Macbeth! Hail to you, Thane of Cawdor!
THIRD WITCH
    All hail, Macbeth, that shall be king hereafter!

BANQUO

Good sir, why do you start, and seem to fear
Things that do sound so fair? — In the name of truth,
Are you fantastical, or that indeed
Which outwardly you show? My noble partner
You greet with present grace, and great prediction
Of noble having and of royal hope
That he seems rapt with it. To me you speak not.
If you can look into the seeds of time
And say which grain will grow and which will not,
Speak then to me who neither beg nor fear
Your favours nor your hate.

FIRST WITCH

Hail!

SECOND WITCH

Hail!

THIRD WITCH

Hail!

FIRST WITCH

Lesser than Macbeth, and greater.

SECOND WITCH

Not so happy, yet much happier.

THIRD WITCH

You shall get kings, though you be none.
So all hail, Macbeth and Banquo!

FIRST WITCH

Banquo and Macbeth, all hail!

MACBETH

Stay, you imperfect speakers! Tell me more!
By Sinel's death I know I am Thane of Glamis;
But how of Cawdor? The Thane of Cawdor lives
A prosperous gentleman. And to be king
Stands not within the prospect of belief—
No more than to be Cawdor. Say from whence
You owe this strange intelligence; or why

Upon this blasted heath you stop our way
With such prophetic greeting? Speak, I charge you!
Witches vanish

BANQUO
The earth has bubbles as the water has,
And these are of them. Whither are they vanished?

MACBETH
Into the air; and what seemed corporal
Melted, as breath into the wind. Would they had
stayed!

BANQUO
Were such things here as we do speak about?
Or have we eaten of the insane root
That takes the reason prisoner?

MACBETH
Your children shall be kings.

BANQUO   You shall be king.

MACBETH
And Thane of Cawdor too, went it not so?

BANQUO
To the selfsame tune and words. Who's here?

Enter ROSS *and* ANGUS

ROSS
The King has happily received, Macbeth,
The news of your success; and when he reads
Your personal venture in the rebels' fight
His wonders and his praises do contend
Which should be yours, or his. Silenced with that,
In viewing over the rest of the selfsame day
He finds you in the stout Norwegian ranks,
Nothing afraid of what yourself did make,
Strange images of death. As thick as hail
Came post with post; and every one did bear

Your praises, in his kingdom's great defence,
And poured them down before him.
ANGUS   We are sent
   To give you from our royal master thanks;
   Only to herald you into his sight,
   Not pay you.
ROSS
   And, for an earnest of a great honour,
   He bade me from him call you Thane of Cawdor
   In which addition, hail, most worthy thane,
   For it is yours.
BANQUO   What! Can the devil speak true?
MACBETH
   The Thane of Cawdor lives. Why do you dress me
   In borrowed robes?
ANGUS   Who was the Thane lives yet;
   But under heavy judgement bears that life
   Which he deserves to lose. Whether he was combined
   With those of Norway, or did line the rebel
   With hidden help and vantage, or that with both
   He laboured in his country's wreck, I know not;
   But treasons capital, confessed, and proved
   Have overthrown him.
MACBETH   *[aside]*   Glamis, and Thane of Cawdor!
   The greatest is behind. — Thanks for your pains.
   [to Banquo] Do you not hope your children shall be
      kings,
   When those that gave the Thane of Cawdor to me
   Promised no less to them?
BANQUO   That trusted home
   Might yet enkindle you unto the crown
   Besides the Thane of Cawdor. It is strange;
   And oftentimes, to win us to your harm,
   The instruments of darkness tell us truths;
   Win us with honest trifles, to betray us

In deepest consequence.
My lords, a word, I pray you.

They walk apart

MACBETH *[aside]*   Two truths are told
  As happy prologues to the swelling Act
  Of the imperial theme. — I thank you, gentlemen.
  [aside] This supernatural soliciting
  Cannot be ill, cannot be good. If ill,
  Why has it given me earnest of success
  Commencing in a truth? I am Thane of Cawdor.
  If good, why do I yield to that suggestion
  Whose horrid image does unfix my hair,
  And make my seated heart knock at my ribs
  Against the use of nature? Present fears
  Are less than horrible imaginings.
  My thought, whose murder yet is but fantastical,
  Shakes so my single state of man
  That function is smothered in surmise,
  And nothing is but what is not.
BANQUO   Look how your partner's rapt.
MACBETH *[aside]*
  If chance will have me king, why chance may crown
    me
  Without my stir.
BANQUO   New honours come upon him
  Like our strange garments, cleave not to their mould
  But with the aid of use.
MACBETH *[aside]*   Come what come may,
  Time and the hour run through the roughest day.
BANQUO
  Worthy Macbeth, we stay upon your leisure.
MACBETH
  Give me your favour. My dull brain was wrought

With things forgotten. Kind gentlemen, your pains
Are registered where every day I turn
The leaf to read them. Let us toward the King.
(*to Banquo*) Think upon what has chanced, and at
    more time,
The interim having weighed it, let us speak
Our free hearts each to other.

BANQUO   Very gladly.

MACBETH

Till then, enough!—Come, friends.   *Exeunt*

SCENE IV
A room in the palace.

Flourish. Enter KING DUNCAN, LENNOX, MALCOLM,
        DONALBAIN, *and Attendants*

KING

Is execution done on Cawdor?
Are not those in commission yet returned?

MALCOLM

My liege,
They are not yet come back. But I have spoken
With one that saw him die, who did report
That very frankly he confessed his treasons,
Implored your highness' pardon, and set forth
A deep repentance. Nothing in his life
Became him like the leaving it. He died
As one that had been studied in his death
To throw away the dearest thing he owed
As though a careless trifle.

KING   There's no art
To find the mind's construction in the face.
He was a gentleman on whom I built
An absolute trust.

Enter MACBETH, BANQUO, ROSS, *and* ANGUS

                    O worthiest cousin!
The sin of my ingratitude even now
Was heavy on me. You are so far before,
That swiftest wing of recompense is slow
To overtake you. Would you had less deserved,
That the proportion both of thanks and payment
Might have been mine. Only I have left to say,
'More is your due than more than all can pay.'
MACBETH
    The service and the loyalty I owe,
In doing it, pays itself. Your highness' part
Is to receive our duties; and our duties
Are to your throne and state, children and servants,
Which do but what they should by doing everything
Safe toward your love and honour.
KING   Welcome hither.
I have begun to plant you, and will labour
To make you full of growing.—Noble Banquo,
That have no less deserved, nor must be known
No less to have done so, let me enfold you
And hold you to my heart.
BANQUO   There if I grow,
The harvest is your own.
KING   My plenteous joys,
Wanton in fulness, seek to hide themselves
In drops of sorrow. Sons, kinsmen, thanes,
And you whose places are the nearest, know
We will establish our estate upon
Our eldest, Malcolm, whom we name hereafter
The Prince of Cumberland: which honour must
Not unaccompanied invest him only;
But signs of nobleness, like stars, shall shine
On all deservers. From hence to Inverness,

And bind us further to you.
MACBETH
　The rest is labour, which is not used for you.
　I'll be myself the harbinger and make joyful
　The hearing of my wife with your approach;
　So humbly take my leave.
KING   My worthy Cawdor!
MACBETH (*aside*)
　The Prince of Cumberland! That is a step
　On which I must fall down, or overleap,
　For in my way it lies. Stars, hide your fires,
　Let not light see my black and deep desires,
　The eye wink at the hand; yet let that be
　Which the eye fears, when it is done, to see.   *Exit*
KING
　True, worthy Banquo; he is full so valiant,
　And in his commendations I am fed;
　It is a banquet to me. Let's after him
　Whose care is gone before to bid us welcome.
　It is a peerless kinsman.   *Flourish. Exeunt*

SCENE V
Inverness. Macbeth's Castle.

Enter Macbeth's Wife alone with a letter

LADY MACBETH *They met me in the day of success,
and I have learned by the perfectest report they have more
in them than mortal knowledge. When I burned in desire
to question them further, they made themselves air, into
which they vanished. While I stood rapt in the wonder of
it, came missives from the King, who all-hailed me
Thane of Cawdor; by which title before these Weird Sisters saluted me, and referred me to the coming of*

time with, 'Hail, king that shall be.' This have I thought
good to deliver to you, my dearest partner of greatness,
that you might not lose the dues of rejoicing by being ig-
norant of what greatness is promised you. Lay it to your
heart, and farewell.
Glamis you are, and Cawdor, and shall be
What you are promised. Yet do I fear your nature:
It is too full of the milk of human-kindness
To catch the nearest way. You would be great,
Are not without ambition, but without
The illness should attend it. What you would highly
That would you holily, would not play false,
And yet would wrongly win. You'd have, great Glamis,
That which cries, 'Thus you must do' if you have it,
And that which rather you do fear to do
That wish should be undone. Hie you hither
That I may pour my spirits in your ear,
And chastise with the valour of my tongue
All that impedes you from the golden round
Which fate and metaphysical aid do seem
To have you crowned with.

Enter Messenger

                                    What are your tidings?
MESSENGER
The King comes here tonight.
LADY M.   You are mad to say it!
Is not your master with him? Who, were it so,
Would have informed for preparation.
MESSENGER
So please you, it is true. Our Thane is coming;
One of my fellows had the speed of him,
Who, almost dead for breath, had scarcely more
Than would make up his message.

LADY M.   Give him tending:
  He brings great news.   *Exit Messenger*
             The raven itself is hoarse
  That croaks the fatal entrance of Duncan
  Under my battlements. Come, you spirits
  That tend on mortal thoughts, unsex me here
  And fill me from the crown to the toe top-full
  Of direst cruelty. Make thick my blood;
  Stop up the access and passage to remorse,
  That no compunctious visitings of nature
  Shake my fell purpose, nor keep peace between
  The effect and it. Come to my woman's breasts
  And take my milk for gall, you murdering ministers,
  Wherever, in your sightless substances,
  You wait on nature's mischief. Come, thick night,
  And pall you in the dunnest smoke of hell,
  That my keen knife sees not the wound it makes,
  Nor heaven peeps through the blanket of the dark
  To cry, 'Hold, hold!'

Enter MACBETH

           Great Glamis, worthy Cawdor!
  Greater than both by the all-hail hereafter;
  Your letters have transported me beyond
  This ignorant present, and I feel now
  The future in the instant.
MACBETH   My dearest love,
  Duncan comes here tonight.
LADY M.   And when goes hence?
MACBETH
  Tomorrow, as he purposes.
LADY M.   O never
  Shall sun that morrow see!
  Your face, my thane, is as a book where men

May read strange matters. To beguile the time
Look like the time, bear welcome in your eye,
Your hand, your tongue; look like the innocent flower,
But be the serpent under it. He that's coming
Must be provided for; and you shall put
This night's great business into my dispatch,
Which shall to all our nights and days to come
Give solely sovereign sway and masterdom.

MACBETH
We will speak further.

LADY M.   Only look up clear:
To alter looks ever is to fear.
Leave all the rest to me.   *Exeunt*

SCENE VI
Before the Castle.

Hautboys and torches. Enter KING DUNCAN, MALCOLM,
DONALBAIN, BANQUO, LENNOX, MACDUFF, ROSS, ANGUS,
and Attendants

KING
This castle has a pleasant seat; the air
Nimbly and sweetly recommends itself
Unto our gentle senses.

BANQUO   This guest of summer,
The temple-haunting martlet, does approve
By his loved mansionry that the heaven's breath
Smells wooingly here; no jutty, frieze,
Buttress, nor coign of vantage, but this bird
Has made his pendent bed and procreant cradle;
Where they most breed and haunt I have observed
The air is delicate.

Enter LADY MACBETH

KING   See, see, our honoured hostess—
  The love that follows us sometime is our trouble,
  Which ever we thank as love. Herein I teach you
  How you shall bid 'God yield us' for your pains,
  And thank us for your trouble.
LADY M.   All our service
  In every point twice done and then done double
  Were poor and single business to contend
  Against those honours, deep and broad, wherewith
  Your majesty loads our house. For those of old,
  And the late dignities heaped up to them,
  We rest your hermits.
KING   Where's the Thane of Cawdor?
  We coursed him at the heels and had a purpose
  To be his purveyor; but he rides well,
  And his great love, sharp as his spur, has helped him
  To his home before us. Fair and noble hostess,
  We are your guest tonight.
LADY M.   Your servants ever
  Have theirs, themselves, and what is theirs, in count,
  To make their audit at your highness' pleasure,
  Ever to return your own.
KING   Give me your hand;
  Conduct me to my host. We love him highly,
  And shall continue our graces towards him.
  By your leave, hostess.   *He kisses her. Exeunt*

SCENE VII
A room in the castle.

*Hautboys. Torches. Enter a Sewer and divers Servants
with dishes and service over the stage. Then enter*
MACBETH

MACBETH

If it were done when 'tis done, then it were well
It were done quickly. If the assassination
Could gather up the consequence, and catch
With the event success—if only this blow
Might be the be-all and the end-all!—here,
But here, upon this bank and shoal of time,
We'd jump the life to come. But in these cases
We still have judgement here—that we but teach
Bloody instructions, which, being taught, return
To plague the inventor. This even-handed justice
Commends the ingredients of our poisoned chalice
To our own lips. He's here in double trust:
First, as I am his kinsman and his subject,
Strong both against the deed; then, as his host,
Who should against his murderer shut the door,
Not bear the knife myself. Besides, this Duncan
Has borne his faculties so meek, has been
So clear in his great office, that his virtues
Will plead like angels, trumpet-tongued against
The deep damnation of his taking-off.
And Pity, like a naked new-born babe
Striding the blast, or heaven's cherubin, horsed
Upon the sightless couriers of the air,
Shall blow the horrid deed in every eye,
That tears shall drown the wind. I have no spur
To prick the sides of my intent but only
Vaulting ambition, which overleaps itself
And falls on the other side.

Enter LADY MACBETH

                              How now? What news?

LADY M.

He has almost supped. Why have you left the chamber?

MACBETH
  Has he asked for me?
LADY M.   Know you not he has?
MACBETH
  We will proceed no further in this business.
  He has honoured me of late, and I have bought
  Golden opinions from all sorts of people,
  Which would be worn now in their newest gloss,
  Not cast aside so soon.
LADY M.   Was the hope drunk
  Wherein you dressed yourself? Has it slept since?
  And wakes it now to look so green and pale
  At what it did so freely? From this time
  Such I account your love. Are you afraid
  To be the same in your own act and valour
  As you are in desire? Would you have that
  Which you esteem the ornament of life,
  And live a coward in your own esteem,
  Letting 'I dare not' wait upon 'I would',
  Like the poor cat in the adage?
MACBETH   Pray you peace.
  I dare do all that may become a man;
  Who dares do more is none.
LADY M.   What beast was it then
  That made you break this enterprise to me?
  When you durst do it, then you were a man;
  And to be more than what you were, you would
  Be so much more the man. Nor time nor place
  Did then adhere, and yet you would make both.
  They have made themselves, and that their fitness now
  Does unmake you. I have given suck, and know
  How tender it is to love the babe that milks me;
  I would while it was smiling in my face
  Have plucked my nipple from his boneless gums
  And dashed the brains out, had I so sworn as you

Have done to this.

MACBETH   If we should fail?

LADY M.   We fail!
But screw your courage to the sticking place,
And we'll not fail. When Duncan is asleep—
Whereto the rather shall his day's hard journey
Soundly invite him—his two chamberlains
Will I with wine and wassail so overcome
That memory, the warder of the brain,
Shall be a-fume, and the receipt of reason
A retort only. When in swinish sleep
Their drenchèd natures lie as in a death,
What cannot you and I perform upon
The unguarded Duncan? What not put upon
His spongy officers, who shall bear the guilt
Of our great end?

MACBETH   Bring forth men-children only!
For your undaunted mettle should compose
Nothing but males. Will it not be received,
When we have marked with blood those sleepy two
Of his own chamber, and used their very daggers,
That they have done it?

LADY M.   Who dares receive it other,
As we shall make our griefs and clamour roar
Upon his death?

MACBETH   I am settled; and bend up
Each corporal agent to this terrible feat.
Away, and mock the time with fairest show:
False face must hide what the false heart does know.

                                          Exeunt

Act II

SCENE I
A court within the castle.

Enter BANQUO, *and* FLEANCE *with a torch before him*

BANQUO
How goes the night, boy?
FLEANCE
The moon is down; I have not heard the clock.
BANQUO
And it goes down at twelve.
FLEANCE   I take it 'tis later, sir.
BANQUO
Hold, take my sword. There's husbandry in heaven:
Their candles are all out. Take you that too.
A heavy summons lies like lead upon me.
And yet I would not sleep. Merciful powers,
Restrain in me the cursèd thoughts that nature
Gives way to in repose.

Enter MACBETH *and a Servant with a torch*

Give me my sword!
Who's there?
MACBETH
A friend.
BANQUO
What, sir, not yet at rest? The King's a-bed.
He has been in unusual pleasure,
And sent forth great largess to your office.

This diamond, he greets your wife with it
By the name of most kind hostess, and shut up
In measureless content.
MACBETH   Being unprepared
Our will became the servant to defect,
Which else should free have wrought.
BANQUO   All's well.
I dreamt last night of the three Weird Sisters.
To you they have showed some truth.
MACBETH   I think not of them.
Yet, when we can entreat an hour to serve,
We would spend it in some words upon that business,
If you would grant the time.
BANQUO   At your kindest leisure.
MACBETH
If you shall cleave to my consent when it is,
It shall make honour for you.
BANQUO   If I lose none
In seeking to augment it, but still keep
My bosom franchised and allegiance clear,
I shall be counselled.
MACBETH   Good repose the while.
BANQUO
Thanks, sir; the like to you.   *Exit Banquo and Fleance*
MACBETH
Go bid your mistress, when my drink is ready
She strike upon the bell. Get you to bed.
                                                        Exit Servant
Is this a dagger which I see before me,
The handle toward my hand? Come, let me clutch you—
I have you not and yet I see you still!
Are you not, fatal vision, sensible
To feeling as to sight? Or are you but
A dagger of the mind, a false creation,
Proceeding from the heat-oppressèd brain?

I see you yet, in form as palpable
As this which now I draw.
You marshall me the way that I was going,
And such an instrument I was to use.—
My eyes are made the fools of the other senses,
Or else worth all the rest.—I see you still;
And, on your blade and handle, gouts of blood,
Which was not so before. There's no such thing.
It is the bloody business which informs
Thus to my eyes. Now over the one half-world
Nature seems dead, and wicked dreams abuse
The curtained sleep. Witchcraft celebrates
Pale Hecat's offerings; and withered Murder,
Alarumed by his sentinel the wolf,
Whose howl is his watch, thus with his stealthy pace,
With Tarquin's ravishing strides, towards his design
Moves like a ghost. You sure and firm-set earth,
Hear not my steps, which way they walk, for fear
Your very stones prate of my whereabouts
And take the present horror from the time
Which now suits with it.—While I threat, he lives:
Words to the heat of deeds too cold breath gives.

A bell rings

I go, and it is done; the bell invites me.
Hear it not, Duncan, for it is a knell
That summons you to heaven or to hell.   *Exit*

SCENE II
The same.

Enter LADY MACBETH

LADY M.

  That which has made them drunk has made me bold;
  What has quenched them has given me fire.—Hark!—
    Peace!
  It was the owl that shrieked, the fatal bellman
  Which gives the sternest good-night. He is about it.
  The doors are open, and the surfeited grooms
  Do mock their charge with snores; I have drugged
    their drink
  That death and nature do contend about them
  Whether they live or die.

MACBETH   (*within*)   Who's there? What, ho!

LADY M.

  Alas, I am afraid they have awaked,
  And 'tis not done. The attempt and not the deed
  Confounds us.—Hark!—I laid their daggers ready;
  He could not miss them. Had he not resembled
  My father as he slept, I had done it.

Enter MACBETH, *carrying two bloodstained daggers*

                            My husband!

MACBETH

  I have done the deed. Did you not hear a noise?

LADY M.

  I heard the owl-scream and the cricket's cry.
  Did not you speak?

MACBETH   When?

LADY M.   Now.

MACBETH   As I descended?

MADY M.

  Ay.

MACBETH

  Hark!
  Who lies in the second chamber?

LADY M.   Donalbain.

MACBETH   *(looks at his hands)*

    This is a sorry sight.

LADY M.

    A foolish thought, to say a sorry sight.

MACBETH

    One did laugh in his sleep, and one cried 'Murder!'
    That they did wake each other. I stood and heard
    them.
    But they did say their prayers and addressed them
    Again to sleep.

LADY M.   There are two lodged together.

MACBETH

    One cried 'God bless us' and 'Amen' the other,
    As they had seen me with these hangman's hands.
    Listening to their fear I could not say 'Amen'
    When they did say 'God bless us.'

LADY M.

    Consider it not so deeply.

MACBETH

    But wherefore could not I pronounce 'Amen'?
    I had most need of blessing, and 'Amen'
    Stuck in my throat.

LADY M.   These deeds must not be thought
    After these ways; so, it will make us mad.

MACBETH

    I thought I heard a voice cry, 'Sleep no more!'
    Macbeth does murder sleep—the innocent sleep,
    Sleep that knits up the tangled skein of care,
    The death of each day's life, sore labour's bath,
    Balm of hurt minds, great nature's second course,
    Chief nourisher in life's feast.

LADY M.   What do you mean?

MACBETH

    Still it cried 'Sleep no more' to all the house;

'Glamis has murdered sleep, and therefore Cawdor
Shall sleep no more, Macbeth shall sleep no more.'
LADY M.
Who was it that thus cried? Why, worthy thane,
You do unbend your noble strength, to think
So brain-sickly of things. Go, get some water,
And wash this filthy witness from your hand.
Why did you bring these daggers from the place?
They must lie there. Go, carry them and smear
The sleepy grooms with blood.
MACBETH   I'll go no more.
I am afraid to think what I have done;
Look on it again I dare not.
LADY M.   Infirm of purpose!
Give me the daggers. The sleeping and the dead
Are but as pictures. It is the eye of childhood
That fears a painted devil. If he does bleed,
I'll gild the faces of the grooms with it,
For it must seem their guilt.   *Exit*

Knock within

MACBETH   Whence is that knocking?
How is it with me when every noise appals me?
What hands are here! Ha—they pluck out my eyes!
Will all great Neptune's ocean wash this blood
Clean from my hand? No, this my hand will rather
The multitudinous seas incarnadine,
Making the green one red.

Enter LADY MACBETH

LADY M.
My hands are of your colour; but I shame
To wear a heart so white.

Knock

               I hear a knocking
At the south entry. Retire we to our chamber.
A little water clears us of this deed;
How easy is it then! Your constancy
Has left you unattended.

Knock

               Hark! more knocking.
Get on your nightgown, lest occasion calls us
And shows us to be watchers. Be not lost
So poorly in your thoughts.
MACBETH
To know my deed it were best not know myself.

Knock

Wake Duncan with your knocking! I would you could!
                            Exeunt

SCENE III
The same.

Enter a Porter. Knocking within

PORTER   Here's a knocking indeed! If a man was porter of
hell-gate he should have his fill of turning the key.

Knock

Knock, knock, knock! Who's there in the name of
Belzebub? Here's a farmer that hanged himself on the

expectation of plenty. Come in time! Have napkins
enough about you; here you'll sweat for it.

Knock

Knock, knock! Who's there in the other devils's name?
Faith, here's an equivocator that could swear in both the
scales against either scale, who committed treason
enough for God's sake, yet could not equivocate to
heaven. O, come in, equivocator.

Knock

Knock, knock, knock! Who's there? Faith, here's an English tailor come hither for stealing out of a tight French
hose. Come in, tailor; here you may roast your goose.

Knock

Knock, knock! Never at quiet! What are you?—But this
place is too cold for hell. I'll devil-porter it no further. I
had thought to have let in some of all professions that go
the primrose way to the everlasting bonfire.

Knock

Anon, anon! I pray you remember the porter.

He opens the gate. Enter MACDUFF *and* LENNOX

MACDUFF
    Was it so late, friend, ere you went to bed,
    That you do lie so late?
PORTER   Faith, sir, we were carousing till the second cock;
and drink, sir, is a great provoker of three things.

MACDUFF What three things does drink especially
provoke?

PORTER Sure, sir, nose-painting, sleep, and urine. Lechery, sir, it provokes and unprovokes: it provokes the desire
but it takes away the performance. Therefore much
drink may be said to be an equivocator with lechery. It
makes him and it mars him; it sets him on and it takes
him off; it persuades him and disheartens him, makes
him stand to and not stand to; in conclusion, equivocates
him in a sleep and giving him the lie, leaves him.

MACDUFF I believe drink gave you the lie last night.

PORTER That it did, sir, in the very throat on me. But I re-
quited him for his lie and, I think, being too strong for
him, though he took up my legs sometime, yet I made a
shift to cast him.

MACDUFF Is your master stirring?

Enter MACBETH

Our knocking has awaked him; here he comes.

LENNOX
Good morrow, noble sir.

MACBETH   Good morrow both.

MACDUFF
Is the King stirring, worthy thane?

MACBETH   Not yet.

MACDUFF
He did command me to call timely on him.
I have almost slipped the hour.

MACBETH   I'll bring you to him.

MACDUFF
I know this is a joyful trouble to you,
But yet 'tis one.

MACBETH

The labour we delight in physics pain.

This is the door.

MACDUFF   I'll make so bold to call,

For it is my limited service.   *Exit*

LENNOX

Goes the King hence today?

MACBETH   He does; he did appoint so.

LENNOX

The night has been unruly. Where we lay,

Our chimneys were blown down and, as they say,

Lamentings heard in the air, strange screams of death,

And prophesying, with accents terrible,

Of dire combustion and confused events

New-hatched to the woeful time. The obscure bird

Clamoured the live-long night. Some say the earth

Was feverish and did shake.

MACBETH   It was a rough night.

LENNOX

My young remembrance cannot parallel

A fellow to it.

Enter MACDUFF

MACDUFF   O horror, horror, horror!

No tongue or heart can conceive or name you!

MACBETH *and* LENNOX

What's the matter?

MACDUFF

Confusion now has made its masterpiece;

Most sacrilegious murder has broken open

The Lord's anointed temple and stolen thence

The life of the building.

MACBETH   What is it you say? The life?

LENNOX

  Mean you his majesty?

MACDUFF

  Approach the chamber and destroy your sight
  With a new Gorgon. Do not bid me speak.
  See, and then speak yourselves.

                              Exeunt Macbeth and Lennox
                                    Awake, awake!
  Ring the alarum bell! Murder and treason!
  Banquo and Donalbain, Malcolm, awake!
  Shake off this downy sleep, death's counterfeit,
  And look on death itself! Up, up, and see
  The Great Doom's image! Malcolm, Banquo,
  As from your graves rise up and walk like sprites
  To countenance this horror. Ring the bell!

                          Bell rings
                    Enter LADY MACBETH

LADY M.

  What's the business,
  That such a hideous trumpet calls to parley
  The sleepers of the house? Speak, speak!

MACDUFF   O gentle lady,

  It is not for you to hear what I can speak.
  The repetition in a woman's ear
  Would murder as it fell.

                    Enter BANQUO

                          O Banquo, Banquo!
  Our royal master's murdered.

LADY M.   Woe, alas!

  What, in our house!

BANQUO   Too cruel, anywhere.

Dear Duff, I pray you contradict yourself
And say it is not so.

Enter MACBETH, LENNOX, *and* ROSS

MACBETH
Had I but died an hour before this chance
I had lived a blessèd time; for from this instant
There is nothing serious in mortality.
All is but toys, renown and grace are dead,
The wine of life is drawn, and the mere lees
Is left this vault to brag of.

Enter MALCOLM *and* DONALBAIN

DONALBAIN
What is amiss?
MACBETH   You are, and do not know it.
The spring, the head, the fountain of your blood
Is stopped, the very source of it is stopped.
MACDUFF
Your royal father's murdered.
MALCOLM   O, by whom?
LENNOX
Those of his chamber, as it seemed, had done it:
Their hands and faces were all marked with blood,
So were their daggers which, unwiped, we found
Upon their pillows. They stared and were distracted;
No man's life was to be trusted with them.
MACBETH
O yet I do repent me of my fury,
That I did kill them.
MACDUFF   Wherefore did you so?
MACBETH
Who can be wise, amazed, temperate and furious,

Loyal and neutral, in a moment? No man.
The expedition of my violent love
Outran the pauser reason. Here lay Duncan,
His silver skin laced with his golden blood,
And his gashed stabs looked like a breach in nature
For ruin's wasteful entrance. There the murderers,
Steeped in the colours of their trade, their daggers
Unmannerly breeched with gore. Who could refrain,
That had a heart to love, and in that heart
Courage to make his love known?
LADY   (*swooning*)   Help me hence, ho!
MACDUFF
Look to the lady!
MALCOLM   (*to Donalbain*) Why do we hold our tongues,
    That most may claim this argument for ours?
DONALBAIN   (*to Malcolm*)
    What should be spoken here where our fate,
    Hid in rat-hole, now may rush and seize us?
    Let's away. Our tears are not yet brewed.
MALCOLM   (*to Donalbain*)
    Nor our strong sorrow upon the foot of motion.
BANQUO
Look to the lady!

               Lady Macbeth *is taken out*

And when we have our naked frailties hid
That suffer in exposure, let us meet
And question this most bloody piece of work,
To know it further. Fears and scruples shake us.
In the great hand of God I stand, and thence
Against the undivulged pretence I fight
Of treasonous malice.
MACDUFF   And so do I.
ALL   So all.

MACBETH

    Let's briefly put on manly readiness,

    And meet in the hall together.

ALL   Well contented.

                Exeunt all but Malcolm and Donalbain

MALCOLM

    What will you do? Let's not consort with them.

    To show an unfelt sorrow is an office

    Which the false man does easy. I'll to England.

DONALBAIN

    To Ireland, I. Our separated fortune

    Shall keep us both the safer. Where we are

    There's daggers in men's smiles. The nearer in blood

    The nearer bloody.

MALCOLM   This murderous shaft that's shot

    Has not yet lighted; and our safest way

    Is to avoid the aim. Therefore to horse,

    And let us not be dainty of leave-taking

    But shift away. There's warrant in that theft

    Which steals itself when there's no mercy left. *Exeunt*

SCENE IV

Outside the Castle.

Enter ROSS *with an Old Man*

OLD MAN

    Threescore and ten I can remember well;

    Within the volume of which time I have seen

    Hours dreadful and things strange; but this sore night

    Has trifled former knowings.

ROSS   Ha, good father,

    You see the heavens, as troubled with man's act,

    Threaten his bloody stage. By the clock 'tis day,

And yet dark night strangles the travelling lamp;
Is it night's predominance or the day's shame
That darkness does the face of earth entomb
When living light should kiss it?
OLD MAN   It is unnatural,
Even like the deed that's done. On Tuesday last,
A falcon towering in her pride of place
Was by a mousing owl hawked at and killed.
ROSS
And Duncan's horses—a thing most strange and
    certain—
Beauteous and swift, the minions of their race,
Turned wild in nature, broke their stalls, flung out,
Contending against obedience, as they would
Make war with mankind.
OLD MAN   'Tis said they ate each other.
ROSS
They did so, to the amazement of my eyes
That looked upon it.

Enter MACDUFF

                              Here comes the good Macduff.
How goes the world, sir, now?
MACDUFF   Why, see you not?
ROSS
Is it known who did this more than bloody deed?
MACDUFF
Those that Macbeth has slain.
ROSS   Alas the day!
What good could they pretend?
MACDUFF   They were suborned.
Malcolm and Donalbain, the King's two sons,
Are stolen away and fled, which puts upon them
Suspicion of the deed.

ROSS   Against nature ever!
  Thriftless ambition that will raven up
  Your own life's means!—Then it is most like
  The sovereignty will fall upon Macbeth?

MACDUFF
  He is already named and gone to Scone
  To be invested.

ROSS   Where is Duncan's body?

MACDUFF
  Carried to Colmekill,
  The sacred storehouse of his predecessors
  And guardian of their bones.

ROSS   Will you to Scone?

MACDUFF
  No, cousin, I'll to Fife.

ROSS   Well, I will thither.

MACDUFF
  Well, may you see things well done there—Adieu!—
  Lest our old robes sit easier than our new.

ROSS
  Farewell, father.

OLD MAN
  God's benison go with you, and with those
  That would make good of bad, and friends of foes!

Exeunt

Act III

SCENE I

A room in the palace.

Enter BANQUO

BANQUO
    You have it now: King, Cawdor, Glamis, all
    As the weird women promised; and I fear
    You played most foully for it. Yet it was said
    It should not stand in your posterity,
    But that myself should be the root and father
    Of many kings. If there comes truth from them,
    As upon you, Macbeth, their speeches shine,
    Why by the verities on you made good
    May they not be my oracles as well
    And set me up in hope? But hush! No more.

Sennet sounded. Enter MACBETH *as King,*
LADY MACBETH, LENNOX, ROSS, LORDS *and Attendants*

MACBETH
    Here is our chief guest.
LADY M.   If he had been forgotten
    It had been as a gap in our great feast
    And all-things unbecoming.
MACBETH
    Tonight we hold a solemn supper, sir,
    And I'll request your presence.
BANQUO   Let your highness
    Command upon me, to which my duties

Are with a most indissoluble tie
Forever knit.

MACBETH

Ride you this afternoon?

BANQUO   Ay, my good lord.

MACBETH

We should have else desired your good advice,
Which ever has been both grave and prosperous,
In this day's council; but we'll take tomorrow.
Is it far you ride?

BANQUO

As far, my lord, as will fill up the time
Between this and supper. Go not my horse the better,
I must become a borrower of the night
For a dark hour or twain.

MACBETH   Fail not our feast.

BANQUO

My lord, I will not.

MACBETH

We hear our bloody cousins are bestowed
In England and in Ireland, not confessing
Their cruel parricide, filling their hearers
With strange invention. But of that tomorrow,
When therewith we shall have cause of state
Craving us jointly. Hie you to horse. Adieu
Till you return at night. Goes Fleance with you?

BANQUO

Ay, my good lord; our time does call upon us.

MACBETH

I wish your horses swift and sure of foot;
And so I do commend you to their backs.
Farewell.   *Exit Banquo*
Let every man be master of his time
Till seven at night.
To make society the sweeter welcome,

We will keep ourself till supper-time alone.
While then, God be with you!

Exeunt Lords and Lady Macbeth
Fellow!
A word with you. Attend those men our pleasure?
SERVANT
They are, my lord, without the palace gate.
MACBETH
Bring them before us.   *Exit Servant*
To be thus is nothing;
But to be safely thus! — Our fears in Banquo
Stick deep; and in his royalty of nature
Reigns that which would be feared. 'Tis much he
    dares,
And to that dauntless temper of his mind
He has a wisdom that does guide his valour
To act in safety. There is none but he
Whose being I do fear; and under him
My genius is rebuked as, it is said,
Mark Antony's was by Caesar. He chid the sisters
When first they put the name of king upon me,
And bade them speak to him. Then, prophet-like,
They hailed him father to a line of kings.
Upon my head they placed a fruitless crown
And put a barren sceptre in my grip,
Thence to be wrenched with an unlineal hand,
No son of mine succeeding. If it be so,
For Banquo's issue have I defiled my mind,
For them the gracious Duncan have I murdered,
Put rancours in the vessel of my peace,
Only for them; and my eternal jewel
Given to be common enemy of man,
To make them kings, the seed of Banquo kings!
Rather than so, come fate into the list
And champion me to the utterance! Who's there?

Enter Servant and two Murderers

Now go to the door, and stay there till we call.
                                    Exit Servant
Was it not yesterday we spoke together?
MURDERERS
   It was, so please your highness.
MACBETH   Well then now,
   Have you considered of my speeches? Know
    That it was he in the times past who held you
   So under fortune, which you thought had been
   Our innocent self. This I made good to you
   In our last conference; passed in probation with you
   How you were deceived, how crossed, the in-
        struments,
   Who wrought with them, and all things else that
        might
   To half a soul and to a notion crazed
   Say, 'Thus did Banquo.'
FIRST MURDERER   You made it known to us.
MACBETH
   I did so; and went further, which is now
   Our point of second meeting. Do you find
   Your patience so predominant in your nature
   That you can let this go? Are you so gospelled,
   To pray for this good man and for his issue,
   Whose heavy hand has bowed you to the grave,
   And beggared yours for ever?
FIRST MURDERER   We are men, my liege.
MACBETH
   Ay, in the catalogue you go for men,
   As hounds and greyhounds, mongrels, spaniels, curs,
   Sheepdogs, water-dogs, half-wolves are called
   All by the name of dogs. The valued file
   Distinguishes the swift, the slow, the subtle,

The house-keeper, the hunter, every one
According to the gift which bounteous nature
Has in him closed. Whereby he does receive
Particular addition from the bill
That writes them all alike. And so of men.
Now, if you have a station in the file,
Not in the worst rank of manhood, say it,
And I will put that business in your bosoms,
Whose execution takes your enemy off,
Grapples you to the heart and love of us;
Who wear our health but sickly in his life,
Which in his death were perfect.

SECOND MURDERER   I am one, my liege,
Whom the vile blows and buffets of the world
Have so incensed that I am reckless what I do
To spite the world.

FIRST MURDERER   And I another,
So weary with disasters, tugged with fortune,
That I would set my life on any chance
To mend it or be rid of it.

MACBETH   Both of you
Know Banquo was your enemy.

MURDERERS   True, my lord.

MACBETH
So is he mine, and in such bloody distance
That every minute of his being thrusts
Against my nearest of life; and though I could
With bare-faced power sweep him from my sight
And bid my will affirm it, yet I must not.
For certain friends that are both his and mine,
Whose loves I may not drop, but wail his fall
Whom I myself struck down. And thence it is
That I to your assistance do make love,
Masking the business from the common eye
For sundry weighty reasons.

SECOND MURDERER   We shall, my lord,
    Perform what you command us.
FIRST MURDERER   Through our lives —
MACBETH
    Your spirits shine through you. Within this hour, at
        most,
    I will advise you where to plant yourselves,
    Acquaint you with the perfect spy of the time,
    The moment too. For it must be done tonight;
    And somewhat from the palace; understand
    That I require a clearance. And with him,
    To leave no rubs nor botches in the work,
    Fleance his son, that keeps him company —
    Whose absence is no less material to me
    Than is his father's—must embrace the fate
    Of that dark hour. Resolve yourselves apart;
    I'll come to you anon.
MURDERERS   We are resolved, my lord.
MACBETH
    I'll call upon you straight. Abide within.

Exeunt Murderers
    It is concluded! Banquo, your soul's flight,
    If it finds heaven, must find it out tonight.   *Exit*

SCENE II
Another room in the palace.

Enter Macbeth's Lady and a Servant

LADY M.
    Is Banquo gone from court?
SERVANT
    Ay, madam, but returns again tonight.

LADY M.
  Say to the King I would attend his leisure
  For a few words.
SERVANT   Madam, I will.   *Exit*
LADY M.   Naught's had, all's spent,
  Where our desire is not without content.
  'Tis safer to be that which we destroy
  Than by destruction dwell in doubtful joy.

                        Enter MACBETH

  How now, my lord? Why do you keep alone,
  Of sorriest fancies your companions making,
  Using those thoughts which should indeed have died
  With them they think on? Things without all remedy
  Should be without regard; what's done is done.
MACBETH
  We have scotched the snake, not killed it;
  She'll close and be herself, while our poor malice
  Remains in danger of her former tooth.
  But let the frame of things disjoint, both the worlds
      suffer
  Ere we will eat our meal in fear, and sleep
  In the affliction of these terrible dreams
  That shake us nightly. Better be with the dead
  Whom we, to gain our peace, have sent to peace,
  Than in the torture of the mind to lie
  In restless madness. Duncan is in his grave;
  After life's fitful fever he sleeps well;
  Treason has done its worst. Nor steel, nor poison,
  Malice domestic, foreign levy, nothing
  Can touch him further.
LADY M.   Come on,
  Gentle my lord, sleek over your rugged looks,
  Be bright and jovial among your guests tonight.

MACBETH

So shall I, love; and so I pray be you.
Let your remembrance apply to Banquo,
Present him eminence both with eye and tongue.
Unsafe the while that we
Must lave our honours in these flattering streams,
And make our faces mask-like to our hearts,
Disguising what they are.

LADY M.   You must leave this.

MACBETH

O, full of scorpions is my mind, dear wife!
You know that Banquo and his Fleance live.

LADY M.

But in them nature's copy is not eternal.

MACBETH

There's comfort yet! They are assailable.
Then be you jovial. Ere the bat has flown
His cloistered flight, ere to black Hecat's summons
The wingèd beetle, with its drowsy hums,
Has rung night's yawning peal, there shall be done
A deed of dreadful note.

LADY M.   What is to be done?

MACBETH

Be innocent of the knowledge, dearest chuck,
Till you applaud the deed. Come, darkling night.
Scarf up the tender eye of pitiful day,
And with your bloody and invisible hand
Cancel and tear to pieces that great bond
Which keeps me pale. Light thickens
And the crow makes wing to the rooky wood;
Good things of day begin to droop and drowse,
While night's black agents to their preys do rouse.
You marvel at my words; but hold you still.
Things bad begun make strong themselves by ill.
So, pray you, go with me.   *Exeunt*

SCENE III

A road beyond the palace.

Enter three Murderers

FIRST MURDERER
  But who did bid you join with us?
THIRD MURDERER   Macbeth.
SECOND MURDERER
  He needs not our mistrust, since he delivers
  Our offices and what we have to do
  To the direction just.
FIRST MURDERER   Then stand with us;
  The west yet glimmers with some streaks of day.
  Now spurs the lated traveller apace
  To gain the timely inn; and near approaches
  The subject of our watch.
THIRD MURDERER   Hark, I hear horses!
BANQUO *[within]*
  Give us a light there, ho!
SECOND MURDERER   Then 'tis he.
  The rest that are within the note of expectation,
  Already are in the court.
FIRST MURDERER   His horses go about.
THIRD MURDERER
  Almost a mile; but he does usually,
  So all men do, from hence to the palace gate
  Make it their walk.

Enter BANQUO *and* FLEANCE, *with a torch*

SECOND MURDERER
  A light, a light!
THIRD MURDERER
            'Tis he.

FIRST MURDERER   Stand to it!
BANQUO
   It will be rain tonight.
FIRST MURDERER   Let it come down!

They attack BANQUO

BANQUO
   O treachery! Fly, good Fleance, fly, fly, fly!
   You may revenge—O slave!

BANQUO *falls.* FLEANCE *escapes*

THIRD MURDERER
   Who did strike out the light?
FIRST MURDERER   Was it not the way?
THIRD MURDERER
   There's but one down; the son is fled.
SECOND MURDERER   We have lost
   Best half of our affair.
FIRST MURDERER
   Well, let's away and say how much is done.   *Exeunt*

SCENE IV
A room of state in the palace.

Banquet prepared. Enter MACBETH, LADY MACBETH,
ROSS, LENNOX, LORDS, *and Attendants*

MACBETH
   You know your own degrees, sit down. At first
   And last, the hearty welcome.
LORDS   Thanks to your majesty.

MACBETH

    Ourself will mingle with society
    And play the humble host.

He walks around the tables

    Our hostess keeps her state; but in best time
    We will require her welcome.

LADY M.

    Pronounce it for me, sir, to all our friends,
    For my heart speaks they are welcome.

Enter First Murderer

MACBETH

    See, they encounter you with their hearts' thanks;
    Both sides are even. Here I'll sit in the midst.
    Be large in mirth. Anon we'll drink a measure
    The table round.

He rises and goes to the Murderer

    There's blood upon your face!

FIRST MURDERER

                  'Tis Banquo's then.

MACBETH

    'Tis better you without than he within.
    Is he dispatched?

FIRST MURDERER   My lord, his throat is cut;
    That I did for him.

MACBETH   You are the best of the cut-throats.
    Yet he's good that did the like for Fleance.
    If you did it, you are the nonpareil.

FIRST MURDERER

    Most royal sir—Fleance has escaped.

MACBETH

Then comes my fit again. I had else been perfect,
Whole as the marble, founded as the rock,
As broad and general as the casing air.
But now I am cabined, cribbed, confined, bound in
To saucy doubts and fears.—But Banquo's safe?

FIRST MURDERER

Ay, my good lord; safe in a ditch he bides,
With twenty trenchèd gashes on his head,
The least a death to nature.

MACBETH   Thanks for that.
There the grown serpent lies. The worm that's fled
Has nature that in time will venom breed,
No teeth for the present. Get you gone. Tomorrow
We'll hear ourselves again.   *Exit Murderer*

LADY M.   My royal lord,
You do not give the cheer. The feast is sold
That is not oft confirmed; while 'tis a-making,
'Tis given with welcome. To feed were best at home;
From thence, the sauce to meat is ceremony;
Meeting were bare without it.

MACBETH   Sweet remembrancer!
Now good digestion wait on appetite,
And health on both!

LENNOX   May it please your highness sit.

*Enter the Ghost of Banquo and
sits in Macbeth's place*

MACBETH

Here had we now our country's honour roofed,
Were the graced person of our Banquo present;
Whom may I rather challenge for unkindness
Than pity for mischance.

ROSS   His absence, sir,

Lays blame upon his promise, Please it your highness
To grace us with your royal company?

MACBETH

The table's full.

LENNOX   Here is a place reserved, sir.

MACBETH

Where?

LENNOX

Here, my good lord. What is it that moves your
    highness?

MACBETH

Which of you have done this?

LORDS   What, my good lord?

MACBETH

You can not say I did it; never shake
Your gory locks at me.

ROSS

Gentlemen, rise. His highness is not well.

LADY M.   *[descends from her throne]*
Sit, worthy friends. My lord is often thus;
And has been from his youth. Pray you keep seat.
The fit is momentary; upon a thought
He will again be well. If much you note him,
You shall offend him and extend his passion.
Feed, and regard him not.—Are you a man?

MACBETH

Ay, and a bold one, that dare look on that
Which might appal the devil.

LADY M.   O proper stuff!
This is the very painting of your fear.
This is the air-drawn dagger which you said
Led you to Duncan. O, these gusts and starts,
Impostors to true fear, would well become
A woman's story at a winter's fire,
Authorized by her grandam. Shame itself!

Why do you make such faces? When all is done
You look but on a stool.
MACBETH   Pray you, see there!
Behold! Look! Lo! — How say you?
Why, what care I if you can nod! Speak, too!
If charnel-houses and our graves must send
Those that we bury, back, our monuments
Shall be the maws of kites.   *Exit Ghost*
LADY M.   What, quite unmanned in folly?
MACBETH
If I stand here, I saw him.
LADY M.   Fie, for shame!
MACBETH
Blood has been shed ere now, in the olden time,
Ere humane statute purged the gentle weal;
Ay, and since too, murders have been performed
Too terrible for the ear. The time has been
That, when the brains were out, the man would die,
And there an end. But now they rise again
With twenty mortal murders on their crowns,
And push us from our stools. This is more strange
Than such a murder is.
LADY M.   My worthy lord,
Your noble friends do lack you.
MACBETH   I do forget.
Do not muse at me, my most worthy friends:
I have a strange infirmity, which is nothing
To those that know me. Come, love and health to all!
Then I'll sit down. Give me some wine; fill full!

Enter Ghost

I drink to the general joy of the whole table,
And to our dear friend Banquo, whom we miss.
Would he were here! To all—and him—we thirst,

And all to all.

LORDS   Our duties and the pledge!

MACBETH   *[sees the Ghost]*

Away, and quit my sight! Let the earth hide you!
Your bones are marrowless, your blood is cold.
You have no certain knowledge in those eyes
Which you do glare with.

LADY M.   Think of this, good peers,
But as a thing of custom; 'tis no other;
Only it spoils the pleasure of the time.

MACBETH

What man dares, I dare.
Approach you like the rugged Russian bear,
The armed rhinoceros, or the Persian tiger,
Take any shape but that, and my firm nerves
Shall never tremble. Or be alive again,
And dare me to the desert with your sword:
If trembling I inhabit then, protest me
The baby of a girl. Hence, horrible shadow!
Unreal mockery, hence!   *Exit Ghost*
                          Why, so; being gone,
I am a man again. — Pray you sit still.

LADY M.

You have displaced the mirth, broke the good meeting
With most strange disorder.

MACBETH   Can such things be,
And overcome us like a summer's cloud,
Without our special wonder? You make me strange
Even to the disposition that I own,
When now I think you can behold such sights
And kept the natural ruby of your cheeks,
When mine is blanched with fear.

ROSS   What sights, my lord?

LADY M.

I pray you speak not; he grows worse and worse.

Question enrages him. At once, good night.
Stand not upon the order of your going;
But go at once.

LENNOX   Good night; and better health
Attend his majesty!

LADY M.   A kind good-night to all!   *Exeunt Lords*

MACBETH
It will have blood, they say; blood will have blood.
Stones have been known to move and trees to speak;
Augurs and understood relations have
By magpies, and choughs, and rooks brought forth
The secretest man of blood. What is the night?

LADY M.
Almost at odds with morning which is which.

MACBETH
How say you, that Macduff denies his person
At our great bidding?

LADY M.   Did you send to him, sir?

MACBETH
I hear it by the way. But I will send.
There's not a one of them, but in his house
I keep a servant fee'd. I will tomorrow—
And betimes I will—to the Weird Sisters.
More shall they speak; for now I am bent to know
By the worst means the worst. For my own good
All causes shall give way. I am in blood
Stepped in so far that, should I wade no more,
Returning were as tedious as go o'er.
Strange things I have in head, that will to hand;
Which must be acted ere they may be scanned.

LADY M.
You lack the season of all natures, sleep.

MACBETH
Come, we'll to sleep. My strange and self-abuse
Is the initiate fear that wants hard use.

We are yet but young in deed.   *Exeunt*

SCENE V
A heath.

Thunder. Enter the three Witches, meeting HECAT

FIRST WITCH
Why, how now, Hecat? You look angrily.
HECAT
    Have I not reason, beldames, as you are
    Saucy and over-bold? How did you dare
    To trade and traffic with Macbeth
    In riddles and affairs of death,
    And I, the mistress of your charms,
    The close contriver of all harms,
    Was never called to bear my part,
    Or show the glory of our art?
    And, which is worse, all you have done
    Has been but for a wayward son,
    Spiteful and wrathful, who, as others do,
    Loves for his own ends, not for you.
    But make amends now: get you gone,
    And at the pit of Acheron
    Meet me in the morning. Thither he
    Will come, to know his destiny.
    Your vessels and your spells provide,
    Your charms and everything beside.
    I am for the air; this night I'll spend
    Unto a dismal and a fatal end.
    Great business must be wrought ere noon.
    Upon the corner of the moon
    There hangs a vaporous drop profound;
    I'll catch it ere it comes to ground;

And that distilled by magic sleights
Shall raise such artificial sprites
As by the strength of their illusion
Shall draw him on to his confusion.
He shall spurn fate, scorn death, and bear
His hopes above wisdom, grace, and fear.
And you know false security
Is mortals' chiefest enemy.

Music and a song

Hark! I am called. My little spirit, see,
Sits in a foggy cloud and stays for me.

Song within: 'Come away, come away,' etc.

FIRST WITCH
Come, let's make haste; she'll soon be back again.

Exeunt

SCENE VI
A room in the palace.

Enter LENNOX *and another Lord*

LENNOX
My former speeches have but hit your thoughts,
Which can interpret further. Only I say,
Things have been strangely borne. The gracious
    Duncan
Was pitied of Macbeth: yet, he was dead!
And the right valiant Banquo walked too late;
Whom you may say, if it please you, Fleance killed,
For Fleance fled. Men must not walk too late.

Who cannot want the thought how monstrous
It was for Malcolm and for Donalbain
To kill their gracious father? Damnèd fact,
How it did grieve Macbeth! Did he not straight—
In pious rage—the two delinquents tear,
That were the slaves of drink, and thralls of sleep?
Was not that nobly done? Ay, and wisely too;
For it would have angered any heart alive
To hear the men deny it. So that I say
He has borne all things well; and I do think
That had he Duncan's sons under his key—
As, if it please heaven, he shall not—they should find
What 'twere to kill a father—so should Fleance.
But, peace! For from broad words, because he failed
His presence at the tyrant's feast, I hear
Macduff lives in disgrace. Sir, can you tell
Where he bestows himself?

LORD   The son of Duncan,
From whom this tyrant holds the due of birth,
Lives in the English court, and is received
Of the most pious Edward with such grace
That the malevolence of fortune nothing
Takes from his high respect. Thither Macduff
Is gone to pray the holy king, upon his aid,
To wake Northumberland and warlike Siward,
That by the help of these—with Him above
To ratify the work—we may again
Give to our tables meat, sleep to our nights,
Free from our feasts and banquets bloody knives,
Do faithful homage and receive free honours—
All which we pine for now. And this report
Has so exasperated the King that he
Prepares for some attempt of war.

LENNOX   Sent he to Macduff?

LORD
  He did. And with an absolute 'Sir, not I!'
  The cloudy messenger turns his back
  And hums, as who should say 'You'll rue the time
  That clogs me with this answer.'
LENNOX   And that well might
  Advise him to a caution to hold what distance
  His wisdom can provide. Some holy angel
  Fly to the court of England and unfold
  His message ere he comes, that a swift blessing
  May soon return to this our suffering country,
  Under a hand accursed!
LORD   I'll send my prayers with him.

                                      Exeunt

Act IV

SCENE I
A cavern with a boiling cauldron.

Thunder. Enter the three Witches

FIRST WITCH
　　Thrice the brindled cat has mewed.
SECOND WITCH
　　　Thrice, and once the hedgehog whined.
THIRD WITCH
　　Harpier cries! 'Tis time, 'tis time!
FIRST WITCH
　　Round about the cauldron go;
　　In the poisoned entrails throw:
　　Toad that under cold stone
　　Days and nights has thirty-one
　　Sweltered venom sleeping got,
　　Boil you first in the charmèd pot.
ALL
　　Double, double, toil and trouble;
　　Fire burn, and cauldron bubble.
SECOND WITCH
　　Fillet of a fenny snake
　　In the cauldron boil and bake;
　　Eye of newt, and toe of frog,
　　Wool of bat, and tongue of dog,
　　Adder's fork, and blind-worm's sting,
　　Lizard's leg and owlet's wing,
　　For a charm of powerful trouble,
　　Like a hell-broth, boil and bubble.

ALL

> Double, double, toil and trouble;
> Fire burn, and cauldron bubble.

THIRD WITCH

> Scale of dragon, tooth of wolf,
> Witch's mummy, maw and gulf
> Of the ravenous sea shark,
> Root of hemlock digged in the dark,
> Liver of blaspheming Jew,
> Gall of goat, and slips of yew
> Slivered in the moon's eclipse,
> Nose of Turk, and Tartar's lips,
> Finger of birth-strangled babe,
> Ditch-delivered by a drab,
> Make the gruel thick and slab.
> Add thereto a tiger's chaudron [entrails]
> For the ingredients of our cauldron.

ALL

> Double, double, toil and trouble;
> Fire burn, and cauldron bubble.

SECOND WITCH

> Cool it with a baboon's blood;
> Then the charm is firm and good

Enter HECAT *and the other three Witches*

HECAT

> O well done! I commend your pains;
> And everyone shall share in the gains.
> And now about the cauldron sing
> Like elves and fairies in a ring,
> Enchanting all that you put in.

Music and a song: 'Black spirits' etc.

Exeunt Hecat and the other three Witches

SECOND WITCH
>   By the pricking of my thumbs,
>   Something wicked this way comes.
>   Open, locks, whoever knocks!

Enter MACBETH

MACBETH
>   How now, you secret, black, and midnight hags!
>   What is it you do?

ALL   A deed without a name.

MACBETH
>   I conjure you, by that which you profess,
>   However you come to know it, answer me—
>   Though you untie the winds and let them fight
>   Against the churches; though the yeasty waves
>   Confound and swallow navigation up;
>   Though bladed corn be lodged and trees blown down;
>   Though castles topple on their warders' heads;
>   Though palaces and pyramids do slope
>   Their heads to their foundations; though the treasure
>   Of nature's seedings tumble all together
>   Even till destruction sickens—answer me
>   To what I ask you.

FIRST WITCH   Speak.

SECOND WITCH   Demand.

THIRD WITCH   We'll answer.

FIRST WITCH
>   Say if you'd rather hear it from our mouths
>   Or from our masters.

MACBETH   Call them. Let me see them.

FIRST WITCH
>   Pour in sow's blood that has eaten
>   Her nine farrow; grease that's sweaten
>   From the murderer's gibbet, throw

Into the flame.
ALL   Come high or low,
Yourself and office deftly show.

Thunder. First Apparition, an Armed Head

MACBETH
Tell me, you unknown power—
FIRST WITCH   He knows your thought.
Hear his speech, but say you naught.
FIRST APPARITION
Macbeth, Macbeth, Macbeth, beware Macduff!
Beware the Thane of Fife! Dismiss me. Enough.
He descends

MACBETH
Whatever you are, for your good caution, thanks;
You have guessed my fear aright. But one word more—
FIRST WITCH
He will not be commanded.Here's another
More potent than the first.

Thunder. Second Apparition, a Bloody Child

SECOND APPARITION
Macbeth, Macbeth, Macbeth!
MACBETH
Had I three ears, I would hear you.
SECOND APPARITION
Be bloody, bold, and resolute; laugh to scorn
The power of man; for none of woman born
Shall harm Macbeth.   *He descends*
MACBETH
Then live Macduff; what need I fear of you?
But yet I'll make assurance double sure,
And take a bond of fate. You shall not live;

That I may tell pale-hearted fear it lies,
And sleep in spite of thunder.

*Thunder. Third Apparition, a Child crowned, with a
tree in his hand*

                         What is this
That rises like the issue of a king,
And wears upon his baby brow the round
And top of sovereignty?
ALL   Listen, but speak not to it.
THIRD APPARITION
Be lion-mettled, proud, and take no care
Who chafes, who frets, or where conspirers are;
Macbeth shall never vanquished be, until
Great Birnam Wood to high Dunsinane Hill
Shall come against him.   *He descends*
MACBETH   That will never be.
Who can impress the forest, bid the tree
Unfix his earth-bound root? Sweet bodings! Good!
Rebellious dead rise never till the wood
Of Birnam rise, and our high-placed Macbeth
Shall live the lease of nature, pay his breath
To time and mortal custom. Yet my heart
Throbs to know one thing: tell me, if your art
Can tell so much, shall Banquo's issue ever
Reign in this kingdom?
ALL   Seek to know no more.
MACBETH
I will be satisfied! Deny me this
And an eternal curse fall on you! Let me know.
Why sinks that cauldron?

Hautboys

              And what noise is this?

FIRST WITCH
  Show!
SECOND WITCH
  Show!
THIRD WITCH
  Show!
ALL
        Show his eyes and grieve his heart;
        Come like shadows, so depart.

A show of eight kings, and BANQUO; *the last king with
a glass in his hand*

MACBETH
  You are too like the spirit of Banquo. Down!
  Your crown does sear my eye-balls. And your hair,
  You other gold-bound brow, is like the first.
  A third is like the former.—Filthy hags,
  Why do you show me this?—A fourth? Start, eyes!
  What, will the line stretch out to the crack of doom?
  Another yet? A seventh? I'll see no more!
  And yet the eighth appears, who bears a glass
  Which shows me many more. And some I see
  That two-fold balls and treble sceptres carry.
  Horrible sight! Now I see it is true,
  For the blood-matted Banquo smiles upon me,
  And points at them for his. What! Is this so?
FIRST WITCH
        Ay, sir, all this is so. But why
        Stands Macbeth thus amazedly?
        Come, sisters, cheer we up his sprites
        And show the best of our delights.
        I'll charm the air to give a sound,

> While you perform your antic round,
> That this great king may kindly say
> Our duties did his welcome pay.

Music. The Witches dance; and vanish

MACBETH

> Where are they? Gone! Let this pernicious hour
> Stand aye accursèd in the calendar.
> Come in, without there.

Enter LENNOX

LENNOX   What is your grace's will?
MACBETH

> Saw you the Weird Sisters?

LENNOX   No, my lord.
MACBETH

> Came they not by you?

LENNOX   No, indeed, my lord.
MACBETH

> Infected be the air whereon they ride,
> And damned all those that trust them. I did hear
> The galloping of horse. Who was it came by?

LENNOX

> It is two or three, my lord, that bring you word
> Macduff is fled to England.

MACBETH   Fled to England!
LENNOX

> Ay, my good lord.

MACBETH

> Time, you anticipate my dread exploits.
> The flighty purpose never is o'ertaken
> Unless the deed goes with it. From this moment

The very firstlings of my heart shall be
The firstlings of my hand. And even now,
To crown my thoughts with acts, be it thought and
   done:
The castle of Macduff I will surprise,
Seize upon Fife, give to the edge of the sword
His wife, his babes, and all unfortunate souls
That trace him in his line. No boasting, like a fool;
This deed I'll do before this purpose cool.
But no more sights!—Where are these gentlemen?
Come, bring me where they are.

Exeunt

SCENE II
Macduff's castle.

Enter MACDUFF'S WIFE, *her Son, and* ROSS

WIFE
What had he done to make him fly the land?
ROSS
You must have patience, madam.
WIFE   .   He had none.
His flight was madness; when our actions do not,
Our fears do make us traitors.
ROSS   You know not
Whether it was his wisdom or his fear.
WIFE
Wisdom! To leave his wife, to leave his babes,
His mansion and his titles, in a place
From whence himself does fly? He loves us not.
He wants the natural touch; for the poor wren,
The most diminutive of birds, will fight,
Her young ones in her nest, against the owl.

All is the fear and nothing is the love,
As little is the wisdom, where the flight
So runs against all reason.
ROSS   Dearest cousin,
   I pray you school yourself. But, for your husband,
   He is noble, wise, judicious, and best knows
   The fits of the season. I dare not speak much further,
   But cruel are the times when we are traitors
   And do not know, ourselves; when we hold rumour
   From what we fear, yet know not what we fear,
   But float upon a wild and violent sea,
   Each way and move. I take my leave of you;
   Shall not be long but I'll be here again.
   Things at the worst will cease or else climb upward
   To what they were before.—My pretty cousin,
   Blessing upon you!
WIFE
   Fathered he is, and yet he's fatherless.
ROSS
   I am so much a fool, should I stay longer
   It would be my disgrace and your discomfort.
   I take my leave at once.   *Exit*
WIFE
   My boy, your father's dead.
   And what will you do now? How will you live?
SON
   As birds do, mother.
WIFE   What, with worms and flies?
SON
   With what I get, I mean; and so do they.
WIFE
   Poor bird, you would never fear
   The net or lime, the pitfall or the gin!
SON
   Why should I, mother? Poor birds they are not set for.

My father is not dead, for all your saying.

WIFE

Yes, he is dead. How will you do for a father?

SON   Nay, how will you do for a husband?

WIFE   Why, I can buy twenty at any market.

SON   Then you'll buy them to sell again.

WIFE

You speak with all your wit;

And yet, in faith, with wit enough for you.

SON   Was my father a traitor, mother?

WIFE   Ay, that he was.

SON   What is a traitor?

WIFE   Why, one that swears and lies.

SON   And are all traitors that do so?

WIFE

Every one that does so is a traitor,

And must be hanged.

SON

And must they all be hanged that swear and lie?

WIFE   Every one.

SON   Who must hang them?

WIFE   Why, the honest men.

SON   Then the liars and swearers are fools; for there are
liars and swearers enough to beat the honest men and
hang up them.

WIFE   Now God help you, poor monkey! But how will
you do for a father?

SON   If he were dead, you would weep for him; if you
would not, it were a good sign that I should quickly have
a new father.

WIFE   Poor prattler, how you talk!

Enter a Messenger

MESSENGER

Bless you, fair dame! I am not to you known,

Though in your state of honour I am perfect.
I fear some danger does approach you nearly.
If you will take a homely man's advice,
Be not found here. Hence with your little ones!
To fright you thus I think I am too savage;
To do worse to you were fell cruelty,
Which is too nigh your person. Heaven preserve you!
I dare abide no longer.   *Exit*
WIFE   Whither should I fly?
I have done no harm. But I remember now
I am in this earthly world, where to do harm
Is often laudable, to do good sometimes
Accounted dangerous folly. Why then, alas,
Do I put up that womanly defence
To say I have done no harm?

Enter Murderers

                          What are these faces?
MURDERER
Where is your husband?
WIFE
I hope in no place so unsanctified
Where such as you may find him.
MURDERER   He is a traitor.
SON
You lie, you shag-haired villain!
MURDERER   What, you egg,
Young fry of treachery!

He stabs him

SON   He has killed me, mother!
Run away, I pray you.
                Son dies. Exit Wife crying 'Murder'

SCENE III
England: before the King's palace

Enter MALCOLM *and* MACDUFF

MALCOLM
  Let us seek out some desolate shade, and there
  Weep our sad bosoms empty.
MACDUFF   Let us rather
  Hold fast the mortal sword; and like good men
  Bestride our down-fallen birthdom. Each new morn
  New widows howl, new orphans cry, new sorrows
  Strike heaven on the face, that it resounds
  As if it felt with Scotland, and yelled out
  Like syllable of dolour.
MALCOLM   What I believe, I'll wail;
  What know, believe; and what I can redress,
  As I shall find the time to friend, I will.
  What you have spoken, it may be so perchance.
  This tyrant, whose sole name blisters our tongues,
  Was once thought honest; you have loved him well;
  He has not touched you yet. I am young; but
      something
  You may deserve of him, through me; and wisdom
  To offer up a weak poor innocent lamb
  To appease an angry god.
MACDUFF
  I am not treacherous.
MALCOLM   But Macbeth is.
  A good and virtuous nature may recoil
  In an imperial charge. But I shall crave your pardon:
  That which you are my thoughts cannot transpose;
  Angels are bright still though the brightest fell.
  Though all things foul would wear the brows of grace,
  Yet grace must still look so.

MACDUFF   I have lost my hopes.

MALCOLM

    Perchance even there where I did find my doubts.
    Why in that rawness left you wife and child,
    Those precious motives, those strong knots of love,
    Without leave-taking? I pray you,
    Let not my doubting thoughts be your dishonours
    But my own safeties. You may be rightly just,
    Whatever I shall think.

MACDUFF   Bleed, bleed, poor country!

    Great tyranny, lay you your basis sure,
    For goodness dares not check you; wear your wrongs,
    The title is confirmed. Fare you well, lord!
    I would not be the villain that you think
    For the whole space that's in the tyrant's grasp,
    And the rich East as well.

MALCOLM   Be not offended;

    I speak not as in absolute fear of you.
    I think our country sinks beneath the yoke,
    It weeps, it bleeds, and each new day a gash
    Is added to her wounds. I think also
    There would be hands uplifted in my right;
    And here from gracious England have I offer
    Of goodly thousands. But for all this,
    When I shall tread upon the tyrant's head
    Or wear it on my sword, yet my poor country
    Shall have more vices than it had before,
    More suffer, and more sundry ways, than ever,
    By him that shall succeed.

MACDUFF   What should he be?

MALCOLM

    It is myself I mean; in whom I know
    All the particulars of vice so grafted
    That, when they shall be opened, black Macbeth
    Will seem as pure as snow and the poor state

Esteem him as a lamb, being compared
With my boundless harms.
MACDUFF   Not in the legions
Of horrid hell can come a devil more damned
In evils to top Macbeth.
MALCOLM   I grant him bloody,
Lustful, avaricious, false, deceitful,
Sudden, malicious, smacking of every sin
That has a name. But there's no bottom, none,
In my voluptuousness. Your wives, your daughters,
Your matrons, and your maids, could not fill up
The cistern of my lust; and my desire
All continent impediments would overbear
That did oppose my will. Better Macbeth
Than such a one to reign.
MACDUFF   Boundless intemperance
In nature is a tyranny. It has been
The untimely emptying of the happy throne,
And fall of many kings. But fear not yet
To take upon you what is yours. You may
Convey your pleasures in a spacious plenty
And yet seem cold; the time you may so hoodwink.
We have willing dames enough. There cannot be
That vulture in you to devour so many
As will to greatness dedicate themselves,
Finding it so inclined.
MALCOLM   With this there grows
In my most ill-composed affection such
A staunchless avarice that, were I king,
I should cut off the nobles for their lands,
Desire his jewels and this other's house.
And my more-having would be as a sauce
To make me hunger more, that I should forge
Quarrels unjust against the good and loyal,
Destroying them for wealth.

MACDUFF   This avarice
  Sticks deeper, grows with more pernicious root
  Than summer-seeming lust; and it has been
  The sword of our slain kings. Yet do not fear:
  Scotland has plenty to fill up your will
  Of your mere own. All these are portable,
  With other graces weighed.
MALCOLM   But I have none.
  The king-becoming graces,
  As justice, verity, temperance, stableness,
  Bounty, persèverance, mercy, lowliness,
  Devotion, patience, courage, fortitude,
  I have no relish of them, but abound
  In the division of each several crime,
  Acting it many ways. Nay, had I power, I should
  Pour the sweet milk of concord into hell,
  Uproar the universal peace, confound
  All unity on earth.
MACDUFF   O Scotland, Scotland!
MALCOLM
  If such a one is fit to govern, speak.
  I am as I have spoken.
MACDUFF   Fit to govern!
  No, not to live! O nation miserable,
  With an untitled tyrant, bloody-sceptred,
  When shall you see your wholesome days again,
  Since now the truest issue of your throne
  By his own interdiction stands accused,
  And does blaspheme his breed? Your royal father
  Was a most sainted king; the queen that bore you,
  Oftener upon her knees than on her feet,
  Died every day she lived. Fare you well!
  These evils you repeat upon yourself
  Have banished me from Scotland. O my breast,
  Your hope ends here!

MALCOLM   Macduff, this noble passion,
  Child of integrity, has from my soul
  Wiped the black scruples, reconciled my thoughts
  To your good truth and honour. Devilish Macbeth
  By many of these trains has sought to win me
  Into his power, and modest wisdom plucks me
  From over-credulous haste. But God above
  Deal between you and me; for even now
  I put myself to your direction, and
  Unspeak my own detraction, here abjure
  The taints and blames I laid upon myself
  For strangers to my nature. I am yet
  Unknown to woman, never was forsworn,
  Scarcely have coveted what was my own,
  At no time broken my faith, would not betray
  The devil to his fellow, and delight
  No less in truth than life. My first false speaking
  Was this upon myself. What I am truly
  Is your and my poor country's to command—
  Whither indeed, before your here-approach,
  Old Siward with ten thousand warlike men,
  Already at a point, was setting forth.
  Now we'll together; and the chance of goodness
  Be like our warranted quarrel! Why are you silent?
MACDUFF
  Such welcome and unwelcome things at once
  It is hard to reconcile.

                    Enter a Doctor

MALCOLM   Well, more shortly.—
  Comes the King forth, I pray you?
DOCTOR
  Ay, sir. There are a crew of wretched souls
  That stay his cure. Their malady defeats

The great assay of art; but at his touch,
Such sanctity has heaven given his hand,
They presently amend.
MALCOLM   I thank you, doctor.

Exit Doctor

MACDUFF
What is the disease he means?
MALCOLM   It is called the Evil—
A most miraculous work in this good king,
Which often since my here-remain in England
I have seen him do. How he solicits heaven
Himself best knows: but strangely visited people,
All swollen and ulcerous, pitiful to the eye,
The mere despair of surgery, he cures,
Hanging a golden stamp about their necks,
Put on with holy prayers. And 'tis spoken,
To the succeeding royalty he leaves
The healing benediction. With this strange virtue
He has a heavenly gift of prophecy,
And sundry blessings hang about his throne
That speak him full of grace.

Enter ROSS

MACDUFF   See who comes here.
MALCOLM
My countryman; but yet I know him not.
MACDUFF
My ever gentle cousin, welcome hither.
MALCOLM
I know him now. Good God betime remove
The means that makes us strangers!
ROSS   Sir, amen.
MACDUFF
Stands Scotland where it did?

ROSS   Alas, poor country,
  Almost afraid to know itself! It cannot
  Be called our mother, but our grave; where nothing
  But who knows nothing is once seen to smile;
  Where sighs and groans and shrieks that rend the air
  Are made, not marked; where violent sorrow seems
  A normal experience. The dead man's knell
  Is there scarce asked for whom, and good men's lives
  Expire before the flowers in their caps,
  Dying before they sicken.
MACDUFF   O relation
  Too nice and yet too true.
MALCOLM   What's the newest grief?
ROSS
  That of an hour's age does hiss the speaker;
  Each minute teems a new one.
MACDUFF   How does my wife?
ROSS
  Why, well.
MACDUFF   And all my children?
ROSS   Well too.
MACDUFF
  The tyrant has not battered at their peace?
ROSS
  No. They were well at peace when I did leave them.
MACDUFF
  Be not a niggard of your speech. How goes it?
ROSS
  When I came hither to transport the tidings
  Which I have heavily borne, there ran a rumour
  Of many worthy fellows that were out;
  Which was to my belief witnessed the rather
  In that I saw the tyrant's power afoot.
  Now is the time of help. (*To Malcolm*) Your eye
    in Scotland

Would create soldiers, make our women fight
To doff their dire distresses.

MALCOLM   Be it their comfort
We are coming thither. Gracious England has
Lent us good Siward and ten thousand men—
An older and a better soldier none
That Christendom gives out.

ROSS   Would I could answer
This comfort with the like. But I have words
That would be howled out in the desert air,
Where hearing should not latch them.

MACDUFF   What concern they?
The general cause, or is it a grief, solely
Due to some single breast?

ROSS   No mind that's honest
But in it shares some woe, though the main part
Pertains to you alone.

MACDUFF   If it is mine,
Keep it not from me; quickly let me have it.

ROSS
Let not your ears despise my tongue for ever,
Which shall possess them with the heaviest sound
That ever yet they heard.

MACDUFF   Hum! I guess at it.

ROSS
Your castle is surprised, your wife and babes
Savagely slaughtered. To relate the manner
Were on the quarry of these murdered deer
To add the death of you.

MALCOLM   Merciful heaven!
What, man! Never pull your hat upon your brows.
Give sorrow words: the grief that does not speak
Whispers the o'erfraught heart and bids it break.

MACDUFF
My children too?

ROSS   Wife, children, servants, all
  That could be found.
MACDUFF   And I must be from thence!
  My wife killed too?
ROSS   I have said.
MALCOLM   Be comforted.
  Let's make us medicines of our great revenge.
  To cure this deadly grief.
MACDUFF   He has no children.
  All my pretty ones? Did you say all?
  O hell-kite! All? What, all my pretty chickens
  And their dam, at one fell swoop?
MALCOLM
  Dispute it like a man.
MACDUFF   I shall do so;
  But I must also feel it as a man.
  I cannot but remember such things were
  That were most precious to me. Did heaven look on
  And would not take their part? Sinful MacDuff!
  They were all struck for you. Naught that I am,
  Not for their own demerits, but for mine,
  Fell slaughter on their souls. Heaven rest them now!
MALCOLM
  Be this the whetstone of your sword; let grief
  Convert to anger; blunt not the heart, enrage it.
MACDUFF
  O, I could play the woman with my eyes
  And braggart with my tongue! But, gentle heavens,
  Cut short all intermission. Front to front
  Bring you this fiend of Scotland and myself.
  Within my sword's length set him; if he escapes,
  Heaven forgive him too.
MALCOLM   This tune goes manly.
  Come, go we to the King; our force is ready;
  Our lack is nothing but our leave. Macbeth

Is ripe for shaking, and the powers above
Put on their instruments. Receive what cheer
   you may:
The night is long that never finds the day.

                               Exeunt

Act V

Dunsinane Castle.

Enter a Doctor of Physic and Gentlewoman

DOCTOR   I have two nights watched with you, but can perceive no truth in your report. When was it she last walked?

GENTLEWOMAN   Since his majesty went into the field I have seen her rise from her bed, throw her nightgown upon her, unlock her closet, take forth paper, fold it, write upon it, read it, afterwards seal it, and again return to bed. Yet all this while in a most fast sleep.

DOCTOR   A great perturbation in nature, to receive at once the benefit of sleep and do the effects of watching. In this slumbery agitation, besides her walking and other actual performances, what, at any time, have you heard her say?

GENTLEWOMAN   That, sir, which I will not report after her.

DOCTOR   You may to me; and it is most meet you should.

GENTLEWOMAN   Neither to you nor anyone, having no witness to confirm my speech.

Enter LADY MACBETH *with a taper*

Lo you! Here she comes. This is her very guise; and, upon my life, fast asleep. Observe her; stand close.

DOCTOR   How came she by that light?

GENTLEWOMAN   Why, it stood by her. She has light by her

347

continually; it is her command.

DOCTOR   You see her eyes are open.

GENTLEWOMAN   Ay, but their sense is shut.

DOCTOR   What is it she does now? Look how she rubs her
hands.

GENTLEWOMAN   It is an accustomed action with her to
seem thus washing her hands. I have known her continue in this a quarter of an hour.

LADY M.   Yet here's a spot.

DOCTOR   Hark! She speaks. I will set down what comes
from her, to satisfy my remembrance the more strongly.

LADY M.   Out, damned spot! Out, I say!—One: two: why
then it is time to do it.—Hell is murky!—Fie, my lord,
fie! A soldier and afraid?—What need we fear who knows
it, when none can call our power to account?—Yet who
would have thought the old man to have had so much
blood in him?

DOCTOR   Do you mark that?

LADY M.   The Thane of Fife had a wife; where is she
now?—What, will these hands never be clean?—No more
of that, my lord, no more of that. You mar all this with
starting.

DOCTOR   Got to, go to: you have known what you should
not.

GENTLEWOMAN   She has spoken what she should not, I
am sure of that. Heaven knows what she has known.

LADY M.   Here's the smell of the blood still. All the perfumes of Arabia will not sweeten this little hand. Oh!
Oh! Oh!

DOCTOR   What a sigh is there! The heart is sorely charged.

GENTLEWOMAN   I would not have such a heart in my bosom for the dignity of the whole body.

DOCTOR   Well, well, well.

GENTLEWOMAN   Pray God it be, sir.

DOCTOR   This disease is beyond my practice; yet I have

known those who have walked in their sleep who have
died holily in their beds.

LADY M.   Wash your hands; put on your nightgown; look
not so pale. I tell you yet again, Banquo's buried; he cannot come out of his grave.

DOCTOR   Even so?

LADY M.   To bed, to bed! There's knocking at the gate.
Come, come, come, come, give me your hand. What's
done cannot be undone. To bed, to bed, to bed.

Exit

DOCTOR
Will she go now to bed?

GENTLEWOMAN   Directly.

DOCTOR
Foul whisperings are abroad, unnatural deeds
Do breed unnatural troubles; infected minds
To their deaf pillows will discharge their secrets.
More needs she the divine than the physician.
God, God forgive us all! Look after her,
Remove from her the means of all annoyance
And ever keep eyes upon her. So, good night.
My mind she has appalled, and amazed my sight.
I think, but dare not speak.

GENTLEWOMAN   Good night, good doctor.

Exeunt

SCENE II
The country near Dunsinane.

Drum and colours. Enter MENTEITH, CAITHNESS,
ANGUS, LENNOX, *Soldiers*

MENTEITH
The English power is near, led on by Malcolm,
His uncle Siward and the good Macduff.

Revenges burn in them; for their dear causes
Would to the bleeding and the grim alarm
Excite the moribund man.
ANGUS   Near Birnam Wood
Shall we meet them; that way are they coming.
CAITHNESS
Who knows if Donalbain is with his brother?
LENNOX
For certain, sir, he is not. I have a file
Of all the gentry: there is Siward's son
And many unrough youths that even now
Protest their first of manhood.
MENTEITH   What does the tyrant?
CAITHNESS
Great Dunsinane he strongly fortifies.
Some say he's mad. Others, that lesser hate him,
Do call it valiant fury; but for certain
He cannot buckle his distempered cause
Within the belt of rule.
ANGUS   Now does he feel
His secret murders sticking on his hands;
Now minutely revolts upbraid his faith-breach.
Those he commands move only in command,
Nothing in love. Now does he feel his title
Hang loose about him like a giant's robe
Upon a dwarfish thief.
MENTEITH   Who then shall blame
His pestered senses to recoil and start,
When all that is within him does condemn
Itself for being there?
CAITHNESS   Well, march we on
To give obedience where 'tis truly owed.
Meet we the medicine of the sickly weal,
And with him pour we in our country's purge
Each drop of us.

LENNOX   Or so much as it needs
   To dew the sovereign flower and drown the weeds.
   Make we our march towards Birnam.

                                                Exeunt, marching

                      SCENE III
                 Dunsinane. The castle.

          Enter MACBETH, *Doctor, and Attendants*

MACBETH
   Bring me no more reports; let them fly all.
   Till Birnam Wood removes to Dunsinane
   I cannot taint with fear. What's the boy Malcolm?
   Was he not born of woman? The spirits that know
   All mortal consequences have pronounced me thus:
   'Fear not, Macbeth; no man that's born of woman
   Shall ever have power upon you.' Then fly, false thanes,
   And mingle with the English sybarites.
   The mind I sway by and the heart I bear
   Shall never sag with doubt or shake with fear.

                      Enter Servant

   The devil damn you black, you cream-faced loon!
   Where got you that goose look?
SERVANT
   There are ten thousand—
MACBETH   Geese, villain?
SERVANT   Soldiers, sir.
MACBETH
   Go prick your face and over-red your fear,
   You lily-livered boy. What soldiers, fool?
   Death of your soul! Those linen cheeks of yours
   Are counsellors to fear. What soldiers, whey-face?
SERVANT
   The English force, so please you.

MACBETH

   Take your face hence.   *Exit Servant*

                          Seton!—I am sick at heart

   When I behold—Seton, I say!—This push

   Will chair me ever or dis-seat me now.

   I have lived long enough: my way of life

   Is fallen into the sere, the yellow leaf;

   And that which should accompany old age,

   As honour, love, obedience, troops of friends,

   I must not look to have. But, in their stead,

   Curses, not loud, but deep, mouth-honour, breath

   Which the poor heart would fain deny and dare not.—

   Seton!

Enter SETON

SETON

   What is your gracious pleasure?

MACBETH   What news more?

SETON

   All is confirmed, my lord, which was reported.

MACBETH

   I'll fight till from my bones my flesh be hacked.

   Give me my armour.

SETON   It is not needed yet.

MACBETH

   I'll put it on.

   Send out more horses, scour the country round,

   Hang those that talk of fear.—Give me my armour.—

   How does your patient, doctor?

DOCTOR   Not so sick, my lord,

   As she is troubled with thick-coming fancies

   That keep her from her rest.

MACBETH   Cure her of that.

   Can you not minister to a mind diseased,

   Pluck from the memory a rooted sorrow,

Raze out the written troubles of the brain,
And with some sweet oblivious antidote
Cleanse the stuffed bosom of that perilous stuff
Which weighs upon the heart?
DOCTOR   Therein the patient
Must minister to himself.
MACBETH
Throw physic to the dogs! I'll none of it.—
Come, put my armour on, give me my staff.
Seton, send out.—Doctor, the thanes fly from me.—
Come, sir, dispatch.—If you could, doctor, test
The water of my land, find her disease
And purge it to a sound and pristine health,
I would applaud you to the very echo
That should applaud again.—Pull it off, I say.—
What rhubarb, senna, or what purgative drug
Would scour these English hence? Hear you of them?
DOCTOR
Ay, my good lord; your royal preparation
Makes us hear something.
MACBETH   —Bring it after me.
I will not be afraid of death and bane
Till Birnam forest comes to Dunsinane.   *Exit*
DOCTOR
Were I from Dunsinane away and clear,
Profit again should hardly draw me here.   *Exit*

SCENE IV
Near Birnam Wood.

Drum and colours. Enter MALCOLM, SIWARD, MACDUFF,
Siward's Son, MENTEITH, CAITHNESS,
ANGUS, *and Soldiers marching*

MALCOLM
Cousins, I hope the days are near at hand

That chambers will be safe.

MENTEITH   We doubt it nothing.

SIWARD

What wood is this before us?

MENTEITH   The wood of Birnam.

MALCOLM

Let every soldier hew him down a bough
And bear it before him; thereby shall we shadow
The numbers of our host and make discovery
Err in report of us.

SOLDIERS   It shall be done.

SIWARD

We learn no other but the confident tyrant
Keeps still in Dunsinane and will endure
Our setting down before it.

MALCOLM   It is his main hope.
For where there is advantage to be given,
Both more and less have given him the revolt,
And none serve with him but constrainèd things
Whose hearts are absent too.

MACDUFF   Let our just censures
Attend the true event, and put we on
Industrious soldiership.

SIWARD   The time approaches
That will with due decision make us know
What we shall say we have, and what we owe [own].
Thoughts speculative their unsure hopes relate,
But certain issue strokes must arbitrate;
Towards which, advance the war.   *Exeunt, marching*

SCENE V
Dunsinane Castle.

Enter MACBETH, SETON,
and Soldiers, with drum and colours

MACBETH

Hang out our banners on the outward walls.
The cry is still, 'They come.' Our castle's strength
Will laugh a siege to scorn. Here let them lie
Till famine and the ague eat them up.
Were they not stuffed with those that should be ours
We might have met them dareful, beard to beard,
And beat them backward home.

A cry within of women

What is that noise?

SETON

It is the cry of women, my good lord.   *Exit*

MACBETH

I have almost forgotten the taste of fears.
The time has been my senses would have cooled
To hear a night-shriek, and my pelt of hair
Would at a dismal story rouse and stir
As life were in it. I have supped full with horrors:
Direness, familiar to my slaughterous thoughts,
Cannot once start me.

Enter SETON

Wherefore was that cry?

SETON

The queen, my lord, is dead.

MACBETH

She should have died hereafter.
There would have been a time for such a word—
Tomorrow, and tomorrow, and tomorrow,
Creeps in this petty pace from day to day
To the last syllable of recorded time;
And all our yesterdays have lighted fools

The way to dusty death. Out, out, brief candle!
Life's but a walking shadow, a poor player
That struts and frets his hour upon the stage
And then is heard no more. It is a tale
Told by an idiot, full of sound and fury,
Signifying nothing.

Enter a Messenger

You come to use your tongue: your story quickly!
MESSENGER
    Gracious my lord,
    I should report that which I say I saw,
    But I know not how to do it.
MACBETH   Well, say, sir.
MESSENGER
    As I did stand my watch upon the hill
    I looked toward Birnam and anon I thought
    The wood began to move.
MACBETH   Liar and slave!
MESSENGER
    Let me endure your wrath if it is not so.
    Within this three mile may you see it coming.
    I say, a moving grove.
MACBETH   If you speak false,
    Upon the next tree shall you hang alive
    Till famine shrinks you. If your speech is true,
    I care not if you do for me as much.
    I pull in resolution, and begin
    To doubt the equivocation of the fiend
    That lies like truth. 'Fear not till Birnam Wood
    Does come to Dunsinane'—and now a wood
    Comes toward Dunsinane. Arm, arm, and out!
    If this that he affirms then does appear,
    There is nor flying hence nor tarrying here.

I begin to be aweary of the sun,
And wish the estate of the world were now undone.—
Ring the alarum bell!—Blow wind, come wrack,
At least we'll die with harness on our back.   *Exeunt*

SCENE VI
Before the Castle.

Drum and colours. Enter MALCOLM, SIWARD,
MACDUFF, *and their army, with boughs*

MALCOLM
Now near enough. Your leafy screens throw down,
And show like those you are. You, worthy uncle,
Shall with my cousin, your right noble son,
Lead our first force. Worthy Macduff and we
Shall take upon us what else remains to do,
According to our order.
SIWARD   Fare you well.
Do we but find but the tyrant's power tonight,
Let us be beaten if we cannot fight.
MACDUFF
Make all our trumpets speak, give them all breath,
Those clamorous harbingers of blood and death.
                                                        Exeunt

Alarums continued
Enter MACBETH

MACBETH
They have tied me to a stake, I cannot fly,
But bear-like I must fight the course. What is he
That was not born of woman? Such a one
Am I to fear, or none.

Enter Young SIWARD

YOUNG SIWARD
  What is your name?
MACBETH   You'll be afraid to hear it.
YOUNG SIWARD
  No, though you call yourself a hotter name
  Than any is in hell.
MACBETH   My name is Macbeth.
YOUNG SIWARD
  The devil himself could not pronounce a title
  More hateful to my ear.
MACBETH   No, nor more fearful.
YOUNG SIWARD
  You lie, abhorrèd tyrant! With my sword
  I'll prove the lie you speak.

Fight, and YOUNG SIWARD *slain*

MACBETH   You were born of woman.
  But swords I smile at, weapons laugh to scorn,
  Brandished by man that's of a woman born.   *Exit*

Alarums. Enter MACDUFF

MACDUFF
  That way the noise is. Tyrant, show your face.
  If you are slain, and with no stroke of mine,
  My wife and children's ghosts will haunt me ever.
  I cannot strike at wretched kerns, whose arms
  Are hired to bear their staves. Either you, Macbeth,
  Or else my sword with an unbattered edge
  I sheathe again undeeded. There you should be:
  By this great clatter one of greatest note
  Seems bruited. Let me find him, fortune!

    And more I beg not.   *Exit*

             Alarums. Enter MALCOLM *and* SIWARD

SIWARD
    This way, my lord. The castle's gently rendered.
    The tyrant's people on both sides do fight;
    The noble thanes do bravely in the war;
    The day almost itself professes yours,
    And little is to do.
MALCOLM   We have met with foes
    That strike beside us.
SIWARD   Enter, sir, the castle.   *Exeunt*

             Alarum. Enter MACBETH

MACBETH
    Why should I play the Roman fool and die
    On my own sword? While I see lives, the gashes
    Do better upon them.

                  Enter MACDUFF

MACDUFF   Turn, hellhound, turn!
MACBETH
    Of all men else I have avoided you.
    But get you back; my soul is too much charged
    With blood of yours already.
MACDUFF   I have no words;
    My voice is in my sword, you bloodier villain
    Than terms can give you out.

                Fight. Alarum

MACBETH   You lose labour.

As easy may you the invisible air
With your keen sword impress, as make me bleed.
Let fall your blade on vulnerable crests,
I bear a charmed life which must not yield
To one of woman born.
MACDUFF   Despair your charm,
And let the angel whom you yet have served
Tell you Macduff was from his mother's womb
Untimely ripped.
MACBETH
Accursèd be that tongue that tells me so;
For it has cowed my better part of man;
And be these juggling fiends no more believed
That palter with us in a double sense,
That keep the word of promise to our ear
And break it to our hope. I'll not fight with you.
MACDUFF
Then yield you, coward;
And live to be the show and gaze of the time.
We'll have you, as our rarer monsters are,
Painted upon a pole, and underwrit,
'Here may you see the tyrant.'
MACBETH   I will not yield
To kiss the ground before young Malcolm's feet
And to be baited with the rabble's curse.
Though Birnam Wood is come to Dunsinane
And you opposed, being of no woman born,
Yet I will try the last. Before my body
I throw my warlike shield. Lay on, Macduff;
And damned be him that first cries, 'Hold enough!'
                                        Exeunt fighting

Alarums. Enter fighting, MACBETH *slain in fight*

                                        Exit Macduff

Retreat and flourish. Enter with drum and colours
MALCOLM, SIWARD, ROSS, THANES, *and Soldiers*

MALCOLM
I would the friends we miss were safe arrived.
SIWARD
Some must go off; and yet, by these I see
So great a day as this is cheaply bought.
MALCOLM
Macduff is missing and your noble son.
ROSS
Your son, my lord, has paid a soldier's debt.
He only lived but till he was a man,
And no sooner had his prowess confirmed
In the unshrinking station where he fought
But, like a man, he died.
SIWARD   Then he is dead?
ROSS
Ay, and brought off the field. Your cause of sorrow
Must not be measured by his worth, for then
It has no end.
SIWARD   Had he his hurts before?
ROSS
Ay, on the front.
SIWARD   Why then, God's soldier is he.
Had I as many sons as I have hairs
I would not wish them to a fairer death.
And so his knell is knolled.
MALCOLM   He's worth more sorrow;
And that I'll spend for him.
SIWARD   He's worth no more:
They say he parted well, and paid his score.
And so God be with him.—Here comes newer
   comfort.

Enter MACDUFF *with* MACBETH'S *head*

MACDUFF
    Hail, King! For so you are. Behold where stands
    The usurper's cursèd head. The time is free
    I see you compassed with your kingdom's pearl
    That speak my salutation in their minds,
    Whose voices I desire aloud with mine.—
    Hail, King of Scotland!
ALL   Hail, King of Scotland!

Flourish

MALCOLM
    We shall not spend a large expense of time
    Before we reckon with your several loves,
    And make us even with you. My thanes and kinsmen,
    Henceforth be earls, the first that ever Scotland
    In such an honour named. What's more to do,
    Which would be planted newly with the time,
    As calling home our exiled friends abroad
    That fled the snares of watchful tyranny,
    Producing forth the cruel ministers
    Of this dead butcher and his fiend-like queen—
    Who, as 'tis thought, by self and violent hands
    Took off her life—this, and what needful else
    That calls upon us, by the grace of Grace
    We will perform in measure, time, and place.
    So thanks to all at once, and to each one,
    Whom we invite to see us crowned at Scone.
                       Flourish. Exeunt

King Richard
The Third

INTRODUCTION

R*ichard III* was Shakespeare's first play to make a permanent mark. It has always held the stage, and been popular with actors no less than audiences. For it provides a superb part for a star actor: Shakespeare's fellow actor, Richard Burbage, was famous and long remembered in the part.

The play itself offers exciting drama, closely integrated as the trilogy of *Henry VI,* its precursors, could hardly hope to achieve, for those were chronicle plays covering a long period of time. *Richard III* covers a short concise space: the few years in which the Yorkist Edward IV had his brother Clarence killed in the Tower of London, and then died; leaving his last brother, Richard, to become Protector, usurp his nephew Edward V's throne and have both young Princes smothered in the Tower. Richard then receives his due at the battle of Bosworth; the Lancastrian heir succeeds to the throne and marries the Yorkist heiress, Elizabeth, uniting the royal houses in the Tudor line.

Shakespeare was not far away from these dramatic events, either in time or place. Bosworth Field was not far from Stratford, and Elizabeth I was the granddaughter of Henry VII, who put paid to Richard and his usurpation—the murder of the boys had turned the country against him.

The up-and-coming dramatist had a reliable source of

information in Sir Thomas More's book, in addition to the chroniclers, Hall and Holinshed. More was not only a truthtelling man, of brilliant intelligence, but a skilled lawyer who ferreted out details of Richard's dark and secret crime. Everybody at the time suspected him, but naturally details were not forthcoming.

Sir Thomas More actually knew some of those who knew Richard only too well. He was a friend of the Surrey who was in the chamber at the Tower when Richard initiated his *coup d'état* with the summary killing of his brother's friend, Lord Hastings, who would not go along with the usurpation. In Shakespeare's day Surrey's grandson, Lord Henry Howard, wrote a book, the *Defensative against Supposed Prophecies* (1583), which reveals the Howard family tradition of Richard's 'heinous crime'. Other crimes in those bloody days might be got away with, but not the killing of children. Shakespeare's repeated word 'homicide' is precisely the charge fixed upon Richard by Parliament, after Bosworth, for the shedding of 'infants' blood'.

Shakespeare, with his unsurpassed insight into human beings, understood the springs of Richard's character, but makes him more interesting, if not more sympathetic, than he was historically. Shakespeare gives him a certain gaiety, at least vivacity, in doing evil—where the historic Richard was morose and unappealing. He is portrayed as a clever, Machiavellian schemer, with a contempt (like Hitler) for those he takes in. He gets round his sister-in-law, Edward IV's widow, and then dismisses her with

Relenting fool, and shallow, changing woman!

This was true enough of the poor woman, in the ambience of those murderous times (our own are not much better.) Other characters too are realised as individuals, if briefly: Hastings, Edward's crony in womanising, a lightweight, too trusting and confident; Stanley, Earl of

Derby, with his politic distrust and reserve; the pious old
Duchess of York who had given birth to this brood; the
unstable Clarence who had played false with both sides.
Shakespeare knew that Clarence's little son was mentally
deficient, and this was historic fact too. Henry VI's widow,
old Queen Margaret has the role of Cassandra carried on
from that trilogy, in which Richard's development is
foreshadowed.

There is an element of the psychotic in Richard; as such
one sees him as a forerunner of such characters as Macbeth
or Iago. For Shakespeare was quite as much the master of
abnormal psychology as Dostoievsky. He came to develop
an extremism in his imagination, and this served a dual
purpose. It not only heightened the dramatic tension, but
it searched more deeply and incisively into the recesses of
character, the unconscious and dark corners in human
nature. Flannery O'Connor has well expressed the artistic
necessity of this: it is at times of crisis, in moments of
emergency, that a man's true character is most sharply
revealed.

Actually Richard is quite conscious and self-aware about
his villainy: he is determined to be a villain and explains
to the audience only too clearly what he is about. This is
early Elizabethan theatre, we must remember, and the
irony is rather too crude for modern taste. It went down
well with an Elizabethan audience, as also the ritual
cursings in antiphony, the one-line slanging matches—
the technical name is stichomythia. So too the combats on
the stage, the marching about, representation of battles,
the drums and trumpets—after all, this was what Elizabethan theatre had chiefly to offer. Nothing complicated
in the way of scenery, but a direct onslaught on eye and
ear and the emotions.

The play is also early in Shakespeare's development—we
shall see how much subtler he was to become. But from
the first, as with his poems and Sonnets, he had rich and

overflowing plenty to offer—his own word for it was 'foison'. Thus *Richard III* is one of the longest of the plays, and for modern production needs cutting and tightening up, particularly the first Act. As the play progresses it gathers speed.

There is little enough variety, though we are given some in the realistic portrayal—as usual—of those lower-class types, Clarence's murderers. The two blackguards are individualised: one is tougher than the other, who is somewhat conscience-smitten. Conscience 'makes a man a coward; a man cannot steal, but it accuses him, a man cannot swear, but it checks him; a man cannot lie with his neighbour's wife, but it detects him. 'Tis a blushing, shamefast spirit, that mutinies in a man's bosom; it fills one full of obstacles: it made me once restore a purse of gold that I found; it beggars any man that keeps it.' Here is the realist, veracious Shakespeare, making a transcript from real life, amid all the rhetoric and high-sounding speeches of the grand and great.

Richard III followed close on the heels of the three parts of *Henry VI,* and is to be dated to 1592. Once he got going, after a long apprenticeship, he worked with intense speed and proliferation. The language of the early plays offers no such difficulties as later—he became more and more difficult as time went on, with the pressure of thought and so much crowding into his mind to express.

CHARACTERS

KING EDWARD the Fourth

EDWARD, Prince of Wales, afterwards
   EDWARD V   } sons to

RICHARD, Duke of York   } the King

GEORGE, Duke of Clarence   } brothers

RICHARD, Duke of Gloucester, afterwards } to the
   RICHARD III   } King

CLARENCE'S SON, EARL OF WARWICK

HENRY, Earl of Richmond, afterwards HENRY VII

CARDINAL BOURCHIER, Archbishop of Canterbury

THOMAS ROTHERHAM, Archbishop of York

JOHN MORTON, Bishop of Ely

DUKE OF BUCKINGHAM

DUKE OF NORFOLK

EARL OF SURREY, his son

ANTHONY WOODVILLE, Earl Rivers, brother to Queen
   Elizabeth

MARQUESS OF DORSET and LORD GREY, her sons

EARL OF OXFORD

LORD HASTINGS

LORD STANLEY (also called EARL OF DERBY)

LORD LOVEL

SIR THOMAS VAUGHAN

SIR RICHARD RATCLIFFE

SIR WILLIAM CATESBY

SIR JAMES TYRREL

SIR JAMES BLOUNT

SIR WALTER HERBERT

SIR ROBERT BRAKENBURY, Lieutenant of the Tower

KEEPER IN THE TOWER

SIR WILLIAM BRANDON

CHRISTOPHER URSWICK, a priest

LORD MAYOR OF LONDON

SHERIFF OF WILTSHIRE

TRESSEL and BERKELEY, gentlemen attending on
    Lady Anne

GHOSTS OF HENRY VI and EDWARD, Prince of Wales,
    his son and other victims of Richard

ELIZABETH, Queen to Edward IV

MARGARET, widow of Henry VI

DUCHESS OF YORK, mother to Edward IV, Gloucester,
    and Clarence

LADY ANNE, widow of Edward, Prince of Wales, son to
    Henry VI; afterwards married to Richard,
    Duke of Gloucester

CLARENCE'S DAUGHTER

LORDS, GENTLEMEN, and other ATTENDANTS;
    a PURSUIVANT, a PAGE, a SCRIVENER, a PRIEST,
    BISHOPS, CITIZENS, ALDERMEN, COUNCILLORS,
    MURDERERS, MESSENGERS, SOLDIERS, & c.

Act 1

SCENE I
London. A street.

Enter Richard, Duke of Gloucester.

RICHARD

  Now is the winter of our discontent
  Made glorious summer by this sun of York;
  And all the clouds that loured upon our house
  In the deep bosom of the ocean buried.
  Now are our brows bound with victorious wreaths,
  Our bruisèd arms hung up for monuments,
  Our stern alarums changed to merry meetings,
  Our dreadful marches to delightful measures.
  Grim-visaged war has smoothed his wrinkled front,
  And now, instead of mounting barbèd steeds
  To fright the souls of fearful adversaries,
  He capers nimbly in a lady's chamber
  To the lascivious pleasing of a lute.
  But I, that am not shaped for sportive tricks
  Nor made to court an amorous looking-glass;
  I, that am rudely stamped, and want love's majesty
  To strut before a wanton ambling nymph;
  I, that am curtailed of this fair proportion,
  Cheated of feature by dissembling Nature,
  Deformed, unfinished, sent before my time
  Into this breathing world, scarce half made up—
  And that so lamely and unfashionable
  That dogs bark at me as I halt by them—
  Why I, in this weak piping time of peace,
  Have no delight to pass away the time,

Unless to see my shadow in the sun
And descant on my own deformity.
And therefore, since I cannot prove a lover
To entertain these fair well-spoken days,
I am determinèd to prove a villain
And hate the idle pleasures of these days.
Plots have I laid, inductions dangerous,
By drunken prophecies, libels, and dreams,
To set my brother Clarence and the king
In deadly hate the one against the other;
And if King Edward be as true and just
As I am subtle, false, and treacherous,
This day should Clarence closely be mewed up
About a prophecy which says that G
Of Edward's heirs the murderer shall be.
Dive, thoughts, down to my soul—here Clarence comes!

Enter Clarence guarded, and Brakenbury.

Brother, good day. What means this armèd guard
That waits upon your grace?
CLARENCE   His majesty,
   Tendering my person's safety, has appointed
   This conduct to convey me to the Tower.
RICHARD
   Upon what cause?
CLARENCE   Because my name is George.
RICHARD
   Alas, my lord, that fault is none of yours:
   He should for that commit your godfathers.
   O, perhaps his majesty has some intent
   That you should be new christened in the Tower.
   But what's the matter, Clarence, may I know?
CLARENCE
   Yea, Richard, when I know; for I protest
   As yet I do not. But, as I can learn,

He hearkens after prophecies and dreams,
And from the alphabet plucks the letter G,
And says a wizard told him that by G
His issue disinherited should be.
Because my name of George begins with G,
It follows in his thought that I am he.
These (as I learn) and suchlike toys as these
Have moved his highness to commit me now.

RICHARD

Why this it is, when men are ruled by women:
'Tis not the king that sends you to the Tower;
My Lady Grey his wife, Clarence, 'tis she
That tempers him to this extremity.
Was it not she, and that good man of worship,
Anthony Woodville, her brother there,
That made him send Lord Hastings to the Tower,
From whence this present day he is deliverèd?
We are not safe, Clarence — we are not safe.

CLARENCE

By heaven, I think there is no man secure
But the queen's kindred, and night-walking heralds
That trudge between the king and Mistress Shore.
Heard you not what an humble suppliant
Lord Hastings was for his delivery?

RICHARD

Humbly complaining to her deity
Got my Lord Chamberlain his liberty.
I'll tell you what, I think it is our way,
If we will keep in favour with the king,
To be her men and wear her livery.
The jealous overworn widow and herself,
Since our brother dubbed them gentlewomen,
Are mighty gossips in our monarchy.

BRAKENBURY

I beseech your graces both to pardon me:
His majesty has straitly given in charge

That no man shall have private conference,
Of what degree soever, with your brother.
RICHARD
Even so? If it please your worship, Brakenbury,
You may partake of anything we say.
We speak no treason, man. We say the king
Is wise and virtuous, and his noble queen
Well struck in years, fair, and not jealous.
We say that Shore's wife has a pretty foot,
A cherry lip, a bonny eye, a passing pleasing tongue;
And that the queen's kindred are made gentlefolks.
How say you, sir? Can you deny all this?
BRAKENBURY
With this, my lord, myself have nought to do.
RICHARD
Naught to do with Mistress Shore? I tell you, fellow,
He that does naught with her, excepting one,
Were best to do it secretly alone.
BRAKENBURY
What one, my lord?
RICHARD
Her husband, knave. Would you betray me?
BRAKENBURY
I do beseech your grace to pardon me, and as well
Forbear your conference with the noble duke.
CLARENCE
We know your charge, Brakenbury, and will obey.
RICHARD
We are the queen's lackeys, and must obey.
Brother, farewell. I will unto the king;
And whatsoever you will employ me in,
Were it to call King Edward's widow sister,
I will perform it to enfranchise you.
Meantime, this deep disgrace in brotherhood
Touches me deeper than you can imagine.

CLARENCE
I know it pleases neither of us well.
RICHARD
Well, your imprisonment shall not be long:
I will deliver you, or else lie for you.
Meantime, have patience.
CLARENCE   I must perforce. Farewell.
                    Exit Clarence, Brakenbury and Guard.
RICHARD
Go, tread the path that you shall never return:
Simple plain Clarence, I do love you so
That I will shortly send your soul to heaven,
If heaven will take the present at our hands.
But who comes here? The new-delivered Hastings?

Enter Lord Hastings.

HASTINGS
Good time of day unto my gracious lord.
RICHARD
As much unto my good Lord Chamberlain.
Well are you welcome to the open air.
How has your lordship brooked imprisonment?
HASTINGS
With patience, noble lord, as prisoners must;
But I shall live, my lord, to give them thanks
That were the cause of my imprisonment.
RICHARD
No doubt, no doubt; and so shall Clarence too,
For they that were your enemies are his
And have prevailed as much on him as you.
HASTINGS
More pity that the eagles should be mewed,
While kites and buzzards prey at liberty.

RICHARD
What news abroad?

HASTINGS
No news so bad abroad as this at home:
The king is sickly, weak, and melancholy,
And his physicians fear for him mightily.

RICHARD
Now, by Saint Paul, that news is bad indeed!
O, he has kept an evil diet long
And overmuch consumed his royal person:
It is very grievous to be thought upon.
What, is he in his bed?

HASTINGS   He is.

RICHARD
Go you before, and I will follow you.   *Exit Hastings.*
He cannot live, I hope, and must not die
Till George be packed with posthorse up to heaven.
I'll in, to urge his hatred more to Clarence
With lies well steeled with weighty arguments;
And, if I fail not in my deep intent,
Clarence has not another day to live.
Which done, God take King Edward to his mercy
And leave the world for me to bustle in!
For then I'll marry Warwick's youngest daughter.
What though I killed her husband and her father?
The readiest way to make the wench amends
Is to become her husband and her father:
And that will I—not all so much for love
As for another secret close intent,
By marrying her, which I must reach unto.
But yet I run before my horse to market:
Clarence still breathes; Edward still lives and reigns;
When they are gone, then must I count my gains. *Exit.*

SCENE II
London. Another street.

Enter the corpse of Henry the Sixth, with halberds to
guard it; Lady Anne as mourner.

ANNE
    Set down, set down your honourable load—
    If honour may be shrouded in a hearse—
    While I awhile obsequiously lament
    The untimely fall of virtuous Lancaster.
    Poor key-cold figure of a holy king,
    Pale ashes of the house of Lancaster,
    You bloodless remnant of that royal blood,
    Be it lawful that I invocate your ghost
    To hear the lamentations of poor Anne,
    Wife to your Edward, to your slaughtered son
    Stabbed by the selfsame hand that made these wounds!
    Lo, in these windows that let forth your life
    I pour the helpless balm of my poor eyes.
    O, cursèd be the hand that made these holes!
    Cursèd the heart that had the heart to do it!
    Cursèd the blood that let this blood from hence!
    More direful hap betide that hated wretch
    That makes us wretched by the death of you
    Than I can wish to wolves—to spiders, toads,
    Or any creeping venomed thing that lives!
    If ever he has child, abortive be it,
    A monster, and untimely brought to light,
    Whose ugly and unnatural aspèct
    May fright the hopeful mother at the view,
    And that be heir to his unhappiness!
    If ever he has wife, let her be made
    More miserable by the life of him
    Than I am made by my young lord and you!
    Come, now towards Chertsey with your holy load,

Taken from Paul's to be interrèd there.
And still, as you are weary of this weight,
Rest you, while I lament King Henry's corpse.

Enter Richard.

RICHARD
Stay, you that bear the corpse, and set it down.
ANNE
What black magician conjures up this fiend
To stop devoted charitable deeds?
RICHARD
Villains, set down the corpse, or, by Saint Paul,
I'll make a corpse of him that disobeys!
GENTLEMAN
My lord, stand back, and let the coffin pass.
RICHARD
Unmannered dog! You stand, when I command!
Advance your halberd higher than my breast,
Or, by Saint Paul, I'll strike you to my foot
And spurn upon you, beggar, for your boldness.
ANNE
What, do you tremble? Are you all afraid?
Alas, I blame you not, for you are mortal,
And mortal eyes cannot endure the devil.
Away, you dreadful minister of hell!
You had but power over his mortal body;
His soul you can not have. Therefore, be gone.
RICHARD
Sweet saint, for charity, be not so bitter.
ANNE
Foul devil, for God's sake hence, and trouble us not,
For you have made the happy earth your hell,
Filled it with cursing cries and deep exclaims.
If you delight to view your heinous deeds,
Behold this pattern of your butcheries.

O gentlemen, see! See dead Henry's wounds
Open their còngealed mouths and bleed afresh!
Blush, blush, you lump of foul deformity;
For 'tis your presence that exhales this blood
From cold and empty veins where no blood dwells.
Your deeds inhuman and unnatural
Provoke this deluge most unnatural.
O God, which this blood made, revenge his death!
O earth, which this blood drinks, revenge his death!
Either heaven with lightning strike the murderer dead;
Or earth gape open wide and eat him quick,
As you do swallow up this good king's blood
Which his hell-governed arm has butcherèd!

RICHARD

Lady, you know no rules of charity,
Which renders good for bad, blessings for curses.

ANNE

Villain, you know nor law of God nor man:
No beast so fierce but knows some touch of pity.

RICHARD

But I know none, and therefore am no beast.

ANNE

O wonderful, when devils tell the truth!

RICHARD

More wonderful, when angels are so angry.
Permit, divine perfection of a woman,
Of these supposèd crimes to give me leave
By circumstance but to acquit myself.

ANNE

Permit, diffused infection of a man,
Of these known evils, but to give me leave
By circumstance to accuse your cursèd self.

RICHARD

Fairer than tongue can name you, let me have
Some patient leisure to excuse myself.

ANNE
>Fouler than heart can think you, you can make
>No excuse current but to hang yourself.

RICHARD
>By such despair I should accuse myself.

ANNE
>And by despairing shall you stand excused
>For doing worthy vengeance on yourself
>That did unworthy slaughter upon others.

RICHARD
>Say that I slew them not?

ANNE   Then say they were not slain.
>But dead they are and, devilish slave, by you.

RICHARD
>I did not kill your husband.

ANNE   Why, then he is alive.

RICHARD
>Nay, he is dead, and slain by Edward's hands.

ANNE
>In your foul throat you lie! Queen Margaret saw
>Your murderous weapon smoking in his blood;
>That which you once did bend against her breast,
>But that your brothers beat aside the point.

RICHARD
>I was provokèd by her slanderous tongue
>That laid their guilt upon my guiltless shoulders.

ANNE
>You were provokèd by your bloody mind
>That never dream on aught but butcheries.
>Did you not kill this king?

RICHARD   I grant you.

ANNE
>Do grant me, hedgehog? Then God grant me too
>You may be damnèd for that wicked deed!
>O, he was gentle, mild, and virtuous!

RICHARD
  The better for the King of Heaven that has him.
ANNE
  He is in heaven, where you shall never come.
RICHARD
  Let him thank me that helped to send him thither;
  For he was fitter for that place than earth.
ANNE
  And you unfit for any place, but hell.
RICHARD
  Yes, one place else, if you will hear me name it.
ANNE
  Some dungeon.
RICHARD   Your bedchamber.
ANNE
  Ill rest betide the chamber where you lie!
RICHARD
  So will it, madam, till I lie with you.
ANNE
  I hope so.
RICHARD   I know so. But, gentle Lady Anne,
  To leave this keen encounter of our wits
  And fall something into a slower method—
  Is not the causer of the timeless deaths
  Of these Plantagenets, Henry and Edward,
  As blameful as the executioner?
ANNE
  You were the cause and most accursed effect.
RICHARD
  Your beauty was the cause of that effect—
  Your beauty, that did haunt me in my sleep
  To undertake the death of all the world,
  So I might live one hour in your sweet bosom.
ANNE
  If I thought that, I tell you, homicide,
  These nails should rend that beauty from my cheeks.

RICHARD
   These eyes could not endure that beauty's wreck;
   You should not blemish it, if I stood by:
   As all the world is cheerèd by the sun,
   So I by that. It is my day, my life.
ANNE
   Black night o'ershade your day, and death your life!
RICHARD
   Curse not yourself, fair creature—you are both.
ANNE
   I would I were, to be revenged on you.
RICHARD
   It is a quarrel most unnatural,
   To be revenged on him that loves you so.
ANNE
   It is a quarrel just and reasonable,
   To be revenged on him that killed my husband.
RICHARD
   He that bereft you, lady, of your husband,
   Did it to help you to a better husband.
ANNE
   His better does not breathe upon the earth.
RICHARD
   He lives, that loves you better than he could.
ANNE
   Name him.
RICHARD   Plantagenet.
ANNE   Why that was he.
RICHARD
   The selfsame name, but one of better nature.
ANNE
   Where is he?
RICHARD   Here.

[She] spits at him.

Why do you spit at me?

ANNE

Would it were mortal poison for your sake!

RICHARD

Never came poison from so sweet a place.

ANNE

Never hung poison on a fouler toad.

Out of my sight! You do infect my eyes.

RICHARD

Your eyes, sweet lady, have infected mine.

ANNE

Would they were basilisks to strike you dead!

RICHARD

I would they were, that I might die at once;
For now they kill me with a living death.
Those eyes of yours from mine have drawn salt tears,
Shamed their aspects with store of childish drops:
These eyes, which never shed remorseful tear—
No, when my father York and Edward wept
To hear the piteous moan that Rutland made,
When black-faced Clifford shook his sword at him.
Nor when your warlike father, like a child,
Told the sad story of my father's death,
And twenty times made pause to sob and weep,
That all the standers-by had wet their cheeks
Like trees bedashed with rain. In that sad time
My manly eyes did scorn an humble tear;
And what these sorrows could not thence exhale,
Your beauty has, and made them blind with weeping.
I never sued to friend nor enemy;
My tongue could never learn sweet smoothing word;
But, now your beauty is proposed my fee,
My proud heart sues, and prompts my tongue to speak.
Teach not your lip such scorn; for it was made
For kissing, lady, not for such contempt.
If your revengeful heart cannot forgive,

Lo, here I lend you this sharp-pointed sword,
Which if you please to hide in this true breast
And let the soul forth that adores you yet,
I lay it naked to the deadly stroke
And humbly beg the death upon my knee.

He lays his breast open. She offers at it with
his sword.

Nay, do not pause: for I did kill King Henry—
But 'twas your beauty that provokèd me.
Nay, now dispatch: 'twas I that stabbed young Edward—
But 'twas your heavenly face that set me on.

She lets fall the sword.

Take up the sword again, or take up me.
ANNE
    Arise, dissembler: though I wish your death,
    I will not be your executioner.
RICHARD
    Then bid me kill myself, and I will do it.
ANNE
    I have already.
RICHARD   That was in your rage:
    Speak it again, and even with the word
    This hand, which for your love did kill your love,
    Shall for your love kill a far truer love;
    To both their deaths shall you be accessary.
ANNE
    I would I knew your heart.
RICHARD
    'Tis figured in my tongue.
ANNE
    I fear me both are false.

RICHARD
  Then never was man true.
ANNE
  Well, well, put up your sword.
RICHARD
  Say then my peace is made.
ANNE
  That shall you know hereafter.
RICHARD
  But shall I live in hope?
ANNE
  All men, I hope, live so.
RICHARD
  Grant me to wear this ring.
ANNE
  To take is not to give.

Richard puts the ring on her finger.

RICHARD
  Look how my ring encompasses your finger,
  Even so your breast encloses my poor heart:
  Wear both of them, for both of them are yours.
  And if your poor devoted servant may
  But beg one favour at your gracious hand,
  You do confirm his happiness for ever.
ANNE   What is it?
RICHARD
  That it may please you leave these sad designs
  To him that has most cause to be a mourner,
  And presently repair to Crosby House;
  Where—after I have solemnly interred
  At Chertsey monastery this noble king
  And wet his grave with my repentant tears—
  I will with all expedient duty see you.
  For divers unknown reasons I beseech you,
  Grant me this boon.

ANNE

    With all my heart; and much it joys me too
    To see you are become so penitent.
    Tressel and Berkeley, go along with me.

RICHARD

    Bid me farewell.

ANNE   'Tis more than you deserve;
    But since you teach me how to flatter you,
    Imagine I have said farewell already.

             Exeunt Tressel and Berkeley, with Lady Anne.

RICHARD

    Sirs, take up the corpse.

GENTLEMAN   Towards Chertsey, noble lord?

RICHARD

    No, to Whitefriars—there attend my coming.

                  Exit all but Gloucester.

    Was ever woman in this humour wooed?
    Was ever woman in this humour won?
    I'll have her, but I will not keep her long.
    What? I that killed her husband and his father
    To take her in her heart's extremest hate,
    With curses in her mouth, tears in her eyes,
    The bleeding witness of my hatred by,
    Having God, her conscience, and these bars against me,
    And I no friends to back my suit at all
    But the plain devil and dissembling looks?
    And yet to win her! All the world to nothing!
    Ha!
    Has she forgot already that brave prince,
    Edward, her lord, whom I, some three months since,
    Stabbed in my angry mood at Tewkesbury?
    A sweeter and a lovelier gentleman,
    Framed in the prodigality of nature—
    Young, valiant, wise, and (no doubt) right royal—
    The spacious world cannot again afford.

And will she yet abase her eyes on me,
That cropped the golden prime of this sweet prince
And made her widow to a woeful bed?
On me, whose all not equals Edward's moiety?
On me, that halts and am misshapen thus?
My dukedom to a beggarly copper,
I do mistake my person all this while!
Upon my life, she finds (although I cannot)
Myself to be a marvellous proper man.
I'll be at charges for a looking-glass
And entertain a score or two of tailors
To study fashions to adorn my body:
Since I am crept in favour with myself,
I will maintain it with some little cost.
But first I'll turn yon fellow in his grave,
And then return lamenting to my love.
Shine out, fair sun, till I have bought a glass,
That I may see my shadow as I pass.   *Exit.*

SCENE III
Westminster. A room in the Palace.

*Enter Queen Elizabeth, Lord Rivers,
and Lord Grey.*

RIVERS
Have patience, madam; there's no doubt his majesty
Will soon recover his accustomed health.
GREY
In that you brook it ill, it makes him worse:
Therefore for God's sake entertain good comfort
And cheer his grace with quick and merry eyes.
QUEEN ELIZABETH
If he were dead, what would betide on me?

GREY

No other harm but loss of such a lord.

QUEEN ELIZABETH

The loss of such a lord includes all harms.

GREY

The heavens have blessed you with a goodly son
To be your comforter when he is gone.

QUEEN ELIZABETH

Ah, he is young; and his minority
Is put unto the trust of Richard Gloucester,
A man that loves not me, nor any of you.

RIVERS

Is it concluded he shall be Protector?

QUEEN ELIZABETH

It is determined, not concluded yet:
But so it must be, if the king miscarries.

Enter Buckingham and Stanley, Earl of Derby.

GREY

Here come the lords of Buckingham and Derby.

BUCKINGHAM

Good time of day unto your royal grace!

DERBY

God make your majesty joyful, as you have been!

QUEEN ELIZABETH

The Countess Richmond, good my Lord of Derby,
To your good prayer will scarcely say 'Amen.'
Yet, Derby, notwithstanding she's your wife
And loves not me, be you, good lord, assured
I hate not you for her proud arrogance.

DERBY

I do beseech you, either not believe
The envious slanders of her false accusers;
Or, if she is accused on true report,
Bear with her weakness, which I think proceeds
From wayward sickness, and no grounded malice.

QUEEN ELIZABETH
  Saw you the king to-day, my Lord of Derby?
DERBY
  But now the Duke of Buckingham and I
  Are come from visiting his majesty.
QUEEN ELIZABETH
  What likelihood of his amendment, lords?
BUCKINGHAM
  Madam, good hope; his grace speaks cheerfully.
QUEEN ELIZABETH
  God grant him health! Did you confer with him?
BUCKINGHAM
  Ay, madam: he desires to make atonement
  Between the Duke of Gloucester and your brothers,
  And between them and my Lord Chamberlain,
  And sent to warn them to his royal presence.
QUEEN ELIZABETH
  Would all were well! but that will never be:
  I fear our happiness is at the height.

              Enter Richard and Lord Hastings.

RICHARD
  They do me wrong, and I will not endure it!
  Who is it that complains unto the king
  That I (indeed) am stern, and love them not?
  By holy Paul, they love his grace but lightly
  That fill his ears with such dissentious rumours.
  Because I cannot flatter and look fair,
  Smile in men's faces, smooth, deceive, and cheat,
  Duck with French nods and apeish courtesy,
  I must be held a rancorous enemy.
  Cannot a plain man live and think no harm,
  But thus his simple truth must be abused
  With silken, sly, insinuating Jacks?

GREY

    To whom in all this presence speaks your grace?

RICHARD

    To you, that have nor honesty nor grace:

    When have I injured you? when done you wrong?

    Or you? or you? or any of your faction?

    A plague upon you all! His royal grace—

    Whom God preserve better than you would wish!—

    Cannot be quiet scarce a breathing while,

    But you must trouble him with lewd complaints.

QUEEN ELIZABETH

    Brother of Gloucester, you mistake the matter:

    The king, on his own royal disposition,

    And not provoked by any suitor else,

    Aiming belike at your interior hatred,

    That in your outward action shows itself

    Against my children, brothers, and myself,

    Makes him to send, that he may learn the ground.

RICHARD

    I cannot tell: the world is grown so bad

    That wrens make prey where eagles dare not perch.

    Since every Jack became a gentleman,

    There's many a gentle person made a Jack.

QUEEN ELIZABETH

    Come, come, we know your meaning, brother Gloucester:

    You envy my advancement and my friends'.

    God grant we never may have need of you!

RICHARD

    Meantime, God grants that I have need of you.

    Our brother is imprisoned by your means,

    Myself disgraced, and the nobility

    Held in contempt, while great promotiòns

    Are daily given to ennoble those

    That scarce, some two days since, were worth a noble.

QUEEN ELIZABETH

>By him that raised me to this careful height
>From that contented hap which I enjoyed,
>I never did incense his majesty
>Against the Duke of Clarence, but have been
>An earnest advocate to plead for him.
>My lord, you do me shameful injury
>Falsely to draw me in these vile suspècts.

RICHARD

>You may deny that you were not the means
>Of my Lord Hastings' late imprisonment.

RIVERS

>She may, my lord, for—

RICHARD

>She may, Lord Rivers! why, who knows not so?
>She may do more, sir, than denying that:
>She may help you to many fair preferments,
>And then deny her aiding hand therein
>And lay those honours on your high desert.
>What may she not? She may—ay, marry, may she—

RIVERS

>What, marry, may she?

RICHARD

>What, marry, may she? Marry with a king,
>A bachelor and a handsome stripling too:
>Sure, your grandam had a worser match.

QUEEN ELIZABETH

>My Lord of Gloucester, I have too long borne
>Your blunt upbraidings and your bitter scoffs.
>By heaven, I will acquaint his majesty
>Of those gross taunts that oft I have endured.
>I had rather be a country servant maid
>Than a great queen with this condition,
>To be so baited, scorned, and stormèd at:

Enter old Queen Margaret, behind.

Small joy have I in being England's queen.
QUEEN MARGARET   [*aside*]
    And lessened be that small, God I beseech him!
    Your honour, state, and seat are due to me.
RICHARD
    What? Threat you me with telling of the king?
    Tell him, and spare not. Look, what I have said
    I will affirm it in presence of the king:
    I dare adventure to be sent to the Tower.
    'Tis time to speak: my pains are quite forgot.
QUEEN MARGARET   [*aside*]
    Out, devil! I do remember them too well:
    You killed my husband Henry in the Tower,
    And Edward, my poor son, at Tewkesbury.
RICHARD
    Ere you were queen, ay, or your husband king,
    I was a packhorse in his great affairs;
    A weeder-out of his proud adversaries,
    A liberal rewarder of his friends:
    To royalize his blood I spent my own.
QUEEN MARGARET   [*aside*]
    Ay, and much better blood than his or yours.
RICHARD
    In all which time you and your husband Grey
    Were factious for the house of Lancaster;
    And, Rivers, so were you. Was not your husband
    In Margaret's battle at Saint Albans slain?
    Let me put in your minds, if you forget,
    What you have been ere this, and what you are;
    As well, what I have been, and what I am.
QUEEN MARGARET   [*aside*]
    A murderous villain, and so still you are.
RICHARD
    Poor Clarence did forsake his father, Warwick;
    Ay, and perjure himself (which Jesu pardon!) —

QUEEN MARGARET   [*aside*]
  Which God revenge!
RICHARD
  To fight on Edward's party for the crown;
  And for reward, poor lord, he is shut up.
  I would to God my heart were flint like Edward's,
  Or Edward's soft and pitiful like mine:
  I am too childish-foolish for this world.
QUEEN MARGARET   [*aside*]
  Hie you to hell for shame, and leave this world,
  You evil demon! there your kingdom is.
RIVERS
  My Lord of Gloucester, in those busy days
  Which here you urge to prove us enemies,
  We followed then our lord, our sovereign king.
  So should we you, if you should be our king.
RICHARD
  If I should be? I had rather be a pedlar:
  Far be it from my heart, the thought thereof!
QUEEN ELIZABETH
  As little joy, my lord, as you suppose
  You should enjoy, were you this country's king—
  As little joy you may suppose in me
  That I enjoy, being the queen thereof.
QUEEN MARGARET   [*aside*]
  A little joy enjoys the queen thereof;
  For I am she, and altogether joyless.
  I can no longer hold me patiènt.

[*Comes forward.*]

Hear me, you wrangling pirates, that fall out
In sharing that which you have pilled from me!
Which of you trembles not that looks on me?
If not, that I am queen, you bow like subjects,

Yet that, by you deposed, you quake like rebels?
Ah, gentle villain, do not turn away!

RICHARD

Foul wrinklèd witch, what make you in my sight?

QUEEN MARGARET

But repetition of what you have marred:
That will I make before I let you go.

RICHARD

Were you not banishèd on pain of death?

QUEEN MARGARET

I was; but I do find more pain in banishment
Than death can yield me here by my abode.
A husband and a son you owe to me—
And you a kingdom—all of you allegiance.
This sorrow that I have, by right is yours,
And all the pleasures you usurp are mine.

RICHARD

The curse my noble father laid on you
When you did crown his warlike brows with paper,
And with your scorns drew rivers from his eyes
And then, to dry them, gave the Duke a rag
Steeped in the faultless blood of pretty Rutland—
His curses then, from bitterness of soul
Denounced against you, are all fallen upon you;
And God, not we, has plagued your bloody deed.

QUEEN ELIZABETH

So just is God, to right the innocent.

HASTINGS

O, 'twas the foulest deed to slay that babe,
And the most merciless, that ever was heard of!

RIVERS

Tyrants themselves wept when it was reported.

DORSET

No man but prophesied revenge for it.

BUCKINGHAM

Northumberland, then present, wept to see it.

QUEEN MARGARET
  What? were you snarling all before I came,
  Ready to catch each other by the throat,
  And turn you all your hatred now on me?
  Did York's dread curse prevail so much with heaven
  That Henry's death, my lovely Edward's death,
  Their kingdom's loss, my woeful banishment,
  Should all but answer for that peevish brat?
  Can curses pierce the clouds and enter heaven?
  Why then, give way, dull clouds, to my quick curses!
  Though not by war, by surfeit die your king,
  As ours by murder, to make him a king!
  Edward your son, that now is Prince of Wales,
  For Edward our son, that was Prince of Wales,
  Die in his youth by like untimely violence!
  Yourself a queen, for me that was a queen,
  Outlive your glory, like my wretched self!
  Long may you live to wail your children's death
  And see another, as I see you now,
  Decked in your rights as you installed in mine!
  Long die your happy days before your death,
  And, after many lengthened hours of grief,
  Die neither mother, wife, nor England's queen!
  Rivers and Dorset, you were standers-by,
  And so were you, Lord Hastings, when my son
  Was stabbed with bloody daggers. God, I pray him
  That none of you may live his natural age,
  But by some unlooked accident cut off!
RICHARD
  Have done your charm, you hateful withered hag!
QUEEN MARGARET
  And leave out you? stay, dog, for you shall hear me.
  If heaven has any grievous plague in store
  Exceeding those that I can wish upon you,
  O, let them keep it till your sins are ripe,
  And then hurl down their indignatiòn

On you, the troubler of the poor world's peace!
The worm of conscience still begnaw your soul!
Your friends suspect for traitors while you live,
And take deep traitors for your dearest friends!
No sleep close up that deadly eye of yours,
Unless it is while some tormenting dream
Affrights you with a hell of ugly devils!
You elvish-marked, abortive, rooting hog!
You that were sealed in your nativity
The slave of nature and the son of hell!
You slander of your heavy mother's womb!
You loathèd issue of your father's loins!
You rag of honour! you detested—

RICHARD
Margaret.

QUEEN MARGARET   Richard!

RICHARD   Ha!

QUEEN MARGARET   I call you not.

RICHARD
I cry you mercy then; for I did think
That you had called me all these bitter names.

QUEEN MARGARET
Why, so I did, but looked for no reply.
O, let me make the period to my curse!

RICHARD
'Tis done by me, and ends in 'Margaret.'

QUEEN ELIZABETH
Thus have you breathed your curse against yourself.

QUEEN MARGARET
Poor painted queen, vain flourish of my fortune!
Why strew you sugar on that bottled spider
Whose deadly web ensnares you now about?
Fool, fool! you whet a knife to kill yourself.
The day will come that you shall wish for me
To help you curse this poisonous bunch-backed toad.

HASTINGS
  False-boding woman, end your frantic curse,
  Lest to your harm you move our patience.
QUEEN MARGARET
  Foul shame upon you! you have all moved mine.
RIVERS
  Were you well served, you would be taught your duty.
QUEEN MARGARET
  To serve me well, you all should do me duty,
  Teach me to be your queen, and you my subjects:
  O, serve me well, and teach yourselves that duty!
DORSET
  Dispute not with her; she is lunatic.
QUEEN MARGARET
  Peace, Master Marquess, you are malapert:
  Your fire-new stamp of honour is scarce current.
  O, that your young nobility could judge
  What it is to lose it and be miserable!
  They that stand high have many blasts to shake them,
  And if they fall, they dash themselves to pieces.
RICHARD
  Good counsel, indeed! Learn it, learn it, Marquess.
DORSET
  It touches you, my lord, as much as me.
RICHARD
  Ay, and much more; but I was born so high:
  Our eyrie builds up in the cedar's top
  And dallies with the wind and scorns the sun.
QUEEN MARGARET
  And turns the sun to shade—alas! alas!
  Witness my son, now in the shade of death,
  Whose bright outshining beams your cloudy wrath
  Has in eternal darkness folded up.
  Your eyrie builds up in our eyrie's nest:
  O God, that see it, do not suffer it!
  As it is won with blood, lost be it so!

BUCKINGHAM
  Peace, peace, for shame! if not, for charity.
QUEEN MARGARET
  Urge neither charity nor shame to me:
  Uncharitably with me have you dealt,
  And shamefully my hopes by you are butchered.
  My charity is outrage, life my shame,
  And in that shame still live my sorrow's rage!
BUCKINGHAM
  Have done, have done.
QUEEN MARGARET
  O princely Buckingham, I'll kiss your hand
  In sign of league and amity with you:
  Now fair befall you and your noble house!
  Your garments are not spotted with our blood,
  Nor you within the compass of my curse.
BUCKINGHAM
  Nor any here; for curses never pass
  The lips of those that breathe them in the air.
QUEEN MARGARET
  I will not think but they ascend the sky
  And there awake God's gentle-sleeping peace.
  O Buckingham, take heed of yonder dog!
  Look when he fawns he bites; and when he bites,
  His venom tooth will rankle to the death.
  Have not to do with him, beware of him:
  Sin, death, and hell have set their marks on him,
  And all their ministers attend on him.
RICHARD
  What does she say, my Lord of Buckingham?
BUCKINGHAM
  Nothing that I respect, my gracious lord.
QUEEN MARGARET
  What, do you scorn me for my gentle counsel?
  And soothe the devil that I warn you from?
  O, but remember this another day,

When he shall split your very heart with sorrow,
And say poor Margaret was a prophetess!
Live each of you the subjects to his hate,
And he to yours, and all of you to God's!   *Exit.*
BUCKINGHAM
    My hair does stand on end to hear her curses.
RIVERS
    And so does mine. I muse why she's at liberty.
RICHARD
    I cannot blame her. By God's holy Mother,
    She has had too much wrong, and I repent
    My part thereof that I have done to her.
QUEEN ELIZABETH
    I never did her any to my knowledge.
RICHARD
    Yet you have all the vantage of her wrong:
    I was too hot to do somebody good
    That is too cold in thinking of it now.
    Indeed, as for Clarence, he is well repaid;
    He is framed up to fatting for his pains —
    God pardon them that are the cause thereof!
RIVERS
    A virtuous and a Christian-like conclusion —
    To pray for them that have done harm to us.
RICHARD
    So do I ever — (*speaks to himself*) being well advised;
    For had I cursed now, I had cursed myself.

Enter Catesby.

CATESBY
    Madam, his majesty does call for you;
    And for your grace; and yours, my gracious lord.
QUEEN ELIZABETH
    Catesby, I come. Lords, will you go with me?

RIVERS
    We wait upon your grace.

                                Exeunt all but Richard.

RICHARD
    I do the wrong, and first begin to brawl.
    The secret mischiefs that I set abroad
    I lay unto the grievous charge of others.
    Clarence, whom I indeed have cast in darkness,
    I do beweep to many simple gulls—
    Namely, to Derby, Hastings, Buckingham—
    And tell them it is the queen and her allies
    That stir the king against the duke my brother.
    Now they believe it, and with that whet me
    To be revenged on Rivers, Dorset, Grey.
    But then I sigh, and, with a piece of Scripture,
    Tell them that God bids us do good for evil:
    And thus I clothe my naked villainy
    With odd old ends stolen forth of holy writ,
    And seem a saint, when most I play the devil.

                    Enter two Murderers.

    But soft! Here come my executioners.
    How now, my hardy, stout, resolved mates!
    Are you now going to dispatch this thing?
1. MURDERER
    We are, my lord, and come to have the warrant,
    That we may be admitted where he is.
RICHARD
    Well thought upon; I have it here about me:

                    Gives the warrant.

    When you have done, repair to Crosby Place.
    But, sirs, be sudden in the execution,
    And obdurate, do not hear him plead;

For Clarence is well-spoken, and perhaps
May move your hearts to pity if you mark him.

1. MURDERER

Tut, tut, my lord! we will not stand to prate;
Talkers are no good doers. Be assured:
We go to use our hands, and not our tongues.

RICHARD

Your eyes drop millstones when fools' eyes drop tears.
I like you, lads: about your business straight.
Go, go, dispatch.

1. MURDERER   We will, my noble lord.   [*Exeunt.*]

SCENE IV
The Tower of London.

Enter Clarence and Keeper.

KEEPER

Why looks your grace so heavily to-day?

CLARENCE

O, I have passed a miserable night,
So full of fearful dreams, of ugly sights,
That, as I am a Christian faithful man,
I would not spend another such a night
Though it were to buy a world of happy days—
So full of dismal terror was the time.

KEEPER

What was your dream, my lord? I pray you tell me.

CLARENCE

I thought that I had broken from the Tower
And was embarked to cross to Burgundy,
And in my company my brother Gloucester,
Who from my cabin tempted me to walk
Upon the hatches. Thence we looked toward England
And cited up a thousand heavy times,

During the wars of York and Lancaster,
That had befallen us. As we paced along
Upon the giddy footing of the hatches,
I thought that Gloucester stumbled, and in falling
Struck me, that thought to stay him, overboard
Into the tumbling billows of the main.
O Lord! I thought what pain it was to drown!
What dreadful noise of waters in my ears!
What sights of ugly death within my eyes!
I thought I saw a thousand fearful wrecks;
A thousand men that fishes gnawed upon;
Wedges of gold, great anchors, heaps of pearl,
Inestimable stones, unvalued jewels,
All scattered in the bottom of the sea.
Some lay in dead men's skulls, and in the holes
Where eyes did once inhabit, there were crept,
As if in scorn of eyes, reflecting gems,
That wooed the slimy bottom of the deep
And mocked the dead bones that lay scattered by.

KEEPER

Had you such leisure in the time of death
To gaze upon these secrets of the deep?

CLARENCE

I thought I had; and often did I strive
To yield the ghost. But still the envious flood
Stopped in my soul, and would not let it forth
To find the empty, vast, and wandering air;
But smothered it within my panting bulk,
Who almost burst to belch it in the sea.

KEEPER

Awaked you not in this sore agony?

CLARENCE

No, no, my dream was lengthened after life.
O, then, began the tempest to my soul!
I passed, I thought, the melancholy flood,
With that sour ferryman which poets write of,

Unto the kingdom of perpetual night.
The first that there did greet my stranger soul
Was my great father-in-law, renownèd Warwick,
Who spoke aloud, 'What scourge for perjury
Can this dark monarchy afford false Clarence?'
And so he vanished. Then came wandering by
A shadow like an angel, with bright hair
Dabbled in blood, and he shrieked out aloud,
'Clarence is come—false, fleeting, perjured Clarence,
That stabbed me in the field by Tewkesbury:
Seize on him, Furies, take him unto torment!'
With that, I thought, a legion of foul fiends
Environed me, and howlèd in my ears
Such hideous cries that with the very noise
I, trembling, waked; and for a season after
Could not believe but that I was in hell,
Such terrible impression made my dream.

KEEPER

No marvel, lord, that it affrighted you;
I am afraid, I think, to hear you tell it.

CLARENCE

Ah, keeper, keeper, I have done these things—
That now give evidence against my soul—
For Edward's sake, and see how he requites me!
O God! if my deep prayers cannot appease you,
But you will be avenged on my misdeeds,
Yet execute your wrath in me alone:
O, spare my guiltless wife and my poor children!
Keeper, I pray you, sit by me awhile.
My soul is heavy, and I fain would sleep.

KEEPER

I will, my lord. God give your grace good rest!

[*Clarence sleeps.*]
Enter Brakenbury, the Lieutenant.

BRAKENBURY

Sorrow breaks seasons and reposing hours,
Makes the night morning and the noontide night:
Princes have but their titles for their glories,
An outward honour for an inward toil;
And for unfelt imaginatiòns
They often feel a world of restless cares.
So that between their titles and low name
There's nothing differs but the outward fame.

Enter two Murderers.

1. MURDERER   Ho! who's here?

BRAKENBURY

What would you, fellow? and how came you hither?

1. MURDERER   I would speak with Clarence, and I came
hither on my legs.

BRAKENBURY   What, so brief?

2. MURDERER   'Tis better, sir, than to be tedious. Let him
see our commission, and talk no more.

Brakenbury reads it.

BRAKENBURY

I am, in this, commanded to deliver
The noble Duke of Clarence to your hands.
I will not reason what is meant hereby,
Because I will be guiltless from the meaning.
There lies the Duke asleep, and there the keys.
I will to the King and signify to him
That thus I have resigned to you my charge.

1. MURDERER   You may, sir; 'tis a point of wisdom. Fare
you well.   *Exit Brakenbury with Keeper.*

2. MURDERER   What? Shall I stab him as he sleeps?

1. MURDERER   No. He'll say 'twas done cowardly when
he wakes.

2. MURDERER   Why, he shall never wake until the great Judgment Day.

1. MURDERER   Why, then he'll say we stabbed him sleeping.

2. MURDERER   The urging of that word 'judgment' has bred a kind of remorse in me.

1. MURDERER   What? Are you afraid?

2. MURDERER   Not to kill him, having a warrant; but to be damned for killing him, from which no warrant can defend me.

1. MURDERER   I thought you had been resolute.

2. MURDERER   So I am—to let him live.

1. MURDERER   I'll back to the Duke of Gloucester and tell him so.

2. MURDERER   Nay, I pray stay a little. I hope this holy humour of mine will change. It was wont to hold me but while one tells twenty.

1. MURDERER   How do you feel yourself now?

2. MURDERER   Faith, some certain dregs of conscience are yet within me.

1. MURDERER   Remember our reward when the deed's done.

2. MURDERER   Zounds, he dies! I had forgot the reward.

1. MURDERER   Where's your conscience now?

2. MURDERER   O, in the Duke of Gloucester's purse.

1. MURDERER   When he opens his purse to give us our reward, your conscience flies out.

2. MURDERER   'Tis no matter; let it go. There's few or none will entertain it.

1. MURDERER   What if it comes to you again?

2. MURDERER   I'll not meddle with it; it makes a man a coward. A man cannot steal, but it accuses him; a man cannot swear, but it checks him; a man cannot lie with his neighbour's wife, but it detects him. 'Tis a blushing shame-faced spirit that mutinies in a man's bosom. It fills a man full of obstacles. It made me once restore a

purse of gold that by chance I found. It beggars any man
that keeps it. It is turned out of towns and cities for a
dangerous thing, and every man that means to live well
endeavours to trust to himself and live without it.

1. MURDERER   Zounds, 'tis even now at my elbow,
persuading me not to kill the duke.

2. MURDERER   Take the devil in your mind, and believe
him not. He would insinuate with you but to make you
sigh.

1. MURDERER   I am strong-framed; he cannot prevail
with me.

2. MURDERER   Spoken like a tall man that respects your
reputation. Come, shall we fall to work?

1. MURDERER   Take him on the nut with the hilts of your
sword, and then throw him into the malmsey butt in
the next room.

2. MURDERER   O excellent device! and make a sop of
him.

1. MURDERER   Soft! he wakes.

2. MURDERER   Strike!

1. MURDERER   No, we'll reason with him.

CLARENCE
Where are you, keeper? Give me a cup of wine.

2. MURDERER
You shall have wine enough, my lord, anon.

CLARENCE
In God's name, what are you?

1. MURDERER
A man, as you are.

CLARENCE
But not as I am, royal.

1. MURDERER
Nor you as we are, loyal.

CLARENCE
Your voice is thunder, but your looks are humble.

1. MURDERER

My voice is now the king's, my looks my own.

CLARENCE

How darkly and how deadly do you speak!
Your eyes do menace me. Why look you pale?
Who sent you hither? Wherefore do you come?

BOTH   To, to, to—

CLARENCE

To murder me?

BOTH   Ay, ay.

CLARENCE

You scarcely have the hearts to tell me so,
And therefore cannot have the hearts to do it.
Wherein, my friends, have I offended you?

1. MURDERER

Offended us you have not, but the king.

CLARENCE

I shall be reconciled to him again.

2. MURDERER

Never, my lord; therefore prepare to die.

CLARENCE

Are you drawn forth among a world of men
To slay the innocent? What is my offence?
Where is the evidence that does accuse me?
What lawful quest have given their verdict up
Unto the frowning judge? or who pronounced
The bitter sentence of poor Clarence' death
Before I am convicted by course of law?
To threaten me with death is most unlawful:
I charge you, as you hope to have redemption
By Christ's dear blood shed for our grievous sins,
That you depart, and lay no hands on me.
The deed you undertake is damnable.

1. MURDERER

What we will do, we do upon command.

2. MURDERER
And he that has commanded is our King.

CLARENCE
Erroneous vassals! the great King of Kings
Has in the table of his law commanded
That you shall do no murder. Will you then
Spurn at his edict, and fulfil a man's?
Take heed; for he holds vengeance in his hand
To hurl upon their heads that break his law.

2. MURDERER
And that same vengeance does he hurl on you
For false perjury and for murder too:
You did receive the sacrament to fight
In quarrel of the house of Lancaster.

1. MURDERER
And like a traitor to the name of God
Did break that vow, and with your treacherous blade
Unrip the bowels of your sovereign's son.

2. MURDERER
Whom you were sworn to cherish and defend.

1. MURDERER
How can you urge God's dreadful law to us
When you have broken it in such dear degree?

CLARENCE
Alas! for whose sake did I that ill deed?
For Edward, for my brother, for his sake.
He sends you not to murder me for this,
For in that sin he is as deep as I.
If God will be avengèd for the deed,
O, know you yet he does it publicly!
Take not the quarrel from his powerful arm.
He needs no indirect or lawless course
To cut off those that have offended him.

1. MURDERER
Who made you then a bloody minister
When gallant-springing brave Plantagenet,
That princely novice, was struck dead by you?

CLARENCE
  My brother's love, the devil, and my rage.
1. MURDERER
  Your brother's love, our duty, and your faults
  Provoke us hither now to slaughter you.
CLARENCE
  O, if you love my brother, hate not me:
  I am his brother, and I love him well.
  If you are hired for pay, go back again,
  And I will send you to my brother Gloucester,
  Who shall reward you better for my life
  Than Edward will for tidings of my death.
2. MURDERER
  You are deceived. Your brother Gloucester hates you.
CLARENCE
  O, no, he loves me and he holds me dear:
  Go you to him from me.
1. MURDERER   Ay, so we will.
CLARENCE
  Tell him, that when our princely father York
  Blessed his three sons with his victorious arm
  And charged us from his soul to love each other,
  He little thought of this divided friendship:
  Bid Gloucester think of this, and he will weep.
1. MURDERER
  Ay, millstones, as he lessoned us to weep.
CLARENCE
  O, do not slander him, for he is kind.
1. MURDERER
  Right as snow in harvest. Come, you deceive yourself;
  'Tis he that sends us to destroy you here.
CLARENCE
  It cannot be, for he bewept my fortune,
  And hugged me in his arms, and swore with sobs
  That he would labour my delivery.

1. MURDERER

Why so he does, when he delivers you
From this earth's thraldom to the joys of heaven.

2. MURDERER

Make peace with God, for you must die, my lord.

CLARENCE

Have you that holy feeling in your souls
To counsel me to make my peace with God,
And are you yet to your own souls so blind
That you will war with God by murdering me?
O, sirs, consider, they that set you on
To do this deed will hate you for the deed.

2. MURDERER

What shall we do?

CLARENCE   Relent, and save your souls.
Which of you, if you were a prince's son,
Pent up from liberty, as I am now,
If two such murderers as yourselves came to you,
Would not entreat for life?

1. MURDERER

Relent? No: 'tis cowardly and womanish.

CLARENCE

Not to relent is beastly, savage, devilish.
My friend [to Second Murderer], I spy some pity in your
    looks.
O, if your eye is not a flatterer,
Come you on my side, and entreat for me
As you would beg, were you in my distress.
A begging prince what beggar pities not?

2. MURDERER

Look behind you, my lord!

1. MURDERER

Take that! and that! (Stabs him.) If all this will not do,
I'll drown you in the malmsey butt within.

                                    Exit with the body.

2. MURDERER

A bloody deed, and desperately dispatched!
How fain, like Pilate, would I wash my hands
Of this most grievous murder!

Enter First Murderer.

1. MURDERER

How now? What mean you that you help me not?
By heavens, the Duke shall know how slack you have
    been.

2. MURDERER

I would he knew that I had saved his brother!
Take you the fee and tell him what I say,
For I repent me that the Duke is slain.   *Exit.*

1. MURDERER

So do not I. Go, coward as you are.
Well, I'll go hide the body in some hole
Till the Duke gives order for his burial.
And when I have my pay, I will away,
For this will out, and then I must not stay.   *Exit.*

Act II

SCENE I
A room in the Palace.

*Flourish. Enter King Edward, sick, the
Queen, Dorset, Rivers,
Hastings, Catesby, and Buckingham.*

KING EDWARD
Why, so: now have I done a good day's work.
You peers, continue this united league.
I every day expect an embassage
From my Redeemer to redeem me hence;
And more at peace my soul shall part to heaven,
Since I have made my friends at peace on earth.
Hastings and Rivers, take each other's hand;
Dissemble not your hatred, swear your love.

RIVERS
By heaven, my soul is purged from grudging hate,
And with my hand I seal my true heart's love.

HASTINGS
So thrive I as I truly swear the like!

KING EDWARD
Take heed you dally not before your King,
Lest he that is the supreme King of Kings
Confounds your hidden falsehood and award
Either of you to be the other's end.

HASTINGS
So prosper I as I swear perfect love!

RIVERS
And I as I love Hastings with my heart!

KING EDWARD
 Madam, yourself is not exempt from this;
 Nor you, son Dorset; Buckingham, nor you:
 You have been factious one against the other.
 Wife, love Lord Hastings, let him kiss your hand,
 And what you do, do it unfeignedly.
QUEEN ELIZABETH
 There, Hastings. I will never more remember
 Our former hatred, so thrive I and mine!
KING EDWARD
 Dorset, embrace him; Hastings, love Lord Marquess.
DORSET
 This interchange of love, I here protest,
 Upon my part shall be inviolable.
HASTINGS
 And so swear I.
KING EDWARD
 Now, princely Buckingham, seal you this league
 With your embracements to my wife's allies,
 And make me happy in your unity.
BUCKINGHAM   [to the Queen]
 Whenever Buckingham does turn his hate
 Upon your grace, but with all duteous love
 Does cherish you and yours, God punish me
 With hate in those where I expect most love!
 When I have most need to employ a friend,
 And most assured that he is a friend,
 Deep, hollow, treacherous, and full of guile
 Be he unto me! This do I beg of God,
 When I am cold in love to you or yours.

They embrace.

KING EDWARD
 A pleasing cordial, princely Buckingham,
 Is this your vow unto my sickly heart.

There wants now but our brother Gloucester here
To make the blessèd period of this peace.
BUCKINGHAM
And in good time, here comes the noble Duke.

Enter Richard.

RICHARD
Good morrow to my sovereign King and Queen;
And, princely peers, a happy time of day!
KING EDWARD
Happy indeed, as we have spent the day:
Gloucester, we have done deeds of charity,
Made peace of enmity, fair love of hate,
Between these swelling wrong-incensèd peers.
RICHARD
A blessèd labour, my most sovereign lord:
Among this princely heap, if any here
By false intelligence or wrong surmise
Holds me a foe—
If I unwittingly, or in my rage,
Have aught committed that is hardly borne
By any in this presence, I desire
To reconcile me to his friendly peace.
It is death to me to be at enmity:
I hate it, and desire all good men's love.
First, madam, I entreat true peace of you,
Which I will purchase with my duteous service;
Of you, my noble cousin Buckingham,
If ever any grudge was lodged between us;
Of you, and you, Lord Rivers, and of Dorset,
That, all without desert, have frowned on me.
Dukes, earls, lords, gentlemen—indeed, of all.
I do not know that Englishman alive
With whom my soul is any jot at odds,
More than the infant that is born to-night.
I thank my God for my humility.

QUEEN ELIZABETH

A holy day shall this be kept hereafter:
I would to God all strifes were well compounded.
My sovereign lord, I do beseech your highness
To take our brother Clarence to your grace.

RICHARD

Why, madam, have I offered love for this,
To be so flouted in this royal presence?
Who knows not that the gentle Duke is dead?

They all start.

You do him injury to scorn his corpse.

KING EDWARD

Who knows not he is dead? Who knows he is?

QUEEN ELIZABETH

All-seeing heaven, what a world is this!

BUCKINGHAM

Look I so pale, Lord Dorset, as the rest?

DORSET

Ay, my good lord; and no man in the presence
But his red colour did forsake his cheeks.

KING EDWARD

Is Clarence dead? The order was reversed.

RICHARD

But he, poor man, by your first order died,
And that a wingèd Mercury did bear:
Some tardy cripple bore the countermand,
That came too lag to see him burièd.
God grant that some, less noble and less loyal,
Nearer in bloody thoughts, but not in blood,
Deserve not worse than wretched Clarence did,
And yet go current from suspiciòn!

Enter Stanley, Earl of Derby.

DERBY

   A favour, my sovereign, for my service done!

KING EDWARD

   I pray you, peace. My soul is full of sorrow.

DERBY

   I will not rise unless your highness hears me.

KING EDWARD

   Then say at once what is it you request.

DERBY

   The forfeit, sovereign, of my servant's life,

   Who slew to-day a riotous gentleman

   Lately attendant on the Duke of Norfolk.

KING EDWARD

   Have I a tongue to doom my brother's death,

   And shall that tongue give pardon to a slave?

   My brother killed no man—his fault was thought—

   And yet his punishment was bitter death.

   Who sued to me for him? Who in my wrath,

   Kneeled at my feet and bid me be advised?

   Who spoke of brotherhood? Who spoke of love?

   Who told me how the poor soul did forsake

   The mighty Warwick and did fight for me?

   Who told me, in the field at Tewkesbury,

   When Oxford had me down, he rescued me

   And said, 'Dear brother, live, and be a king'?

   Who told me, when we both lay in the field

   Frozen almost to death, how he did lap me

   Even in his garments, and did give himself,

   All thin and naked, to the numb-cold night?

   All this from my remembrance brutish wrath

   Sinfully plucked, and not a man of you

   Had so much grace to put it in my mind.

   But when your carters or your waiting vassals

   Have done a drunken slaughter and defaced

   The precious image of our dear Redeemer,

   You straight are on your knees for pardon, pardon;

And I, unjustly too, must grant it you.

[Derby rises.]

But for my brother not a man would speak,
Nor I, ungracious, speak unto myself
For him, poor soul! The proudest of you all
Have been beholding to him in his life;
Yet none of you would once beg for his life.
O God! I fear your justice will take hold
On me and you, and mine and yours, for this.
                                      Exeunt some with King and Queen.

RICHARD
This is the fruit of rashness! Marked you not
How now the guilty kindred of the queen
Looked pale when they did hear of Clarence' death?
O, they did urge it ever unto the king!
God will revenge it. Come, lords, will you go
To comfort Edward with our company?

BUCKINGHAM
We wait upon your grace.   *Exeunt.*

SCENE II
The same.

*Enter the old Duchess of York, with the two
Children of Clarence.*

BOY
Good grandam, tell us, is our father dead?

DUCHESS OF YORK   No, boy.

GIRL
Why do you weep so oft, and beat your breast,
And cry 'O Clarence, my unhappy son'?

BOY

Why do you look on us, and shake your head,
And call us orphans, wretches, castaways,
If yet our noble father is alive?

DUCHESS OF YORK

My pretty children, you mistake me both.
I do lament the sickness of the King,
As loath to lose him, not your father's death:
It were lost sorrow to wail one that's lost.

BOY

Then you conclude, my grandam, he is dead.
The King my uncle is to be blamed for it:
God will revenge it, whom I will importune
With earnest prayers all to that effect.

GIRL

And so will I.

DUCHESS OF YORK

Peace, children, peace! The King does love you well.
Incapable and shallow innocents,
You cannot guess who caused your father's death.

BOY

Grandam, we can; for my good uncle Gloucester
Told me the King, provoked to it by the Queen,
Devised impeachments to imprison him.
And when my uncle told me so, he wept,
And pitied me, and kindly kissed my cheek;
Bade me rely on him as on my father,
And he would love me dearly as a child.

DUCHESS OF YORK

Ah, that deceit should steal such gentle shape
And with a virtuous mask should hide deep vice!
He is my son—ay, and therein my shame;
Yet from my dugs he drew not this deceit.

BOY

Think you my uncle did dissemble, grandam?

DUCHESS OF YORK   Ay, boy.

BOY
> I cannot think it. Hark! What noise is this?

> *Enter the Queen dishevelled,*
> *Rivers and Dorset after her.*

QUEEN ELIZABETH
> Ah, who shall hinder me to wail and weep,
> To chide my fortune, and torment myself?
> I'll join with black despair against my soul
> And to myself become an enemy.

DUCHESS OF YORK
> What means this scene of rude impatiènce?

QUEEN ELIZABETH
> To make an act of tragic violence.
> Edward, my lord, your son, our King, is dead!
> Why grow the branches when the root is gone?
> Why wither not the leaves that want their sap?
> If you will live, lament; if die, be brief,
> That our swift-wingèd souls may catch the King's,
> Or like obedient subjects follow him
> To his new kingdom of never-changing night.

DUCHESS OF YORK
> Ah, so much interest have I in your sorrow
> As I had title in your noble husband.
> I have bewept a worthy husband's death,
> And lived with looking on his images;
> But now two mirrors of his princely semblance
> Are cracked in pieces by malignant death,
> And I for comfort have but one false glass
> That grieves me when I see my shame in him.
> You are a widow; yet you are a mother,
> And have the comfort of your children left.
> But death has snatched my husband from my arms
> And plucked two crutches from my feeble hands,
> Clarence and Edward. O, what cause have I—

Yours being but a moiety of my moan —
To overgo your woes and drown your cries!

BOY

Ah, aunt! you wept not for our father's death.
How can we aid you with our kindred tears?

GIRL

Our fatherless distress was left unmoaned:
Your widow-dolour likewise be unwept!

QUEEN ELIZABETH

Give me no help in lamentatiòn;
I am not barren to bring forth complaints.
All springs reduce their currents to my eyes,
That I, being governed by the watery moon,
May send forth plenteous tears to drown the world.
Ah for my husband, for my dear lord Edward!

CHILDREN

Ah for our father, for our dear lord Clarence!

DUCHESS OF YORK

Alas for both, both mine, Edward and Clarence!

QUEEN ELIZABETH

What stay had I but Edward? and he's gone.

CHILDREN

What stay had we but Clarence? and he's gone.

DUCHESS OF YORK

What stays had I but they? and they are gone.

QUEEN ELIZABETH

Was never widow had so dear a loss.

CHILDREN

Were never orphans had so dear a loss.

DUCHESS OF YORK

Was never mother had so dear a loss.
Alas! I am the mother of these griefs:
Their woes are parcelled, mine is general.
She for an Edward weeps, and so do I;
I for a Clarence weep, so does not she:
These babes for Clarence weep, and so do I;

I for an Edward weep, so do not they.
Alas, you three on me, threefold distressed,
Pour all your tears! I am your sorrow's nurse,
And I will pamper it with lamentation.

DORSET
Comfort, dear mother; God is much displeased
That you take with unthankfulness his doing.
In common worldly things 'tis called ungrateful
With dull unwillingness to repay a debt,
Which with a bounteous hand was kindly lent;
Much more to be thus opposite with heaven
For it requires the royal debt it lent you.

RIVERS
Madam, bethink you like a careful mother
Of the young prince your son. Send straight for him;
Let him be crowned; in him your comfort lives.
Drown desperate sorrow in dead Edward's grave,
And plant your joys in living Edward's throne.

        Enter Richard, Buckingham, Stanley Earl of
             Derby, Hastings, and Ratcliffe.

RICHARD
Sister, have comfort. All of us have cause
To wail the dimming of our shining star;
But none can help our harms by wailing them.
Madam, my mother, I do cry you mercy;
I did not see your grace. Humbly on my knee
I crave your blessing.

DUCHESS OF YORK
God bless you, and put meekness in your breast,
Love, charity, obedience, and true duty!

RICHARD
Amen!—[*aside*] and make me die a good old man!
That is the butt-end of a mother's blessing;
I marvel that her grace did leave it out.

BUCKINGHAM
    You cloudy princes and heart-sorrowing peers
    That bear this heavy mutual load of moan,
    Now cheer each other in each other's love.
    Though we have spent our harvest of this king,
    We are to reap the harvest of his son.
    The broken rancour of your high-swollen hates,
    But lately splintered, knit, and joined together,
    Must gently be preserved, cherished, and kept.
    It seems good that with some little train
    Forthwith from Ludlow the young prince be fetched
    Hither to London, to be crowned our king.
RIVERS
    Why with some little train, my Lord of Buckingham?
BUCKINGHAM
    Surely, my lord, lest by a multitude
    The new-healed wound of malice should break out,
    Which would be so much the more dangerous
    By how much the estate is green and yet ungoverned.
    Where every horse bears his commanding rein
    And may direct his course to please himself,
    As well the fear of harm as harm apparent,
    In my opinion, ought to be prevented.
RICHARD
    I hope the king made peace with all of us;
    And the compact is firm and true in me.
RIVERS
    And so in me; and so, I think, in all.
    Yet, since it is but green, it should be put
    To no apparent likelihood of breach,
    Which haply by much company might be urged.
    Therefore I say with noble Buckingham
    That it is meet so few should fetch the prince.
HASTINGS
    And so say I.

RICHARD
    Then be it so; and go we to determine
    Who they shall be that straight shall post to Ludlow.
    Madam, and you, my sister, will you go
    To give your censures in this business?
BOTH
    With all our hearts.
                        Exeunt. Buckingham and Richard remain.
BUCKINGHAM
    My lord, whoever journeys to the prince,
    For God's sake let not us two stay at home;
    For by the way I'll sort occasiòn,
    As index to the story we late talked of,
    To part the queen's proud kindred from the prince.
RICHARD
    My other self, my counsel's consistory,
    My oracle, my prophet, my dear cousin,
    I, as a child, will go by your direction.
    Toward Ludlow then, for we'll not stay behind. *Exeunt.*

SCENE III
A street.

Enter one Citizen at one door and another at the other.

1. CITIZEN
    Good morrow, neighbour. Whither away so fast?
2. CITIZEN
    I promise you, I scarcely know myself.
    Hear you the news abroad?
1. CITIZEN   Yes, that the king is dead.

2. CITIZEN
    Ill news, by our Lady, seldom comes the better:
    I fear, I fear 'twill prove a giddy world.

Enter another Citizen.

3. CITIZEN
    Neighbours, God speed!
1. CITIZEN   Give you good morrow, sir.
3. CITIZEN
    Does the news hold of good King Edward's death?
2. CITIZEN
    Ay, sir, it is too true. God help the while!
3. CITIZEN
    Then, masters, look to see a troublous world.
1. CITIZEN
    No, no! By God's good grace his son shall reign.
3. CITIZEN
    Woe to that land that's governed by a child!
2. CITIZEN
    In him there is a hope of government,
    Which, in his nonage, council under him,
    And, in his full and ripened years, himself,
    No doubt shall then, and till then, govern well.
1. CITIZEN
    So stood the state when Henry the Sixth
    Was crowned in Paris but at nine months old.
3. CITIZEN
    Stood the state so? No, no, good friends, God knows!
    For then this land was famously enriched
    With politic grave counsel; then the king
    Had virtuous uncles to protect his grace.
1. CITIZEN
    Why, so has this, both by his father and mother.

3. CITIZEN

> Better it were they all came by his father,
> Or by his father there were none at all;
> For emulation who shall now be nearest
> Will touch us all too near, if God prevents not.
> O, full of danger is the Duke of Gloucester,
> And the queen's sons and brothers haughty and proud;
> And were they to be ruled, and not to rule,
> This sickly land might solace as before.

1. CITIZEN

> Come, come, we fear the worst. All will be well.

3. CITIZEN

> When clouds are seen, wise men put on their cloaks;
> When great leaves fall, then winter is at hand;
> When the sun sets, who does not look for night?
> Untimely storms makes men expect a dearth.
> All may be well; but if God sorts it so,
> 'Tis more than we deserve or I expect.

2. CITIZEN

> Truly, the hearts of men are full of fear:
> You cannot reason almost with a man
> That looks not heavily and full of dread.

3. CITIZEN

> Before the days of change, ever it's so.
> By a divine instinct men's minds mistrust
> Ensuing danger; as by proof we see
> The water swell before a boisterous storm.
> But leave it all to God. Whither away?

2. CITIZEN

> Sure, we were sent for to the justices.

3. CITIZEN

> And so was I. I'll bear you company.   *Exeunt.*

SCENE IV
A room in the Palace.

Enter the Archbishop of York, the young
Duke of York, the Queen, and the Duchess of York.

ARCHBISHOP

Last night, I hear, they lay at Stony Stratford;
And at Northampton they do rest to-night;
To-morrow, or next day, they will be here.

DUCHESS OF YORK

I long with all my heart to see the prince:
I hope he is much grown since last I saw him.

QUEEN ELIZABETH

But I hear no. They say my son of York
Has almost overtaken him in his growth.

YORK

Ay, mother; but I would not have it so.

DUCHESS OF YORK

Why, my good cousin? it is good to grow.

YORK

Grandam, one night as we did sit at supper,
My uncle Rivers talked how I did grow
More than my brother. 'Ay,' quoth my uncle Gloucester,
'Small herbs have grace; great weeds do grow apace.'
And since, I think, I would not grow so fast,
Because sweet flowers are slow and weeds make haste.

DUCHESS OF YORK

Good faith, good faith, the saying did not hold
In him that did object the same to you:
He was the wretchedest thing when he was young,
So long a-growing and so leisurely
That, if his rule were true, he should be gracious.

ARCHBISHOP

And so no doubt he is, my gracious madam.

DUCHESS OF YORK

I hope he is; but yet let mothers doubt.

YORK
    Now, by my faith, if I had rememberèd,
    I could have given my uncle's grace a flout
    To touch his growth nearer than he touched mine.
DUCHESS OF YORK
    How, my young York? I pray you, let me hear it.
YORK
    Truly they say, my uncle grew so fast
    That he could gnaw a crust at two hours old:
    'Twas full two years ere I could get a tooth.
    Grandam, this would have been a biting jest.
DUCHESS OF YORK
    I pray you, pretty York, who told you this?
YORK
    Grandam, his nurse.
DUCHESS OF YORK
    His nurse? Why, she was dead ere you were born.
YORK
    If 'twere not she, I cannot tell who told me.
QUEEN ELIZABETH
    A forward boy! Go to, you are too shrewd.
DUCHESS OF YORK
    Good madam, be not angry with the child.
QUEEN ELIZABETH
    Pitchers have ears.

Enter a Messenger.

ARCHBISHOP
    Here comes a messenger. What news?
MESSENGER
    Such news, my lord, as grieves me to report.
QUEEN ELIZABETH
    How does the prince?
MESSENGER   Well, madam, and in health.

DUCHESS OF YORK
　　What is your news?
MESSENGER
　　Lord Rivers and Lord Grey are sent to Pomfret,
　　And with them Sir Thomas Vaughan, prisoners.
DUCHESS OF YORK
　　Who has committed them?
MESSENGER　　　　　　　　　The mighty dukes,
　　Gloucester and Buckingham.
ARCHBISHOP　　　　　　　For what offence?
MESSENGER
　　The sum of all I can I have disclosed.
　　Why or for what the nobles were committed
　　Is all unknown to me, my gracious lord.
QUEEN ELIZABETH
　　Ay me! I see the ruin of my house.
　　The tiger now has seized the gentle hind;
　　Insulting tyranny begins to thrust
　　Upon the innocent and aweless throne:
　　Welcome destruction, blood, and massacre!
　　I see as in a map the end of all.
DUCHESS OF YORK
　　Accursèd and unquiet wrangling days,
　　How many of you have my eyes beheld!
　　My husband lost his life to get the crown,
　　And often up and down my sons were tossed
　　For me to joy and weep their gain and loss.
　　And being seated, and domestic broils
　　Clean overblown, themselves the conquerors
　　Make war upon themselves, brother to brother,
　　Blood to blood, self against self. O preposterous
　　And frantic outrage, end your damnèd malice,
　　Or let me die, to look on death no more!
QUEEN ELIZABETH
　　Come, come, my boy; we will to sanctuary.
　　Madam, farewell.

DUCHESS OF YORK   Stay, I will go with you.
QUEEN ELIZABETH
  You have no cause.
ARCHBISHOP   [*to the Queen*] My gracious lady, go,
  And thither bear your treasure and your goods.
  For my part, I'll resign unto your grace
  The seal I keep; and so betide to me
  As well I tender you and all of yours!
  Go, I'll conduct you to the sanctuary.   *Exeunt.*

Act III

SCENE I
A street.

*The trumpets sound. Enter young Prince
Wales, the Dukes of Gloucester and
Buckingham, Cardinal Bourchier, Catesby,
with others.*

BUCKINGHAM
Welcome, sweet prince, to London, to your chamber.
RICHARD
Welcome, dear cousin, my thoughts' sovereign:
The weary way has made you melancholy.
PRINCE EDWARD
No, uncle; but our crosses on the way
Have made it tedious, wearisome, and heavy.
I want more uncles here to welcome me.
RICHARD
Sweet prince, the untainted virtue of your years
Has not yet dived into the world's deceit:
Nor more can you distinguish of a man
Than of his outward show, which, God he knows,
Seldom or never is in accord with the heart.
Those uncles whom you want were dangerous;
Your grace attended to their sugared words
But looked not on the poison of their hearts:
God keep you from them, and from such false friends!
PRINCE EDWARD
God keep me from false friends!—but they were none.

RICHARD
  My lord, the Mayor of London comes to greet you.

  Enter Lord Mayor and his Train.

LORD MAYOR
  God bless your grace with health and happy days!
PRINCE EDWARD
  I thank you, good my lord, and thank you all.

  Mayor and his Train stand aside.

  I thought my mother and my brother York
  Would long ere this have met us on the way.
  Fie, what a slug is Hastings that he comes not
  To tell us whether they will come or no!

  Enter Lord Hastings.

BUCKINGHAM
  And, in good time, here comes the sweating lord.
PRINCE EDWARD
  Welcome, my lord. What, will our mother come?
HASTINGS
  On what occasion God he knows, not I,
  The queen your mother and your brother York
  Have taken sanctuary. The tender prince
  Would fain have come with me to meet your grace,
  But by his mother was perforce withheld.
BUCKINGHAM
  Fie, what an indirect and peevish course
  Is this of hers! Lord Cardinal, will your grace
  Persuade the queen to send the Duke of York
  Unto his princely brother immediately?
  If she denies, Lord Hastings, go with him
  And from her jealous arms pluck him perforce.

CARDINAL BOURCHIER
   My Lord of Buckingham, if my weak oratory
   Can from his mother win the Duke of York,
   Expect him here; but if she is obdurate
   To mild entreaties, God in heaven forbid
   We should infringe the holy privilege
   Of blessèd sanctuary! Not for all this land
   Would I be guilty of so deep a sin.

BUCKINGHAM
   You are too senseless-obstinate, my lord,
   Too ceremonious and traditional.
   Weigh it but with the grossness of this age,
   You break not sanctuary in seizing him.
   The benefit thereof is always granted
   To those whose dealings have deserved the place,
   And those who have the wit to claim the place.
   This prince has neither claimed it nor deserved it,
   And therefore, in my opinion, cannot have it.
   Then, taking him from thence that is not there,
   You break no privilege nor charter there.
   Oft have I heard of sanctuary men,
   But sanctuary children never till now.

CARDINAL BOURCHIER
   My lord, you shall overrule my mind for once.
   Come on, Lord Hastings, will you go with me?

HASTINGS
   I go, my lord.

PRINCE EDWARD
   Good lords, make all the speedy haste you may.
                      Exeunt Cardinal and Hastings.
   Say, uncle Gloucester, if our brother comes,
   Where shall we sojourn till our coronation?

RICHARD
   Where it seems best unto your royal self.
   If I may counsel you, some day or two
   Your highness shall repose you at the Tower.

Then where you please, and shall be thought most fit
For your best health and recreation.
PRINCE EDWARD
    I do not like the Tower, of any place.
    Did Julius Caesar build that place, my lord?
BUCKINGHAM
    He did, my gracious lord, begin that place,
    Which, since, succeeding ages have re-edified.
PRINCE EDWARD
    Is it upon record, or else reported
    Successively from age to age, he built it?
BUCKINGHAM
    Upon record, my gracious lord.
PRINCE EDWARD
    But say, my lord, it were not registered,
    I think the truth should live from age to age,
    As it were retailed to all posterity,
    Even to the general all-ending day.
RICHARD   [aside]
    So wise so young, they say, do never live long.
PRINCE EDWARD
    What say you, uncle?
RICHARD
    I say, without characters fame lives long.

                        [Aside]

    Thus, like the formal Vice, Iniquity,
    I moralize two meanings in one word.
PRINCE EDWARD
    That Julius Caesar was a famous man:
    With what his valour did enrich his wit,
    His wit set down to make his valour live.
    Death makes no conquest of this conqueror,
    For now he lives in fame, though not in life.
    I'll tell you what, my cousin Buckingham—

BUCKINGHAM
   What, my gracious lord?
PRINCE EDWARD
   If I do live until I am a man,
   I'll win our ancient right in France again,
   Or die a soldier as I lived a king.
RICHARD   [*aside*]
   Short summers lightly have a forward spring.

   Enter the young Duke of York, Hastings,
   and Cardinal Bourchier.

BUCKINGHAM
   Now in good time, here comes the Duke of York.
PRINCE EDWARD
   Richard of York, how fares our loving brother?
YORK
   Well, my dread lord—so must I call you now.
PRINCE EDWARD
   Ay, brother—to our grief, as it is yours:
   Too soon he died that might have kept that title,
   Which by his death has lost much majesty.
RICHARD
   How fares our cousin, noble Lord of York?
YORK
   I thank you, gentle uncle. O, my lord,
   You said that idle weeds are fast in growth:
   The prince my brother has outgrown me far.
RICHARD
   He has, my lord.
YORK   And therefore is he idle?
RICHARD
   O my fair cousin, I must not say so.
YORK
   Then he is more beholding to you than I.

RICHARD

He may command me as my sovereign,

But you have power in me as in a kinsman.

YORK

I pray you, uncle, give me this dagger.

RICHARD

My dagger, little cousin? With all my heart.

PRINCE EDWARD

A beggar, brother?

YORK

Of my kind uncle, that I know will give,

And being but a toy, which is no grief to give.

RICHARD

A greater gift than that I'll give my cousin.

YORK

A greater gift? O, that's the sword to it.

RICHARD

Ay, gentle cousin, were it light enough.

YORK

O, then I see you will part but with light gifts!

In weightier things you'll say a beggar nay.

RICHARD

It is too heavy for your grace to wear.

YORK

I weigh it lightly, were it heavier.

RICHARD

What, would you have my weapon, little lord?

YORK

I would, that I might thank you as you call me.

RICHARD   How?

YORK   Little.

PRINCE EDWARD

My Lord of York will still be cross in talk.

Uncle, your grace knows how to bear with him.

YORK

> You mean, to bear me, not to bear with me.
> Uncle, my brother mocks both you and me:
> Because that I am little, like an ape,
> He thinks that you should bear me on your shoulders.

BUCKINGHAM   [*aside to Hastings*]

> With what a sharp-provided wit he reasons!
> To mitigate the scorn he gives his uncle,
> He prettily and aptly taunts himself:
> So cunning, and so young, is wonderful.

RICHARD

> My lord, will it please you pass along?
> Myself and my good cousin Buckingham
> Will to your mother, to entreat of her
> To meet you at the Tower and welcome you.

YORK

> What, will you go unto the Tower, my lord?

PRINCE EDWARD

> My Lord Protector needs will have it so.

YORK

> I shall not sleep in quiet at the Tower.

RICHARD

> Why, what should you fear?

YORK

> For sure, my uncle Clarence's angry ghost:
> My grandam told me he was murdered there.

PRINCE EDWARD

> I fear no uncles dead.

RICHARD

> Nor none that live, I hope.

PRINCE EDWARD

> Well, if they live, I hope I need not fear.
> But come, my lord; with a heavy heart,
> Thinking on them, go I unto the Tower.

A sennet. Exeunt all but Richard, Buckingham,
and Catesby.

BUCKINGHAM
    Think you, my lord, this little prating York
    Was not incensèd by his subtle mother
    To taunt and scorn you thus opprobriously?
RICHARD
    No doubt, no doubt. O, 'tis a perilous boy,
    Bold, quick, ingenious, forward, capable:
    He is all the mother's, from the top to toe.
BUCKINGHAM
    Well, let them rest. Come hither, Catesby.
    You are sworn as deeply to effect what we intend
    As closely to conceal what we impart.
    You know our reasons urged upon the way.
    What think you? Is it not an easy matter
    To make William Lord Hastings of our mind
    For the instalment of this noble duke
    In the seat royal of this famous isle?
CATESBY
    He for his father's sake so loves the prince
    That he will not be won to aught against him.
BUCKINGHAM
    What think you then of Stanley? Will not he?
CATESBY
    He will do all in all as Hastings does.
BUCKINGHAM
    Well then, no more but this: go, gentle Catesby,
    And, as it were far off, sound you Lord Hastings
    How he does stand affected to our purpose,
    And summon him to-morrow to the Tower
    To sit about the coronatiòn.
    If you do find him tractable to us,
    Encourage him, and tell him all our reasons,
    If he is leaden, icy, cold, unwilling,

Be you so too, and so break off the talk,
And give us notice of his inclination.
For we to-morrow hold divided councils,
Wherein yourself shall highly be employed.
RICHARD
Commend me to Lord William. Tell him, Catesby,
His ancient knot of dangerous adversaries
To-morrow are let blood at Pomfret Castle;
And bid my lord, for joy of this good news,
Give Mistress Shore one gentle kiss the more.
BUCKINGHAM
Good Catesby, go effect this business soundly.
CATESBY
My good lords both, with all the heed I can.
RICHARD
Shall we hear from you, Catesby, ere we sleep?
CATESBY
You shall, my lord.
RICHARD
At Crosby House, there shall you find us both.

Exit Catesby.

BUCKINGHAM
Now, my lord, what shall we do if we perceive
Lord Hastings will not yield to our complots?
RICHARD
Chop off his head! Something we will determine.
And look when I am king, claim you of me
The earldom of Hereford and all the moveables
Whereof the king my brother was possessed.
BUCKINGHAM
I'll claim that promise at your grace's hand.
RICHARD
And look to have it yielded with all kindness.
Come, let us sup betimes, that afterwards
We may digest our complots in some form.   *Exeunt.*

SCENE II
Before Lord Hastings' house.

Enter a Messenger.

MESSENGER
  My lord! my lord!
HASTINGS   [*within*]
  Who knocks?
MESSENGER
  One from the Lord Stanley.

Enter Lord Hastings.

HASTINGS
  What is it a clock?
MESSENGER
  Upon the stroke of four.
HASTINGS
  Cannot my Lord Stanley sleep these tedious nights?
MESSENGER
  So it appears by that I have to say:
  First, he commends him to your noble self.
HASTINGS
  What then?
MESSENGER
  Then certifies your lordship that this night
  He dreamt the boar had rasèd off his helm.
  Besides, he says there are two councils kept;
  And that may be determined at the one
  Which may make you and him to rue at the other.
  Therefore he sends to know your lordship's pleasure,
  If you will now at once take horse with him
  And with all speed post with him toward the North
  To shun the danger that his soul divines.

HASTINGS

Go, fellow, go, return unto your lord;
Bid him not fear the separated council.
His honour and myself are at the one,
And at the other is my good friend Catesby;
Where nothing can proceed that touches us
Whereof I shall not have intelligence.
Tell him his fears are shallow, without instance;
And for his dreams, I wonder he's so simple
To trust the mockery of unquiet slumbers.
To fly the boar before the boar pursues
Were to incense the boar to follow us,
And make pursuit where he did mean no chase.
Go, bid your master rise and come to me,
And we will both together to the Tower,
Where he shall see the boar will use us kindly.

MESSENGER

I'll go, my lord, and tell him what you say.   *Exit.*

Enter Catesby.

CATESBY

Many good morrows to my noble lord!

HASTINGS

Good morrow, Catesby; you are early stirring.
What news, what news, in this our tottering state?

CATESBY

It is a reeling world indeed, my lord,
And I believe will never stand upright
Till Richard wear the garland of the realm.

HASTINGS

How! wear the garland! Do you mean the crown?

CATESBY

Ay, my good lord.

HASTINGS

    I'll have this crown of mine cut from my shoulders
    Before I'll see the crown so foul misplaced.
    But can you guess that he does aim at it?

CATESBY

    Ay, on my life, and hopes to find you forward
    Upon his party for the gain thereof.
    And thereupon he sends you this good news,
    That this same very day your enemies,
    The kindred of the queen, must die at Pomfret.

HASTINGS

    Indeed I am no mourner for that news,
    Because they have been long my adversaries;
    But that I'll give my voice on Richard's side
    To bar my master's heirs in true descent—
    God knows I will not do it, to the death!

CATESBY

    God keep your lordship in that gracious mind!

HASTINGS

    But I shall laugh at this a twelvemonth hence,
    That they who brought me in my master's hate,
    I live to look upon their tragedy.
    Well, Catesby, ere a fortnight makes me older,
    I'll send some packing that yet think not of it.

CATESBY

    'Tis a vile thing to die, my gracious lord,
    When men are unprepared and look not for it.

HASTINGS

    O monstrous, monstrous! and so falls it out
    With Rivers, Vaughan, Grey; and so 'twill do
    With some men else, that think themselves as safe
    As you and I, who, as you know, are dear
    To princely Richard and to Buckingham.

CATESBY

    The princes both make high account of you—

[Aside]

For they account his head upon the Bridge.
HASTINGS
    I know they do, and I have well deserved it.

Enter Lord Stanley Earl of Derby.

    Come on, come on! Where is your boar-spear, man?
    Fear you the boar, and go so unprovided?
DERBY
    My lord, good morrow. Good morrow, Catesby.
    You may jest on, but, by the Holy Rood,
    I do not like these separate councils, I.
HASTINGS
    My lord,
    I hold my life as dear as you do yours,
    And never in my days, I do protest,
    Was it so precious to me as it is now.
    Think you but that I know our state secure,
    I would be so triumphant as I am?
DERBY
    The lords at Pomfret, when they rode from London,
    Were jocund and supposed their states were sure,
    And they indeed had no cause to mistrust;
    But yet you see how soon the day o'ercast.
    This sudden stab of rancour I mistrust:
    Pray God, I say, I prove a needless coward!
    What, shall we toward the Tower? The day is spent.
HASTINGS
    Come, come, have with you. Know you what, my lord?
    To-day the lords you talked of are beheaded.
DERBY
    They, for their truth, might better wear their heads
    Than some that have accused them wear their hats.
    But come, my lord, let's away.

Enter a Pursuivant.

HASTINGS
Go on before. I'll talk with this good fellow.
                          Exeunt Stanley and Catesby.
How now, fellow? How goes the world with you?
PURSUIVANT
The better that your lordship pleases to ask.
HASTINGS
I tell you, man, 'tis better with me now
Than when you met me last where now we meet.
Then was I going prisoner to the Tower,
By the suggestion of the queen's allies.
But now I tell you, keep it to yourself,
This day those enemies are put to death,
And I in better state than ever I was.
PURSUIVANT
God hold it, to your honour's good content!
HASTINGS
Much thanks, fellow. There, drink that for me.

Throws him his purse.

PURSUIVANT   I thank your honour.   *Exit Pursuivant.*

Enter a Priest.

PRIEST
Well met, my lord. I am glad to see your honour.
HASTINGS
I thank you, good Sir John, with all my heart.
I am in your debt for your last exercise;
Come the next Sabbath, and I will content you.

[*He whispers in his ear.*]

PRIEST

   I'll wait upon your lordship.

           Enter Buckingham.

BUCKINGHAM

   What, talking with a priest, Lord Chamberlain?
   Your friends at Pomfret, they do need the priest;
   Your honour has no shriving work in hand.

HASTINGS

   Good faith, and when I met this holy man,
   The men you talk of came into my mind.
   What, go you toward the Tower?

BUCKINGHAM

   I do, my lord, but long I cannot stay there.
   I shall return before your lordship thence.

HASTINGS

   Nay, like enough, for I stay dinner there.

BUCKINGHAM   [*aside*]

   And supper too, although you know it not.—
   Come, will you go?

HASTINGS   I'll wait upon your lordship.   *Exeunt.*

SCENE III
Pomfret Castle.

Enter Ratcliffe, with halberds, leading Rivers,
Grey, and Vaughan to execution.

RATCLIFFE   Come, bring forth the prisoners.

RIVERS

   Sir Richard Ratcliffe, let me tell you this:
   To-day shall you behold a subject die
   For truth, for duty, and for loyalty.

GREY

God bless the prince from all the pack of you!
A knot you are of damnèd bloodsuckers.

VAUGHAN

You live that shall cry woe for this hereafter.

RATCLIFFE

Dispatch! The limit of your lives is out.

RIVERS

O Pomfret, Pomfret! O you bloody prison,
Fatal and ominous to noble peers!
Within the guilty closure of your walls
Richard the Second here was hacked to death;
And, for more slander to your dismal seat,
We give to you our guiltless blood to drink.

GREY

Now Margaret's curse is fallen upon our heads,
When she exclaimed on Hastings, you, and me,
For standing by when Richard stabbed her son.

RIVERS

Then cursed she Richard, then cursed she Buckingham,
Then cursed she Hastings. O, remember, God,
To hear her prayer for them, as now for us!
And for my sister and her princely sons,
Be satisfied, dear God, with our true blood,
Which, as you know, unjustly must be spilt.

RATCLIFFE

Make haste. The hour of death is expiate.

RIVERS

Come, Grey; come, Vaughan; let us here embrace.
Farewell, until we meet again in heaven.   *Exeunt.*

SCENE IV
London. The Tower.

Enter Buckingham, Derby, Hastings, Bishop of Ely, Norfolk,
Ratcliffe, Lovel, with others, at a table.

HASTINGS
> Now, noble peers, the cause why we are met
> Is to determine of the coronation.
> In God's name, speak. When is the royal day?

BUCKINGHAM
> Are all things ready for the royal time?

DERBY
> It is, and wants but nomination.

BISHOP OF ELY
> To-morrow then I judge a happy day.

BUCKINGHAM
> Who knows the Lord Protector's mind herein?
> Who is most inward with the noble duke?

BISHOP OF ELY
> Your grace, we think, should soonest know his mind.

BUCKINGHAM
> We know each other's faces; for our hearts,
> He knows no more of mine than I of yours;
> Or I of his, my lord, than you of mine.
> Lord Hastings, you and he are near in love.

HASTINGS
> I thank his grace, I know he loves me well;
> But, for his purpose in the coronation,
> I have not sounded him, nor he delivered
> His gracious pleasure any way therein.
> But you, my honourable lords, may name the time,
> And in the duke's behalf I'll give my voice,
> Which, I presume, he'll take in gentle part.

Enter Richard.

BISHOP OF ELY
> In happy time, here comes the duke himself.

RICHARD

> My noble lords and cousins all, good morrow.
> I have been long a sleeper; but I trust
> My absence does neglect no great design
> Which by my presence might have been concluded.

BUCKINGHAM

> Had you not come upon your cue, my lord,
> William Lord Hastings had pronounced your part—
> I mean, your voice for crowning of the king.

RICHARD

> Than my Lord Hastings no man might be bolder.
> His lordship knows me well, and loves me well.
> My Lord of Ely, when I was last in Holborn
> I saw good strawberries in your garden there.
> I do beseech you send for some of them.

BISHOP OF ELY

> Indeed and will, my lord, with all my heart. *Exit Bishop.*

RICHARD

> Cousin of Buckingham, a word with you.

[*Takes him aside.*]

> Catesby has sounded Hastings in our business:
> And finds the testy gentleman so hot,
> That he will lose his head ere give consent
> His master's child, as worshipfully he terms it,
> Shall lose the royalty of England's throne.

BUCKINGHAM

> Withdraw yourself awhile. I'll go with you.
>   *Exeunt Richard and Buckingham.*

DERBY

> We have not yet set down this day of triumph:
> To-morrow, in my judgment, is too sudden;
> For I myself am not so well provided
> As else I would be, were the day prolonged.

Enter the Bishop of Ely.

BISHOP OF ELY
  Where is my lord the Duke of Gloucester?
  I have sent for these strawberries.
HASTINGS
  His grace looks cheerfully and smooth this morning;
  There's some conceit or other likes him well
  When that he bids good morrow with such spirit.
  I think there's never a man in Christendom
  Can lesser hide his love or hate than he,
  For by his face straight shall you know his heart.
DERBY
  What of his heart perceive you in his face
  By any liveliness he showed to-day?
HASTINGS
  Sure, that with no man here he is offended;
  For were he, he had shown it in his looks.
DERBY
  I pray God he is not, I say.

Enter Richard and Buckingham.

RICHARD
  I pray you all, tell me what they deserve
  That do conspire my death with devilish plots
  Of damnèd witchcraft, and that have prevailed
  Upon my body with their hellish charms.
HASTINGS
  The tender love I bear your grace, my lord,
  Makes me most forward in this princely presence
  To judge the offenders, whosoever they are:
  I say, my lord, they have deserved death.
RICHARD
  Then be your eyes the witness of their evil.
  Look how I am bewitched. Behold, my arm

Is like a blasted sapling, withered up;
And this is Edward's wife, that monstrous witch,
Consorted with that harlot, strumpet Shore,
That by their witchcraft thus have markèd me.

HASTINGS

If they have done this deed, my noble lord—

RICHARD

If? You protector of this damnèd strumpet,
Talk you to me of ifs? You are a traitor.
Off with his head! Now by Saint Paul, I swear
I will not dine until I see the same.
Lovel and Ratcliffe, look that it is done:
The rest that love me, rise and follow me.

Exeunt, all but Lovel, Ratcliffe, and Hastings.

HASTINGS

Woe, woe for England, not a whit for me!
For I, too sure, might have prevented this.
Stanley did dream the boar did raze our helms;
But I did scorn it and disdain to fly.
Three times to-day my footcloth horse did stumble,
And started when he looked upon the Tower,
As loath to bear me to the slaughterhouse.
O, now I need the priest that spoke to me!
I now repent I told the pursuivant,
As too triumphing, how my enemies
To-day at Pomfret bloodily were butchered,
And I myself secure, in grace and favour.
O Margaret, Margaret, now your heavy curse
Is lighted on poor Hastings' wretched head!

RATCLIFFE

Come, come, dispatch! The duke would be at dinner.
Make a short shrift; he longs to see your head.

HASTINGS

O momentary grace of mortal men,
Which we more hunt for than the grace of God!
Who builds his hope in air of your good looks

Lives like a drunken sailor on a mast,
Ready with every nod to tumble down
Into the fatal bowels of the deep.

LOVEL

Come, come, dispatch! 'Tis useless to exclaim.

HASTINGS

O bloody Richard! Miserable England!
I prophesy the fearfullest time to you
That ever wretched age has looked upon.
Come, lead me to the block; bear him my head.
They smile at me who shortly shall be dead.   *Exeunt.*

SCENE V
The Tower Walls.

*Enter Richard, and
Buckingham, in rotten armour.*

RICHARD

Come, cousin, can you quake and change your colour,
Murder your breath in middle of a word,
And then again begin, and stop again,
As if you were distraught and mad with terror?

BUCKINGHAM

Tut, I can counterfeit the deep tragedian,
Speak and look back, and pry on every side,
Tremble and start at wagging of a straw:
Intending deep suspicion, ghastly looks
Are at my service, like enforcèd smiles;
And both are ready in their offices,
At any time to grace my stratagems.
But what, is Catesby gone?

RICHARD

He is; and see, he brings the Mayor along.

Enter the Mayor and Catesby.

BUCKINGHAM
　Lord Mayor —
RICHARD
　Look to the drawbridge there!
BUCKINGHAM
　Hark! a drum.
RICHARD
　Catesby, overlook the walls.
BUCKINGHAM
　Lord Mayor, the reason we have sent —
RICHARD
　Look back! defend you! Here are enemies!
BUCKINGHAM
　God and our innocence defend and guard us!

Enter Lovel and Ratcliffe, with Hastings' head.

RICHARD
　Be patient, they are friends — Ratcliffe and Lovel.
LOVEL
　Here is the head of that ignoble traitor,
　The dangerous and unsuspected Hastings.
RICHARD
　So dear I loved the man that I must weep:
　I took him for the plainest harmless creature
　That breathed upon the earth a Christian;
　Made him my book, wherein my soul recorded
　The history of all her secret thoughts.
　So smooth he daubed his vice with show of virtue
　That, his apparent open guilt omitted —
　I mean, his conversation with Shore's wife —
　He lived from all attainder of suspects.

BUCKINGHAM

    Well, well, he was the covertest sheltered traitor

    That ever lived. Look you, my Lord Mayor.

    Would you imagine, or almost believe,

    Were it not that by great preservatiòn

    We live to tell it, that the subtle traitor

    This day had plotted, in the Council House,

    To murder me and my good Lord of Gloucester?

MAYOR

    Had he done so?

RICHARD

    What? Think you we are Turks or infidels?

    Or that we would, against the form of law,

    Proceed thus rashly in the villain's death

    But that the extreme peril of the case,

    The peace of England, and our persons' safety

    Enforced us to this executiòn?

MAYOR

    Now fair befall you! He deserved his death,

    And your good graces both have well proceeded

    To warn false traitors from the like attempts.

    I never looked for better at his hands

    After he once fell in with Mistress Shore.

BUCKINGHAM

    Yet had we not determined he should die

    Until your lordship came to see his end,

    Which now the loving haste of these our friends,

    Something against our meanings, have forestalled.

    Because, my lord, I would have had you heard

    The traitor speak, and timorously confess

    The manner and the purpose of his treasons;

    That you might well have signified the same

    Unto the citizens, who haply may

    Miscònstrue us in him and wail his death.

MAYOR

But, my good lord, your grace's words shall serve,
As well as I had seen, and heard him speak;
And do not doubt, right noble princes both,
But I'll acquaint our duteous citizens
With all your just proceedings in this cause.

RICHARD

And to that end we wished your lordship here,
To avoid the censures of the carping world.

BUCKINGHAM

But since you come too late of our intent,
Yet witness what you hear we did intend.
And so, my good Lord Mayor, we bid farewell.

Exit Mayor.

RICHARD

Go after, after, cousin Buckingham.
The Mayor towards Guildhall hurries in all post:
There, at your meetest advantage of the time,
Infer the bastardy of Edward's children.
Tell them how Edward put to death a citizen
Only for saying he would make his son
Heir to the Crown—meaning indeed his house,
Which by the sign thereof was termèd so.
Moreover, urge his hateful lustfulness
And bestial appetite in change of lust,
Which stretched unto their servants, daughters, wives,
Even where his raging eye or savage heart,
Without control, lusted to make a prey.
Nay, for a need, thus far come near my person:
Tell them, that when my mother went with child
Of that insatiate Edward, noble York,
My princely father, then had wars in France,
And by true computation of the time
Found that the issue was not his begot;
Which well appearèd in his lineaments,
Being nothing like the noble duke my father.

Yet touch this sparingly, as if far off,
Because, my lord, you know my mother lives.
BUCKINGHAM
Doubt not, my lord, I'll play the orator
As if the golden fee for which I plead
Were for myself—and so, my lord, adieu.
RICHARD
If you thrive well, bring them to Baynard's Castle,
Where you shall find me well accompanied
With reverend fathers and well-learnèd bishops.
BUCKINGHAM
I go; and towards three or four o'clock
Look for the news that the Guildhall affords.

Exit Buckingham.

RICHARD
Go, Lovel, with all speed to Doctor Shaw—

[*To Catesby*]

Go you to Friar Penker.—Bid them both
Meet me within this hour at Baynard's Castle.

Exeunt Lovel, Catesby, and Ratcliffe.

Now will I go to take some privy order
To draw the brats of Clarence out of sight,
And to give order that no manner of person
Has any time recourse unto the princes.   *Exit.*

SCENE VI
A street.

Enter a Scrivener.

SCRIVENER
Here is the indictment of the good Lord Hastings,
Which in a set hand fairly is engrossed

That it may be to-day read over in Paul's.
And mark how well the sequel hangs together.
Eleven hours I have spent to write it over,
For yesternight by Catesby was it sent me;
The precedent was full as long a-doing;
And yet within these five hours Hastings lived,
Untainted, unexamined, free, at liberty.
Here's a good world the while! Who is so gross
That cannot see this palpable device?
Yet who's so bold but says he sees it not?
Bad is the world, and all will come to nought
When such ill dealing must be seen in thought.

Exit.

SCENE VII
Baynard's Castle.

*Enter Richard and
Buckingham at separate doors.*

RICHARD

How now, how now? What say the citizens?

BUCKINGHAM

Now, by the holy Mother of our Lord,
The citizens are mum, say not a word.

RICHARD

Touched you the bastardy of Edward's children?

BUCKINGHAM

I did, with his contràct with Lady Lucy,
And his contràct by deputy in France;
The insatiate greediness of his desire
And his enforcement of the city wives;
His tyranny for trifles; his own bastardy,
As being got, your father then in France,
And his resemblance, being not like the duke.

Also I did infer your lineaments,
Being the right idea of your father
Both in your form and nobleness of mind;
Laid open all your victories in Scotland,
Your discipline in war, wisdom in peace,
Your bounty, virtue, fair humility;
Indeed, left nothing fitting for your purpose
Untouched, or slightly handled in discourse.
And when my oratory drew to an end,
I bid them that did love their country's good
Cry, 'God save Richard, England's royal king!'

RICHARD

And did they so?

BUCKINGHAM

No, so God help me, they spoke not a word,
But, like dumb statuas or breathing stones,
Stared each on other, and looked deadly pale.
Which when I saw, I reprehended them,
And asked the Mayor what meant this wilful silence.
His answer was, the people were not used
To be spoken to but by the Recorder.
Then he was urged to tell my tale again:
'Thus says the duke, thus has the duke inferred,'—
But nothing spoke in warrant from himself.
When he had done, some followers of my own,
At lower end of the hall, hurled up their caps,
And some ten voices cried, 'God save King Richard!'
And thus I took the vantage of those few:
'Thanks, gentle citizens and friends,' said I.
'This general applause and cheerful shout
Argue your wisdoms and your love to Richard'—
And even here broke off and came away.

RICHARD

What tongueless blocks were they! Would they not speak?

BUCKINGHAM

No, by my faith, my lord.

RICHARD

Will not the Mayor then and his brethren come?

BUCKINGHAM

The Mayor is here at hand. Pretend some fear;
Be not you spoken with but by mighty suit.
And look you get a prayer book in your hand
And stand between two churchmen, good my lord;
For on that ground I'll make a holy descant.
And be not easily won to our requests.
Play the maid's part: still answer nay, and take it.

RICHARD

I go; and if you plead as well for them
As I can say nay to you for myself,
No doubt we bring it to a happy issue.

BUCKINGHAM

Go, go, up to the leads! The Lord Mayor knocks.

[*Exit Richard.*]

Enter the Mayor, Aldermen, and Citizens.

Welcome, my lord. I dance attendance here;
I think the duke will not be spoken with.

Enter Catesby.

Now, Catesby, what says your lord to my request?

CATESBY

He does entreat your grace, my noble lord,
To visit him to-morrow or next day.
He is within, with two right reverend fathers,
Divinely bent to meditatiòn,
And in no worldly suits would he be moved
To draw him from his holy exercise.

BUCKINGHAM
    Return, good Catesby, to the gracious Duke:
    Tell him, myself, the Mayor and Aldermen,
    In deep designs, in matter of great moment,
    No less importing than our general good,
    Are come to have some conference with his grace.
CATESBY
    I'll signify so much unto him straight.   *Exit.*
BUCKINGHAM
    Ah ha, my lord! this prince is not an Edward.
    He is not lolling on a lewd love-bed,
    But on his knees at meditatiòn;
    Not dallying with a brace of courtesans,
    But meditating with two deep divines;
    Not sleeping, to engross his idle body,
    But praying, to enrich his watchful soul.
    Happy were England, would this virtuous prince
    Take on his grace the sovereignty thereof;
    But sure I fear we shall not win him to it.
MAYOR
    Well, God defend his grace should say us nay!
BUCKINGHAM
    I fear he will. Here Catesby comes again.

Enter Catesby.

    Now, Catesby, what says his grace?
CATESBY   My lord,
    He wonders to what end you have assembled
    Such troops of citizens to come to him,
    His grace not being warned thereof before.
    He fears, my lord, you mean no good to him.
BUCKINGHAM
    Sorry I am my noble cousin should
    Suspect me that I mean no good to him:
    By heaven, we come to him in perfect love;

And so once more return and tell his grace.

Exit Catesby.

When holy and devout religious men
Are at their beads, 'tis much to draw them thence,
So sweet is zealous contemplatiòn.

Enter Richard aloft, between two Bishops. Catesby returns.

MAYOR

See where his grace stands, between two clergymen.

BUCKINGHAM

Two props of virtue for a Christian prince,
To stay him from the fall of vanity;
And see, a book of prayèr in his hand—
True ornaments to know a holy man.
Famous Plantagenet, most gracious prince,
Lend favourable ear to our requests,
And pardon us the interruptiòn
Of your devotion and right Christian zeal.

RICHARD

My lord, there needs no such apology:
I do beseech your grace to pardon me,
Who, earnest in the service of my God,
Deferred the visitation of my friends.
But, leaving this, what is your grace's pleasure?

BUCKINGHAM

Even that, I hope, which pleases God above
And all good men of this ungoverned isle.

RICHARD

I do suspect I have done some offence
That seems disgracious in the city's eye,
And that you come to reprehend my ignorance.

BUCKINGHAM

You have, my lord. Would it might please your grace,
On our entreaties, to amend your fault!

RICHARD
    Else wherefore breathe I in a Christian land?
BUCKINGHAM
    Know then it is your fault that you resign
    The supreme seat, the throne majestical,
    The sceptered office of your ancestors,
    Your state of fortune and your due of birth,
    The lineal glory of your royal house,
    To the corruption of a blemished stock.
    While, in the mildness of your sleepy thoughts,
    Which here we waken to our country's good,
    The noble isle does want her proper limbs;
    Her face defaced with scars of infamy,
    Her royal stock grafted with ignoble plants,
    And almost shouldered in the swallowing gulf
    Of dark forgetfulness and deep oblivion.
    Which to restore, we heartily solicit
    Your gracious self to take on you the charge
    And kingly government of this your land.
    Not as Protector, steward, substitute,
    Or lowly factor for another's gain;
    But as successively, from blood to blood,
    Your right of birth, your empery, your own.
    For this, consorted with the citizens,
    Your very worshipful and loving friends,
    And by their vehement instigation,
    In this just cause come I to move your grace.
RICHARD
    I cannot tell if to depart in silence,
    Or bitterly to speak in your reproof,
    Best fits now my degree or your condition.
    If not to answer, you might haply think
    Tongue-tied ambition, not replying, yielded
    To bear the golden yoke of sovereignty
    Which fondly you would here impose on me.
    If to reprove you for this suit of yours,

So seasoned with your faithful love to me,
Then, on the other side, I checked my friends.
Therefore—to speak, and to avoid the first,
And then, in speaking, not to incur the last—
Definitively thus I answer you.
Your love deserves my thanks, but my desert
Unmeritable shuns your high request.
First, if all obstacles were cut away,
And that my path were even to the crown,
As the ripe revenue and due of birth,
Yet so much is my poverty of spirit,
So mighty and so many my defects,
That I would rather hide me from my greatness,
Being a bark to brook no mighty sea,
Than in my greatness covet to be hid
And in the vapour of my glory smothered.
But, God be thanked, there is no need of me,
And much I need to help you, if there is need:
The royal tree has left us royal fruit,
Which, mellowed by the stealing hours of time,
Will well become the seat of majesty
And make, no doubt, us happy by his reign.
On him I lay that you would lay on me,
The right and fortune of his happy stars,
Which God defend that I should wring from him!

BUCKINGHAM
My lord, this argues conscience in your grace,
But the respects thereof are fine and trivial,
All circumstances well consider èd.
You say that Edward is your brother's son:
So say we too, but not by Edward's wife;
For first was he contracted to Lady Lucy—
Your mother lives a witness to his vow—
And afterward by substitute betrothed
To Bona, sister to the King of France.
These both put off, a poor petitioner,

A care-crazed mother to her many sons,
A beauty-waning and distressèd widow,
Even in the afternoon of her best days,
Made prize and purchase of his wanton eye,
Seduced the pitch and height of his degree
To base declension and loathed bigamy.
By her, in his unlawful bed, he got
This Edward, whom our manners call the prince.
More bitterly could I expostulate,
Save that, for reverence to some alive,
I give a sparing limit to my tongue.
Then, good my lord, take to your royal self
This proffered benefit of dignity;
If not to bless us and the land as well,
Yet to draw forth your noble ancestry
From the corruption of abusing times
Unto a lineal true-derivèd course.

MAYOR
Do, good my lord; your citizens entreat you.

BUCKINGHAM
Refuse not, mighty lord, this proffered love.

CATESBY
O, make them joyful, grant their lawful suit!

RICHARD
Alas, why would you heap this care on me?
I am unfit for state and majesty:
I do beseech you take it not amiss,
I cannot and I will not yield to you.

BUCKINGHAM
If you refuse it—as, in love and zeal,
Loath to depose the child, your brother's son;
As well we know your tenderness of heart
And gentle, kind, effeminate remorse,
Which we have noted in you to your kindred
And equally indeed to all estates—
Yet know, whether you accept our suit or no,

Your brother's son shall never reign our king,
But we will plant some other in the throne
To the disgrace and downfall of your house;
And in this resolution here we leave you.
Come, citizens. Zounds, I'll entreat no more!
RICHARD
O, do not swear, my lord of Buckingham.

Exeunt Buckingham, Mayor, Aldermen,
and Citizens.

CATESBY
Call him again, sweet prince, accept their suit:
If you deny them, all the land will rue it.
RICHARD
Will you enforce me to a world of cares?
Call them again. I am not made of stones,
But penetrable to your kind entreaties,
Albeit against my conscience and my soul.

Enter Buckingham and the rest.

Cousin of Buckingham, and sage grave men,
Since you will buckle fortune on my back,
To bear her burden, whether I will or no,
I must have patience to endure the load.
But if black scandal or foul-faced reproach
Attend the sequel of your imposition,
Your mere enforcement shall acquittance me
From all the impure blots and stains thereof.
For God does know, and you may partly see,
How far I am from the desire of this.
MAYOR
God bless your grace! We see it and will say it.
RICHARD
In saying so you shall but say the truth.

BUCKINGHAM

Then I salute you with this royal title—
Long live King Richard, England's worthy king!

ALL

Amen.

BUCKINGHAM

To-morrow may it please you to be crowned?

RICHARD

Even when you please, for you will have it so.

BUCKINGHAM

To-morrow then we will attend your grace,
And so most joyfully we take our leave.

RICHARD   [*to the Bishops*]

Come, let us to our holy work again.
Farewell, my cousin; farewell, gentle friends.   *Exeunt.*

Act IV

SCENE I
Before the Tower.

*Enter the Queen, the Duchess of
York, and Dorset at one door;
Anne Duchess of Gloucester
Clarence's young daughter, at
another door.*

DUCHESS OF YORK
Who meets us here? My niece Plantagenet,
Led in the hand of her kind aunt of Gloucester?
Now, for my life, she's wandering to the Tower
On pure heart's love, to greet the tender prince.
Daughter, well met.

ANNE   God give your graces both
A happy and a joyful time of day!

QUEEN ELIZABETH
As much to you, good sister. Whither away?

ANNE
No farther than the Tower and, as I guess,
Upon the like devotion as yourselves,
To gratulate the gentle princes there.

QUEEN ELIZABETH
Kind sister, thanks. We'll enter all together.

Enter the Lieutenant.

And in good time, here the Lieutenant comes.
Master Lieutenant, pray you, by your leave,
How do the prince and my young son of York?

LIEUTENANT
  Right well, dear madam. By your patiènce,
  I may not suffer you to visit them;
  The King has strictly charged the contrary.
QUEEN ELIZABETH
  The King? Who's that?
LIEUTENANT   I mean the Lord Protector.
QUEEN ELIZABETH
  The Lord protect him from that kingly title!
  Has he set bounds between their love and me?
  I am their mother; who shall bar me from them?
DUCHESS OF YORK
  I am their father's mother; I will see them.
ANNE
  Their aunt I am in law, in love their mother;
  Then bring me to their sights. I'll bear your blame
  And take your office from you on my peril.
LIEUTENANT
  No, madam, no! I may not leave it so:
  I am bound by oath, and therefore pardon me.
                                   Exit Lieutenant.

            Enter Stanley, Earl of Derby.

DERBY
  Let me but meet you, ladies, an hour hence,
  And I'll salute your grace of York as mother
  And reverend looker-on of two fair queens.

                  [*To Anne*]

  Come, madam, you must straight to Westminster,
  There to be crownèd Richard's royal queen.
QUEEN ELIZABETH
  Ah, cut my lace asunder,
  That my pent heart may have some scope to beat,
  Or else I swoon with this dead-killing news!

ANNE

Despiteful tidings! O unpleasing news!

DORSET

Be of good cheer. Mother, how fares your grace?

QUEEN ELIZABETH

O Dorset, speak not to me, get you gone!
Death and destruction dog you at your heels;
Your mother's name is ominous to children.
If you will outstrip death, go cross the seas,
And live with Richmond, from the reach of hell.
Go hie you, hie you from this slaughterhouse,
Lest you increase the number of the dead
And make me die the thrall of Margaret's curse,
Nor mother, wife, nor England's counted queen.

DERBY

Full of wise care is this your counsel, madam:
Take all the swift advantage of the hours.
You shall have letters from me to my son
In your behalf, to meet you on the way:
Be not taken tardy by unwise delay.

DUCHESS OF YORK

O ill-dispersing wind of misery!
O my accursèd womb, the bed of death!
A basilisk have you hatched to the world,
Whose unavoided eye is murderous.

DERBY

Come, madam, come! I in all haste was sent.

ANNE

And I with all unwillingness will go.
O, would to God that the inclusive verge
Of golden metal that must round my brow
Were red-hot steel, to sear me to the brains!
Anointed let me be with deadly venom
And die ere men can say, 'God save the queen!'

QUEEN ELIZABETH
  Go, go, poor soul! I envy not your glory.
  To feed my humour wish yourself no harm.
ANNE
  No? Why! when he that is my husband now
  Came to me as I followed Henry's corpse,
  When scarce the blood was well washed from his hands
  Which issued from my other angel husband
  And that dear saint which then I weeping followed —
  O when, I say, I looked on Richard's face,
  This was my wish: 'Be you,' said I, 'accursed
  For making me, so young, so old a widow!
  And when you wed, let sorrow haunt your bed;
  And be your wife, if any are so mad,
  More miserable by the life of you
  Than you have made me by my dear lord's death!'
  Lo, ere I can repeat this curse again,
  Within so small a time, my woman's heart
  Grossly grew captive to his honey words,
  And proved the subject of my own soul's curse,
  Which hitherto has held my eyes from rest.
  For never yet one hoùr in his bed
  Did I enjoy the golden dew of sleep,
  But with his fearful dreams was still awaked.
  Besides, he hates me for my father Warwick.
  And will, no doubt, shortly be rid of me.
QUEEN ELIZABETH
  Poor heart, adieu! I pity your complaining.
ANNE
  No more than with my soul I mourn for yours.
DORSET
  Farewell, you woeful welcomer of glory.
ANNE
  Adieu, poor soul, that take your leave of it.

DUCHESS OF YORK   [*to Dorset*]
  Go you to Richmond, and good fortune guide you!

                    [*To Anne*]

  Go you to Richard, and good angels tend you!

              [*To Queen Elizabeth*]

  Go you to sanctuary, and good thoughts possess you!
  I to my grave, where peace and rest lie with me!
  Eighty odd years of sorrow have I seen,
  And each hour's joy racked with a week of grief.
QUEEN ELIZABETH
  Stay, yet look back with me unto the Tower.
  Pity, you ancient stones, those tender babes
  Whom envy has immured within your walls—
  Rough cradle for such little pretty ones!
  Rude ragged nurse, old sullen playfellow
  For tender princes—use my babies well!
  So foolish sorrow bids your stones farewell. *Exeunt.*

                   SCENE II
       A room of state in the Palace.

       A sennet. Enter Richard crowned,
     Buckingham, Catesby, Ratcliffe, Lovel,
              and others.

KING RICHARD
  Stand all apart. Cousin of Buckingham—
BUCKINGHAM
  My gracious sovereign.

KING RICHARD
> Give me your hand.

> *He ascends the throne.*

> Thus high, by your advice
> And your assistance, is King Richard seated.
> But shall we wear these glories for a day?
> Or shall they last, and we rejoice in them?

BUCKINGHAM
> Ever live they, and for ever let them last!

KING RICHARD
> Ah, Buckingham, now do I play the touch,
> To try if you be current gold indeed:
> Young Edward lives. Think now what I would speak.

BUCKINGHAM
> Say on, my loving lord.

KING RICHARD
> Why, Buckingham, I say I would be king.

BUCKINGHAM
> Why, so you are, my thrice-renownèd liege.

KING RICHARD
> Ha! Am I king? It is so. But Edward lives.

BUCKINGHAM
> True, noble prince.

KING RICHARD   O bitter consequence,
> That Edward still should live true noble prince!
> Cousin, you were not wont to be so dull.
> Shall I be plain? I wish the bastards dead,
> And I would have it suddenly performed.
> What say you now? Speak suddenly, be brief.

BUCKINGHAM
> Your grace may do your pleasure.

KING RICHARD
  Tut, tut, you are all ice; your kindness freezes.
  Say, have I your consent that they shall die?
BUCKINGHAM
  Give me some little breath, some pause, dear lord,
  Before I positively speak in this:
  I will resolve you herein presently.   *Exit Buckingham.*
CATESBY [*aside to another*]
  The King is angry. See, he gnaws his lip.
KING RICHARD
  I will converse with iron-witted fools
  And unrespective boys. None are for me
  That look into me with considerate eyes.
  High-reaching Buckingham grows circumspect.
  Boy!
PAGE
  My lord?
KING RICHARD
  Know you not any whom corrupting gold
  Will tempt unto a close exploit of death?
PAGE
  I know a discontented gentleman
  Whose humble means match not his haughty spirit.
  Gold were as good as twenty orators,
  And will, no doubt, tempt him to anything.
KING RICHARD
  What is his name?
PAGE   His name, my lord, is Tyrrel.
KING RICHARD
  I partly know the man. Go call him hither, boy.
                          Exit [Page].
  The deep-revolving clever Buckingham
  No more shall be the neighbour to my counsels.
  Has he so long held out with me, untired,
  And stops he now for breath? Well, be it so.

Enter Stanley Earl of Derby

How now, Lord Stanley? What's the news?
DERBY   Know, my loving lord,
   The Marquess Dorset, as I hear, is fled
   To Richmond in the parts where he abides.

Stands aside.

KING RICHARD
   Come hither, Catesby. Rumour it abroad
   That Anne my wife is very grievous sick:
   I will take order for her keeping close.
   Inquire me out some mean poor gentleman,
   Whom I will marry straight to Clarence' daughter.
   The boy is foolish, and I fear not him.
   Look how you dream! I say again, give out
   That Anne, my queen, is sick and like to die.
   About it! for it stands me much upon
   To stop all hopes whose growth may damage me.
                                          Exit Catesby.
   I must be married to my brother's daughter,
   Or else my kingdom stands on brittle glass:
   Murder her brothers, and then marry her—
   Uncertain way of gain! But I am in
   So far in blood that sin will pluck on sin.
   Tear-falling pity dwells not in this eye.

Enter Page, with Tyrrel.

   Is your name Tyrrel?
TYRREL
   James Tyrrel, and your most obedient subject.
KING RICHARD
   Are you indeed?
TYRREL   Prove me, my gracious lord.

KING RICHARD
    Dare you resolve to kill a friend of mine?
TYRREL
    Please you;
    But I had rather kill two enemies.
KING RICHARD
    Why, there you have it! Two deep enemies,
    Foes to my rest and my sweet sleep's disturbers,
    Are they that I would have you deal upon:
    Tyrrel, I mean those bastards in the Tower.
TYRREL
    Let me have open means to come to them,
    And soon I'll rid you from the fear of them.
KING RICHARD
    You sing sweet music. Hark, come hither, Tyrrel.
    Go, by this token. Rise, and lend your ear.

Whispers.

    There is no more but so: say it is done,
    And I will love you and prefer you for it.
TYRREL
    I will dispatch it straight.   *Exit*

Enter Buckingham.

BUCKINGHAM
    My lord, I have considered in my mind
    The late request that you did sound me in.
KING RICHARD
    Well, let that rest. Dorset is fled to Richmond.
BUCKINGHAM
    I hear the news, my lord.
KING RICHARD
    Stanley, he is your wife's son. Well, look unto it.

BUCKINGHAM

My lord, I claim the gift, my due by promise,
For which your honour and your faith are pawned:
The earldom of Hereford and the moveables
Which you have promisèd I shall possess.

KING RICHARD

Stanley, look to your wife: if she conveys
Letters to Richmond, you shall answer for it.

BUCKINGHAM

What says your highness to my just request?

KING RICHARD

I do remember that Henry the Sixth
Did prophesy that Richmond should be king,
When Richmond was a little peevish boy.
A king!—perhaps—perhaps—

BUCKINGHAM

My lord—

KING RICHARD

How chance the prophet could not at that time
Have told me, I being by, that I should kill him?

BUCKINGHAM

My lord, your promise for the earldom!

KING RICHARD

Richmond! When last I was at Exeter,
The Mayor in courtesy showed me the castle,
And called it Rougemont; at which name I started,
Because a bard of Ireland told me once
I should not live long after I saw Richmond.

BUCKINGHAM

My lord—

KING RICHARD

Ay, what's o'clock?

BUCKINGHAM

I am thus bold to put your grace in mind
Of what you promised me.

KING RICHARD   Well, but what's o'clock?

BUCKINGHAM
Upon the stroke of ten.
KING RICHARD   Well, let it strike.
BUCKINGHAM
Why let it strike?
KING RICHARD
Because that like a Jack you keep the stroke
Between your begging and my meditation.
I am not in the giving vein to-day.
BUCKINGHAM
May it please you to resolve me in my suit.
KING RICHARD
You trouble me; I am not in the vein.
Exeunt all but Buckingham.
BUCKINGHAM
And is it thus? Repays he my deep service
With such contempt? Made I him king for this?
O, let me think on Hastings, and be gone
To Brecknock while my fear-ful head is on!   *Exit.*

SCENE III
The same.

Enter Tyrrel.

TYRREL
The tyrannous and bloody act is done,
The most arch deed of piteous massacre
That ever yet this land was guilty of.
Dighton and Forrest, whom I did suborn
To do this piece of ruthless butchery,
Albeit they were fleshed villains, bloody dogs,
Melted with tenderness and kind compassion,
Wept like children in their death's sad story.
'O, thus,' said Dighton, 'lay the gentle babes.'

'Thus, thus,' said Forrest, 'girdling one another
Within their alabaster innocent arms.
Their lips were four red roses on a stalk,
Which in their summer beauty kissed each other.
A book of prayèrs on their pillow lay,
Which once,' said Forrest, 'almost changed my mind;
But O! the devil'—there the villain stopped—
When Dighton thus told on—'We smothered
The most replenishèd sweet work of nature
That from the prime creation ever she framed.'
Hence both are gone with conscience and remorse:
They could not speak; and so I left them both,
To bear this tidings to the bloody king.

Enter Richard.

And here he comes. All health, my sovereign lord!
KING RICHARD
Kind Tyrrel, am I happy in your news?
TYRREL
If to have done the thing you gave in charge
Begets your happiness, be happy then,
For it is done.
KING RICHARD   But did you see them dead?
TYRREL
I did, my lord.
KING RICHARD   And buried, gentle Tyrrel?
TYRREL
The chaplain of the Tower has buried them;
But where, to say the truth, I do not know.
KING RICHARD
Come to me, Tyrrel, soon after supper,
When you shall tell the process of their death.
Meantime, but think how I may do you good,
And be inheritor of your desire.
Farewell till then.

TYRREL   I humbly take my leave.   [*Exit.*]
KING RICHARD
   The son of Clarence have I pent up close,
   His daughter meanly have I matched in marriage,
   The sons of Edward sleep in Abraham's bosom,
   And Anne my wife has bid this world good night.
   Now, for I know the Breton Richmond aims
   At young Elizabeth, my brother's daughter,
   And by that knot looks proudly on the crown,
   To her go I, a jolly thriving wooer.

Enter Ratcliffe.

RATCLIFFE
   My lord—
KING RICHARD
   Good or bad news, that you come in so bluntly?
RATCLIFFE
   Bad news, my lord. Morton is fled to Richmond,
   And Buckingham, backed with the hardy Welshmen,
   Is in the field, and still his power increases.
KING RICHARD
   Ely with Richmond troubles me more near
   Than Buckingham and his rash-levied strength.
   Come! I have learned that fearful commenting
   Is leaden servitor to dull delay;
   Delay leads impotent and snail-paced beggary.
   Then fiery expedition be my wing,
   Jove's Mercury, and herald for a king!
   Go, muster men. My counsel is my shield;
   We must be brief when traitors brave the field. *Exeunt.*

SCENE IV
Before the Palace.

Enter old Queen Margaret.

QUEEN MARGARET

 So now prosperity begins to mellow
 And drop into the rotten mouth of death.
 Here in these confines slily have I lurked
 To watch the waning of my enemies.
 A dire induction am I witness to,
 And will to France, hoping the consequence
 Will prove as bitter, black, and tragical.
 Withdraw, wretched Margaret! Who comes here?
                                              [*Retires.*]

 Enter Duchess of York and Queen Elizabeth.

QUEEN ELIZABETH

 Ah, my poor princes! ah, my tender babes!
 My unblown flowers, new-appearing sweets!
 If yet your gentle souls fly in the air
 And be not fixed in doom perpetual,
 Hover about me with your airy wings
 And hear your mother's lamentation!
QUEEN MARGARET   [*aside*]
 Hover about her. Say that right for right
 Has dimmed your infant morn to agèd night.
DUCHESS OF YORK
 So many miseries have crazed my voice
 That my woe-wearied tongue is still and mute.
 Edward Plantagenet, why are you dead?
QUEEN MARGARET   [*aside*]
 Plantagenet does quit Plantagenet;
 Edward for Edward pays a dying debt.
QUEEN ELIZABETH
 Will you, O God, fly from such gentle lambs
 And throw them in the entrails of the wolf?
 When did you sleep when such a deed was done?

QUEEN MARGARET   [*aside*]
  When holy Harry died, and my sweet son.
DUCHESS OF YORK
  Dead life, blind sight, poor mortal-living ghost,
  Woe's scene, world's shame, grave's due by life usurped,
  Brief abstract and recòrd of tedious days,
  Rest your unrest on England's lawful earth,

[*Sits down.*]

  Unlawfully made drunk with innocent blood!
QUEEN ELIZABETH
  Ah that you would as soon afford a grave
  As you can yield a melancholy seat!
  Then would I hide my bones, not rest them here.
  Ah, who has any cause to mourn but we?

[*Sits down by her.*]

QUEEN MARGARET   [*comes forward*]
  If ancient sorrow be most reverent,
  Give mine the benefit of seniory
  And let my griefs frown on the upper hand.
  If sorrow can admit society,

[*Sits down with them.*]

  Tell over your woes again by viewing mine.
  I had an Edward, till a Richard killed him;
  I had a Harry, till a Richard killed him:
  You had an Edward, till a Richard killed him;
  You had a Richard, till a Richard killed him.
DUCHESS OF YORK
  I had a Richard too, and you did kill him;
  I had a Rutland too, you helped to kill him.

QUEEN MARGARET
    You had a Clarence too, and Richard killed him.
    From forth the kennel of your womb has crept
    A hellhound that does hunt us all to death:
    That dog, that had his teeth before his eyes,
    To worry lambs and lap their gentle blood,
    That foul defacer of God's handiwork,
    That excellent grand tyrant of the earth
    That reigns in gallèd eyes of weeping souls,
    Your womb let loose to chase us to our graves.
    O upright, just, and true-disposing God,
    How do I thank you that this carnal cur
    Preys on the issue of his mother's body,
    And makes her pew-fellow with others' moan!
DUCHESS OF YORK
    O Harry's wife, triumph not in my woes!
    God witness with me, I have wept for yours.
QUEEN MARGARET
    Bear with me! I am hungry for revenge,
    And now I cloy me with beholding it.
    Your Edward he is dead, that killed my Edward;
    Your other Edward dead, to quit my Edward;
    Young York he is thrown in, because both they
    Matched not the high perfection of my loss.
    Your Clarence he is dead that stabbed my Edward,
    And the beholders of this frantic play,
    The adulterous Hastings, Rivers, Vaughan, Grey,
    Untimely smothered in their dusky graves.
    Richard yet lives, hell's black intelligencer;
    Only reserved their factor to buy souls
    And send them thither. But at hand, at hand,
    Ensues his piteous and unpitied end.
    Earth gapes, hell burns, fiends roar, saints pray,
    To have him suddenly conveyed from hence.
    Cancel his bond of life, dear God, I pray,
    That I may live and say, 'The dog is dead.'

QUEEN ELIZABETH
   O, you did prophesy the time would come
   That I should wish for you to help me curse
   That bottled spider, that foul bunch-backed toad!
QUEEN MARGARET
   I called you then vain flourish of my fortune;
   I called you then poor shadow, painted queen,
   The presentation of but what I was,
   The flattering index of a direful pageant,
   One heaved a-high to be hurled down below;
   A mother only mocked with two fair babes,
   A dream of what you were, a garish flag,
   To be the aim of every dangerous shot;
   A sign of dignity, a breath, a bubble,
   A queen in jest, only to fill the scene.
   Where is your husband now? Where are your brothers?
   Where are your two sons? Wherein do you joy?
   Who sues and kneels and says, 'God save the queen'?
   Where are the bending peers that flattered you?
   Where are the thronging troops that followed you?
   Decline all this, and see what now you are:
   For happy wife, a most distressèd widow;
   For joyful mother, one that wails the name;
   For one being sued to, one that humbly sues;
   For queen, a very cripple crowned with care;
   For she that scorned at me, now scorned of me;
   For she being feared of all, now fearing one;
   For she commanding all, obeyed of none.
   Thus has the course of justice whirled about
   And left you but a very prey to time,
   Having no more but thought of what you were,
   To torture you the more, being what you are,
   You did usurp my place, and do you not
   Usurp the just proportion of my sorrow?
   Now your proud neck bears half my burdened yoke,
   From which even here I slip my weary head

And leave the burden of it all on you.
Farewell, York's wife, and queen of sad mischance!
These English woes shall make me smile in France.

QUEEN ELIZABETH
O you well skilled in curses, stay awhile
And teach me how to curse my enemies!

QUEEN MARGARET
Forbear to sleep the nights, and fast the days;
Compare dead happiness with living woe;
Think that your babes were sweeter than they were
And he that slew them fouler than he is:
Bettering your loss makes the bad causer worse;
Revolving this will teach you how to curse.

QUEEN ELIZABETH
My words are dull. O, quicken them with thine!

QUEEN MARGARET
Your woes will make them sharp and pierce like mine.
                                    Exit Queen Margaret.

DUCHESS OF YORK
Why should calamity be full of words?

QUEEN ELIZABETH
Windy attorneys to their client's woes,
Airy succeeders of intestate joys,
Poor breathing orators of miseries,
Let them have scope! Though what they will impart
Help nothing else, yet do they ease the heart.

DUCHESS OF YORK
If so, then be not tongue-tied: go with me,
And in the breath of bitter words let's smother
My damnèd son that your two sweet sons smothered.
The trumpet sounds. Be copious in exclaims.

Enter King Richard and his train marching.

KING RICHARD
Who intercepts me in my expedition?

DUCHESS OF YORK
    O, she that might have intercepted you,
    By strangling you in her accursèd womb,
    From all the slaughters, wretch, that you have done!
QUEEN ELIZABETH
    Hide you that forehead with a golden crown
    Where should be branded, if that right were right,
    The slaughter of the prince that owned that crown
    And the dire death of my poor sons and brothers?
    Tell me, you villain-slave, where are my children?
DUCHESS OF YORK
    You toad, you toad, where is your brother Clarence?
    And little Ned Plantagenet, his son?
QUEEN ELIZABETH
    Where are the gentle Rivers, Vaughan, Grey?
DUCHESS OF YORK
    Where is kind Hastings?
KING RICHARD
    A flourish, trumpets! Strike alarum, drums!
    Let not the heavens hear these telltale women
    Rail on the Lord's anointed. Strike, I say!

Flourish. Alarums.

    Either be patient and entreat me fair,
    Or with the clamorous report of war
    Thus will I drown your exclamatiòns.
DUCHESS OF YORK
    Are you my son?
KING RICHARD
    Ay, I thank God, my father, and yourself.
DUCHESS OF YORK
    Then patiently hear my impatiènce.
KING RICHARD
    Madam, I have a touch of your condition
    That cannot brook the accent of reproof.

DUCHESS OF YORK
  O, let me speak!
KING RICHARD   Do then, but I'll not hear.
DUCHESS OF YORK
  I will be mild and gentle in my words.
KING RICHARD
  And brief, good mother, for I am in haste.
DUCHESS OF YORK
  Are you so hasty? I have stayed for you,
  God knows, in torment and in agony.
KING RICHARD
  And came I not at last to comfort you?
DUCHESS OF YORK
  No, by the Holy Rood, you know it well,
  You came on earth to make the earth my hell.
  A grievous burden was your birth to me;
  Tetchy and wayward was your infancy;
  Your schooldays frightful, desperate, wild, and furious;
  Your prime of manhood daring, bold, and venturous;
  Your age confirmed, proud, subtle, sly, and bloody,
  More mild, but yet more harmful—kind in hatred.
  What comfortable hour can you name
  That ever graced me with your company?
KING RICHARD
  Faith, none, but Humphrey Hour, that called your grace
  To breakfast once, forth of my company.
  If I be so disgracious in your eye,
  Let me march on and not offend you, madam.
  Strike up the drum.
DUCHESS OF YORK   I pray you, hear me speak.
KING RICHARD
  You speak too bitterly.
DUCHESS OF YORK   Hear me a word;
  For I shall never speak to you again.

KING RICHARD
  So.
DUCHESS OF YORK
  Either you will die by God's just ordinance
  Ere from this war you return a conqueror,
  Or I with grief and extreme age shall perish
  And never more behold your face again.
  Therefore take with you my most grievous curse,
  Which in the day of battle attire you more
  Than all the còmplete armour that you wear!
  My prayèrs on the adverse party fight,
  And there the little souls of Edward's children
  Whisper the spirits of your enemies
  And promise them success and victory!
  Bloody you are, bloody will be your end;
  Shame serves your life and does your death attend. *Exit.*
QUEEN ELIZABETH
  Though far more cause, yet much less spirit to curse
  Abides in me. I say amen to her.
KING RICHARD
  Stay, madam; I must talk a word with you.
QUEEN ELIZABETH
  I have no more sons of the royal blood
  For you to slaughter. For my daughters, Richard,
  They shall be praying nuns, not weeping queens;
  And therefore level not to hit their lives.
KING RICHARD
  You have a daughter called Elizabeth,
  Virtuous and fair, royal and gracious.
QUEEN ELIZABETH
  And must she die for this? O, let her live,
  And I'll corrupt her manners, stain her beauty,
  Slander myself as false to Edward's bed,
  Throw over her the veil of infamy,
  So she may live unscarred of bleeding slaughter,
  I will confess she was not Edward's daughter.

KING RICHARD
  Wrong not her birth; she is a royal princess.
QUEEN ELIZABETH
  To save her life, I'll say she is not so.
KING RICHARD
  Her life is safest only in her birth.
QUEEN ELIZABETH
  And only in that safety died her brothers.
KING RICHARD
  Lo, at their birth good stars were opposite.
QUEEN ELIZABETH
  No, to their lives ill friends were contrary.
KING RICHARD
  All unavoided is the lot of destiny.
QUEEN ELIZABETH
  True, when avoided grace makes destiny:
  My babes were destined to a fairer death
  If grace had blessed you with a fairer life.
KING RICHARD
  You speak as if I had slain my cousins [nephews]!
QUEEN ELIZABETH
  Cousins indeed, and by their uncle cozened
  Of comfort, kingdom, kindred, freedom, life:
  Whose hand soever lanced their tender hearts,
  Your head, all indirectly, gave direction.
  No doubt the murderous knife was dull and blunt,
  Till it was whetted on your stone-hard heart
  To revel in the entrails of my lambs.
  But constant use of grief makes wild grief tame,
  My tongue should to your ears not name my boys
  Till that my nails were anchored in your eyes.
  And I, in such a desperate bay of death,
  Like a poor bark of sails and tackling reft,
  Rush all to pieces on your rocky bosom.

KING RICHARD
Madam, so thrive I in my enterprise
And dangerous outcome of bloody wars
As I intend more good to you and yours,
Than ever you or yours by me were harmed!
QUEEN ELIZABETH
What good is covered with the face of heaven,
To be discovered, that can do me good?
KING RICHARD
The advancement of your children, gentle lady.
QUEEN ELIZABETH
Up to some scaffold, there to lose their heads!
KING RICHARD
Unto the dignity and height of fortune,
The high imperial type of this earth's glory.
QUEEN ELIZABETH
Flatter my sorrow with report of it:
Tell me, what state, what dignity, what honour
Can you demise to any child of mine?
KING RICHARD
Even all I have—ay, and myself and all—
Will I with that endow a child of yours,
If in the Lethe of your angry soul
You drown the sad remembrance of those wrongs
Which you suppose that I have done to you.
QUEEN ELIZABETH
Be brief, lest the process of your kindness
Lasts longer telling than your kindness' date.
KING RICHARD
Then know that from my soul I love your daughter.
QUEEN ELIZABETH
My daughter's mother thinks it with her soul.
KING RICHARD
What do you think?

QUEEN ELIZABETH

    That you do love my daughter from your soul.
    So from your soul's love did you love her brothers,
    And from my heart's love I do thank you for it.

KING RICHARD

    Be not so hasty to confound my meaning:
    I mean that with my soul I love your daughter
    And do intend to make her Queen of England.

QUEEN ELIZABETH

    Well then, who do you mean shall be her king?

KING RICHARD

    Even he that makes her queen. Who should be else?

QUEEN ELIZABETH

    What, you?

KING RICHARD   Even so. How think you of it?

QUEEN ELIZABETH

    How can you woo her?

KING RICHARD   That would I learn of you,
    As one being best acquainted with her humour.

QUEEN ELIZABETH

    And will you learn of me?

KING RICHARD   Madam, with all my heart.

QUEEN ELIZABETH

    Send to her by the man that slew her brothers
    A pair of bleeding hearts; thereon engrave
    'Edward' and 'York'; then haply will she weep.
    Therefore present to her—as sometime Margaret
    Did to your father, steeped in Rutland's blood—
    A handkerchief, which say to her did drain
    The purple sap from her sweet brother's body,
    And bid her wipe her weeping eyes with that.
    If this inducement moves her not to love,
    Send her a letter of your noble deeds:
    Tell her you made away her uncle Clarence,
    Her uncle Rivers; ay, and for her sake.
    Made quick conveyance of her good aunt Anne.

KING RICHARD
    You mock me, madam; this is not the way
    To win your daughter.
QUEEN ELIZABETH   There is no other way,
    Unless you could put on some other shape,
    And not be Richard that has done all this.
KING RICHARD
    Say that I did all this for love of her.
QUEEN ELIZABETH
    Nay, then indeed she cannot choose but hate you,
    Having bought love with such a bloody spoil.
KING RICHARD
    Look, what is done cannot be now amended.
    Men shall deal unadvisedly sometimes,
    Which after-hours give leisure to repent.
    If I did take the kingdom from your sons,
    To make amends I'll give it to your daughter;
    If I have killed the issue of your womb,
    To quicken your increase I will beget
    My issue of your blood upon your daughter.
    A grandam's name is little less in love
    Than is the doting title of a mother.
    They are as children but one step below,
    Even of your metal, of your very blood,
    Of all one pain, save for a night of groans
    Endured of her for whom you bid like sorrow.
    Your children were vexation to your youth,
    But mine shall be a comfort to your age.
    The loss you have is but a son being king,
    And by that loss your daughter is made queen.
    I cannot make you what amends I would;
    Therefore accept such kindness as I can.
    Dorset your son, that with a fearful soul
    Leads discontented steps in foreign soil,
    This fair alliance quickly shall call home

To high promotions and great dignity.
The king, that calls your beauteous daughter wife,
Familiarly shall call your Dorset brother:
Again shall you be mother to a king,
And all the ruins of distressful times
Repaired with double riches of content.
What! we have many goodly days to see:
The liquid drops of tears that you have shed
Shall come again, transformed to orient pearl,
Advantaging their love with interest
Often times double gain of happiness.
Go then, my mother; to your daughter go;
Make bold her bashful years with your experience;
Prepare her ears to hear a wooer's tale;
Put in her tender heart the aspiring flame
Of golden sovereignty; acquaint the princess
With the sweet silent hours of marriage joys.
And when this arm of mine has chastisèd
The petty rebel, dull-brained Buckingham,
Bound with triumphant garlands will I come
And lead your daughter to a conqueror's bed;
To whom I will retail my conquest won,
And she shall be sole victoress, Caesar's Caesar.

QUEEN ELIZABETH
What were I best to say? Her father's brother
Would be her lord? Or shall I say her uncle?
Or he that slew her brothers and her uncles?
Under what title shall I woo for you
That God, the law, my honour, and her love
Can make seem pleasing to her tender years?

KING RICHARD
Infer fair England's peace by this alliance.

QUEEN ELIZABETH
Which she shall purchase with still-lasting war.

KING RICHARD
  Tell her the King, that may command, entreats.
QUEEN ELIZABETH
  That at her hands which the King's King forbids.
KING RICHARD
  Say she shall be a high and mighty queen.
QUEEN ELIZABETH
  To wail the title, as her mother does.
KING RICHARD
  Say I will love her everlastingly.
QUEEN ELIZABETH
  But how long shall that title 'ever' last?
KING RICHARD
  Sweetly in force unto her fair life's end.
QUEEN ELIZABETH
  But how long fairly shall her sweet life last?
KING RICHARD
  As long as heaven and nature lengthen it.
QUEEN ELIZABETH
  As long as hell and Richard like of it.
KING RICHARD
  Say I, her sovereign, am her subject low.
QUEEN ELIZABETH
  But she, your subject, loathes such sovereignty.
KING RICHARD
  Be eloquent in my behalf to her.
QUEEN ELIZABETH
  An honest tale speeds best being plainly told.
KING RICHARD
  Then plainly to her tell my loving tale.
QUEEN ELIZABETH
  Plain and not honest is too harsh a style.
KING RICHARD
  Your reasons are too shallow and too quick.

QUEEN ELIZABETH
  O no, my reasons are too deep and dead—
  Too deep and dead, poor infants, in their graves.
KING RICHARD
  Harp not on that string, madam; that is past.
QUEEN ELIZABETH
  Harp on it still shall I till heartstrings break.
KING RICHARD
  Now, by my George, my garter, and my crown—
QUEEN ELIZABETH
  Profaned, dishonoured, and the third usurped.
KING RICHARD
  I swear—
QUEEN ELIZABETH   By nothing, for this is no oath:
  Your George, profaned, has lost its lordly honour;
  Your garter, blemished, pawned its knightly virtue;
  Your crown, usurped, disgraced its kingly glory.
  If something you would swear to be believed,
  Swear then by something that you have not wronged.
KING RICHARD
  Then by myself—
QUEEN ELIZABETH   Yourself is self-misused.
KING RICHARD
  Now by the world—
QUEEN ELIZABETH   It is full of your foul wrongs.
KING RICHARD
  My father's death—
QUEEN ELIZABETH   Your life has it dishonoured.
KING RICHARD
  Why then, by God—
QUEEN ELIZABETH   God's wrong is most of all.
  If you did fear to break an oath with him,
  The unity the King my husband made
  You had not broken, nor my brothers died.
  If you had feared to break an oath by him,
  The imperial metal, circling now your head,

Had graced the tender temples of my child;
And both the princes had been breathing here,
Who now, two tender bedfellows for dust,
Your broken faith has made the prey for worms.
What can you swear by now?
KING RICHARD   The time to come.
QUEEN ELIZABETH
That you have wronged in the time overpast;
For I myself have many tears to wash
Hereafter time, for time past wronged by you.
The children live whose fathers you have slaughtered,
Ungoverned youth, to wail it in their age.
The parents live whose children you have butchered,
Old barren plants, to wail it with their age.
Swear not by time to come, for that you have
Misused ere used, by times ill-used o'erpast.
KING RICHARD
As I intend to prosper and repent,
So thrive I in my dangerous affairs
Of hostile arms! Myself myself confound!
Heaven and fortune bar me happy hours!
Day, yield me not your light, nor, night, your rest!
Be opposite all planets of good luck
To my proceeding if, with dear heart's love,
Immaculate devotion, holy thoughts,
I tender not your beauteous princely daughter!
In her consists my happiness and yours;
Without her, follows to myself and you,
Herself, the land, and many a Christian soul,
Death, desolation, ruin, and decay.
It cannot be avoided but by this;
It will not be avoided but by this.
Therefore, dear mother (I must call you so),
Be the attorney of my love to her:
Plead what I will be, not what I have been—
Not my deserts, but what I will deserve;

Urge the necessity and state of times,
And be not peevish-fond in great designs.

QUEEN ELIZABETH
Shall I be tempted of the devil thus?

KING RICHARD
Ay, if the devil tempts you to do good.

QUEEN ELIZABETH
Shall I forget myself to be myself?

KING RICHARD
Ay, if yourself's remembrance wrong yourself.

QUEEN ELIZABETH
Yet you did kill my children.

KING RICHARD
But in your daughter's womb I bury them,
Where, in that nest of spicery, they will breed
Selves of themselves, to your recomforture.

QUEEN ELIZABETH
Shall I go win my daughter to your will?

KING RICHARD
And be a happy mother by the deed.

QUEEN ELIZABETH
I go. Write to me very shortly,
And you shall understand from me her mind.

KING RICHARD
Bear her my true love's kiss; and so farewell—

Exit Queen Elizabeth.

Relenting fool, and shallow, changing woman!

Enter Ratcliffe, Catesby following.

How now? What news?

RATCLIFFE
Most mighty sovereign, on the western coast
Rides a powerful navy; to our shores
Throng many doubtful hollow-hearted friends,
Unarmed, and unresolved to beat them back.

It is thought that Richmond is their admiral;
And there they hull, expecting but the aid
Of Buckingham to welcome them ashore.

KING RICHARD
Some light-foot friend post to the Duke of Norfolk:
Ratcliffe, yourself—or Catesby—where is he?

CATESBY
Here, my good lord.

KING RICHARD   Catesby, fly to the Duke.

CATESBY
I will, my lord, with all convenient haste.

KING RICHARD
Ratcliffe, come hither. Post to Salisbury.
When you come thither—

[*To Catesby*]

Dull unmindful villain,
Why stay you here and go not to the Duke?

CATESBY
First, mighty king, tell me your highness' pleasure,
What from your grace I shall deliver to him.

KING RICHARD
O, true, good Catesby: bid him levy straight
The greatest strength and power that he can make
And meet me suddenly at Salisbury.

CATESBY
I go.   *Exit.*

RATCLIFFE
What, may it please you, shall I do at Salisbury?

KING RICHARD
Why, what would you do there before I go?

RATCLIFFE
Your highness told me I should post before.

KING RICHARD
My mind is changed.

Enter Lord Stanley Earl of Derby.

Stanley, what news with you?

DERBY

None good, my liege, to please you with the hearing,
Nor none so bad but well may be reported.

KING RICHARD

Hoyday, a riddle! Neither good nor bad!
What need you run so many miles about,
When you may tell your tale the nearest way?
Once more, what news?

DERBY   Richmond is on the seas.

KING RICHARD

There let him sink, and be the seas on him!
White-livered runagate, what does he there?

DERBY

I know not, mighty sovereign, but by guess.

KING RICHARD

Well, as you guess?

DERBY

Stirred up by Dorset, Buckingham, and Morton,
He makes for England, here to claim the crown.

KING RICHARD

Is the chair empty? is the sword unswayed?
Is the king dead? the empire unpossessed?
What heir of York is there alive but we?
And who is England's king but great York's heir?
Then tell me, what makes he upon the seas?

DERBY

Unless for that, my liege, I cannot guess.

KING RICHARD

Unless for that he comes to be your liege,
You cannot guess wherefore the Welshman comes.
You will revolt and fly to him, I fear.

DERBY
No, my good lord; therefore mistrust me not.
KING RICHARD
Where is your power then to beat him back?
Where are your tenants and your followers?
Are they not now upon the western shore,
Safe-conducting the rebels from their ships?
DERBY
No, my good lord, my friends are in the North.
KING RICHARD
Cold friends to me! What do they in the North
When they should serve their sovereign in the West?
DERBY
They have not been commanded, mighty king.
Please it your majesty to give me leave,
I'll muster up my friends and meet your grace
Where and what time your majesty shall please.
KING RICHARD
Ay, you would be gone to join with Richmond:
But I'll not trust you.
DERBY   Most mighty sovereign,
You have no cause to hold my friendship doubtful.
I never was nor ever will be false.
KING RICHARD
Go then and muster men. But leave behind
Your son, George Stanley. Look your heart be firm,
Or else his head's assurance is but frail.
DERBY
So deal with him as I prove true to you.   *Exit.*

Enter a Messenger.

1. MESSENGER
My gracious sovereign, now in Devonshire,
As I by friends am well advèrtisèd,

Sir Edward Courtney and the haughty prelate,
Bishop of Exeter, his elder brother,
With many more confederates, are in arms.

Enter another Messenger.

2. MESSENGER
In Kent, my liege, the Guildfords are in arms,
And every hour more competitors
Flock to the rebels, and their power grows strong.

Enter another Messenger.

3. MESSENGER
My lord, the army of great Buckingham—
KING RICHARD
Out on you, owls! Nothing but songs of death?

He strikes him.

There, take that, till you bring better news.
3. MESSENGER
The news I have to tell your majesty
Is that by sudden floods and fall of waters
Buckingham's army is dispersed and scattered,
And he himself wandered away alone,
No man knows whither.
KING RICHARD   I cry you mercy:
There is my purse to cure that blow of yours.
Has any well-advisèd friend proclaimed
Reward to him that brings the traitor in?
3. MESSENGER
Such proclamation has been made, my lord.

Enter another Messenger.

4. MESSENGER

    Sir Thomas Lovel and Lord Marquess Dorset,
    'Tis said, my liege, in Yorkshire are in arms.
    But this good comfort bring I to your highness:
    The Breton navy is dispersed by tempest;
    Richmond in Dorsetshire sent out a boat
    Unto the shore to ask those on the banks
    If they were his assistants, yea or no;
    Who answered him they came from Buckingham
    Upon his party. He, mistrusting them,
    Hoisted sail, and made his course for Brittany.

KING RICHARD

    March on, march on, since we are up in arms;
    If not to fight with foreign enemies,
    Yet to beat down these rebels here at home.

Enter Catesby.

CATESBY

    My liege, the Duke of Buckingham is taken.
    That is the best news. That the Earl of Richmond
    Is with a mighty power landed at Milford
    Is colder tidings, but yet they must be told.

KING RICHARD

    Away towards Salisbury! While we reason here,
    A royal battle might be won and lost.
    Some one take order Buckingham be brought
    To Salisbury; the rest march on with me.

                      Flourish. Exeunt.

SCENE V
Lord Stanley's house.

*Enter Lord Stanley Earl of Derby, and
Christopher Urswick, a priest.*

DERBY

    Sir Christopher, tell Richmond this from me:
    That in the sty of the most deadly boar
    My son George Stanley is shut up in hold;
    If I revolt, off goes young George's head;
    The fear of that holds off my present aid.
    So get you gone; commend me to your lord.
    Say that the Queen has heartily consented
    He should espouse Elizabeth her daughter.
    But tell me, where is princely Richmond now?

CHRISTOPHER

    At Pembroke, or at Ha'rford-West in Wales.

DERBY

    What men of name resort to him?

CHRISTOPHER

    Sir Walter Herbert, a renownèd soldier,
    Sir Gilbert Talbot, Sir William Stanley,
    Oxford, redoubted Pembroke, Sir James Blount,
    And Rice ap Thomas, with a valiant crew,
    And many others of great name and worth;
    And towards London do they bend their power,
    If by the way they are not fought with now.

DERBY

    Well, haste you to your lord. I kiss his hand:
    My letter will resolve him of my mind.

Gives letter.

Farewell.   *Exeunt.*

Act V

SCENE I
Near Salisbury.

*Enter Buckingham with halberds and the Sheriff,
led to execution.*

BUCKINGHAM
Will not King Richard let me speak with him?
SHERIFF
No, my good lord; therefore be patiènt.
BUCKINGHAM
Hastings, and Edward's children, Grey and Rivers,
Holy King Henry and your fair son Edward,
Vaughan and all that have miscarrièd
By underhand corrupted foul injustice,
If your moody discontented souls
Do through the clouds behold this present hour,
Even for revenge mock my destructiòn!
This is All Souls' day, fellow, is it not?
SHERIFF
It is, my lord.
BUCKINGHAM
Why, then All Souls' day is my body's doomsday.
This is the day which in King Edward's time
I wished might fall on me, when I was found
False to his children and his wife's allies.
This is the day wherein I wished to fall
By the false faith of him whom most I trusted.
This, this All Souls' day to my fearful soul
Is the determined respite of my wrongs:
That high All-seer whom I dallied with

Has turned my feignèd prayer on my head
And given in earnest what I begged in jest.
Thus does he force the swords of wicked men
To turn their own points in their masters' bosoms.
Thus Margaret's curse falls heavy on my neck:
'When he,' said she, 'shall split your heart with sorrow,
Remember Margaret was a prophetess.' —
Come lead me, officers, to the block of shame.
Wrong has but wrong, and blame the due of blame.
                    Exeunt Buckingham with Officers.

SCENE II
Near Tamworth.

*Enter Richmond, Oxford, Sir James Blount, Sir
Walter Herbert, and others, with drum and colours.*

RICHMOND
Fellows in arms, and my most loving friends,
Bruised underneath the yoke of tyranny,
Thus far into the bowels of the land
Have we marched on without impediment;
And here receive we from our father Stanley
Lines of fair comfort and encouragement.
The wretched, bloody, and usurping boar,
That spoiled your summer fields and fruitful vines,
Swills your warm blood like wash, and makes his trough
In your embowelled bosoms — this foul swine
Is now even in the centre of this isle,
Near to the town of Leicester, as we learn:
From Tamworth thither is but one day's march.
In God's name cheerily on, courageous friends,
To reap the harvest of perpetual peace
By this one bloody trial of sharp war.

OXFORD
    Every man's conscience is a thousand men,
    To fight against this guilty homicide.
HERBERT
    I doubt not but his friends will turn to us.
BLOUNT
    He has no friends but what are friends for fear,
    Who in his dearest need will fly from him.
RICHMOND
    All for our vantage. Then in God's name march!
    True hope is swift and flies with swallow's wings;
    Kings it makes gods, and meaner creatures kings.

                                                    Exeunt.

SCENE III
Bosworth Field.

*Enter King Richard in arms, with Norfolk, Ratcliffe,
the Earl of Surrey, and soldiers.*

KING RICHARD
    Here pitch our tent, even here in Bosworth field.
    My Lord of Surrey, why look you so sad?
SURREY
    My heart is ten times lighter than my looks.
KING RICHARD
    My Lord of Norfolk—
NORFOLK   Here, most gracious liege.
KING RICHARD
    Norfolk, we must have knocks. Ha! must we not?
NORFOLK
    We must both give and take, my loving lord.
KING RICHARD
    Up with my tent! Here will I lie to-night;

Soldiers begin to set up the King's tent.

But where to-morrow? Well, all's one for that.
Who has descried the number of the traitors?
NORFOLK
Six or seven thousand is their utmost power.
KING RICHARD
Why, our army trebles that account;
Besides, the king's name is a tower of strength,
Which they upon the adverse faction want.
Up with the tent! Come, noble gentlemen,
Let us survey the vantage of the ground.
Call for some men of sound directiòn:
Let's lack no discipline, make no delay,
For, lords, to-morrow is a busy day.   *Exeunt.*

Enter Richmond, Sir William Brandon, Oxford,
Dorset, Herbert, and Blount. Soldiers
pitch Richmond's tent.

RICHMOND
The weary sun has made a golden set
And by the bright tract of his fiery car
Gives token of a goodly day to-morrow.
Sir William Brandon, you shall bear my standard.
Give me some ink and paper in my tent:
I'll draw the form and model of our battle,
Limit each leader to his several charge,
And part in just proportion our small power.
My Lord of Oxford—you, Sir William Brandon—
And you, Sir Walter Herbert—stay with me.
The Earl of Pembroke keeps his regiment;
Good Captain Blount, bear my good-night to him,
And by the second hoùr in the morning
Desire the earl to see me in my tent.

Yet one thing more, good captain, do for me—
Where is Lord Stanley quartered, do you know?
BLOUNT
  Unless I have mistaken his colours much—
  Which well I am assured I have not done—
  His regiment lies half a mile at least
  South from the mighty powèr of the king.
RICHMOND
  If without peril it is possible,
  Sweet Blount, make some good means to speak with
    him
  And give him from me this most needful note.
BLOUNT
  Upon my life, my lord, I'll undertake it;
  And so God give you quiet rest to-night!
RICHMOND
  Good night, good Captain Blount.   *Exit Blount.*
                        Come, gentlemen,
  Let us consult upon to-morrow's business.
  In to my tent; the dew is raw and cold.

                    They withdraw into the tent.
          Enter, to his tent, King Richard, Ratcliffe,
                Norfolk, and Catesby.

KING RICHARD
  What is it o'clock?
CATESBY   It's supper time, my lord;
  It's nine o'clock.
KING RICHARD   I will not sup to-night.
  Give me some ink and paper.
  What? is my beaver easier than it was?
  And all my armour laid into my tent?
CATESBY
  It is, my liege, and all things are in readiness.

KING RICHARD
  Good Norfolk, hie you to your charge;
  Use careful watch, choose trusty sentinels.
NORFOLK
  I go, my lord.
KING RICHARD
  Stir with the lark to-morrow, gentle Norfolk.
NORFOLK
  I warrant you, my lord.   *Exit.*
KING RICHARD
  Catesby!
CATESBY
  My lord?
KING RICHARD   Send out a pursuivant-at-arms
  To Stanley's regiment; bid him bring his power
  Before sunrising, lest his son George fall
  Into the blind cave of eternal night.   *Exit Catesby.*
  Fill me a bowl of wine. Give me a watch.
  Saddle white Surrey for the field to-morrow.
  Look that my staves be sound and not too heavy.
  Ratcliffe!
RATCLIFFE
  My lord?
KING RICHARD
  Saw you the melancholy Lord Northumberland?
RATCLIFFE
  Thomas the Earl of Surrey and himself,
  Much about cockshut time, from troop to troop
  Went through the army, cheering up the soldiers.
KING RICHARD
  So, I am satisfied. Give me a bowl of wine.
  I have not that alacrity of spirit
  Nor cheer of mind that I was wont to have.

                        Wine brought.

Set it down. Are ink and paper ready?
RATCLIFFE
   They are, my lord.
KING RICHARD
   Bid my guard watch. Leave me. Ratcliffe,
   About the mid of night come to my tent
   And help to arm me. Leave me, I say.   *Exit Ratcliffe.*
                                  King Richard withdraws
                                  into his tent, and sleeps.

         Enter Lord Stanley Earl of Derby, to Richmond
            in his tent, Lords and others attending.

DERBY
   Fortune and victory sit on your helm!
RICHMOND
   All comfort that the dark night can afford
   Be to your person, noble father-in-law!
   Tell me, how fares our loving mother?
DERBY
   I, by attorney, bless you from your mother,
   Who prays continually for Richmond's good:
   So much for that. The silent hours steal on
   And flaky darkness breaks within the east.
   In brief, for so the season bids us be,
   Prepare your army early in the morning
   And put your fortune to the arbitrament
   Of bloody strokes and mortal-staring war.
   I, as I may—that which I would I cannot—
   With best advantage will deceive the time
   And aid you in this doubtful shock of arms.
   But on your side I may not be too forward,
   Lest, being seen, your brother, tender George,
   Be executed in his father's sight.
   Farewell. The leisure and the fearful time
   Cut off the ceremonious vows of love

And ample interchange of sweet discourse,
Which so long-sundered friends should dwell upon.
God give us leisure for these rites of love!
Once more adieu: be valiant, and speed well!
RICHMOND
Good lords, conduct him to his regiment.
I'll strive with troubled thoughts, to take a nap,
Lest leaden slumber weigh me down to-morrow,
When I should mount with wings of victory.
Once more, good night, kind lords and gentlemen.
                    Exeunt. Richmond remains.
O you, whose captain I account myself,
Look on my forces with a gracious eye;
Put in their hands your bruising irons of wrath,
That they may crush down with a heavy fall
The usurping helmets of our adversaries.
Make us your ministers of chastisement,
That we may praise you in the victory.
To you I do commend my watchful soul
Ere I let fall the windows of my eyes.
Sleeping and waking, O, defend me still!

                    Sleeps.
        Enter the Ghost of Prince Edward, son to
                Henry the Sixth.

GHOST   *(to Richard)*
Let me sit heavy on your soul to-morrow!
Think how you stabbed me in my prime of youth
At Tewkesbury: despair therefore, and die!

            (To Richmond)

Be cheerful, Richmond; for the wrongèd souls
Of butchered princes fight in your behalf.
King Henry's issue, Richmond, comforts you.

Enter the Ghost of Henry the Sixth.

GHOST   *(to Richard)*
When I was mortal, my anointed body
By you was punchèd full of deadly holes.
Think on the Tower, and me: despair, and die!
Harry the Sixth bids you despair, and die!

(To Richmond)

Virtuous and holy, be you conqueror!
Harry, that prophesied you should be king,
Does comfort you in your sleep: live, and flourish!

Enter the Ghost of Clarence.

GHOST   [*to Richard*]
Let me sit heavy in your soul to-morrow—
I that was washed to death with fulsome wine,
Poor Clarence by your guile betrayed to death!
To-morrow in the battle think on me,
Let fall your edgeless sword: despair, and die!

(To Richmond)

You offspring of the house of Lancaster,
The wrongèd heirs of York do pray for you;
Good angels guard your army! live, and flourish!

Enter the Ghosts of Rivers, Grey, and Vaughan.

RIVERS   [*to Richard*]
Let me sit heavy in your soul to-morrow,
Rivers, that died at Pomfret! despair, and die!
GREY
Think upon Grey, and let your soul despair!

VAUGHAN
    Think upon Vaughan, and with guilty fear
    Let fall your lance: despair, and die!
ALL   (to Richmond)
    Awake, and think our wrongs in Richard's bosom
    Will conquer him! Awake, and win the day!

        Enter the Ghost of Lord Hastings.

GHOST   [*to Richard*]
    Bloody and guilty, guiltily awake
    And in a bloody battle end your days!
    Think on Lord Hastings: despair, and die!

            (To Richmond)

    Quiet untroubled soul, awake, awake!
    Arm, fight, and conquer, for fair England's sake!

        Enter the Ghosts of the two young Princes.

GHOSTS   [*to Richard*]
    Dream on your nephews smothered in the Tower.
    Let us be lead within your bosom, Richard,
    And weigh you down to ruin, shame, and death!
    Your nephews' souls bid you despair, and die!

            (To Richmond)

    Sleep, Richmond, sleep in peace and wake in joy.
    Good angels guard you from the boar's annoy!
    Live, and beget a happy race of kings!
    Edward's unhappy sons do bid you flourish.

Enter the Ghost of Anne, his wife.

GHOST   *(to Richard)*
   Richard, your wife, that wretched Anne your wife,
   That never slept a quiet hour with you,
   Now fills your sleep with perturbatiòns:
   To-morrow in the battle think on me,
   Let fall your edgeless sword: despair, and die!

                  (To Richmond)

   You quiet soul, sleep now a quiet sleep.
   Dream of success and happy victory!
   Your adversary's wife does pray for thee.

              Enter the Ghost of Buckingham.

GHOST   *(to Richard)*
   The first was I that helped you to the crown;
   The last was I that felt your tyranny.
   O, in the battle think on Buckingham,
   And die in terror of your guiltiness!
   Dream on, dream on, of bloody deeds and death:
   Fainting, despair; despairing, yield your breath!

                  (To Richmond)

   I died for hope ere I could lend you aid;
   But cheer your heart and be you not dismayed:
   God and good angels fight on Richmond's side,
   And Richard falls in height of all his pride!

   The Ghosts vanish. Richard starts out of his dream.

KING RICHARD

> Give me another horse! Bind up my wounds!
> Have mercy, Jesu! Soft! I did but dream.
> O coward conscience, how do you afflict me!
> The lights burn blue. It is now dead midnight.
> Cold fearful drops stand on my trembling flesh.
> What do I fear? Myself? There's none else by.
> Richard loves Richard: that is, I am I.
> Is there a murderer here? No. Yes, I am:
> Then fly. What, from myself? Great reason why—
> Lest I revenge. What, myself upon myself?
> Alas, I love myself. Wherefore? For any good
> That I myself have done unto myself?
> O no! Alas, I rather hate myself
> For hateful deeds committed by myself.
> I am a villain. Yet I lie, I am not.
> Fool, of yourself speak well. Fool, do not flatter.
> My conscience has a thousand separate tongues,
> And every tongue brings in a separate tale,
> And every tale condemns me for a villain.
> Perjury, perjury, in the highest degree,
> Murder, stern murder, in the direst degree,
> All separate sins, all used in each degree,
> Throng to the bar, crying all, 'Guilty! guilty!'
> I shall despair. There is no creature loves me;
> And if I die, no soul will pity me.
> And, wherefore should they, since I myself
> Find in myself no pity to myself?
> I thought the souls of all that I had murdered
> Came to my tent, and every one did threaten
> To-morrow's vengeance on the head of Richard.

Enter Ratcliffe.

RATCLIFFE
    My lord!
KING RICHARD
    Zounds, who is there?
RATCLIFFE
    Ratcliffe, my lord, 'tis I. The early village cock
    Has twice done salutation to the morn:
    Your friends are up and buckle on their armour.
KING RICHARD
    O Ratcliffe, I have dreamed a fearful dream!
    What think you? Will our friends prove all true?
RATCLIFFE
    No doubt, my lord.
KING RICHARD   O Ratcliffe, I fear, I fear!
RATCLIFFE
    Nay, good my lord, be not afraid of shadows.
KING RICHARD
    By the apostle Paul, shadows to-night
    Have struck more terror to the soul of Richard
    Than can the substance of ten thousand soldiers,
    Armèd in proof and led by shallow Richmond.
    It is not yet near day. Come, go with me.
    Under our tents I'll play the eavesdropper,
    To see if any mean to shrink from me.
                            Exeunt Richard and Ratcliffe.

    Enter the Lords to Richmond sitting in his tent.

LORDS
    Good morrow, Richmond.
RICHMOND
    Cry mercy, lords and watchful gentlemen,
    That you have taken a tardy sluggard here.
LORDS
    How have you slept, my lord?

RICHMOND

    The sweetest sleep, and fairest-boding dreams
    That ever entered in a drowsy head
    Have I since your departure had, my lords.
    I thought their souls whose bodies Richard murdered
    Came to my tent and cried on victory.
    I promise you my soul is very joyful
    In the remembrance of so fair a dream.
    How far into the morning is it, lords?

LORDS

    Upon the stroke of four.

RICHMOND

    Why, then 'tis time to arm and give direction.

His Oration to his Soldiers.

    More than I have said, loving countrymen,
    The leisure and enforcement of the time
    Forbid to dwell upon. Yet remember this:
    God and our good cause fight upon our side;
    The prayers of holy saints and wrongèd souls,
    Like high-reared bulwarks, stand before our faces.
    Richard except, those whom we fight against
    Had rather have us win than him they follow.
    For what is he they follow? Truly, gentlemen,
    A bloody tyrant and a homicide;
    One raised in blood and one in blood established;
    One that made means to come by what he has,
    And slaughtered those that were the means to help him;
    A base foul stone, made precious by the foil
    Of England's chair, where he is falsely set;
    One that has ever been God's enemy.
    Then if you fight against God's enemy,
    God will in justice ward you as his soldiers;
    If you do sweat to put a tyrant down,
    You sleep in peace, the tyrant being slain,

If you do fight against your country's foes,
Your country's fat shall pay your pains the hire;
If you do fight in safeguard of your wives,
Your wives shall welcome home the conquerors;
If you do free your children from the sword,
Your children's children requite it in your age.
Then in the name of God and all these rights,
Advance your standards, draw your willing swords.
For me, the ransom of my bold attempt
Shall be this cold corpse on the earth's cold face;
But if I thrive, the gain of my attempt
The least of you shall share his part thereof.
Sound drums and trumpets boldly and cheerfully:
God and Saint George! Richmond and victory!

Exeunt.

Enter King Richard, Ratcliffe and soldiers.

KING RICHARD
What said Northumberland as touching Richmond?
RATCLIFFE
That he was never trainèd up in arms.
KING RICHARD
He said the truth. And what said Surrey then?
RATCLIFFE
He smiled and said, 'The better for our purpose.'
KING RICHARD
He was in the right, and so indeed it is.

Clock strikes.

Tell the clock there. Give me a calendar.
Who saw the sun to-day?
RATCLIFFE   Not I, my lord.

KING RICHARD
> Then he disdains to shine; for by the book
> He should have braved the east an hour ago.
> A black day will it be to somebody.
> Ratcliffe!

RATCLIFFE
> My lord?

KING RICHARD   The sun will not be seen to-day;
> The sky does frown and lour upon our army.
> I would these dewy tears were from the ground.
> Not shine to-day? Why, what is that to me
> More than to Richmond? For the selfsame heaven
> That frowns on me looks sadly upon him.

Enter Norfolk.

NORFOLK
> Arm, arm, my lord; the foe vaunts in the field.

KING RICHARD
> Come, bustle, bustle! Caparison my horse!
> Call up Lord Stanley, bid him bring his power.
> I will lead forth my soldiers to the plain,
> And thus my army shall be orderèd:
> My foreward shall be drawn out all in length,
> Consisting equally of horse and foot;
> Our archers shall be placèd in the midst;
> John Duke of Norfolk, Thomas Earl of Surrey,
> Shall have the leading of this foot and horse.
> They thus directed, we will follow
> In the main army, whose force on either side
> Shall be well wingèd with our chiefest horse.
> This, and Saint George to help! What think you,
>   Norfolk?

NORFOLK
> A good direction, warlike sovereign.
> This found I on my tent this morning.

He shows him a paper.

'Jockey of Norfolk, be not so bold,
For Dickon your master is bought and sold.'
KING RICHARD
    A thing devisèd by the enemy.
    Go, gentlemen, every man unto his charge.
    Let not our babbling dreams affright our souls;
    Conscience is but a word that cowards use,
    Devised at first to keep the strong in awe:
    Our strong arms be our conscience, swords our law!
    March on, join bravely, let us to it pell-mell,
    If not to heaven, then hand in hand to hell.

His Oration to his Army.

    What shall I say more than I have inferred?
    Remember whom you are to cope with here—
    A sort of vagabonds, rascals, and runaways,
    A scum of Bretons and base lackey peasants,
    Whom their o'ercloyed country vomits forth
    To desperate adventures and assured destruction.
    You sleeping safe, they bring to you unrest;
    You having lands, and blessed with beauteous wives,
    They would restrain the one and stain the other.
    And who does lead them but a paltry fellow,
    Long kept in Britain at our mother's cost,
    A milksop, one that never in his life
    Felt so much cold as over-shoes in snow?
    Let's whip these stragglers over the seas again,
    Lash hence these overweening rags of France,
    These famished beggars, weary of their lives,
    Who—but for dreaming on this mad exploit—
    For want of means, poor rats, had hanged themselves.
    If we are conquered, let men conquer us,
    And not these bastard Bretons, whom our fathers

Have in their own land beaten, bobbed, and thumped,
And, in recòrd, left them the heirs of shame.
Shall these enjoy our lands? lie with our wives?
Ravish our daughters?

Drum afar off.

Hark! I hear their drum.
Fight, gentlemen of England! Fight, bold yeomen!
Draw, archers, draw your arrows to the head!
Spur your proud horses hard, and ride in blood!
Amaze the heavens with your broken staves!

Enter a Messenger.

What says Lord Stanley? Will he bring his power?
MESSENGER
My lord, he does deny to come.
KING RICHARD
Off with his son George's head!
NORFOLK
My lord, the enemy is past the marsh:
After the battle let George Stanley die.
KING RICHARD
A thousand hearts are great within my bosom!
Advance our standards, set upon our foes.
Our ancient word of courage, fair Saint George,
Inspire us with the spirit of fiery dragons!
Upon them! Victory sits on our helms.   *Exeunt.*

SCENE IV
Another part of the field.

*Alarum; excursions. Enter Norfolk and forces;
to him Catesby.*

CATESBY
    Rescue, my Lord of Norfolk, rescue, rescue!
    The King enacts more wonders than a man,
    Daring an opposite to every danger:
    His horse is slain, and all on foot he fights,
    Seeking for Richmond in the throat of death.
    Rescue, fair lord, or else the day is lost!

       Alarums. Enter King Richard.

KING RICHARD
    A horse! a horse! my kingdom for a horse!
CATESBY
    Withdraw, my lord; I'll help you to a horse.
KING RICHARD
    Slave, I have set my life upon a cast,
    And I will stand the hazard of the die.
    I think there are six Richmonds in the field;
    Five have I slain to-day instead of him.
    A horse! a horse! my kingdom for a horse! [*Exeunt.*]

    Alarum. Enter King Richard and Richmond; they
    fight; Richard is slain. Retreat and flourish.
    Enter Richmond, Lord Stanley Earl of Derby,
    bearing the crown, with divers other Lords.

RICHMOND
    God and your arms be praised, victorious friends!
    The day is ours; the bloody dog is dead.
DERBY
    Courageous Richmond, well you acquit yourself.
    Lo, here this long usurpèd royalty
    From the dead temples of this bloody wretch
    Have I plucked off, to grace your brows with it.
    Wear it, enjoy it, and make much of it.

RICHMOND

> Great God of heaven, say amen to all!
> But tell me, is young George Stanley living?

DERBY

> He is, my lord, and safe in Leicester town,
> Whither, if it please you, we may now withdraw us.

RICHMOND

> What men of name are slain on either side?

DERBY

> John Duke of Norfolk, Walter Lord Ferrers,
> Sir Robert Brakenbury, and Sir William Brandon.

RICHMOND

> Inter their bodies as become their births.
> Proclaim a pardon to the soldiers fled
> That in submission will return to us;
> And then, as we have taken the sacrament,
> We will unite the White Rose and the Red.
> Smile heaven upon this fair conjunctiòn,
> That long has frowned upon their enmity!
> What traitor hears me, and says not amen?
> England has long been mad and scarred herself;
> The brother blindly shed the brother's blood;
> The father rashly slaughtered his own son;
> The son, compelled, been butcher to the sire.
> All this divided York and Lancaster,
> Divided in their dire divisiòn,
> O, now let Richmond and Elizabeth,
> The true succeeders of each royal house,
> By God's fair ordinance conjoin together!
> And let their heirs—God, if your will be so—
> Enrich the time to come with smooth-faced peace,
> With smiling plenty, and fair prosperous days!
> Blunt the edge of traitors, gracious Lord,
> That would reduce these bloody days again
> And make poor England weep in streams of blood!
> Let them not live to taste this land's increase

That would with treason wound this fair land's peace!
Now civil wounds are stopped, peace lives again:
That she may long live here, God say amen!

Exeunt.

The Taming of the Shrew

INTRODUCTION

Of no play of Shakespeare is it more important to see it in terms of its own time than *The Taming of the Shrew*. It is fatal—loses its whole point—to regard it anachronistically and think of its theme in modern terms, still less those of Women's Lib, with which Elizabethans would not have agreed, even the women themselves. Traditional society was hierarchical and ordered, with the husband as head of the family. This did not prevent strong-minded women from taking the lead—after all the Age itself took its name from the strongest-minded of them all, though the actual administration of the country was in the hands of her right-hand man, Lord Burghley (who had, by the way, a very strong-minded, blue-stocking of a wife). The theme is the reduction of an intolerably hoydenish girl, quite out of hand, to order, to make of her a proper partner for a husband who loves her and sees good material for a wife beneath the pranks of a spoiled young lady. What is wrong with that?

This theme is a traditional one, so embedded in life as to be virtually folklore, often told and re-told. But the main plot, of the younger sister Bianca and the suitors who are forced to pay their addresses to her in disguise, came from George Gascoigne's *The Supposes*, which in turn came from Ariosto's comedy of that name. We are reminded of that in the last Act, when the confusions are cleared up which rested

on 'counterfeit supposes'. Shakespeare married the two
themes together and made an admirably unified and amus-
ing play of it, all the more so for so much of it being farcical.

Ingenious as always, he then put it in the further farce
of being performed for the pleasure of the drunken tinker,
Christopher Sly, persuaded out of his stupor that he is a
lord—a game to amuse a real lord (or, rather, stage-lord)
returned from hunting. Of this framework we have the
Induction in two scenes; fragments of Sly's comments at
intervals and of an epilogue appeared in a pirated version
in 1594. These were omitted from the collected plays in
1623—it does not appear that much was lost by that. The
play fairly clearly belongs to 1592–3.

The Induction is of fascinating interest to those interested
in Shakespeare the man, for it refers to places, and perhaps
people, in the immediate vicinity of his home town in
veracious and corroborative detail. Christopher Sly tells
us he comes from Barton-on-the-heath; this was where
Shakespeare's aunt and uncle, the Lamberts, lived—who
bought some of his mother's inheritance when his father's
affairs went downhill.[1] 'Ask Marian Hacket, the fat ale-
wife of Wincot'—a hamlet south of Clifton Chambers
(where the poet Drayton used to reside in summer with the
Gooderes). In his drunken stupor Sly would call out for
Cicely Hacket; and we know that there *were* Hackets
thereabouts, as there were Slys in Stratford. Along with
Stephen Sly 'old John Naps of Greet' is named, and editors
have been pedantic enough to retain the unlikely 'Greece'
for a hamlet across the more familiar, the endearing,
Cotswolds. (It still retains its manor farmhouse of the time.)

We see the author too, notably in these early days, in his
fascination for out-door sports. There is a good deal about
hunting the deer, with knowledgeable talk about the qualities of the hounds; we have hare-coursing—as in *Venus*

[1] cf my *Shakespeare the Man*, 35.

and Adonis contemporaneously—and falconry, along with the (then) gentlemanly addiction to bowls. We know from the Sonnets his feeling for horses, and here, in Act III Scene II, we have a comic virtuoso passage on all the diseases that they could possibly be afflicted with—incidentally setting an almost impossible task to render into modern English. We need have no doubt that in those early years, before the exigencies of his theatre career closed in on him, he had a thoroughly good time out of doors in the country. Even here we have reference to the simple ways of the stage, when the boy in the Induction needs tears:

> An onion will do well for such a shift,
> Which in a napkin close conveyed
> Shall in despite enforce a watery eye.

Schooldays are not far behind, with the Latin citation from Lily's Grammar, the text book in general use in Elizabethan schools. A couple of lines from the favourite Ovid—he was himself to be hailed as the English Ovid—are used for comic effect in the bogus instruction of Bianca by her supposed teacher, her suitor in disguise, courting her. His rival describes him as 'Pedascule', a Shakespearean coinage for pedagogue. Even more pointed is the use of the regular formula for licensing the printing of a book, 'cum privilegio ad imprimendum solum', for he himself was shortly to lay claim as an author with his first book. The very subject running in his head is echoed here:

> Adonis painted by a running brook,
> And Cytherea all in sedges hidden,

i.e. Venus and Adonis.

This same passage shows the awakening of his artistic tastes with his introduction into the Southampton circle.

The translated tinker is asked, 'Do you love pictures?' If so, he shall be shown the couple,

As lively painted as the deed was done;

or Daphne, equally realistic:

So workmanly the blood and tears are drawn.

We see, as again from references in later plays, what Elizabethans looked for in painting—the representational and the real, accurately limned.

The provincial dramatist's new and enthusiastic response to high life in London appears along with this: burning sweet wood in the chambers; perfumes, hangings, pictures; a silver basin full of rose-water to wash the hands, a serving man to bear the ewer, another the diaper; music when the bemused 'lord' awakes. An even more enthusiastic note is heard later in describing the contents of Gremio's house: basins and ewers again—those characteristic pieces of contemporary silver-ware; ivory coffers and cypress chests, tapestries, arras counterpanes, Turkey cushions and Venice valences.

A realistic note is sounded when the players who are to present the comedy are sent into the buttery for their welcome—as no doubt he had experienced often enough himself as a provincial player. A recent editor comments: 'Shakespeare is clearly drawing on direct personal experience in his depiction of country people and their activities. The setting is outside an ale-house in the playwright's native Warwickshire; and then, for the second scene, in a large country house.' But Petruchio's own country house in the play proper, the hills and miry ways to it, the chatter and gossip of the servants bidden to make ready for the master and new mistress—all are even more realistic. 'Where's the cook? Is supper ready, the house trimmed, rushes strewed, cobwebs swept, the servingmen in their new fustian, their white stockings, and every officer his wedding garment on? Are the Jacks fair within, the Jills fair without, the carpets laid [i.e. on tables, in those days] and everything in order? . . . Let their heads be slickly combed, their blue coats brushed, and their garters of an indifferent [modest] knit.' Blue was the regular colour for servants' clothes.

Do we detect a recent experience in his unique use of the word 'proceeders'? 'Proceeding' to a degree is a university term; that summer Southampton, a Cambridge man, proceeded Master of Arts at Oxford, with fairly certainly his poet attending on the proceedings.[2]

We should remember, not only from the rhyming of the word with 'owe', etc, that the pronunciation of the word 'shrew' in those days was shrow, as in Shrewsbury (in upper-class speech) today. What is original about Shakespeare's treatment of the Shrew theme is that she is 'broken in'—as we say of spirited horses—by a combination of love with firmness. Kate is not physically maltreated; though she strikes Petruchio, he does not retaliate that way. He reduces her, true, but she certainly needed reducing. Elizabethans had a short way with lower-class scolds: they ducked them in the village pond, sometimes gagged them. But Kate is a lady, a good match; moreover, Petruchio loves her—as she comes to do him, when he shows her who is master. Though her final summing up seems excessive to modern taste, it expresses the Elizabethan view of the matter— Shakespeare shows himself, as over everything, in conformity with the regular commonsense view of things in his time. Nothing so crude as the old stage habit of bringing Petruchio on, whip in hand—completely out of keeping with Shakespeare's spirit, who was given to sharing the woman's point of view. Kate's final speech sums up the

---

[2] cf my edition of *A Midsummer Night's Dream*.

situation from the Elizabethan point of view (and, for that matter, the Biblical).

And, in fact, what woman would not prefer an adult man to an ephebe?

CHARACTERS

INDUCTION

CHRISTOPHER SLY, a tinker, HOSTESS, A LORD, PAGE, HUNTSMEN, PLAYERS, SERVANTS

BAPTISTA MINOLA, a gentleman of Padua
KATHERINA, his elder daughter
PETRUCHIO, a gentleman of Verona, suitor to Katherina
GRUMIO ⎫
CURTIS ⎬ Petruchio's servants
BIANCA, younger daughter of Baptista
GREMIO ⎫
HORTENSIO ⎬ suitors to Bianca
LUCENTIO, a gentleman of Pisa, in love with Bianca
TRANIO ⎫
BIONDELLO ⎬ servants to Lucentio
VINCENTIO, a citizen of Pisa, father of Lucentio

A PEDANT, A WIDOW, SERVANT attending on Baptista, A TAILOR, A HABERDASHER, SERVANTS

536

INDUCTION

SCENE I
Before an alehouse.

Enter Christopher Sly and the Hostess

SLY I'll fix you, in faith.

HOSTESS A pair of stocks, you rogue!

SLY You are a baggage, the Slys are no rogues. Look in the Chronicles, we came in with Richard Conqueror. Therefore no words, let the world slide. Sessa! [Shut up!]

HOSTESS You will not pay for the glasses you have burst?

SLY No, not a penny. Go by, Saint Jeronimy, go to your cold bed and warm you.

He lies on the ground

HOSTESS I know my remedy, I must go fetch the third-borough [constable].   *Exit*

SLY Third, or fourth, or fifth borough, I'll answer him by law. I'll not budge an inch, boy. Let him come, and kindly.

He falls asleep
Wind horns. Enter a Lord from hunting, with his train

LORD
Huntsman, I charge you, tender well my hounds.
Breathe Merriman, the poor cur is foaming,
And couple Clowder with the deep-mouthed bitch.
Saw you not, boy, how Silver made it good

At the hedge corner, in the coldest fault? [scent]
I would not lose the dog for twenty pound.

FIRST HUNTSMAN

Why, Belman is as good as he, my lord.
He cried upon it at the merest loss,
And twice today picked out the dullest scent.
Trust me, I take him for the better dog.

LORD

You are a fool. If Echo were as fleet,
I would esteem him worth a dozen such.
But sup them well, and look unto them all.
Tomorrow I intend to hunt again.

FIRST HUNTSMAN

I will, my lord.

LORD

What's here? One dead, or drunk? See, does he breathe?

SECOND HUNTSMAN

He breathes, my lord. Were he not warmed with ale,
This were a bed but cold to sleep so soundly.

LORD

O monstrous beast, how like a swine he lies!
Grim death, how foul and loathsome is your image!
Sirs, I will practise on this drunken man.
What think you, if he were conveyed to bed,
Wrapped in sweet clothes, rings put upon his fingers,
A most delicious banquet by his bed,
And brave attendants near him when he wakes,
Would not the beggar then forget himself?

FIRST HUNTSMAN

Believe me, lord, I think he cannot choose.

SECOND HUNTSMAN

It would seem strange unto him when he waked.

LORD

Even as a flattering dream or worthless fancy.
Then take him up, and manage well the jest.
Carry him gently to my fairest chamber,

And hang it round with all my wanton pictures.
Balm his foul head in warm distillèd waters,
And burn sweet wood to make the lodging sweet.
Procure me music ready when he wakes,
To make a dulcet and a heavenly sound.
If he chances to speak, be ready straight
And with a low submissive reverence
Say 'What is it your honour will command?'
Let one attend him with a silver basin
Full of rose-water and bestrewed with flowers,
Another bear the ewer, the third a diaper,
And say 'Will it please your lordship cool your hands?'
Some one be ready with a costly suit,
And ask him what apparel he will wear.
Another tell him of his hounds and horse,
And that his lady mourns at his disease.
Persuade him that he has been lunatic,
And when he says he is Sly, say that he dreams,
For he is nothing but a mighty lord.
This do, and do it kindly, gentle sirs.
It will be pastime passing excellent,
If it is husbanded with modesty.

FIRST HUNTSMAN
My lord, I warrant you we will play our part
As he shall think by our true diligence
He is no less than what we say he is.

LORD
Take him up gently and to bed with him,
And each one to his office when he wakes.

Sly is carried away

A trumpet sounds

Fellow, go see what trumpet it is that sounds—

Exit Servingman

Perhaps some noble gentleman that means,
Travelling some journey, to repose him here.

Enter Servingman

How now? Who is it?
SERVINGMAN   If it pleases your honour, players
That offer service to your lordship.
LORD
Bid them come near.

Enter Players

Now, fellows, you are welcome.
PLAYERS
We thank your honour.
LORD
Do you intend to stay with me tonight?
FIRST PLAYER
So please your lordship to accept our duty.
LORD
With all my heart. This fellow I remember
Since once he played a farmer's eldest son.
'Twas where you wooed the gentlewoman so well.
I have forgotten your name; but, sure, that part
Was aptly fitted and naturally performed.
FIRST PLAYER
I think it was Soto that your honour means.
LORD
'Tis very true, you did it excellently.
Well, you are come to me in happy time,
The rather for I have some sport in hand
Wherein your cunning can assist me much.
There is a lord will hear you play tonight;
But I am doubtful of your modesties,
Lest over-eyeing of his odd behaviour—
For yet his honour never heard a play—

You break into some merry passiòn
And so offend him. For I tell you, sirs,
If you should smile, he grows impatiènt.
FIRST PLAYER
Fear not, my lord, we can contain ourselves,
Were he the veriest oddity in the world.
LORD
Go, fellow, take them to the buttery,
And give them friendly welcome every one.
Let them want nothing that my house affords.
                                        Exit one with the Players
Fellow, go you to Bartholomew my page,
And see him dressed in all suits like a lady.
That done, conduct him to the drunkard's chamber,
And call him 'madam', do him obeisance.
Tell him from me—as he will win my love—
To bear himself with honourable action,
Such as he has observed in noble ladies
Unto their lords, by them accomplishèd.
Such duty to the drunkard let him do,
With soft low tongue and lowly courtesy,
And say 'What is it your honour will command,
Wherein your lady and your humble wife
May show her duty and make known her love?'
And then with kind embracements, tempting kisses,
And with declining head into his bosom,
Bid him shed tears, as being overjoyed
To see her noble lord restored to health:
Who for these seven years has esteemèd him
No better than a poor and loathsome beggar.
And if the boy has not a woman's gift
To rain a shower of commanded tears,
An onion will do well for such a shift,
Which in a napkin being close conveyed,
Shall in despite enforce a watery eye.

See this dispatched with all the haste you can,
Anon I'll give you more instructiòns.

Exit a Servingman

I know the boy will well usurp the grace,
Voice, gait, and action of a gentlewoman.
I long to hear him call the drunkard husband,
And how my men will stay themselves from laughter
When they do homage to this simple peasant.
I'll in to counsel them. Haply my presence
May well abate the over-merry spirit
Which otherwise would grow into extremes.   *Exeunt*

SCENE II
A lord's bedchamber.

*Enter aloft Sly, with attendants; some with apparel, basin
and ewer, and other appurtenances; and Lord*

SLY   For God's sake, a pot of small ale.
FIRST SERVINGMAN
Will it please your lordship drink a cup of sack?
SECOND SERVINGMAN
Will it please your honour taste of these conserves?
THIRD SERVINGMAN
What raiment will your honour wear today?
SLY   I am Christophero Sly, call not me 'honour' nor
'lordship'. I never drank sack in my life. And if you give
me any conserves, give me conserves of beef. Never ask
me what raiment I'll wear, for I have no more doublets
than backs, no more stockings than legs, and no more
shoes than feet—nay, sometimes more feet than shoes,
or such shoes as my toes look through the overleather.
LORD
Heaven cease this idle humour in your honour!
O, that a mighty man of such descent,

Of such possessions, and so high esteem,
Should be infusèd with so foul a spirit!

SLY   What, would you make me mad? Am not I Christopher
Sly, old Sly's son of Barton-heath, by birth a pedlar, by
education a cardmaker, by transmutation a bear-herd,
and now by present profession a tinker? Ask Marian
Hacket, the fat ale-wife of Wincot, if she knows me not.
If she says I am not fourteen pence on the score for sheer
ale, score me up for the lyingest knave in Christendom.

A Servingman brings him a pot of ale

What! I am not distracted. Here's—

He drinks

THIRD SERVINGMAN
   O, this it is that makes your lady mourn.
SECOND SERVINGMAN
   O, this is it that makes your servants droop.
LORD
   Hence comes it that your kindred shuns your house,
   As beaten hence by your strange lunacy.
   O noble lord, bethink you of your birth,
   Call home your ancient thoughts from banishment,
   And banish hence these abject lowly dreams.
   Look how your servants do attend on you,
   Each in his office ready at your beck.
   Will you have music? Hark, Apollo plays,

Music

   And twenty cagèd nightingales do sing.
   Or will you sleep? We'll have you to a couch
   Softer and sweeter than the lustful bed
   On purpose trimmed up for Semiramis.
   Say you will walk; we will bestrew the ground.

Or will you ride? Your horses shall be trapped,
Their harness studded all with gold and pearl.
Do you love hawking? You have hawks will soar
Above the morning lark. Or will you hunt?
Your hounds shall make the heavens answer them
And fetch shrill echoes from the hollow earth.

FIRST SERVINGMAN
Say you will course, your greyhounds are as swift
As breathèd stags, ay, fleeter than the roe.

SECOND SERVINGMAN
Do you love pictures? We will fetch you straight
Adonis painted by a running brook,
And Cytherea all in sedges hidden,
Which seem to move and wanton with her breath
Even as the waving sedges play with the wind.

LORD
We'll show you Io as she was a maid,
And how she was beguilèd and surprised,
As lively painted as the deed was done.

THIRD SERVINGMAN
Or Daphne roaming through a thorny wood,
Scratching her legs that one shall swear she bleeds,
And at that sight shall sad Apollo weep,
So workmanly the blood and tears are drawn.

LORD
You are a lord, and nothing but a lord.
You have a lady far more beautiful
Than any woman in this waning age.

FIRST SERVINGMAN
And till the tears that she has shed for you
Like envious floods o'errun her lovely face,
She was the fairest creature in the world—
And yet she is inferior to none.

SLY
Am I a lord and have I such a lady?
Or do I dream? Or have I dreamed till now?

I do not sleep. I see, I hear, I speak.
I smell sweet savours and I feel soft things.
Upon my life, I am a lord indeed,
And not a tinker nor Christophero Sly.
Well, bring our lady hither to our sight,
And once again a pot of the smallest ale.

SECOND SERVINGMAN
  Will it please your mightiness to wash your hands?
  O, how we joy to see your wit restored!
  O, that once more you knew but what you are!
  These fifteen years you have been in a dream,
  Or when you waked, so waked as if you slept.

SLY
  These fifteen years! By my faith, a goodly nap.
  But did I never speak in all that time?

FIRST SERVINGMAN
  O, yes, my lord, but very idle words,
  For though you lay here in this goodly chamber,
  Yet would you say ye were beaten out of door,
  And rail upon the hostess of the house;
  And say you would present her at the court,
  Because she brought stone jugs and no sealed quarts.
  Sometimes you would call out for Cicely Hacket.

SLY
  Ay, the woman's maid of the house.

THIRD SERVINGMAN
  Why, sir, you know no house, nor any such maid,
  Nor any such men as you have reckoned up,
  As Stephen Sly, and old John Naps of Greet,
  And Peter Turph, and Henry Pimpernell,
  And twenty more such names and men as these,
  Who never were nor any man ever saw.

SLY
  Now Lord be thankèd for my good amends.

ALL   Amen.

Enter Page as a lady, with attendants

SLY   I thank you, you shall not lose by it.

PAGE   How fares my noble lord?

SLY   Sure, I fare well, for here is cheer enough.
   Where is my wife?

PAGE

   Here, noble lord, what is your will with her?

SLY

   Are you my wife, and will not call me husband?
   My men should call me 'lord', I am your goodman.

PAGE

   My husband and my lord, my lord and husband,
   I am your wife in all obedience.

SLY   I know it well. What must I call her?

LORD   Madam.

SLY   Alice madam, or Joan madam?

LORD

   Madam and nothing else, so lords call ladies.

SLY

   Madam wife, they say that I have dreamed
   And slept above some fifteen years or more.

PAGE

   Ay, and the time seems thirty unto me,
   Being all this time abandoned from your bed.

SLY

   'Tis much. Servants, leave me and her alone.
                              Exeunt Lord and Servingmen
   Madam, undress you and come now to bed.

PAGE

   Thrice-noble lord, let me entreat of you
   To pardon me yet for a night or two,
   Or, if not so, until the sun is set.
   For your physicians have expressly charged,
   In peril to incur your former malady,

That I should yet absent me from your bed.

I hope this reason stands for my excuse.

SLY   Ay, it stands so that I may hardly tarry so long. But
I would be loath to fall into my dreams again. I will
therefore tarry in despite of the flesh and the blood.

Enter the Lord as a Messenger

LORD

Your honour's players, hearing your amendment,

Are come to play a pleasant comedy;

For so your doctors hold it very meet,

Seeing too much sadness has congealed your blood,

And melancholy is the nurse of frenzy.

Therefore they thought it good you hear a play

And frame your mind to mirth and merriment,

Which bars a thousand harms and lengthens life.

SLY   Sure, I will. Let them play it. Is not a comonty
[comedy] a Christmas gambol or a tumbling-trick?

PAGE

No, my good lord, it is more pleasing stuff.

SLY   What, household stuff?

PAGE   It is a kind of history.

SLY   Well, we'll see it. Come, madam wife, sit by my side
and let the world slip, we shall never be younger.

A flourish of trumpets

Act I

SCENE I
Padua. A square.

Enter Lucentio and his man Tranio

LUCENTIO

Tranio, since for the great desire I had
To see fair Padua, nursery of arts,
I am arrived for fruitful Lombardy,
The pleasant garden of great Italy,
And by my father's love and leave am armed
With his good will and your good company,
My trusty servant well approved in all—
Here let us breathe and haply institute
A course of learning and ingenious studies.
Pisa renownèd for grave citizens
Gave me my being and my father first,
A merchant of great traffic through the world,
Vincentio come of the Bentivolii.
Vincentio's son, brought up in Florence,
It shall become to serve all hopes conceived
To deck his fortune with his virtuous deeds.
And therefore, Tranio, for the time I study
Virtue, and that part of philosophy
Will I apply that treats of happiness
By virtue specially to be achieved.
Tell me your mind, for I have Pisa left
And am to Padua come as he that leaves
A shallow plash to plunge him in the deep,
And with satiety seeks to quench his thirst.

TRANIO

   Mi perdonato, [Pardon me] gentle master mine.
   I am in all affected as yourself,
   Glad that you thus continue your resolve
   To suck the sweets of sweet philosophy.
   Only, good master, while we do admire
   This virtue and this moral discipline,
   Let us be no stoics and no stocks, I pray,
   Or so devoted to Aristotle's checks
   As Ovid is an outcast quite abjured.
   Chop logic with acquaintance that you have,
   And practise rhetoric in your common talk,
   Music and poesy use to quicken you,
   The mathematics and the metaphysics
   Fall to them as you find your stomach serves you.
   No profit grows where is no pleasure taken.
   In brief, sir, study what you most affect.

LUCENTIO

   Many thanks, Tranio, well do you advise.
   If, Biondello, you were come ashore,
   We could at once put us in readiness,
   And take a lodging fit to entertain
   Such friends as time in Padua shall beget.

   Enter Baptista with his two daughters Katherina
   and Bianca; Gremio, a pantaloon, and Hortensio,
   suitor to Bianca. Lucentio and Tranio stand by

   But stay awhile, what company is this?

TRANIO

   Master, some show to welcome us to town.

BAPTISTA

   Gentlemen, importune me no farther,
   For how I firmly am resolved you know;
   That is, not to bestow my younger daughter

Before I have a husband for the elder.
If either of you both love Katherina,
Because I know you well and love you well,
Leave shall you have to court her at your pleasure.

GREMIO
To cart her rather. She's too rough for me.
There, there, Hortensio, will you any wife?

KATHERINA   (to Baptista)
I pray you, sir, is it your will
To make a jest of me among these mates?

HORTENSIO
Mates, maid, how mean you that? No mates for you
Unless you were of gentler, milder mould.

KATHERINA
In faith, sir, you shall never need to fear.
Sure it is not halfway to her heart.
But if it were, doubt not her care should be
To comb your noddle with a three-legged stool,
And paint your face, and use you like a fool.

HORTENSIO
From all such devils, good Lord deliver us!

GREMIO
And me too, good Lord!

TRANIO   (aside to Lucentio)
Hush, master, here's some good pastime toward.
That wench is stark mad or wonderful froward.

LUCENTIO   (aside to Tranio)
But in the other's silence do I see
Maid's mild behaviour and sobriety.
Peace, Tranio.

TRANIO   (aside to Lucentio)
Well said, master. Mum! And gaze your fill.

BAPTISTA
Gentlemen, that I may soon make good
What I have said—Bianca, get you in.

And let it not displease you, good Bianca,
For I will love you never the less, my girl.
KATHERINA
A pretty pet! It is best
Put finger in the eye, if she knew why.
BIANCA
Sister, content you in my discontent.
Sir, to your pleasure humbly I subscribe.
My books and instruments shall be my company,
On them to look and practise by myself.
LUCENTIO   (aside)
Hark, Tranio, you may hear Minerva speak.
HORTENSIO
Signor Baptista, will you be so strange?
Sorry am I that our good will effects
Bianca's grief.
GREMIO   Why will you mew her up,
Signor Baptista, for this fiend of hell,
And make her bear the penance of her tongue?
BAPTISTA
Gentlemen, content you. I am resolved.
Go in, Bianca.   Exit Bianca
And since I know she takes her most delight
In music, instruments, and poetry,
Schoolmasters will I keep within my house
Fit to instruct her youth. If you, Hortensio,
Or Signor Gremio, you, know any such,
Prefer them hither; for to cunning men
I will be very kind, and liberal
To my own children in good bringing-up.
And so farewell. Katherina, you may stay,
For I have more to commune with Bianca.   Exit
KATHERINA
Why, and I trust I may go too, may I not?
What, shall I be appointed hours, as though, perhaps,
I knew not what to take and what to leave? Ha?   Exit

GREMIO You may go to the devil's dam. Your gifts are so good here's none will hold you. There! Love is not so great, Hortensio, but we may blow our nails together, and fast it fairly out. Our cake's dough on both sides. Farewell. Yet, for the love I bear my sweet Bianca, if I can by any means light on a fit man to teach her that wherein she delights, I will wish him to her father.

HORTENSIO So will I, Signor Gremio. But a word, I pray. Though the nature of our quarrel yet never brooked parleys know now, upon advice, it touches us both—that we may yet again have access to our fair mistress and be happy rivals in Bianca's love—to labour and effect one thing specially.

GREMIO What is that, I pray?

HORTENSIO Indeed, sir, to get a husband for her sister.

GREMIO A husband? A devil.

HORTENSIO I say a husband.

GREMIO I say a devil. Think you, Hortensio, though her father is very rich, any man is so very a fool to be married to hell?

HORTENSIO Tush, Gremio. Though it passes your patience and mine to endure her loud alarums, why, man, there are good fellows in the world, if a man could light on them, would take her with all faults, and money enough.

GREMIO I cannot tell. But I had as soon take her dowry with this condition—to be whipped at the high-cross every morning.

HORTENSIO Faith, as you say, there's small choice in rotten apples. But come, since this bar in law makes us friends, it shall be so far forth friendly maintained, till by helping Baptista's elder daughter to a husband we set his younger free for a husband, and then have to it afresh. Sweet Bianca! Happy man be his lot. He that runs fastest gets the ring. How say you, Signor Gremio?

GREMIO I am agreed, and would I had given him the best horse in Padua to begin his wooing that would

thoroughly woo her, wed her, and bed her, and rid the
house of her. Come on.   *Exeunt Gremio and Hortensio*

TRANIO

I pray, sir, tell me, is it possible
That love should of a sudden take such hold?

LUCENTIO

O Tranio, till I found it to be true,
I never thought it possible or likely.
But see, while idly I stood looking on,
I found the effect of love in idleness,
And now in plainness do confess to you,
That are to me as secret and as dear
As Anna to the Queen of Carthage was—
Tranio, I burn, I pine, I perish, Tranio,
If I achieve not this young modest girl.
Counsel me, Tranio, for I know you can.
Assist me, Tranio, for I know you will.

TRANIO

Master, it is no time to chide you now;
Affection is not rated from the heart.
If love has touched you, naught remains but so—
Redime te captum quam queas minimo.[1]

LUCENTIO

Many thanks, lad. Go forward, this contents.
The rest will comfort, for your counsel's sound.

TRANIO

Master, you looked so longingly on the maid,
Perhaps you marked not what's the pith of all.

LUCENTIO

O yes, I saw sweet beauty in her face,
Such as the daughter of Agenor had,
That made great Jove to humble him to her hand,
When with his knees he kissed the Cretan strand.

---

[1]Redeem yourself when captured at the lowest you can.

TRANIO

    Saw you no more? Marked you not how her sister
    Began to scold and raise up such a storm
    That mortal ears might hardly endure the din?

LUCENTIO

    Tranio, I saw her coral lips to move,
    And with her breath she did perfume the air.
    Sacred and sweet was all I saw in her.

TRANIO

    Then it is time to stir him from his trance.
    I pray, awake, sir. If you love the maid,
    Bend thoughts and wits to achieve her. Thus it stands:
    Her elder sister is so perverse and cross
    That till the father rids his hands of her,
    Master, your love must live a maid at home.
    And therefore has he closely mewed her up,
    Because she shall not be annoyed with suitors.

LUCENTIO

    Ah, Tranio, what a cruel father's he!
    But are you not advised he took some care
    To get her cunning schoolmasters to instruct her?

TRANIO

    Ay, indeed, am I, sir—and now it is plotted.

LUCENTIO

    I have it, Tranio.

TRANIO   Master, for my hand,
    Both our inventions meet and agree in one.

LUCENTIO

    Tell me yours first.

TRANIO   You will be schoolmaster,
    And undertake the teaching of the maid—
    That is your device.

LUCENTIO   It is. May it be done?

TRANIO

    Not possible. For who shall bear your part
    And be in Padua here Vincentio's son,

Keep house and ply his book, welcome his friends,
Visit his countrymen and banquet them?

LUCENTIO

Enough, content you, for I have it fully.
We have not yet been seen in any house,
Nor can we be distinguished by our faces
For man or master. Then it follows thus—
You shall be master, Tranio, in my stead,
Keep house and state and servants, as I should.
I will some other be—some Florentine,
Some Neapolitan, or meaner man of Pisa.
'Tis hatched, and shall be so. Tranio, at once
Undress and take my coloured hat and cloak.
When Biondello comes, he waits on you,
But I will charm him first to keep his tongue.

TRANIO

So had you need.

They exchange garments

In brief, sir, since it your pleasure is,
And I am tied to be obedient—
For so your father charged me at our parting:
'Be serviceable to my son', said he,
Although I think it was in another sense—
I am content to be Lucentio,
Because so well I love Lucentio.

LUCENTIO

Tranio, be so, because Lucentio loves.
And let me be a slave to achieve that maid
Whose sudden sight has thralled my wounded eye.

Enter Biondello

Here comes the rogue. Fellow, where have you been?

BIONDELLO   Where have I been? Nay, how now, where are
   you? Master, has my fellow Tranio stolen your clothes,
   or you stolen his, or both? Pray, what's the news?
LUCENTIO
   Fellow, come hither. 'Tis no time to jest,
   And therefore frame your manners to the time.
   Your fellow Tranio here, to save my life,
   Puts my apparel and my countenance on,
   And I for my escape have put on his.
   For in a quarrel since I came ashore
   I killed a man, and fear I was descried.
   Wait you on him, I charge you, as becomes,
   While I make way from hence to save my life.
   You understand me?
BIONDELLO   I, sir? Never a whit.
LUCENTIO
   And not a jot of Tranio in your mouth.
   Tranio is changed into Lucentio.
BIONDELLO
   The better for him, would I were so too!
TRANIO
   So could I, faith, boy, to have the next wish after,
   That Lucentio indeed had Baptista's younger daughter.
   But not for my sake but your master's, I advise
   You use your manners discreetly in all kind of companies.
   When I am alone, why then I am Tranio,
   But in all places else your master Lucentio.
LUCENTIO
   Tranio, let's go.
   One thing more rests, that yourself execute—
   To make one among these wooers. If you ask me why,
   Suffice it, my reasons are both good and weighty. *Exeunt*

The Presenters above speak

LORD
  My lord, you nod, you do not mind the play.
SLY   Yes, by Saint Anne, do I. A good matter, surely.
  Comes there any more of it?
PAGE   My lord, it is but begun.
SLY   'Tis a very excellent piece of work, madam lady.
  Would it were done!

SCENE II
Before Hortensio's house.

Enter Petruchio and Grumio

PETRUCHIO
  Verona, for a while I take my leave,
  To see my friends in Padua, but of all
  My best belovèd and approvèd friend,
  Hortensio; and I trust this is his house.
  Here you ass Grumio, knock, I say.
GRUMIO   Knock, sir? Whom should I knock? Is there any
  man has abused your worship?
PETRUCHIO   Villain, I say, knock me here soundly.
GRUMIO   Knock you here, sir? Why, sir, what am I, sir,
  that I should knock you here, sir?
PETRUCHIO
  Villain, I say, knock for me at this gate,
  And rap well too, or I'll knock your knave's pate.
GRUMIO
  My master is grown quarrelsome. I should knock you
      first,
  And then I know after who comes by the worst.
PETRUCHIO
  Will it not be?
  Faith, varlet, if you'll not knock, I'll ring it.
  I'll try how you can *sol-fa* and sing it.

He wrings him by the ears

GRUMIO
Help, masters, help! My master is mad.
PETRUCHIO
Now knock when I bid you, silly villain.

Enter Hortensio

HORTENSIO   How now, what's the matter? My old friend
Grumio and my good friend Petruchio! How do you all
at Verona?
PETRUCHIO
Signor Hortensio, come you to part the fray?
Con tutto il cuore ben trovato,[2] may I say.
HORTENSIO
Alla nostra casa ben venuto,
Molto honorato signor mio Petruchio.[3]
Rise, Grumio, rise. We will compound this quarrel.
GRUMIO   Nay, 'tis no matter, sir, what he alleges in
Latin. If this is not a lawful cause for me to leave his
service, look you, sir. He bid me knock him and rap
him soundly, sir. Well, was it fit for a servant to use his
master so, being perhaps, for aught I see, two and thirty,
a pip out?
Whom would to God I had well knocked at first,
Then had not Grumio come by the worst.
PETRUCHIO
A senseless villain. Good Hortensio,
I bade the rascal knock upon your gate,
And could not get him for my heart to do it.

---

[2]With all my heart well met.
[3]Welcome to our house, my much honoured sir, Petruchio.

GRUMIO   Knock at the gate? O heavens! Spoke you not
these words plain, 'Fellow, knock me here, rap me here,
knock me well, and knock me soundly'? And come you
now with 'knocking at the gate'?
PETRUCHIO
Man, be gone, or talk not, I advise you.
HORTENSIO
Petruchio, patience, I am Grumio's pledge.
This is a heavy chance between him and you,
Your ancient, trusty, pleasant servant Grumio.
And tell me now, sweet friend, what happy gale
Blows you to Padua here from old Verona?
PETRUCHIO
Such wind as scatters young men through the world
To seek their fortunes farther than at home,
Where small experience grows. But in few words,
Signor Hortensio, thus it stands with me:
Antonio, my father, is deceased,
And I have thrust myself into this maze,
Haply to wive and thrive as best I may.
Crowns in my purse I have, and goods at home,
And so am come abroad to see the world.
HORTENSIO
Petruchio, shall I then come roundly to you
And wish you to a shrewd ill-favoured wife?
You would thank me but a little for my counsel,
And yet I'll promise you she shall be rich,
And very rich. But you are too much my friend,
And I'll not wish you to her.
PETRUCHIO
Signor Hortensio, between such friends as we
Few words suffice; and therefore, if you know
One rich enough to be Petruchio's wife—
As wealth is burden of my wooing dance—
Be she as foul as was Florentius' love,

As old as Sibyl, and as cross and mean
As Socrates' Xanthippe, or a worse,
She moves me not, or not removes at least
Affection's edge in me, were she as rough
As are the swelling Adriatic seas.
I come to wive it wealthily in Padua;
If wealthily, then happily in Padua.

GRUMIO   Nay, look you, sir, he tells you flatly what his
mind is. Why, give him gold enough and marry him to
a puppet or death's head, or an old hag with never a
tooth in her head, though she has as many diseases as
two and fifty horses. Why, nothing comes amiss, if
money comes with it.

HORTENSIO
Petruchio, since we are stepped thus far in,
I will continue what I broached in jest.
I can, Petruchio, help you to a wife
With wealth enough, and young and beauteous,
Brought up as best becomes a gentlewoman.
Her only fault—and that is faults enough—
Is that she is of intolerable temper,
Perverse and froward so beyond all measure
That, were my state far worse now than it is,
I would not wed her for a mine of gold.

PETRUCHIO
Hortensio, peace. You know not gold's effect.
Tell me her father's name and 'tis enough.
For I will board her though she chides as loud
As thunder when the clouds in autumn crack.

HORTENSIO
Her father is Baptista Minola,
An affable and courteous gentleman.
Her name is Katherina Minola,
Renowned in Padua for her scolding tongue.

PETRUCHIO
    I know her father, though I know not her,
    And he knew my deceasèd father well.
    I will not sleep, Hortensio, till I see her;
    And therefore let me be thus bold with you
    To give you over at this first encounter,
    Unless you will accompany me thither.
GRUMIO   I pray you, sir, let him go while the humour
    lasts. On my word, if she knew him as well as I do, she
    would think scolding would do little good upon him.
    She may perhaps call him half a score knaves or so.
    Why, that's nothing; if he begins once, he'll rail in his
    rhetorics. I'll tell you what, sir, if she stands him but a
    little, he will throw a figure in her face, and so disfigure
    her with it that she shall have no more eyes to see with
    than a cat. You know him not, sir.
HORTENSIO
    Tarry, Petruchio, I must go with you,
    For in Baptista's keep my treasure is.
    He has the jewel of my life in hold,
    His younger daughter, beautiful Bianca;
    And her withholds from me and others too,
    Suitors to her and rivals in my love,
    Supposing it a thing impossible,
    For those defects I have before rehearsed,
    That ever Katherina will be wooed.
    Therefore this order has Baptista taken,
    That none shall have access unto Bianca
    Till Katherine the curst has got a husband.
GRUMIO
    Katherine the curst,
    A title for a maid of all titles the worst.
HORTENSIO
    Now shall my friend Petruchio do me grace,
    And offer me disguised in sober robes
    To old Baptista as a schoolmaster

Well seen in music, to instruct Bianca;
That so I may by this device at least
Have leave and leisure to make love to her,
And unsuspected court her by herself.
GRUMIO   Here's no knavery! See, to beguile the old folks,
how the young folks lay their heads together.

Enter Gremio, and Lucentio disguised as Cambio,
a schoolmaster

Master, master, look about you. Who goes there, ha?
HORTENSIO
Peace, Grumio. It is the rival of my love.
Petruchio, stand by a while.
GRUMIO
A proper stripling and an amorous!

They stand aside

GREMIO
O, very well—I have perused the note.
Hark you, sir, I'll have them very fairly bound—
All books of love, see that at any hand—
And see you read no other lectures to her.
You understand me. Over and beside
Signor Baptista's liberality,
I'll mend it with a largess. Take your paper too.
And let me have them very well perfùmed,
For she is sweeter than perfùme itself
To whom they go. What will you read to her?
LUCENTIO
Whatever I read to her, I'll plead for you
As for my patron, stand you so assured,
As firmly as yourself were still in place—
Yea, and perhaps with more successful words
Than you, unless you were a scholar, sir.

GREMIO

O this learning, what a thing it is!

GRUMIO   *(aside)*

O this woodcock, what an ass it is!

PETRUCHIO   *(aside)*

Peace, fellow.

HORTENSIO   *(aside)*

Grumio, mum! *(Coming forward)* God save you, Signor
   Gremio.

GREMIO

And you are well met, Signor Hortensio.

Know you whither I am going? To Baptista Minola.

I promised to enquire carefully

About a schoolmaster for the fair Bianca;

And by good fortune I have lighted well

On this young man, for learning and behaviour

Fit for her turn, well read in poetry

And other books—good ones, I warrant you.

HORTENSIO

'Tis well. And I have met a gentleman

Has promised me to help me to another,

A fine musician to instruct our mistress.

So shall I no whit be behind in duty

To fair Bianca, so beloved of me.

GREMIO

Beloved of me, and that my deeds shall prove.

GRUMIO   *(aside)*

And that his bags shall prove.

HORTENSIO

Gremio, 'tis now no time to vent our love.

Listen to me, and if you speak me fair,

I'll tell you news equally good for either.

Here is a gentleman whom by chance I met,

Upon agreement from us to his liking,

Will undertake to woo curst Katherine,

Yea, and to marry her, if her dowry pleases.

GREMIO

So said, so done, is well.

Hortensio, have you told him all her faults?

PETRUCHIO

I know she is an irksome brawling scold.

If that is all, masters, I hear no harm.

GREMIO

No, say you me so, friend? What countryman?

PETRUCHIO

Born in Verona, old Antonio's son.

My father dead, my fortune lives for me,

And I do hope good days and long to see.

GREMIO

O sir, such a life with such a wife were strange.

But if you have a stomach, to it in God's name —

You shall have me assisting you in all.

But will you woo this wildcat?

PETRUCHIO   Will I live?

GRUMIO

Will he woo her? Ay, or I'll hang her.

PETRUCHIO

Why came I hither but to that intent?

Think you a little din can daunt my ears?

Have I not in my time heard lions roar?

Have I not heard the sea, puffed up with winds,

Rage like an angry boar chafèd with sweat?

Have I not heard great ordnance in the field,

And heaven's artillery thunder in the skies?

Have I not in a pitchèd battle heard

Loud alarums, neighing steeds, and trumpets' clang?

And do you tell me of a woman's tongue,

That gives not half so great a blow to hear

As will a chestnut in a farmer's fire?

Tush, tush, fright boys with bogeys!

GRUMIO   He fears none.

GREMIO
    Hortensio, hark.
    This gentleman is happily arrived,
    My mind presumes, for his own good and yours.
HORTENSIO
    I promised we would be contributors
    And bear his charge of wooing, whatsoever.
GREMIO
    And so we will—provided that he wins her.
GRUMIO
    I would I were as sure of a good dinner.

    Enter Tranio, dressed as Lucentio, and Biondello

TRANIO
    Gentlemen, God save you. If I may be bold,
    Tell me, I beseech you, which is the readiest way
    To the house of Signor Baptista Minola?
BIONDELLO   He that has the two fair daughters—is it he
    you mean?
TRANIO   Even he, Biondello.
GREMIO
    Hark you, sir, you mean not her too?
TRANIO
    Perhaps him and her, sir. What have you to do?
PETRUCHIO
    Not her that chides, sir, at any hand, I pray.
TRANIO
    I love no chiders, sir. Biondello, let's away.
LUCENTIO   *(aside)*
    Well begun, Tranio.
HORTENSIO   Sir, a word ere you go.
    Are you a suitor to the maid you talk of, yea or no?
TRANIO
    And if I am, sir, is it any offence?

GREMIO
No, if without more words you will get you hence.
TRANIO
Why, sir, I pray, are not the streets as free
For me as for you?
GREMIO   But so is not she.
TRANIO
For what reason, I beseech you?
GREMIO   For this reason, if you'll know,
That she's the choice love of Signor Gremio.
HORTENSIO
That she's the chosen of Signor Hortensio.
TRANIO
Softly, my masters! If you are gentlemen,
Do me this right—hear me with patiènce.
Baptista is a noble gentleman,
To whom my father is not all unknown,
And were his daughter fairer than she is,
She may more suitors have and me for one.
Fair Leda's daughter had a thousand wooers,
Then well one more may fair Bianca have.
And so she shall. Lucentio shall make one,
Though Paris came, in hope to speed alone.
GREMIO
What, this gentleman will out-talk us all!
LUCENTIO
Sir, give him head, I know he will prove a jade.
PETRUCHIO
Hortensio, to what end are all these words?
HORTENSIO
Sir, let me be so bold as ask you,
Did you yet ever see Baptista's daughter?

TRANIO

No, sir, but hear I do that he has two;
The one as famous for a scolding tongue
As is the other for beauteous modesty.

PETRUCHIO

Sir, sir, the first's for me, let her go by.

GREMIO

Yea, leave that labour to great Hercules,
And let it be more than Alcides' twelve.

PETRUCHIO

Sir, understand you this of me in fact,
The younger daughter whom you hearken for
Her father keeps from all access of suitors,
And will not promise her to any man
Until the elder sister first is wedded.
The younger then is free, and not before.

TRANIO

If it is so, sir, that you are the man
Must aid us all—and me among the rest—
And if you break the ice and do this feat,
Achieve the elder, set the younger free
For our access—whose hap shall be to have her
Will not so graceless be to be ingrate.

HORTENSIO

Sir, you say well, and well you do conceive.
And since you do profess to be a suitor,
You must, as we do, gratify this gentleman,
To whom we all rest generally beholding.

TRANIO

Sir, I shall not be slack. In sign whereof,
Please you we may contrive this afternoon,
And quaff carouses to our mistress' health,
And do as adversaries do in law,
Strive mightily, but eat and drink as friends.

GRUMIO *and* BIONDELLO
    O excellent motion! Fellows, let's be gone.
HORTENSIO
    The motion's good indeed, and be it so.
    Petruchio, I shall be your *ben venuto*. [host]   *Exeunt*

Act II

SCENE I
Baptista's house.

Enter Katherina, and Bianca with her hands bound

BIANCA

    Good sister, wrong me not, nor wrong yourself,
    To make a bondmaid and a slave of me.
    That I disdain. But for these fripperies,
    Unbind my hands, I'll pull them off myself,
    Yea, all my raiment, to my petticoat,
    Or what you will command me will I do,
    So well I know my duty to my elders.

KATHERINA

    Of all your suitors here I charge you tell
    Whom you love best. See you dissemble not.

BIANCA

    Believe me, sister, of all men alive
    I never yet beheld that special face
    Which I could fancy more than any other.

KATHERINA

    Minion, you lie. Is it not Hortensio?

BIANCA

    If you affect him, sister, here I swear
    I'll plead for you myself that you shall have him.

KATHERINA

    O then, perhaps, you fancy riches more.
    You will have Gremio to keep you fair.

BIANCA
    Is it for him you do envỳ me so?
    Nay then you jest, and now I well perceive
    You have but jested with me all this while.
    I pray you, sister Kate, untie my hands.
KATHERINA

Strikes her

If that is jest, then all the rest was so.

Enter Baptista

BAPTISTA
    Why, how now, dame, whence grows this insolence?
    Bianca, stand aside. Poor girl, she weeps.

He unties her hands

    Go ply your needle, meddle not with her.
    (to Katherina) For shame, you bitch of a devilish spirit,
    Why do you wrong her that did never wrong you?
    When did she cross you with a bitter word?
KATHERINA
    Her silence flouts me, and I'll be revenged.

She flies after Bianca

BAPTISTA
    What, in my sight? Bianca, get you in.   *Exit Bianca*
KATHERINA
    What, will you not suffer me? Nay, now I see
    She is your treasure, she must have a husband.
    I must dance bare-foot on her wedding-day,

And for your love to her lead apes in hell.[1]
Talk not to me, I will go sit and weep,
Till I can find occasion of revenge.   *Exit Katherina*
BAPTISTA
Was ever gentleman thus grieved as I?
But who comes here?

Enter Gremio, with Lucentio, disguised as Cambio;
Petruchio, with Hortensio disguised as Licio; and Tranio,
disguised as Lucentio, with his boy, Biondello,
bearing a lute and books

GREMIO   Good morrow, neighbour Baptista.
BAPTISTA   Good morrow, neighbour Gremio. God save
you, gentlemen.
PETRUCHIO
And you, good sir. Pray have you not a daughter
Called Katherina, fair and virtuous?
BAPTISTA
I have a daughter, sir, called Katherina.
GREMIO
You are too blunt, go to it orderly.
PETRUCHIO
You wrong me, Signor Gremio, give me leave.
I am a gentleman of Verona, sir,
That hearing of her beauty and her wit,
Her affability and bashful modesty,
Her wondrous qualities and mild behaviour,
Am bold to show myself a forward guest
Within your house, to make my eye the witness
Of that report which I so oft have heard.
And for an entrance to my entertainment
I do present you with a man of mine,

(presenting Hortensio)

---

[1]The fate of an old maid, according to folklore.

Cunning in music and the mathematics,
To instruct her fully in those sciences,
Whereof I know she is not ignorant.
Accept of him, or else you do me wrong.
His name is Licio, born in Mantua.

BAPTISTA

You are welcome, sir, and he for your good sake.
But for my daughter Katherine, this I know,
She is not for your turn, the more my grief.

PETRUCHIO

I see you do not mean to part with her,
Or else you like not of my company.

BAPTISTA

Mistake me not, I speak but as I find.
Whence are you, sir? What may I call your name?

PETRUCHIO

Petruchio is my name, Antonio's son,
A man well known throughout all Italy.

BAPTISTA

I know him well. You are welcome for his sake.

GREMIO

Saving your tale, Petruchio, I pray
Let us that are poor petitioners speak too.
Give way! You are marvellous forward.

PETRUCHIO

O pardon me, Signor Gremio, I would fain be doing.

GREMIO

I doubt it not, sir, but you will curse your wooing.
(to Baptista) Neighbour, this is a gift very grateful, I am
sure of it. To express the like kindness, myself, that
have been more kindly beholding to you than any,
freely give unto you this young scholar (presenting
Lucentio) that has been long studying at Rheims, as
cunning in Greek, Latin, and other languages, as the
other in music and mathematics. His name is Cambio.
Pray accept his service.

BAPTISTA A thousand thanks, Signor Gremio. Welcome,
good Cambio. (*To Tranio*) But, gentle sir, it seems you
walk like a stranger. May I be so bold to know the cause
of your coming?
TRANIO
Pardon me, sir, the boldness is my own
That, being a stranger in this city here,
Do make myself a suitor to your daughter,
Unto Bianca, fair and virtuous.
Nor is your firm resolve unknown to me
In the preferment of the elder sister.
This liberty is all that I request—
That, upon knowledge of my parentage,
I may have welcome among the rest that woo,
And free access and favour as the rest.
And toward the education of your daughters
I here bestow a simple instrument,
And this small packet of Greek and Latin books.
If you accept them, then their worth is great.
BAPTISTA
Lucentio is your name? Of whence, I pray?
TRANIO
Of Pisa, sir, son to Vincentio.
BAPTISTA
A mighty man of Pisa. By report
I know him well. You are very welcome, sir.
(*to Hortensio*) Take you the lute, (*to Lucentio*) and you
    the set of books.
You shall go see your pupils immediately.
Holla, within!

Enter a Servant

Fellow, lead these gentlemen
To my daughters, and tell them both
These are their tutors. Bid them use them well.

Exit Servant, with Hortensio, Lucentio, and Biondello

We will go walk a little in the orchard,
And then to dinner. You are passing welcome,
And so I pray you all to think yourselves.
PETRUCHIO
Signor Baptista, my business asks some haste,
And every day I cannot come to woo.
You knew my father well, and in him me,
Left solely heir to all his lands and goods,
Which I have bettered rather than decreased.
Then tell me, if I get your daughter's love,
What dowry shall I have with her to wife?
BAPTISTA
After my death the one half of my lands,
And in possession twenty thousand crowns.
PETRUCHIO
And for that dowry I'll assure her of
Her widowhood—be it that she survives me—
In all my lands and leases whatsoever.
Let specialties be therefore drawn between us,
That covenants may be kept on either hand.
BAPTISTA
Ay, when the special thing is well obtained,
That is, her love; for that is all in all.
PETRUCHIO
Why, that is nothing. For I tell you, father,
I am as pèremptòry as she proud-minded;
And where two raging fires meet together,
They do consume the thing that feeds their fury.
Though little fire grows great with little wind,
Yet extreme gusts will blow out fire and all.
So I to her, and so she yields to me,
For I am rough and woo not like a babe.

BAPTISTA

    Well may you woo, and happy be your luck.

    But be you armed for some unhappy words.

PETRUCHIO

    Ay, to the proof, as mountains are for winds,

    That shake not though they blow perpetually.

Enter Hortensio with his head bruised

BAPTISTA

    How now, my friend, why do you look so pale?

HORTENSIO

    For fear, I promise you, if I look pale.

BAPTISTA

    What, will my daughter prove a good musician?

HORTENSIO

    I think she'll sooner prove a soldier.

    Iron may hold with her, but never lutes.

BAPTISTA

    Why then, you can not break her to the lute?

HORTENSIO

    Why no, for she has broken the lute to me.

    I did but tell her she mistook her frets,

    And bowed her hand to teach her fingering,

    When, with a most impatient devilish spirit,

    'Frets, call you these?' said she, 'I'll fume with them.'

    And with that word she struck me on the head,

    And through the instrument my pate made way;

    And there I stood amazèd for a while,

    As on a pillory, looking through the lute,

    While she did call me rascal fiddler

    And twangling Jack, with twenty such vile terms,

    As had she studied to misuse me so.

PETRUCHIO
> Now, by the world, it is a lusty wench.
> I love her ten times more than ever I did.
> O, how I long to have some chat with her!

BAPTISTA
> Well, go with me, and be not so discomfited.
> Proceed in practice with my younger daughter,
> She's apt to learn and thankful for good turns.
> Signor Petruchio, will you go with us,
> Or shall I send my daughter Kate to you?

PETRUCHIO
> I pray you do.   *Exeunt all but Petruchio*
>   I'll attend her here,
> And woo her with some spirit when she comes.
> Say that she rails, why then I'll tell her plain
> She sings as sweetly as a nightingale.
> Say that she frowns, I'll say she looks as clear
> As morning roses newly washed with dew.
> Say she is mute and will not speak a word,
> Then I'll commend her volubility,
> And say she utters piercing eloquence.
> If she does bid me go, I'll give her thanks,
> As though she bids me stay by her a week.
> If she denies to wed, I'll crave the day
> When I shall ask the banns, and when be married.
> But here she comes, and now, Petruchio, speak.

Enter Katherina

> Good morrow, Kate—for that's your name, I hear.

KATHERINA
> Well have you heard, but something hard of hearing;
> They call me Katherine that do talk of me.

PETRUCHIO
> You lie, in faith, for you are called plain Kate,
> And bonny Kate, and sometimes Kate the curst.

But Kate, the prettiest Kate in Christendom,
Kate of Kate Hall, my super-dainty Kate,
For dainties are all Kates, and therefore, Kate,
Take this of me, Kate of my consolation—
Hearing your mildness praised in every town,
Your virtues spoken of, and your beauty sounded,
Yet not so deeply as to you belongs,
Myself am moved to woo you for my wife.

KATHERINA
Moved, in good time! Let him that moved you hither
Remove you hence. I knew you at the first
You were a movable.

PETRUCHIO   Why, what's a movable?

KATHERINA
A joint-stool.

PETRUCHIO   You have hit it. Come, sit on me.

KATHERINA
Asses are made to bear, and so are you.

PETRUCHIO
Women are made to bear, and so are you.

KATHERINA
No such jade as you, if me you mean.

PETRUCHIO
Alas, good Kate, I will not burden you!
For knowing you to be but young and light—

KATHERINA
Too light for such a swain as you to catch,
And yet as heavy as my weight should be.

PETRUCHIO
Should be? Should—buzz!

KATHERINA   Well taken, and like a buzzard.

PETRUCHIO
O slow-winged dove, shall a buzzard take you?

KATHERINA
Ay, for a dove, as he does take a buzzard.

PETRUCHIO
Come, come, you wasp, in faith, you are too angry.
KATHERINA
If I am waspish, best beware my sting.
PETRUCHIO
My remedy is then to pluck it out.
KATHERINA
Ay, if the fool could find it where it lies.
PETRUCHIO
Who knows not where a wasp does wear his sting?
In his tail.
KATHERINA   In his tongue.
PETRUCHIO   Whose tongue?
KATHERINA
Yours, if you talk of tales, and so farewell.
PETRUCHIO
What, with my tongue in your tail? Nay, come again.
Good Kate, I am a gentleman—
KATHERINA   That I'll try.

She strikes him

PETRUCHIO
I swear I'll cuff you, if you strike again.
KATHERINA
So may you loose your arms.
If you strike me, you are no gentleman,
And if no gentleman, why then no arms.
PETRUCHIO
A herald, Kate? O, put me in your books!
KATHERINA
What is your crest—a coxcomb?
PETRUCHIO
A combless cock, if Kate will be my hen.

KATHERINA
No cock of mine, you crow too like a craven.
PETRUCHIO
Nay, come, Kate, come, you must not look so sour.
KATHERINA
It is my fashion when I see a crab.
PETRUCHIO
Why, here's no crab, and therefore look not sour.
KATHERINA
There is, there is.
PETRUCHIO
Then show it me.
KATHERINA   Had I a glass, I would.
PETRUCHIO
What, you mean my face?
KATHERINA   Well aimed of such a young one.
PETRUCHIO
Now, by Saint George, I am too young for you.
KATHERINA
Yet you are withered.
PETRUCHIO   'Tis with cares.
KATHERINA   I care not.
PETRUCHIO
Nay, hear you, Kate—
                     In fact, you escape not so.
KATHERINA
I chafe you, if I tarry. Let me go.
PETRUCHIO
No, not a whit. I find you passing gentle.
'Twas told me you were rough, and coy, and sullen,
And now I find report a very liar.
For you are pleasant, gamesome, passing courteous,
But slow in speech, yet sweet as spring-time flowers.
You can not frown, you can not look askance,
Nor bite the lip, as angry wenches will,
Nor have you pleasure to be cross in talk.

But you with mildness entertain your wooers,
With gentle conference, soft and affable.
Why does the world report that Kate does limp?
O slanderous world! Kate like the hazel-twig
Is straight and slender, and as brown in hue
As hazel-nuts and sweeter than the kernels.
O, let me see you walk. You do not halt.

KATHERINA
Go, fool, and whom you keep command.

PETRUCHIO
Did ever Dian so become a grove
As Kate this chamber with her princely gait?
O, be you Dian, and let her be Kate,
And then let Kate be chaste and Dian sportful.

KATHERINA
Where did you study all this goodly speech?

PETRUCHIO
It is extempore, from my mother-wit.

KATHERINA
A witty mother, witless else her son.

PETRUCHIO
Am I not wise?

KATHERINA   Yes, keep you warm [so-so].

PETRUCHIO
So I mean, sweet Katherine, in your bed.
And therefore, setting all this chat aside,
Thus in plain terms—your father has consented
That you shall be my wife; your dowry agreed on;
And will you, nill you, I will marry you.
Now, Kate, I am a husband for your turn,
For by this light whereby I see your beauty,
Your beauty that does make me like you well,
You must be married to no man but me.
For I am he am born to tame you, Kate,
And bring you from a wild Kate to a Kate
Conformable as other household Kates.

Enter Baptista, Gremio, and Tranio

Here comes your father. Never make denial;
I must and will have Katherine to my wife.
BAPTISTA
Now, Signor Petruchio, how speed you with my daughter?
PETRUCHIO
How but well, sir? How but well?
It were impossible I should speed amiss.
BAPTISTA
Why, how now, daughter Katherine? In your dumps?
KATHERINA
Call you me daughter? Now I promise you
You have showed a tender fatherly regard
To wish me wed to one half lunatic,
A madcap ruffian and a swearing Jack,
That thinks with oaths to face the matter out.
PETRUCHIO
Father, 'tis thus—yourself and all the world
That talked of her have talked amiss of her.
If she is curst, it is for policy,
For she's not froward, but modest as the dove.
She is not hot, but temperate as the morn.
For patience she will prove a second Grissel,
And Roman Lucrece for her chastity.
And to conclude, we have agreed so well together
That upon Sunday is the wedding-day.
KATHERINA
I'll see you hanged on Sunday first.
GREMIO
Hark, Petruchio, she says she'll see you hanged first.
TRANIO
Is this your speeding? Nay then, good night our part.

PETRUCHIO

> Be patient, gentlemen, I choose her for myself.
> If she and I are pleased, what's that to you?
> 'Tis bargained between us twain, being alone,
> That she shall still be curst in company.
> I tell you it is incredible to believe
> How much she loves me—O, the kindest Kate!
> She hung about my neck, and kiss on kiss
> She plied so fast, protesting oath on oath,
> That in a twink she won me to her love.
> O, you are novices! 'Tis a world to see
> How tame, when men and women are alone,
> A feeble wretch can make the curstest shrew.
> Give me your hand, Kate, I will unto Venice,
> To buy apparel before the wedding-day.
> Provide the feast, father, and bid the guests.
> I will be sure my Katherine shall be fine.

BAPTISTA

> I know not what to say—but give me your hands.
> God send you joy! Petruchio, 'tis a match.

GREMIO *and* TRANIO

> Amen, say we. We will be witnesses.

PETRUCHIO

> Father, and wife, and gentlemen, adieu,
> I will to Venice—Sunday comes apace.
> We will have rings, and things, and fine array,
> And kiss me, Kate, we will be married on Sunday.
>
> *Exeunt Petruchio and Katherina*

GREMIO

> Was ever match clapped up so suddenly?

BAPTISTA

> Faith, gentlemen, now I play a merchant's part,
> And venture madly on a desperate mart.

TRANIO

> It was a commodity lay fretting by you,
> It will bring you gain, or perish on the seas.

BAPTISTA
  The gain I seek is quiet in the match.
GREMIO
  No doubt but he has got a quiet catch.
  But now, Baptista, to your younger daughter—
  Now is the day we long have lookèd for.
  I am your neighbour, and was suitor first.
TRANIO
  And I am one that love Bianca more
  Than words can witness or your thoughts can guess.
GREMIO
  Youngster, you can not love so dear as I.
TRANIO
  Greybeard, your love does freeze.
GREMIO   But yours does fry.
  Skipper, stand back, 'tis age that nourishes.
TRANIO
  But youth in ladies' eyes that flourishes.
BAPTISTA
  Content you, gentlemen, I will compound this strife.
  'Tis deeds must win the prize, and he of both
  That can assure my daughter greatest dower
  Shall have my Bianca's love.
  Say, Signor Gremio, what can you assure her?
GREMIO
  First, as you know, my house within the city
  Is richly furnishèd with plate and gold,
  Basins and ewers to lave her dainty hands—
  My hangings all of Tyrian tapestry.
  In ivory coffers I have stuffed my crowns,
  In cypress chests my arras counterpoints,
  Costly apparel, tents, and canopies,
  Fine linen, Turkey cushions bossed with pearl,
  Valance of Venice gold in needlework,
  Pewter and brass, and all things that belong
  To house or housekeeping. Then at my farm

I have a hundred milch-kine to the pail,
Six score fat oxen standing in my stalls,
And all things answerable to this portion.
Myself am struck in years, I must confess,
And if I die tomorrow this is hers,
If while I live she will be only mine.

TRANIO
That 'only' came well in. Sir, listen to me.
I am my father's heir and only son.
If I may have your daughter to my wife,
I'll leave her houses three or four as good,
Within rich Pisa walls, as any one
Old Signor Gremio has in Padua;
Besides two thousand ducats by the year
Of fruitful land, all which shall be her jointure.
What, have I pinched you, Signor Gremio?

GREMIO
Two thousand ducats by the year of land!
(aside) My land amounts not to so much in all.
(to them) That she shall have, besides an argosy
That now is lying in Marseilles road.
What, have I choked you with an argosy?

TRANIO
Gremio, it is known my father has no less
Than three great argosies, besides two galliasses
And twelve tight galleys. These I will assure her,
And twice as much whatever you offer next.

GREMIO
Nay, I have offered all, I have no more,
And she can have no more than all I have.
If you like me, she shall have me and mine.

TRANIO
Why, then the maid is mine from all the world
By your firm promise. Gremio is out-vied.

BAPTISTA

    I must confess your offer is the best,
    And let your father make her the assurance,
    She is your own. Else, you must pardon me,
    If you should die before him, where's her dower?

TRANIO

    That's but a cavil. He is old, I young.

GREMIO

    And may not young men die as well as old?

BAPTISTA

    Well, gentlemen,
    I am thus resolved. On Sunday next you know
    My daughter Katherine is to be married.
    Now, on the Sunday following shall Bianca
    Be bride to you, if you make this assurance;
    If not, to Signor Gremio.
    And so I take my leave, and thank you both.

GREMIO

    Adieu, good neighbour.   *Exit Baptista*
                Now I fear you not.
    Youngster, young gamester, your father was a fool
    To give you all, and in his waning age
    Set foot under your table. Tut, a toy!
    An old Italian fox is not so kind, my boy.   *Exit*

TRANIO

    A vengeance on your crafty withered hide!
    Yet I have faced it with a card of ten.
    'Tis in my head to do my master good.
    I see no reason but supposed Lucentio
    Must get a father, called supposed Vincentio.
    And that's a wonder. Fathers commonly
    Do get their children; but in this case of wooing
    A child shall get a sire, if I fail not of my cunning. *Exit*

Act III

SCENE I
The same.

Enter Lucentio as Cambio, Hortensio as Licio, and Bianca

LUCENTIO
    Fiddler, forbear, you grow too forward, sir.
    Have you so soon forgotten the entertainment
    Her sister Katherine welcomed you with?
HORTENSIO
    But, wrangling pedant, this is
    The patroness of heavenly harmony.
    Then give me leave to have prerogative,
    And when in music we have spent an hour,
    Your lecture shall have leisure for as much.
LUCENTIO
    Preposterous ass, that never read so far
    To know the cause why music was ordained!
    Was it not to refresh the mind of man
    After his studies or his usual pain?
    Then give me leave to read philosophy,
    And while I pause serve in your harmony.
HORTENSIO
    Sir, I will not bear these flouts of yours.
BIANCA
    Why, gentlemen, you do me double wrong
    To strive for that which rests in my own choice.
    I am no breeching scholar in the schools,
    I'll not be tied to hours nor appointed times,
    But learn my lessons as I please myself.

And, to cut off all strife, here sit we down.
Take you your instrument, play you the while—
His lecture will be done ere you have tuned.
HORTENSIO
You'll leave his lecture when I am in tune?
LUCENTIO
That will be never. Tune your instrument.
BIANCA   Where left we last?
LUCENTIO   Here, madam.
       (He reads)
       'Hic ibat Simois, hic est Sigeia tellus,
       Hic steterat Priami regia celsa senis.'[1]
BIANCA   Construe them.
LUCENTIO   *'Hic ibat'*, as I told you before—*'Simois'*, I am
    Lucentio—*'hic est'*, son unto Vincentio of Pisa—*'Sigeia*
    tellus', disguised thus to get your love—*'Hic steterat'*,
    and that Lucentio that comes a-wooing—*'Priami'*, is my
    man Tranio—*'regia'*, bearing my part—*'celsa senis'*, that
    we might beguile the old pantaloon.
HORTENSIO   Madam, my instrument's in tune.
BIANCA   Let us hear. *(He plays)* O fie! The treble jars.
LUCENTIO   Spit in the hole, man, and tune again.
BIANCA   Now let me see if I can construe it. *'Hic ibat*
    Simois', I know you not—*'hic est Sigeia tellus'*, I trust
    you not—*'Hic steterat Priami'*, take heed he hears us
    not—*'regia'*, presume not—*'celsa senis'*, despair not.
HORTENSIO
Madam, it is now in tune.
LUCENTIO   All but the bass.
HORTENSIO
The bass is right, 'tis the base knave that jars.
(aside) How fiery and forward our pedant is.
Now, for my life, the knave does court my love.

---

[1]Here ran the Simois; here is Sigeian land (i.e. Troy); here
stood the lofty palace of old Priam.

Pedagogue, I'll watch you better yet.

BIANCA

In time I may believe, yet I mistrust.

LUCENTIO

Mistrust it not—for, sure, Aeacides
Was Ajax, called so from his grandfather.

BIANCA

I must believe my master, else, I promise you,
I should be arguing still upon that doubt.
But let it rest. Now, Licio, to you.
Good master, take it not unkindly, pray,
That I have been thus pleasant with you both.

HORTENSIO   *(to Lucentio)*

You may go walk, and give me leave awhile.
My lessons make no music in three parts.

LUCENTIO

Are you so formal, sir? Well, I must wait—
(aside) And watch too, for, unless I am deceived,
Our fine musician grows too amorous.

HORTENSIO

Madam, before you touch the instrument
To learn the order of my fingering,
I must begin with rudiments of art,
To teach you gamut in a briefer sort,
More pleasant, pithy, and effectual,
Than has been taught by any of my trade.
And there it is in writing fairly drawn.

BIANCA

Why, I am past my gamut long ago.

HORTENSIO

Yet read the gamut of Hortensio.

BIANCA   *(reads)*

'Gamut *I am, the ground of all accord*—
A re, *to plead Hortensio's passion*—
B mi, *Bianca, take him for your lord*—
C fa ut, *that loves with all affection*—

D sol re, *one clef, two notes have I—*
E la mi, *show pity or I die.'*
Call you this gamut? Tut, I like it not!
Old fashions please me best. I am not so nice
To change true rules for odd inventiòns.

Enter a Servant

SERVANT
Mistress, your father prays you leave your books,
And help to dress your sister's chamber up.
You know tomorrow is the wedding-day.
BIANCA
Farewell, sweet masters both, I must be gone.
Exeunt Bianca and Servant
LUCENTIO
Faith, mistress, then I have no cause to stay.   *Exit*
HORTENSIO
But I have cause to pry into this pedant,
I think he looks as though he were in love.
Yet if your thoughts, Bianca, are so humble
To cast your wandering eyes on every ass,
Seize you that likes. If once I find you ranging,
Hortensio will be quit with you by changing.   *Exit*

SCENE II
Before Baptista's house.

Enter Baptista, Gremio, Tranio as Lucentio, Katherina,
Bianca, Lucentio as Cambio, and attendants

BAPTISTA   *(to Tranio)*
Signor Lucentio, this is the appointed day
That Katherine and Petruchio should be married,
And yet we hear not of our son-in-law.

What will be said? What mockery will it be
To want the bridegroom when the priest attends
To speak the ceremonial rites of marriage!
What says Lucentio to this shame of ours?

KATHERINA
No shame but mine. I must forsooth be forced
To give my hand, opposed against my heart,
Unto a mad-brain roughneck, full of whims
Who wooed in haste and means to wed at leisure.
I told you, I, he was a frantic fool,
Hiding his bitter jests in blunt behaviour.
And to be noted for a merry man,
He'll woo a thousand, appoint the day of marriage,
Make feast, invite friends, and proclaim the banns,
Yet never means to wed where he has wooed.
Now must the world point at poor Katherine,
And say 'Lo, there is mad Petruchio's wife,
If it would please him come and marry her.'

TRANIO
Patience, good Katherine, and Baptista too.
Upon my life, Petruchio means but well,
Whatever fortune stays him from his word.
Though he is blunt, I know him passing wise,
Though he is merry, yet with that he's honest.

KATHERINA
Would Katherine had never seen him though.
Exit weeping, followed by Bianca and the other women

BAPTISTA
Go, girl, I cannot blame you now to weep,
For such an injury would vex a saint,
Much more a shrew of your impatient humour.

Enter Biondello

BIONDELLO   Master, master, news! And such old news as
you never heard of.

BAPTISTA   Is it new and old too? How may that be?

BIONDELLO   Why, is it not news to hear of Petruchio's coming?

BAPTISTA   Is he come?

BIONDELLO   Why, no, sir.

BAPTISTA   What then?

BIONDELLO   He is coming.

BAPTISTA   When will he be here?

BIONDELLO   When he stands where I am and sees you there.

TRANIO   But say, what to your old news?

BIONDELLO   Why, Petruchio is coming in a new hat and an old jerkin; a pair of old breeches thrice turned; a pair of boots that have been candle-cases, one buckled, another laced. An old rusty sword taken out of the town armoury, with a broken hilt, and sheathless; with two broken points; his horse hipped—with an old mothy saddle and stirrups of no kindred. Besides,[2] possessed with the glanders and likely to drip in the chine, troubled with the lampass, infected with the fashions, full of tumours, thick with swellings, foul with jaundice, past cure of the fives, stark spoiled with the staggers, gnawed by worms, sprained in the back and shoulder-cut, near-legged before. With a half-cheeked bit and a headstall of sheep's leather, which, being restrained to keep him from stumbling, has been often burst and new-repaired with knots; one girth six times pieced, and a woman's crupper of velvet, which has two letters for her name fairly set down in studs, and here and there pieced with string.

BAPTISTA   Who comes with him?

BIONDELLO   O sir, his lackey, for all the world caparisoned like the horse. With a linen stocking on one leg and a kersey boot-hose on the other, gartered with red and

_____

[2] A virtuoso passage on various horse-diseases.

blue cloth; an old hat, and the humour of forty fancies
pricked in it for a feather; a monster, a very monster in
apparel, and not like a Christian footboy or a gentleman's
lackey.

TRANIO
'Tis some odd humour pricks him to this fashion.
Yet oftentimes he goes but mean-apparelled.

BAPTISTA   I am glad he's come, howsoever he comes.

BIONDELLO   Why, sir, he comes not.

BAPTISTA   Did you not say he comes?

BIONDELLO   Who? That Petruchio came?

BAPTISTA   Ay, that Petruchio came.

BIONDELLO   No, sir. I say his horse comes with him on
his back.

BAPTISTA   Why, that's all one.

BIONDELLO
            Nay, by Saint Jamy,
            I hold you a penny,
            A horse and a man
            Is more than one,
            And yet not many.

                Enter Petruchio and Grumio

PETRUCHIO   Come, where are these gallants? Who's at
home?

BAPTISTA   You are welcome, sir.

PETRUCHIO   And yet I come not well?

BAPTISTA   And yet you halt not.

TRANIO   Not so well apparelled as I wish you were.

PETRUCHIO
Were it not better I should rush in thus?
But where is Kate? Where is my lovely bride?
How does my father? Gentles, I think you frown.
And wherefore gaze this goodly company

As if they saw some wondrous monument,
Some comet, or unusual prodigy?

BAPTISTA
Why, sir, you know this is your wedding-day.
First were we sad, fearing you would not come,
Now sadder that you come so unprovided.
Fie, doff this habit, shame to your estate,
An eye-sore to our solemn festival.

TRANIO
And tell us what occasion of import
Has all so long detained you from your wife
And sent you hither so unlike yourself?

PETRUCHIO
Tedious it were to tell, and harsh to hear—
Suffice it I am come to keep my word,
Though in some part enforcèd to digress;
Which at more leisure I will so excuse
As you shall well be satisfied with it.
But where is Kate? I stay too long from her.
The morning wears, 'tis time we were at church.

TRANIO
See not your bride in these unreverent robes,
Go to my chamber, put on clothes of mine.

PETRUCHIO
Not I, believe me. Thus I will visit her.

BAPTISTA
But thus, I trust, you will not marry her.

PETRUCHIO
Good faith, even thus. Therefore have done with words;
To me she's married, not unto my clothes.
Could I repair what she will wear in me
As I can change these poor accoutrements,
'Twere well for Kate and better for myself.
But what a fool am I to chat with you,
When I should bid good morrow to my bride,
And seal the title with a lovely kiss.

                                        Exit with Grumio

TRANIO
    He has some meaning in his mad attire.
    We will persuade him, be it possible,
    To put on better ere he goes to church.
BAPTISTA
    I'll after him and see the event of this.
        Exit followed by Gremio, Biondello, and attendants
TRANIO
    But, sir, to love concerns us now to add
    Her father's liking; which to bring to pass,
    As I before imparted to your worship,
    I am to get a man—whatever he is
    It matters not much, we'll fit him to our turn—
    And he shall be Vincentio of Pisa;
    And make assurance here in Padua
    Of greater sums than I have promisèd.
    So shall you quietly enjoy your hope
    And marry sweet Bianca with consent.
LUCENTIO
    Were it not that my fellow schoolmaster
    Does watch Bianca's steps so narrowly,
    'Twere good I think to steal our marriage;
    Which once performed, let all the world say no,
    I'll keep my own despite of all the world.
TRANIO
    That by degrees we mean to look into
    And watch our vantage in this business.
    We'll overreach the greybeard Gremio,
    The narrow-prying father Minola,
    The quaint musician, amorous Licio—
    All for my master's sake, Lucentio.

               Enter Gremio

    Signor Gremio, came you from the church?

GREMIO

As willingly as ever I came from school.

TRANIO

And are the bride and bridegroom coming home?

GREMIO

A bridegroom, say you? 'Tis a groom indeed,
A grumbling groom, and that the girl shall find.

TRANIO

Curster than she? Why, 'tis impossible.

GREMIO

Why, he's a devil, a devil, a very fiend.

TRANIO

Why, she's a devil, a devil, the devil's dam.

GREMIO

Tut, she's a lamb, a dove, a fool to him.
I'll tell you, Sir Lucentio—when the priest
Should ask if Katherine should be his wife,
'Ay, by gogs-woun's[3] said he, and swore so loud
That all-amazed the priest let fall the book;
And as he stooped again to take it up,
This mad-brained bridegroom took him such a cuff
That down fell priest and book, and book and priest.
'Now take them up', said he, 'if any likes.'

TRANIO

What said the wench when he rose up again?

GREMIO

Trembled and shook. For why, he stamped and swore
As if the vicar meant to cozen him.
But after many ceremonies done
He calls for wine. 'A health!' said he, as if
He had been aboard, carousing to his mates
After a storm; quaffed off the muscadel,
And threw the sops all in the sexton's face—
Having no other reason

---

[3]God's wounds—modern, Zounds.

But that his beard grew thin and hungerly
And seemed to ask him sops as he was drinking.
This done, he took the bride about the neck,
And kissed her lips with such a clamorous smack
That at the parting all the church did echo.
And I seeing this came thence for very shame,
And after me, I know, the rout is coming.
Such a mad marriage never was before.
Hark, hark! I hear the minstrels play.

Music plays
Enter Petruchio, Katherina, Bianca, Baptista, Hortensio,
Grumio, and attendants

PETRUCHIO
Gentlemen and friends, I thank you for your pains.
I know you think to dine with me today,
And have prepared great store of wedding cheer,
But so it is, my haste does call me hence,
And therefore here I mean to take my leave.
BAPTISTA
Is it possible you will away tonight?
PETRUCHIO
I must away today before night comes.
Make it no wonder. If you knew my business,
You would entreat me rather go than stay.
And, honest company, I thank you all
That have beheld me give away myself
To this most patient, sweet, and virtuous wife.
Dine with my father, drink a health to me,
For I must hence, and farewell to you all.
TRANIO
Let us entreat you stay till after dinner.
PETRUCHIO
It may not be.
GREMIO   Let me entreat you.

PETRUCHIO
  It cannot be.
KATHERINA   Let me entreat you.
PETRUCHIO
  I am content.
KATHERINA   Are you content to stay?
PETRUCHIO
  I am content you shall entreat me stay—
  But yet not stay, entreat me how you can.
KATHERINA
  Now if you love me stay.
PETRUCHIO   Grumio, my horse.
GRUMIO   Ay, sir, they are ready—the oats have eaten the
  horses.
KATHERINA
  Nay then,
  Do what you can, I will not go today,
  No, nor tomorrow—not till I please myself.
  The door is open, sir, there lies your way,
  You may be jogging while your boots are green.
  For me, I'll not be gone till I please myself.
  'Tis likely you'll prove a jolly surly groom
  That take it on you at the first so roundly.
PETRUCHIO
  O Kate, content you, pray you be not angry.
KATHERINA
  I will be angry—what have you to do?
  Father, be quiet—he shall stay my leisure.
GREMIO
  Ay indeed, sir, now it begins to work.
KATHERINA
  Gentlemen, forward to the bridal dinner.
  I see a woman may be made a fool
  If she had not a spirit to resist.

PETRUCHIO
    They shall go forward, Kate, at your command.
    Obey the bride, you that attend on her.
    Go to the feast, revel and domineer,
    Carouse full measure to her maidenhead,
    Be mad and merry, or go hang yourselves.
    But for my bonny Kate, she must with me.
    Nay, look not big, nor stamp, nor stare, nor fret,
    I will be master of what is my own.
    She is my goods, my chattels, she is my house,
    My household stuff, my field, my barn,
    My horse, my ox, my ass, my any thing,
    And here she stands. Touch her whoever dares!
    I'll bring my action on the proudest he
    That stops my way in Padua. Grumio,
    Draw forth your weapon, we are beset with thieves,
    Rescue your mistress if you are a man.
    Fear not, sweet wench, they shall not touch you, Kate.
    I'll buckler you against a million.
                    Exeunt Petruchio, Katherina, and Grumio
BAPTISTA
    Nay, let them go, a couple of quiet ones.
GREMIO
    Went they not quickly, I should die with laughing.
TRANIO
    Of all mad matches never was the like.
LUCENTIO
    Mistress, what's your opinion of your sister?
BIANCA
    That being mad herself, she's madly mated.
GREMIO
    I warrant him, Petruchio is Kated.
BAPTISTA
    Neighbours and friends, though bride and bridegroom
        want
    Now to supply the places at the table,

You know there want no junkets at the feast.
Lucentio, you shall supply the bridegroom's place,
And let Bianca take her sister's room.

TRANIO
Shall sweet Bianca practise how to bride it?

BAPTISTA
She shall, Lucentio. Come, gentlemen, let's go. *Exeunt*

Act IV

SCENE 1
Petruchio's house.

Enter Grumio

GRUMIO   Fie, fie on all tired jades, on all mad masters, and all foul ways! Was ever man so beaten? Was ever man so dirtied? Was ever man so weary? I am sent before to make a fire, and they are coming after to warm them. Now were not I a little pot and soon hot, my very lips might freeze to my teeth, my tongue to the roof of my mouth, my heart in my belly, ere I should come by a fire to thaw me. But I with blowing the fire shall warm myself, for, considering the weather, a taller man than I will take cold. Holla, ho! Curtis!

Enter Curtis

CURTIS   Who is that calls so coldly?
GRUMIO   A piece of ice. If you doubt it, you may slide from my shoulder to my heel with no greater a run but my head and my neck. A fire, good Curtis.
CURTIS   Are my master and his wife coming, Grumio?
GRUMIO   O ay, Curtis, ay—and therefore fire, fire, cast on no water.
CURTIS   Is she so hot a shrew as she is reported?
GRUMIO   She was, good Curtis, before this frost. But you know winter tames man, woman, and beast; for it has tamed my old master, and my new mistress, and myself, fellow Curtis.

CURTIS   Away, you three-inch fool! I am no beast.

GRUMIO   Am I but three inches? Why, your horn is a
foot, and so long am I at the least. But will you make a
fire, or shall I complain of you to our mistress, whose
hand—she being now at hand—you shall soon feel, to
your cold comfort, for being slow in your hot office?

CURTIS   I pray, good Grumio, tell me how goes the world?

GRUMIO   A cold world, Curtis, in every office but yours—
and therefore fire. Do your duty, and have your duty, for
my master and mistress are almost frozen to death.

CURTIS   There's fire ready—and therefore, good Grumio,
the news.

GRUMIO   Why [sings] 'Jack boy, ho boy!' and as much
news as will you.

CURTIS   Come, you are so full of cony-catching.

GRUMIO   Why therefore fire, for I have caught extreme
cold. Where's the cook? Is supper ready, the house
trimmed, rushes strewed, cobwebs swept, the servingmen
in their new fustian, their white stockings, and every
officer his wedding-garment on? Are the Jacks fair within,
the Jills fair without, the carpets laid, and everything in
order?

CURTIS   All ready—and therefore, I pray you, news.

GRUMIO   First know my horse is tired, my master and
mistress fallen out.

CURTIS   How?

GRUMIO   Out of their saddles into the dirt, and thereby
hangs a tale.

CURTIS   Let's have it, good Grumio.

GRUMIO   Lend your ear.

CURTIS   Here.

GRUMIO   There.

[Cuffs him]

CURTIS   This it is to feel a tale, not to hear a tale.

GRUMIO   And therefore it is called a sensible tale; and this cuff was but to knock at your ear and beseech listening. Now I begin. *Imprimis,* [first] we came down a foul hill, my master riding behind my mistress—

CURTIS   Both on one horse?

GRUMIO   What's that to you?

CURTIS   Why, a horse.

GRUMIO   Tell you the tale. But had you not crossed me, you should have heard how her horse fell, and she under her horse. You should have heard in how miry a place, how she was befouled, how he left her with the horse upon her; how he beat me because her horse stumbled, how she waded through the dirt to pluck him off me; how he swore, how she prayed that never prayed before, how I cried; how the horses ran away, how her bridle was burst, how I lost my crupper—with many things of worthy memory, which now shall die in oblivion, and you return unexperienced to your grave.

CURTIS   By this reckoning he is more shrew than she.

GRUMIO   Ay, and that you and the proudest of you all shall find when he comes home. But what talk I of this? Call forth Nathaniel, Joseph, Nicholas, Philip, Walter, Sugarsop, and the rest. Let their heads be slickly combed, their blue coats brushed, and their garters of a modest knit. Let them curtsy with their left legs, and not presume to touch a hair of my master's horse-tail till they kiss their hands. Are they all ready?

CURTIS   They are.

GRUMIO   Call them forth.

CURTIS   Do you hear, ho? You must meet my master to countenance my mistress.

GRUMIO   Why, she has a face of her own.

CURTIS   Who knows not that?

GRUMIO   You, it seems, that call for company to countenance her.

CURTIS   I call them forth to credit her.

GRUMIO   Why, she comes to borrow nothing of them.

Enter four or five Servingmen

NATHANIEL   Welcome home, Grumio.
PHILIP   How now, Grumio.
JOSEPH   What, Grumio.
NICHOLAS   Fellow Grumio.
NATHANIEL   How now, old lad.
GRUMIO   Welcome, you. How now, you. What, you.
   Fellow, you. And thus much for greeting. Now, my
   spruce companions, is all ready, and all things neat?
NATHANIEL   All things are ready. How near is our master?
GRUMIO   Even at hand, alighted by this. And therefore
   be not—Cock's [God's] passion, silence! I hear my master.

Enter Petruchio and Katherina

PETRUCHIO
   Where are these knaves? What, no man at door
   To hold my stirrup nor to take my horse?
   Where are Nathaniel, Gregory, Philip?
ALL SERVINGMEN   Here, here sir, here sir.
PETRUCHIO
   Here sir, here sir, here sir, here sir!
   You logger-headed and unpolished grooms!
   What, no attendance? No regard? No duty?
   Where is the foolish knave I sent before?
GRUMIO
   Here sir, as foolish as I was before.
PETRUCHIO
   You peasant swain, you blasted malt-horse drudge!
   Did I not bid you meet me in the park
   And bring along these rascal knaves with you?

GRUMIO
    Nathaniel's coat, sir, was not fully made,
    And Gabriel's pumps were all ragged in the heel.
    There was no blacking to colour Peter's hat,
    And Walter's dagger was not come from sheathing.
    There were none fine but Adam, Rafe, and Gregory—
    The rest were ragged, old, and beggarly.
    Yet, as they are, here are they come to meet you.
PETRUCHIO
    Go, rascals, go and fetch my supper in.

Exeunt Servingmen

He sings

        Where is the life that late I led?
        Where are those—
    Sit down, Kate, and welcome. Food, food, food, food!

Enter Servants with supper

    Why, when, I say? Nay, good sweet Kate, be merry.
    Off with my boots, you rogues! You villains, when?

He sings

        It was the friar of orders grey,
        As he forth walkèd on his way—
    Out, you rogue! You pluck my foot awry.

He strikes the Servant

    Take that, and mend the plucking off the other.
    Be merry, Kate. Some water here. What ho!

Enter one with water

Where's my spaniel Troilus? Fellow, get you hence,
And bid my cousin Ferdinand come hither.

Exit another Servingman

One, Kate, that you must kiss and be acquainted with.
Where are my slippers? Shall I have some water?
Come, Kate, and wash, and welcome heartily.

He knocks the basin out of the Servant's hands

You silly villain, will you let it fall?

He strikes the Servant

KATHERINA
Patience, I pray you, it was a fault unwilling.
PETRUCHIO
A stupid, beetle-headed, flap-eared knave!
Come, Kate, sit down, I know you have a stomach.
Will you give thanks, sweet Kate, or else shall I?
What's this? Mutton?
FIRST SERVINGMAN   Ay.
PETRUCHIO   Who brought it?
PETER   I.
PETRUCHIO
'Tis burnt, and so is all the meat.
What dogs are these! Where is the rascal cook?
How durst you, villains, bring it from the dresser
And serve it thus to me that love it not?
There, take it to you, trenchers, cups, and all.

He throws the food and dishes at them

You heedless blockheads and unmannered slaves!
What, do you grumble? I'll be with you straight.

Exeunt Servants

KATHERINA
  I pray you, husband, be not so disquiet.
  The meat was well, if you were so contented.
PETRUCHIO
  I tell you, Kate, 'twas burnt and dried away,
  And I expressly am forbidden to touch it,
  For it engenders choler and plants anger.
  And better it is that both of us did fast,
  Since, of ourselves, ourselves are choleric,
  Than feed it with such over-roasted flesh.
  Be patient, tomorrow it shall be mended,
  And for this night we'll fast for company.
  Come, I will bring you to your bridal chamber. *Exeunt*

Enter Servants severally

NATHANIEL   Peter, did you ever see the like?
PETER   He kills her in her own humour.

Enter Curtis

GRUMIO   Where is he?
CURTIS
  In her chamber,
  Making a sermon of continency to her,
  And rails, and swears, and rates, that she, poor soul,
  Knows not which way to stand, to look, to speak,
  And sits as one new-risen from a dream.
  Away, away, for he is coming hither.   *Exeunt*

Enter Petruchio

PETRUCHIO
  Thus have I politicly begun my reign,
  And 'tis my hope to end successfully.
  My falcon now is sharp and passing empty,

And till she stoops she must not be full-gorged,
For then she never looks upon her lure.
Another way I have to man my falcon,
To make her come and know her keeper's call,
That is, to watch her, as we watch these kites
That flap and beat and will not be obedient.
She ate no meat today, and none shall eat.
Last night she slept not, and tonight she shall not.
As with the meat, some undeservèd fault
I'll find about the making of the bed,
And here I'll fling the pillow, there the bolster,
This way the coverlet, another way the sheets.
Ay, and amid this bustle I intend
That all is done in reverend care of her.
And, in conclusion, she shall watch all night,
And if she chances to nod I'll rail and brawl,
And with the clamour keep her wide awake.
This is a way to kill a wife with kindness,
And thus I'll curb her mad and headstrong humour.
He that knows better how to tame a shrew,
Now let him speak—'tis charity to show.   *Exit*

SCENE II
Before Baptista's house.

Enter Tranio as Lucentio, and Hortensio as Licio

TRANIO
  Is it possible, friend Licio, that Mistress Bianca
  Does fancy any other than Lucentio?
  I tell you, sir, she takes me fairly in.
HORTENSIO
  Sir, to satisfy you in what I have said,
  Stand by and mark the manner of his teaching.

They stand aside
Enter Bianca, and Lucentio as Cambio

LUCENTIO
Now, mistress, profit you in what you read?
BIANCA
What, master, read you? First resolve me that.
LUCENTIO
I read that I profess, *The Art to Love.*
BIANCA
And may you prove, sir, master of your art.
LUCENTIO
While you, sweet dear, prove mistress of my heart.

They retire

HORTENSIO
Quick proceeders, indeed! Now tell me, I pray,
You that durst swear that your mistress Bianca
Loved none in the world so well as Lucentio.
TRANIO
O despiteful love, unconstant womankind!
I tell you, Licio, this is wonderful.
HORTENSIO
Mistake no more, I am not Licio,
Nor a musician as I seem to be;
But one that scorn to live in this disguise
For such a one as leaves a gentleman
And makes a god of such a scullion.
Know, sir, that I am called Hortensio.
TRANIO
Signor Hortensio, I have often heard
Of your entire affection to Bianca,
And since my eyes are witness of her lightness,
I will with you, if you are so contented,
Forswear Bianca and her love for ever.

HORTENSIO
  See how they kiss and court! Signor Lucentio,
  Here is my hand, and here I firmly vow
  Never to woo her more, but do forswear her,
  As one unworthy all the former favours
  With which I have foolishly flattered her.
TRANIO
  And here I take the like unfeignèd oath,
  Never to marry her though she would entreat.
  Fie on her! See how beastly she does court him.
HORTENSIO
  Would all the world but he had quite forsworn!
  For me, that I may surely keep my oath,
  I will be married to a wealthy widow
  Ere three days pass, who has as long loved me
  As I have loved this proud disdainful bird.
  And so farewell, Signor Lucentio.
  Kindness in women, not their beauteous looks,
  Shall win my love—and so I take my leave,
  In resolution as I swore before.   *Exit*

              Tranio joins Lucentio and Bianca

TRANIO
  Mistress Bianca, bless you with such grace
  As should belong to a lover's blessèd case!
  Nay, I have taken you napping, gentle love,
  And have forsworn you with Hortensio.
BIANCA
  Tranio, you jest—but have you both forsworn me?
TRANIO
  Mistress, we have.
LUCENTIO   Then we are rid of Licio.
TRANIO
  In faith, he'll have a lusty widow now,
  That shall be wooed and wedded in a day.

BIANCA
  God give him joy!
TRANIO
  Ay, and he'll tame her.
BIANCA   He says so, Tranio.
TRANIO
  Faith, he is gone unto the taming-school.
BIANCA
  The taming-school? What, is there such a place?
TRANIO
  Ay, mistress, and Petruchio is the master,
  That teaches tricks eleven and twenty long,
  To tame a shrew and charm her chattering tongue.

Enter Biondello

BIONDELLO
  O master, master, I have watched so long
  That I'm dog-weary, but at last I spied
  An ancient angel coming down the hill
  Will serve the turn.
TRANIO   What is he, Biondello?
BIONDELLO
  Master, a merchant type or a pedant,
  I know not what—but formal in apparel,
  In gait and countenance surely like a father.
LUCENTIO
  And what of him, Tranio?
TRANIO
  If he is credulous and trusts my tale,
  I'll make him glad to seem Vincentio,
  And give assurance to Baptista Minola
  As if he were the right Vincentio.
  Take in your love, and then let me alone.
                    Exeunt Lucentio and Bianca

Enter a Pedant

PEDANT
  God save you, sir.
TRANIO   And you, sir. You are welcome.
  Travel you farther on, or are you at the farthest?
PEDANT
  Sir, at the farthest for a week or two,
  But then up farther, and as far as Rome,
  And so to Tripoli, if God lends me life.
TRANIO
  What countryman, I pray?
PEDANT   Of Mantua.
TRANIO
  Of Mantua? Sir, indeed, God forbid!
  And come to Padua, careless of your life?
PEDANT
  My life, sir? How, I pray? For that goes hard.
TRANIO
  It is death for any one in Mantua
  To come to Padua. Know you not the cause?
  Your ships are stayed at Venice, and the Duke,
  For private quarrel between your Duke and him,
  Has published and proclaimed it openly.
  'Tis marvel—but that you are newly come,
  You might have heard it else proclaimed about.
PEDANT
  Alas, sir, it is worse for me than so!
  For I have bills for money by exchange
  From Florence, and must here deliver them.
TRANIO
  Well, sir, to do you courtesy,
  This will I do, and this I will advise you—
  First tell me, have you ever been at Pisa?

PEDANT
　　Ay, sir, in Pisa have I often been,
　　Pisa renownèd for grave citizens.
TRANIO
　　Among them know you one Vincentio?
PEDANT
　　I know him not, but I have heard of him,
　　A merchant of incomparable wealth.
TRANIO
　　He is my father, sir, and truth to say,
　　In countenance somewhat does resemble you.
BIONDELLO　　(aside) As much as an apple does an oyster,
and all one.
TRANIO
　　To save your life in this extremity,
　　This favour will I do you for his sake—
　　And think it not the worst of all your fortunes
　　That you are so like Sir Vincentio—
　　His name and credit shall you undertake,
　　And in my house you shall be friendly lodged.
　　Look that you take upon you as you should.
　　You understand me, sir. So shall you stay
　　Till you have done your business in the city.
　　If this is courtesy, sir, accept of it.
PEDANT
　　O, sir, I do, and will repute you ever
　　The patron of my life and liberty.
TRANIO
　　Then go with me to make the matter good.
　　This, by the way, I let you understand—
　　My father is here looked for every day
　　To pass assurance of a dower in marriage
　　Between me and one Baptista's daughter here.
　　In all these circumstances I'll instruct you.
　　Go with me, sir, to clothe you as becomes you.
　　　　　　　　　　　　　　　　　　　　　　　　　　　Exeunt

SCENE III
Petruchio's house.

Enter Katherina and Grumio

GRUMIO
    No, no, forsooth, I dare not for my life.
KATHERINA
    The more my wrong, the more his spite appears.
    What, did he marry me to famish me?
    Beggars that come unto my father's door
    Upon entreaty have immediate alms,
    If not, elsewhere they meet with charity.
    But I, who never knew how to entreat,
    Nor ever needed that I should entreat,
    Am starved for meat, giddy for lack of sleep,
    With oaths kept waking, and with brawling fed.
    And that which spites me more than all these wants,
    He does it under name of perfect love,
    As who should say, if I should sleep or eat,
    'Twere deadly sickness or else present death.
    I pray you go and get me some repast,
    I care not what, so it is wholesome food.
GRUMIO
    What say you to a calf's foot?
KATHERINA
    'Tis passing good, I pray you let me have it.
GRUMIO
    I fear it is too choleric a meat.
    How say you to a fat tripe finely broiled?
KATHERINA
    I like it well. Good Grumio, fetch it me.
GRUMIO
    I cannot tell, I fear it is choleric.
    What say you to a piece of beef and mustard?

KATHERINA
A dish that I do love to feed upon.
GRUMIO
Ay, but the mustard is too hot a little.
KATHERINA
Why then, the beef, and let the mustard rest.
GRUMIO
Nay then, I will not. You shall have the mustard,
Or else you get no beef of Grumio.
KATHERINA
Then both, or one, or anything you will.
GRUMIO
Why then, the mustard without the beef.
KATHERINA
Go, get you gone, you false deluding slave,

She beats him

That feed me with the very name of meat.
Sorrow on you and all the pack of you
That triumph thus upon my misery!
Go, get you gone, I say.

Enter Petruchio and Hortensio with meat

PETRUCHIO
How fares my Kate? What, sweeting, in the dumps?
HORTENSIO
Mistress, what cheer?
KATHERINA   Faith, as cold as can be.
PETRUCHIO
Pluck up your spirits, look cheerfully upon me.
Here, love, you see how diligent I am,
To dress your meat myself, and bring it you.

He sets the dish down

I am sure, sweet Kate, this kindness merits thanks.
What, not a word? Nay then, you love it not,
And all my pains are taken to no point.
Here, take away this dish.
KATHERINA   I pray you, let it stand.
PETRUCHIO
The poorest service is repaid with thanks,
And so shall mine before you touch the meat.
KATHERINA
I thank you, sir.
HORTENSIO
Signor Petruchio, fie, you are to blame.
Come, Mistress Kate, I'll bear you company.
PETRUCHIO   *(aside to Hortensio)*
Eat it up all, Hortensio, if you love me.
(to Katherina) Much good do it unto your gentle heart!
Kate, eat apace. And now, my honey love,
Will we return unto your father's house
And revel it as bravely as the best,
With silken coats and caps, and golden rings,
With ruffs and cuffs and farthingales and things,
With scarfs and fans and double change of bravery,
With amber bracelets, beads, and all this knavery.
What, have you dined? The tailor stays your leisure,
To deck your body with his ruffling treasure.

Enter Tailor

Come, tailor, let us see these ornaments.
Lay forth the gown.

Enter Haberdasher

What news with you, sir?
HABERDASHER
Here is the cap your worship did bespeak.

PETRUCHIO
   Why, this was moulded on a porringer—
   A velvet dish. Fie, fie, 'tis lewd and filthy!
   Why, it is a cockle or a walnut-shell,
   A knack, a toy, a trick, a baby's cap.
   Away with it! Come, let me have a bigger.
KATHERINA
   I'll have no bigger. This does fit the time,
   And gentlewomen wear such caps as these.
PETRUCHIO
   When you are gentle, you shall have one too,
   And not till then.
HORTENSIO   *(aside)* That will not be in haste.
KATHERINA
   Why sir, I trust I may have leave to speak,
   And speak I will. I am no child, no babe.
   Your betters have endured me say my mind,
   And if you cannot, best you stop your ears.
   My tongue will tell the anger of my heart,
   Or else my heart concealing it will break;
   And rather than it shall, I will be free
   Even to the uttermost, as I please, in words.
PETRUCHIO
   Why, you say true—it is a paltry cap,
   A custard-coffin, a bauble, a silken pie.
   I love you well in that you like it not.
KATHERINA
   Love me or love me not, I like the cap,
   And it I will have, or I will have none.
PETRUCHIO
   Your gown? Why, ay. Come, tailor, let us see it.
                             Exit Haberdasher
   O mercy, God! What masquing stuff is here?
   What's this? A sleeve? 'Tis like a demi-cannon.
   What, up and down carved like an apple-tart?
   Here's snip and nip and cut and slish and slash,

Like to a censer in a barber's shop.
Why, what a devil's name, tailor, call you this?
HORTENSIO   *(aside)*
I see she's likely to have neither cap nor gown.
TAILOR
You bid me make it orderly and well,
According to the fashion and the time.
PETRUCHIO
Indeed, and did. But if you will remember,
I did not bid you mar it to the time.
Go, hop me over every kennel home,
For you shall hop without my custom, sir.
I'll none of it. Hence, make your best of it.
KATHERINA
I never saw a better-fashioned gown,
More quaint, more pleasing, nor more commendable.
Perhaps you mean to make a puppet of me.
PETRUCHIO
Why, true, he means to make a puppet of you.
TAILOR
She says your worship means to make a puppet of her.
PETRUCHIO
O monstrous arrogance! You lie, you thread, you thimble,
You yard, three-quarters, half-yard, quarter, inch,
You flea, you nit, you winter-cricket you!
Braved in my own house with a skein of thread?
Away, you rag, you quantity, you remnant,
Or I shall so bemeasure you with your yard
As you shall think before prating while you live.
I tell you, I, that you have marred her gown.
TAILOR
Your worship is deceived—the gown is made
Just as my master had direction.
Grumio gave order how it should be done.
GRUMIO   I gave him no order, I gave him the stuff.

TAILOR
But how did you desire it should be made?

GRUMIO   Sure, sir, with needle and thread.

TAILOR
But did you not request to have it cut?

GRUMIO   You have faced many things.

TAILOR   I have.

GRUMIO   Face not me. You have braved many men, brave
not me. I will neither be faced nor braved. I say unto
you, I bid your master cut out the gown, but I did not
bid him cut it to pieces. Therefore, you lie.

TAILOR   Why, here is the note of the fashion to testify.

PETRUCHIO   Read it.

GRUMIO   The note lies in his throat, if he says I said so.

TAILOR   (reads) 'Imprimis [first] a loose-bodied gown.'

GRUMIO   Master, if ever I said loose-bodied gown, sew
me in the skirts of it and beat me to death with a ball of
brown thread. I said a gown.

PETRUCHIO   Proceed.

TAILOR   'With a small compassed cape.'

GRUMIO   I confess the cape.

TAILOR   'With a trunk sleeve.'

GRUMIO   I confess two sleeves.

TAILOR   'The sleeves curiously cut.'

PETRUCHIO   Ay, there's the villainy.

GRUMIO   Error in the bill, sir, error in the bill! I commanded the sleeves should be cut out, and sewed up
again; and that I'll prove upon you, though your little
finger is armed with a thimble.

TAILOR   This is true that I say; if I had you in place
where, you should know it.

GRUMIO   I am for you straight. Take you the bill, give me
your tape-measure, and spare not me.

HORTENSIO   God-a-mercy, Grumio, then he shall have
no odds.

PETRUCHIO   Well sir, in brief, the gown is not for me.

GRUMIO   You are in the right, sir, it is for my mistress.

PETRUCHIO   Go, take it up unto your master's use.

GRUMIO   Villain, not for your life! Take up my mistress'
gown for your master's use!

PETRUCHIO   Why sir, what's your meaning in that?

GRUMIO

O sir, the meaning is deeper than you think.
Take up my mistress' gown to his master's use!
O fie, fie, fie!

PETRUCHIO   (aside)

Hortensio, say you will see the tailor paid.

(to the Tailor) Go take it hence, be gone, and say no
more.

HORTENSIO   (aside)

Tailor, I'll pay you for your gown tomorrow.
Take no unkindness of his hasty words.
Away, I say, commend me to your master.   Exit Tailor

PETRUCHIO

Well, come my Kate, we will unto your father's
Even in these honest mean habiliments.
Our purses shall be proud, our garments poor,
For 'tis the mind that makes the body rich,
And as the sun breaks through the darkest clouds,
So honour peers out in the meanest habit.
What, is the jay more precious than the lark
Because his feathers are more beautiful?
Or is the adder better than the eel
Because his painted skin contents the eye?
O no, good Kate, neither are you the worse
For this poor furniture and mean array.
If you account it shame, lay it on me.
And therefore frolic. We will hence forthwith
To feast and sport us at your father's house.
(to Grumio) Go call my men, and let us straight to him,
And bring our horses unto Long-lane end,
There will we mount, and thither walk on foot.

Let's see, I think 'tis now some seven o'clock,
And well we may come there by dinner-time.
KATHERINA
I dare assure you, sir, 'tis almost two,
It will be supper-time ere you come there.
PETRUCHIO
It shall be seven ere I go to horse.
Look what I speak, or do, or think to do,
You are still crossing it. Sirs, let it alone,
I will not go today, and ere I do,
It shall be what o'clock I say it is.
HORTENSIO
Why, so this gallant will command the sun.

Exeunt

SCENE IV
Before Baptista's house.

Enter Tranio as Lucentio,
and the Pedant dressed like Vincentio

TRANIO
Sir, this is the house—please it you that I call?
PEDANT
Ay, what else? Unless I am deceived
Signor Baptista may remember me
Near twenty years ago in Genoa,
Where we were lodgers at the Pegasus.
TRANIO
'Tis well, and hold your own, in any case,
With such austerity as belongs to a father.

Enter Biondello

PEDANT

    I warrant you. But sir, here comes your boy.

    It were good he were schooled.

TRANIO

    Fear you not him. Good Biondello,

    Now do your duty thoroughly, I advise you.

    Imagine it were the right Vincentio.

BIONDELLO

    Tut, fear not me.

TRANIO

    But have you done your errand to Baptista?

BIONDELLO

    I told him that your father was at Venice,

    And that you looked for him this day in Padua.

TRANIO

    You are a tall fellow, hold you that to drink.

Enter Baptista, and Lucentio as Cambio

    Here comes Baptista. Set your countenance, sir.

    Signor Baptista, you are happily met.

    (to the Pedant) Sir, this is the gentleman I told you of.

    I pray you stand good father to me now,

    Give me Bianca for my patrimony.

PEDANT

    Soft, son!

    Sir, by your leave, having come to Padua

    To gather in some debts, my son Lucentio

    Made me acquainted with a weighty cause

    Of love between your daughter and himself.

    And—for the good report I hear of you,

    And for the love he bears now to your daughter,

    And she to him—to stay him not too long,

    I am content, in a good father's care,

    To have him matched. And, if you please to like

    No worse than I, upon some agreement

Me shall you find ready and willing
With one consent to have her so bestowed.
For niggling I cannot be with you,
Signor Baptista, of whom I hear so well.

BAPTISTA

Sir, pardon me in what I have to say.
Your plainness and your shortness please me well.
Right true it is your son Lucentio here,
Does love my daughter, and she indeed loves him,
Or both dissemble deeply their affections.
And therefore if you say no more than this,
That like a father you will deal with him,
And pass my daughter a sufficient dower,
The match is made, and all is done—
Your son shall have my daughter with consent.

TRANIO

I thank you, sir. Where then do you know best
We come to terms and such assurance take
As shall with either part's agreement stand?

BAPTISTA

Not in my house, Lucentio, for you know
Pitchers have ears, and I have many servants.
Besides, old Gremio is hearkening still,
And happily we might be interrupted.

TRANIO

Then at my lodging, if it likes you.
There does my father lie; and there this night
We'll pass the business privately and well.
Send for your daughter by your servant here.
My boy shall fetch the scrivener presently.
The worst is this, that at so slender warning
You are likely to have a thin and slender pittance.

BAPTISTA

It likes me well. Cambio, hie you home,
And bid Bianca make her ready straight.
And, if you will, tell what has happenèd—

Lucentio's father is arrived in Padua,
And how she's likely to be Lucentio's wife. *Exit Lucentio*
BIONDELLO
I pray the gods she may, with all my heart.
TRANIO
Dally not with the gods, but get you gone.

Exit Biondello

Enter Peter, a Servingman

Signor Baptista, shall I lead the way?
Welcome! One dish is likely to be your cheer.
Come sir, we will better it in Pisa.
BAPTISTA
I follow you.   ⸀   *Exeunt*

Enter Lucentio and Biondello

BIONDELLO
Cambio.
LUCENTIO   What say you, Biondello?
BIONDELLO
You saw my master wink and laugh upon you?
LUCENTIO   Biondello, what of that?
BIONDELLO   Faith, nothing—but he has left me here
behind to expound the meaning or moral of his signs
and tokens.
LUCENTIO   I pray you explain them.
BIONDELLO   Then thus—Baptista is safe, talking with
the deceiving father of a deceitful son.
LUCENTIO   And what of him?
BIONDELLO   His daughter is to be brought by you to the
supper.
LUCENTIO   And then?
BIONDELLO   The old priest at Saint Luke's church is at
your command at all hours.

LUCENTIO   And what of all this?

BIONDELLO   I cannot tell, except they are busied about a
counterfeit assurance. Take you assurance of her, *cum
privilegio ad imprimendum solum*.[1] To the church! Take
the priest, clerk, and some sufficient honest witnesses.
If this is not that you look for, I have no more to say,
But bid Bianca farewell for ever and a day.

LUCENTIO   Hear you, Biondello?

BIONDELLO   I cannot tarry. I knew a wench married in
an afternoon as she went to the garden for parsley to
stuff a rabbit. And so may you, sir; and so adieu, sir. My
master has appointed me to go to Saint Luke's to bid the
priest be ready to come by the time you come with your
appendix.   *Exit*

LUCENTIO
I may and will, if she is so contented.
She will be pleased, then wherefore should I doubt?
Hap what hap may, I'll roundly go about her.
It shall go hard if Cambio goes without her.

                                                 Exit

SCENE V
The road to Padua.

Enter Petruchio, Katherina, Hortensio and Servants

PETRUCHIO
Come on, in God's name, once more toward our father's.
Good Lord, how bright and goodly shines the moon!

KATHERINA
The moon? The sun! It is not moonlight now.

---

[1]With the privilege of sole printing (inscription stamped
on title pages of books).

PETRUCHIO
    I say it is the moon that shines so bright.
KATHERINA
    I know it is the sun that shines so bright.
PETRUCHIO
    Now by my mother's son, and that's myself,
    It shall be moon, or star, or what I like,
    If ever I journey to your father's house.
    (to the Servants) Go on and fetch our horses back again.
    Evermore crossed and crossed, nothing but crossed!
HORTENSIO
    Say as he says, or we shall never go.
KATHERINA
    Forward, I pray, since we have come so far,
    And be it moon, or sun, or what you please.
    And if you please to call it a rush-candle,
    Henceforth I vow it shall be so for me.
PETRUCHIO
    I say it is the moon.
KATHERINA   I know it is the moon.
PETRUCHIO
    Nay, then you lie. It is the blessèd sun.
KATHERINA
    Then, God be blessed, it is the blessèd sun.
    But sun it is not, when you say it is not,
    And the moon changes even as your mind.
    What you will have it named, even that it is,
    And so it shall be so for Katherine.
HORTENSIO   (aside)
    Petruchio, go your ways, the field is won.
PETRUCHIO
    Well, forward, forward! Thus the bowl should run,
    And not unluckily against the bias.
    But soft, company is coming here.

Enter Vincentio

(to Vincentio) Good morrow, gentle mistress, where
  away?
Tell me, sweet Kate, and tell me truly too,
Have you beheld a fresher gentlewoman?
Such war of white and red within her cheeks!
What stars do spangle heaven with such beauty
As those two eyes become that heavenly face?
Fair lovely maid, once more good day to you.
Sweet Kate, embrace her for her beauty's sake.
HORTENSIO   (aside) He will make the man mad, to make
a woman of him.
KATHERINA
Young budding virgin, fair and fresh and sweet,
Whither away, or where is your abode?
Happy the parents of so fair a child,
Happier the man whom favourable stars
Allots you for his lovely bedfellow.
PETRUCHIO
Why, how now, Kate, I hope you are not mad!
This is a man, old, wrinkled, faded, withered,
And not a maiden, as you say he is.
KATHERINA
Pardon, old father, my mistaking eyes,
That have been so bedazzled with the sun
That everything I look on seems so green.
Now I perceive you are a reverend father.
Pardon, I pray you, for my mad mistaking.
PETRUCHIO
Do, good old grandsire, and also make known
Which way you travel—if along with us,
We shall be joyful of your company.
VINCENTIO
Fair sir, and you my merry mistress,
That with your strange encounter much amazed me,
My name is called Vincentio, my dwelling Pisa,
And bound I am to Padua, there to visit

A son of mine, whom long I have not seen.

PETRUCHIO
What is his name?

VINCENTIO   Lucentio, gentle sir.

PETRUCHIO
Happily met—the happier for your son.
And now by law, as well as reverend age,
I may entitle you my loving father.
The sister to my wife, this gentlewoman,
Your son by this has married. Wonder not,
Nor be you grieved—she is of good esteem,
Her dowry wealthy, and of worthy birth;
Besides so qualified as may beseem
The spouse of any noble gentleman.
Let me embrace with old Vincentio,
And wander we to see your honest son,
Who will of your arrival be full joyous.

VINCENTIO
But is this true, or is it else your pleasure,
Like pleasant travellers, to break a jest
Upon the company you overtake?

HORTENSIO
I do assure you, father, so it is.

PETRUCHIO
Come, go along and see the truth hereof,
For our first merriment has made you doubtful.
                              Exeunt all but Hortensio

HORTENSIO
Well, Petruchio, this has put me in heart.
Have to my widow! And if she is froward,
Then have you taught Hortensio to be untoward.
                                              Exit

Act V

SCENE I
Before Lucentio's house.

Enter Biondello, Lucentio as himself, and Bianca. Gremio is out before

BIONDELLO   Softly and swiftly, sir, for the priest is ready.
LUCENTIO   I fly, Biondello. But they may chance to need you at home, therefore leave us.
Exeunt Lucentio and Bianca
BIONDELLO   Nay, faith, I'll see the church at your back, and then come back to my master's as soon as I can.
Exit

GREMIO
I marvel Cambio comes not all this while.

Enter Petruchio, Katherina, Vincentio and Grumio, with attendants

PETRUCHIO
Sir, here's the door, this is Lucentio's house.
My father's bears more toward the market-place.
Thither must I, and here I leave you, sir.
VINCENTIO
You shall not choose but drink before you go.
I think I shall command your welcome here,
And by all likelihood some cheer is toward.

He knocks

GREMIO   They're busy within. You were best knock louder.

PEDANT   What's he that knocks as he would beat down the gate?

VINCENTIO   Is Signor Lucentio within, sir?

PEDANT   He's within, sir, but not to be spoken with.

VINCENTIO   What if a man brings him a hundred pound or two to make merry with?

PEDANT   Keep your hundred pounds to yourself. He shall need none so long as I live.

PETRUCHIO   Nay, I told you your son was well beloved in Padua. Do you hear, sir? To leave frivolous circumstances, I pray you tell Signor Lucentio that his father is come from Pisa, and is here at the door to speak with him.

PEDANT   You lie. His father is come from Mantua, and here looking out at the window.

VINCENTIO   Are you his father?

PEDANT   Ay sir, so his mother says, if I may believe her.

PETRUCHIO   (to Vincentio) Why how now, gentleman! Why, this is flat knavery, to take upon you another man's name.

PEDANT   Lay hands on the villain. I believe he means to cozen somebody in this city under my countenance.

Enter Biondello

BIONDELLO   (aside) I have seen them in the church together. God send them good shipping! But who is here? My old master Vincentio! Now we are undone and brought to nothing.

VINCENTIO   Come hither, gallows bird.

BIONDELLO   I hope I may choose, sir.

VINCENTIO   Come hither, you rogue. What, have you forgotten me?

BIONDELLO   Forgotten you? No, sir. I could not forget you, for I never saw you before in all my life.

VINCENTIO What, you notorious villain, did you never
see your master's father, Vincentio?
BIONDELLO What, my old worshipful old master? Yes,
indeed, sir—see where he looks out of the window.
VINCENTIO   Is it so, indeed?

He beats Biondello

BIONDELLO Help, help, help! Here's a madman will
murder me.   *Exit*
PEDANT   Help, son! Help, Signor Baptista!
PETRUCHIO   Pray, Kate, let's stand aside and see the end
of this controversy.

They stand aside
Enter Pedant below, with Servants, Baptista, and Tranio

TRANIO   Sir, what are you that offer to beat my servant?
VINCENTIO   What am I, sir? Nay, what are you, sir? O
immortal gods! O fine villain! A silken doublet, a velvet
hose, a scarlet cloak, and a high-crowned hat! O, I am
undone, I am undone! While I play the good husband at
home, my son and my servant spend all at the university.
TRANIO   How now, what's the matter?
BAPTISTA   What, is the man lunatic?
TRANIO   Sir, you seem a sober ancient gentleman by your
habit, but your words show you a madman. Why, sir,
what concerns it you if I wear pearl and gold? I thank
my good father, I am able to maintain it.
VINCENTIO   Your father? O villain, he is a sail-maker in
Bergamo.
BAPTISTA   You mistake, sir, you mistake, sir. Pray, what
do you think is his name?
VINCENTIO   His name? As if I knew not his name! I have
brought him up ever since he was three years old, and
his name is Tranio.

PEDANT   Away, away, mad ass! His name is Lucentio,
  and he is my only son, and heir to the lands of me,
  Signor Vincentio.
VINCENTIO   Lucentio? O, he has murdered his master!
  Lay hold on him, I charge you, in the Duke's name. O,
  my son, my son! Tell me, you villain, where is my son
  Lucentio?
TRANIO   Call forth an officer.

                    Enter an Officer

  Carry this mad knave to the gaol. Father Baptista, I
  charge you see that he is forthcoming.
VINCENTIO   Carry me to the gaol?
GREMIO   Stay, officer. He shall not go to prison.
BAPTISTA   Talk not, Signor Gremio. I say he shall go to
  prison.
GREMIO   Take heed, Signor Baptista, lest you be cheated
  in this business. I dare swear this is the right Vincentio.
PEDANT   Swear if you dare.
GREMIO   Nay, I dare not swear it.
TRANIO   Then you were best say that I am not Lucentio.
GREMIO   Yes, I know you to be Signor Lucentio.
BAPTISTA   Away with the dotard, to the gaol with him!
VINCENTIO   Thus strangers may be haled and abused. O
  monstrous villain!

        Enter Biondello, with Lucentio and Bianca

BIONDELLO   O, we are spoiled, and yonder he is! Deny
  him, forswear him, or else we are all undone.
LUCENTIO   *(kneeling)*
  Pardon, sweet father.
VINCENTIO   Lives my sweet son?

      Exeunt Biondello, Tranio and Pedant, as fast as may be

BIANCA
  Pardon, dear father.
BAPTISTA   How have you offended?
  Where is Lucentio?
LUCENTIO   Here's Lucentio,
  Right son to the right Vincentio,
  That have by marriage made your daughter mine,
  While counterfeit supposes bleared thine eyne [eyes].
GREMIO
  Here's plotting, with a witness, to deceive us all.
VINCENTIO
  Where is that damnèd villain, Tranio,
  That faced and braved me in this matter so?
BAPTISTA
  Why, tell me, is not this my Cambio?
BIANCA
  Cambio is changed into Lucentio.
LUCENTIO
  Love wrought these miracles. Bianca's love
  Made me exchange my state with Tranio,
  While he did bear my countenance in the town,
  And happily I have arrived at last
  Unto the wishèd haven of my bliss.
  What Tranio did, myself enforced him to;
  Then pardon him, sweet father, for my sake.
VINCENTIO   I'll slit the villain's nose that would have
  sent me to the gaol.
BAPTISTA   (to Lucentio) But do you hear, sir? Have you
  married my daughter without asking my good will?
VINCENTIO   Fear not, Baptista, we will content you, go
  to. But I will in to be revenged for this villainy.   *Exit*
BAPTISTA   And I to sound the depth of this knavery. *Exit*
LUCENTIO   Look not pale, Bianca—your father will not
  frown.   *Exeunt Lucentio and Bianca*

GREMIO
  My cake is dough, but I'll in among the rest,
  Out of hope of all but my share of the feast.   *Exit*
  KATHERINA   Husband, let's follow to see the end of this
  ado.
  PETRUCHIO   First kiss me, Kate, and we will.
  KATHERINA   What, in the midst of the street?
  PETRUCHIO   What, are you ashamed of me?
  KATHERINA   No, sir, God forbid—but ashamed to kiss.
  PETRUCHIO
  Why then, let's home again.
  (to Grumio) Come, fellow, let's away.
  KATHERINA
  Nay, I will give you a kiss.

                    She kisses him

  Now pray you, love, stay.
  PETRUCHIO
  Is not this well? Come, my sweet Kate.
  Better once than never, for never too late.   *Exeunt*

                    SCENE II
                 Lucentio's house.

  Enter Baptista with Vincentio, Gremio with the Pedant,
     Lucentio with Bianca, Petruchio with Katherina,
  Hortensio with the Widow; followed by Tranio, Biondello,
  and Grumio, with the Servingmen bringing in a banquet

LUCENTIO
  At last, though long, our jarring notes agree,
  And time it is when raging war is done
  To smile at escapes and perils overblown.
  My fair Bianca, bid my father welcome,

While I with self-same kindness welcome yours.
Brother Petruchio, sister Katherina,
And you, Hortensio, with your loving widow,
Feast with the best, and welcome to my house.
My banquet is to close our stomachs up
After our great good cheer. Pray you, sit down,
For now we sit to chat as well as eat.

They sit

PETRUCHIO
Nothing but sit and sit, and eat and eat!
BAPTISTA
Padua affords this kindness, son Petruchio.
PETRUCHIO
Padua affords nothing but what is kind.
HORTENSIO
For both our sakes I would that word were true.
PETRUCHIO
Now, for my life, Hortensio frightens his widow.
WIDOW
Then never trust me if I am afraid.
PETRUCHIO
You are very sensible, and yet you miss my sense:
I mean Hortensio is afraid of you.
WIDOW
He that is giddy thinks the world turns round.
PETRUCHIO
Roundly replied.
KATHERINA   Mistress, how mean you that?
WIDOW
Thus I conceive by him.
PETRUCHIO
Conceives by me! How likes Hortensio that?

HORTENSIO
  My widow says thus she conceives her tale.
PETRUCHIO
  Very well mended. Kiss him for that, good widow.
KATHERINA
  'He that is giddy thinks the world turns round' —
  I pray you tell me what you meant by that.
WIDOW
  Your husband, being troubled with a shrew,
  Measures my husband's sorrow by his woe.
  And now you know my meaning.
KATHERINA
  A very mean meaning.
WIDOW   Right, I mean you.
KATHERINA
  And I am mean, indeed, respecting you.
PETRUCHIO
  To her, Kate!
HORTENSIO
  To her, widow!
PETRUCHIO
  A hundred marks, my Kate does put her down.
HORTENSIO
  That's my office.
PETRUCHIO
  Spoken like an officer — here's to you, lad.

                 He drinks to Hortensio

BAPTISTA
  How likes Gremio these quick-witted folks?
GREMIO
  Believe me, sir, they butt together well.
BIANCA
  Head and butt! A hasty-witted body
  Would say your head and butt were head and horn.

VINCENTIO
    Ay, mistress bride, has that awakened you?
BIANCA
    Ay, but not frighted me, therefore I'll sleep again.
PETRUCHIO
    Nay, that you shall not. Since you have begun,
    Have at you for a bitter jest or two.
BIANCA
    Am I your bird? I mean to shift my bush,
    And then pursue me as you draw your bow.
    You are welcome all.
                    Exeunt Bianca, Katherina, and Widow
PETRUCHIO
    She has forestalled me. Here, Signor Tranio,
    This bird you aimed at, though you hit her not—
    Therefore a health to all that shot and missed.
TRANIO
    O sir, Lucentio slipped me like his greyhound,
    Which runs himself, and catches for his master.
PETRUCHIO
    A good swift simile, but something currish.
TRANIO
    It is well, sir, that you hunted for yourself.
    'Tis thought your deer does hold you at a bay.
BAPTISTA
    O, O, Petruchio! Tranio hits you now.
LUCENTIO
    I thank you for that gird, good Tranio.
HORTENSIO
    Confess, confess, has he not hit you here?
PETRUCHIO
    He has a little galled me, I confess;
    And as the jest did glance away from me,
    'Tis ten to one it maimed you two outright.

BAPTISTA
  Now, in good sadness, son Petruchio,
  I think you have the veriest shrew of all.
PETRUCHIO
  Well, I say no. And therefore for assurance
  Let's each one send unto his wife,
  And he whose wife is most obedient,
  To come at first when he does send for her,
  Shall win the wager which we will propose.
HORTENSIO
  Content. What's the wager?
LUCENTIO   Twenty crowns.
PETRUCHIO
  Twenty crowns?
  I'll venture so much of my hawk or hound,
  But twenty times so much upon my wife.
LUCENTIO
  A hundred then.
HORTENSIO   Content.
PETRUCHIO   A match! 'Tis done.
HORTENSIO
  Who shall begin?
LUCENTIO   That will I. Biondello,
  Go bid your mistress come to me.
BIONDELLO   I go.   *Exit*
BAPTISTA
  Son, I'll be your half Bianca comes.
LUCENTIO
  I'll have no halves. I'll bear it all myself.

                    Enter Biondello

  How now, what news?
BIONDELLO   Sir, my mistress sends you word
  That she is busy and she cannot come.

PETRUCHIO
  How? She's busy, and she cannot come!
  Is that an answer?
GREMIO   Ay, and a kind one too.
  Pray God, sir, your wife send you not a worse.
PETRUCHIO
  I hope better.
HORTENSIO
  Fellow Biondello, go and entreat my wife
  To come to me forthwith.   *Exit Biondello*
PETRUCHIO   O ho, entreat her!
  Nay, then she must needs come.
HORTENSIO   I am afraid, sir,
  Do what you can, yours will not be entreated.

Enter Biondello

  Now, where is my wife?
BIONDELLO
  She says you have some goodly jest in hand.
  She will not come. She bids you come to her.
PETRUCHIO
  Worse and worse, she will not come! O vile,
  Intolerable, not to be endured!
  Fellow Grumio, go to your mistress,
  Say I command her come to me.   *Exit Grumio*
HORTENSIO
  I know her answer.
PETRUCHIO   What?
HORTENSIO   She will not.
PETRUCHIO
  The fouler fortune mine, and there an end.

Enter Katherina

BAPTISTA
  Now, by my word, here comes Katherina.
KATHERINA
  What is your will, sir, that you send for me?
PETRUCHIO
  Where is your sister, and Hortensio's wife?
KATHERINA
  They sit conferring by the parlour fire.
PETRUCHIO
  Go fetch them hither. If they deny to come,
  Swinge them soundly forth unto their husbands.
  Away, I say, and bring them hither straight.

Exit Katherina

LUCENTIO
  Here is a wonder, if you talk of a wonder.
HORTENSIO
  And so it is. I wonder what it bodes.
PETRUCHIO
  Well, peace it bodes, and love, and quiet life,
  Respectful rule, and right supremacy,
  And, to be short, what not that's sweet and happy.
BAPTISTA
  Now fair befall you, good Petruchio!
  The wager you have won, and I will add
  Unto their losses twenty thousand crowns—
  Another dowry to another daughter,
  For she is changed, as she had never been.
PETRUCHIO
  Nay, I will win my wager better yet,
  And show more sign of her obedience,
  Her new-built virtue and obedience.

Enter Katherina with Bianca and Widow

  See where she comes, and brings your froward wives
  As prisoners to her womanly persuasion.

Katherine, that cap of yours becomes you not.
Off with that bauble, throw it under foot.

She obeys

WIDOW
  Lord, let me never have a cause to sigh
  Till I be brought to such a silly pass!
BIANCA
  Fie, what a foolish duty call you this?
LUCENTIO
  I would your duty were as foolish too!
  The wisdom of your duty, fair Bianca,
  Has cost me a hundred crowns since supper-time.
BIANCA
  The more fool you for laying on my duty.
PETRUCHIO
  Katherine, I charge you, tell these headstrong women
  What duty they do owe their lords and husbands.
WIDOW
  Come, come, you're mocking. We will have no telling.
PETRUCHIO
  Come on, I say, and first begin with her.
WIDOW
  She shall not.
PETRUCHIO
  I say she shall. And first begin with her.
KATHERINA
  Fie, fie, unknit that threatening unkind brow,
  And dart not scornful glances from those eyes
  To wound your lord, your king, your governor.
  It blots your beauty as frosts do bite the meads,
  Confounds your fame as whirlwinds shake fair buds,
  And in no sense is meet or amiable.
  A woman angry is like a fountain troubled,
  Muddy, ill-seeming, thick, bereft of beauty,

And while it is so, none so dry or thirsty
Will deign to sip or touch one drop of it.
Your husband is your lord, your life, your keeper,
Your head, your sovereign; one that cares for you,
And for your maintenance; commits his body
To painful labour both by sea and land,
To watch the night in storms, the day in cold,
While you lie warm at home, secure and safe;
And craves no other tribute at your hands
But love, fair looks, and true obedience—
Too little payment for so great a debt.
Such duty as the subject owes the prince,
Even such a woman owes then to her husband.
And when she is froward, peevish, sullen, sour,
And not obedient to his honest will,
What is she but a foul contending rebel
And graceless traitor to her loving lord?
I am ashamed that women are so simple
To offer war where they should kneel for peace,
Or seek for rule, supremacy, and sway,
When they are bound to serve, love, and obey.
Why are our bodies soft, and weak, and smooth,
Unapt to toil and trouble in the world,
But that our soft conditions and our hearts
Should well agree with our external parts?
Come, come, you froward and unable worms,
My mind has been as big as one of yours,
My heart as great, my reason haply more,
To bandy word for word and frown for frown.
But now I see our lances are but straws,
Our strength as weak, our weakness past compare,
That seeming to be most which we indeed least are.
Then lower your pride, for it is no boot, [good]
And place your hands below your husband's foot.
In token of which duty, if he please,
My hand is ready, may it do him ease.

PETRUCHIO
  Why, there's a wench! Come on, and kiss me, Kate.
LUCENTIO
  Well, go your ways, old lad, for you shall ha't. [have it]
VINCENTIO
  'Tis a good hearing when children are toward.
LUCENTIO
  But a harsh hearing when women are froward.
PETRUCHIO
  Come, Kate, we'll to bed.
  We three are married, but you two are sped [done for].
  (to Lucentio) 'Twas I won the wager, though you hit the
     white,
  And being a winner, God give you good night!
                              Exeunt Petruchio and Katherina
HORTENSIO
  Now go your ways, you have tamed a curst shrew.
LUCENTIO
  'Tis a wonder, by your leave, she will be tamed so.
                                                    Exeunt